SHAPING THE METROPOLIS

McGILL-QUEEN'S STUDIES IN URBAN GOVERNANCE
Series editors: Kristin Good and Martin Horak

In recent years there has been an explosion of interest in local politics and the governance of cities – both in Canada and around the world. Globally, the city has become a consequential site where instances of social conflict and of cooperation play out. Urban centres are increasingly understood as vital engines of innovation and prosperity and a growing body of interdisciplinary research on urban issues suggests that high-performing cities have become crucial to the success of nations, even in the global era. Yet at the same time, local and regional governments continue to struggle for political recognition and for the policy resources needed to manage cities, to effectively govern, and to achieve sustainable growth.

The purpose of the McGill-Queen's Studies in Urban Governance series is to highlight the growing importance of municipal issues, local governance, and the need for policy reform in urban spaces. The series aims to answer the question "why do cities matter?" while exploring relationships between levels of government and examining the changing dynamics of metropolitan and community development. By taking a four-pronged approach to the study of urban governance, the series encourages debate and discussion of: (1) actors, institutions, and how cities are governed; (2) policy issues and policy reform; (3) the city as case study; and (4) urban politics and policy through a comparative framework.

With a strong focus on governance, policy, and the role of the city, this series welcomes manuscripts from a broad range of disciplines and viewpoints.

Shaping the Metropolis

Institutions and Urbanization in the United States and Canada

ZACK TAYLOR

To John —
Thanks for your interest!
Zack T

McGill-Queen's University Press
Montreal & Kingston • London • Chicago

ISBN 978-0-7735-5704-8 (cloth)
ISBN 978-0-7735-5705-5 (paper)
ISBN 978-0-7735-5842-7 (ePDF)
ISBN 978-0-7735-5843-4 (ePUB)

Legal deposit second quarter 2019
Bibliothèque nationale du Québec

Printed in Canada on acid-free paper that is 100% ancient forest free
(100% post-consumer recycled), processed chlorine free

This book has been published with the help of a grant from the Canadian
Federation for the Humanities and Social Sciences, through the Awards to
Scholarly Publications Program, using funds provided by the Social Sciences
and Humanities Research Council of Canada. Funding was also received
from the J.B. Smallman Publication Fund, and the Faculty of Social Science,
The University of Western Ontario.

Funded by the Government of Canada   Financé par le gouvernement du Canada   Canada   Canada Council for the Arts   Conseil des arts du Canada

We acknowledge the support of the Canada Council for the Arts, which
last year invested $153 million to bring the arts to Canadians throughout
the country.

Nous remercions le Conseil des arts du Canada de son soutien. L'an dernier,
le Conseil a investi 153 millions de dollars pour mettre de l'art dans la vie
des Canadiennes et des Canadiens de tout le pays.

Library and Archives Canada Cataloguing in Publication

Title: Shaping the metropolis: institutions and urbanization in the United States
and Canada / Zack Taylor.

Names: Taylor, Zachary Todd, 1973– author.

Series: McGill-Queen's studies in urban governance; 11.

Description: Series statement: McGill-Queen's studies in urban governance;
11 | Includes bibliographical references and index.

Identifiers: Canadiana (print) 20190051914 | Canadiana (eBOOK)
20190051957 | ISBN 9780773557055 (softcover) | ISBN 9780773557048
(hardcover) | ISBN 9780773558427 (ePDF) | ISBN 9780773558434 (ePUB)

Subjects: LCSH: Municipal government—Canada—Case studies. | LCSH:
Municipal government—United States—Case studies. | LCSH: Urbanization—
Canada—Case studies. | LCSH: Urbanization—United States—Case studies. |
LCGFT: Case studies.

Classification: LCC JS1710 .T39 2019 | DDC 320.8/50971—dc23

This book was typeset by Marquis Interscript in 10.5/13 Sabon.

Contents

Figures and Tables

FIGURES

TABLES

Acknowledgments

Although neither of us knew it at the time, my friend Celia Moore set this book in motion over a decade ago when she handed me a dog-eared copy of *The Myth of the North American City* and said, "I think this is your kind of thing." It was. Born in Canada to American parents, and now married to an American émigrée, I have spent most of my life traversing the world's longest undefended border, wondering how these two societies and their cities could be so similar and yet so different. As a trained urban planner attuned to the physical and spatial order of cities, I have come to understand that Canadian and American urban built environments differ in important respects, and that these differences have important social, economic, environmental, and even political consequences. As a student of politics and history, I questioned whether these differences are the direct outcomes of divergent political cultures and patterns of social conflict, or are reducible to economic forces. This book investigates how physical environments are shaped by the ways in which urban development policy decisions are made – in essence, how contention among interests, and the ideas they champion, is organized by political institutions. I hope that as a result of this work we know more than we did before, and can ask new questions.

This book began as a doctoral dissertation at the University of Toronto. I am grateful for the support of my committee, my supervisor David Wolfe and committee members Phil Triadafilopoulos and André Sorensen, each of whom provided valuable insights, encouragement, and direction along the way, and also my internal and external readers, Graham White and Ron Vogel. The field research would not have been possible without generous funding from the Social Sciences and

Humanities Research Council of Canada through a Joseph-Armand Bombardier Canada Graduate Scholarship and a Michael Smith Foreign Study Supplement, and by the School of Graduate Studies at the University of Toronto. I gained important insights from discussants and others as I presented portions of the research at annual meetings of the American Political Science Association, the Association of Collegiate Schools of Planning, the Canadian Political Science Association, and the Society for American City and Regional Planning History. I benefited from graduate fellowships at the University of Toronto's Centre for the Study of the United States and the Institute on Municipal Finance and Governance, and the opportunity to present in the University of Minnesota Geography Department's Coffee Hour speakers' series and at Simon Fraser University's fourth Rethinking the Region conference. Many faculty at the University of Toronto and other universities have influenced, assisted, and mentored me over the years, especially Don Abelson, Larry Bourne, Neil Bradford, David R. Cameron, Pierre Filion, Frances Frisken, Gunter Gad, Kristin Good, Paul Hess, Martin Horak, David Y. Miller, Eric Miller, Neil Nevitte, Ted Relph, Andrew Sancton, Ed Schatz, Enid Slack, Clarence Stone, Richard Stren, and Bob Whelan. I am grateful to have received the Urban Politics Section of the American Political Science Association's award for best dissertation.

 I am honoured to have had the opportunity to immerse myself deeply in the history and landscapes of specific places as I sought to understand how they were shaped. I acknowledge the generosity of my interviewees, many of whom gave me extraordinary amounts of their time and took my questions and follow-up queries seriously. My field research was smoothed and enriched by local friends and the generosity of many local archivists, librarians, journalists, and scholars. In the Twin Cities, I am grateful to John and Sue Hall for allowing me to stay in their St. Paul *pied-à-terre* and to their daughters Brenna and Sarah for accommodating an unexpected housemate during their summer of freedom. I am also grateful to Barney and Sandra Hall for their kindness and for sharing their intimate knowledge of the place. The late Judith Martin of the University of Minnesota connected me to many valuable interviewees. The extraordinary staff of the Minnesota Historical Society and State Archives accommodated my every need. In Portland, I must thank Kyle and Tara Dawkins for their friendship. Archivist *sans-pareil* Becky Shoemaker gave me the run of Portland Metro's basement storage rooms and, more importantly, her time. Carl Abbott and Sy Adler of Portland State University took care to correct superficial interpretations of the Portland story. In British Columbia, my childhood friend Iain McCormick generously hosted me for a month in Vancouver. His mother, Pat, who sadly has since passed way, and stepfather Neil Boyle put me up in Victoria. Staff at the UBC Archives and Metro Vancouver's Harry Lash Library were exceptionally helpful, as were Ken Cameron and Narissa Chadwick. Back in Toronto, I am indebted to Frances Frisken, Almos Tassonyi, Lionel Feldman, Don Stevenson, and especially Richard White for their historical insights. Susan Fletcher ably transcribed literally days of taped interviews.

Finally, I am grateful to several local experts who commented on early drafts of individual chapters: in Portland, the late Lloyd Anderson, Richard Benner, David Bragdon, and A. McKay Rich; in Vancouver, Ken Cameron and Christina DeMarco; in the Twin Cities, John Adams, Steven Dornfeld, and Iric Nathanson; and in Toronto, Ted Relph, Don Stevenson, and Richard White. Martin Horak provided invaluable comments on an early draft. Alan Martinson schooled me on the contract clause of the US constitution. The two anonymous reviewers provided useful comments and direction. All errors are, of course, my own. At McGill-Queen's University Press, Philip Cercone, Jacqueline Mason, and Kathleen Kearns have been extraordinarily supportive, generous, and patient as this project has developed. I am grateful to Barbara Tessman for her diligent copy-editing of the manuscript.

I would not have completed this journey without the support of friends and colleagues inside and outside of academe: David Ainsworth and Maeve Haldane, Ahmed Allahwala, Karlo Basta, Leah Birnbaum, Michelle Buckley, Kristin Cavoukian, Joanna Clarke, Chris Cochrane, Carey Doberstein, Mike Ekers, Gabriel Eidelman, Bill Flanik, Suzanne Hindmarch, Seth Jaffe, Andrea Janzen and Paul Jorgensen, Olga Kesarchuk, Dave Ley and Rebecca Smollet, Jack Lucas, Waye Mason, Neil McCormick, Jen Nelles, Nick Radia, Abby Spinak, Debra Thompson, and Jeff and Joanna Zuk.

Finally, I must thank my family. My partner, Jenny Hall, made many sacrifices as I pursued this project and has been more patient than I deserve. I dedicate this book to her and to our son Sam. I also dedicate it to my late grandparents, Mary Justine Rapp (1917–2006) and Charles Eugene Rapp (1914–2014). They would have been so proud.

Abbreviations

ACIR	Advisory Commission on Intergovernmental Relations
AIP	American Institute of Planners
ALC	Agricultural Land Commission (British Columbia)
ALR	Agricultural Land Reserve (British Columbia)
AOC	Association of Ontario Counties
ASPO	American Society of Planning Officials
BMRS	Bureau of Municipal Research and Service (Oregon)
CCF	Co-operative Commonwealth Federation
CED	Committee for Economic Development
CFVRD	Central Fraser Valley Regional District
CIO	Congress of Industrial Organizations
CMA	census metropolitan area (Canada)
CMHC	Central Mortgage and Housing Corporation
COG	council of governments
CPAC	Community Planning Association of Canada
CRAG	Columbia Region Association of Governments
CSD	Council of State Governments
DARD	Dewdney-Alouette Regional District
DBI	Density Balance Index
DFL	Democratic Farmer-Labor Party (Minnesota)
DLCD	Department of Land Conservation and Development (Oregon)
FVRD	Fraser Valley Regional District
GTA	Greater Toronto Area
GTCC	Greater Toronto Coordinating Committee
GTSB	Greater Toronto Services Board
GVRD	Greater Vancouver Regional District

GVSDD	Greater Vancouver Sewerage and Drainage District
HB	House Bill (Oregon)
ICMA	International City Managers Association
ISTEA	Intermodal Surface Transportation and Efficiency Act
JPACT	Joint Policy Advisory Committee on Transportation (Portland)
LCDC	Land Conservation and Development Commission (Oregon)
LMM	League of Minnesota Municipalities
LMRPB	Lower Mainland Regional Planning Board
LOC	League of Oregon Cities
LRP	Livable Region Program
LRSP	Livable Region Strategic Plan
LUTRAQ	Making the Land Use–Transportation–Air Quality Connection program (Portland)
LWV	League of Women Voters
MAC	Metropolitan Airports Commission (Twin Cities)
MAP	Metropolitan Area Perspectives (Portland)
MHI	Minnesota Housing Institute
MMC	Minnesota Municipal Commission
MPC	Metropolitan Planning Commission (in both Twin Cities and Portland)
MPO	metropolitan planning organization
MPP	member of Provincial Parliament (Ontario)
MRB	Municipal Reference Bureau (Minnesota)
MSA	metropolitan statistical areas (United States)
MSD	Metropolitan Service District (Portland)
MSPB	Minnesota State Planning Board
MSSD	Minneapolis–St. Paul Sanitation District
MTARTS	Metropolitan Toronto and Region Transportation Study
MTC	Metropolitan Transit Commission (Twin Cities)
MTPB	Metropolitan Toronto Planning Board
MTRCA	Metropolitan Toronto and Region Conservation Authority
MUSA	metropolitan urban service area (Twin Cities)
NACO	National Association of Counties (United States)
NAPA	National Academy of Public Administration
NDP	New Democratic Party
NRPB	National Resources Planning Board
OGTA	Office for the Greater Toronto Area

OMB	Ontario Municipal Board
ORMB	Ontario Railway and Municipal Board
ORP	Official Regional Plan (British Columbia)
OSPB	Oregon State Planning Board
OSPIRG	Oregon State Public Interest Research Group
OWRC	Ontario Water Resources Commission
P-V MTS	Portland-Vancouver Metropolitan Transportation Study
PAC	Urban Growth Management Policy Advisory Committee (Portland)
PCB	Pollution Control Board (British Columbia)
PIBC	Planning Institute of British Columbia
PMPC	Portland Metropolitan Planning Commission
PMSC	Portland Metropolitan Study Commission
PRT	personal rapid transit
PWA	Public Works Administration
PWRC	Post-War Rehabilitation Council
RUGGOS	Regional Urban Growth Goals and Objectives (Portland)
SB	Senate Bill (Oregon)
SPA	State Planning Agency (Minnesota)
TCR	Toronto-Centred Region policy statement
TPC	Town Planning Commission (Vancouver)
TTC	Toronto Transit Commission
TVA	Tennessee Valley Authority
UBC	University of British Columbia
UGB	urban growth boundary (Oregon)
VKT	vehicle kilometres travelled
WPA	Works Progress Administration

SHAPING THE METROPOLIS

It is not a failure of ideas that constrains political possibilities ... but
a state apparatus that, for all its divisions and internal conflicts, has
variously absorbed, dissolved, and deflected alternative visions with
remarkable consistency.

Karen Orren and Stephen Skowronek,
The Search for American Political Development

The American model of metropolitan development represents the
cumulative outcome of processes occurring over an extended period of
time, something that is often overlooked in comparisons of Canadian
and American cities. It thus suggests that the model's usefulness as a guide
to Canadian urban analysis will depend on an understanding of the way
governments in the United States have responded to urban growth at
successive stages of the country's development.

Frances Frisken, "Canadian Cities and the American Example:
A Prologue to Urban Policy Analysis"

1

Shaping the Metropolis

In only a few generations, Western societies have been transformed by urbanization, and the rest of the world is not far behind. North America's urban population has more than tripled, and the urban housing stock almost quintupled, since the end of the Second World War (see figure 1.1). At the turn of the twentieth century, only a small minority of Americans and Canadians lived in cities. Now four in five North Americans live in urban areas, and most are concentrated in large metropolitan areas. In an urban society, almost all governance is *urban* governance. Most contemporary policy problems, and their solutions, are to be found in cities.

These problems are legion. Urbanization's encroachment on sensitive ecosystems and fertile agricultural land risks undermining urban water supplies, species habitats, and food security, leading environmentalists to make common cause with working farmers and outer suburbanites in pursuit of "growth management."[1] Governments struggle to pay for new and expanded urban infrastructure and services while existing systems crumble.[2] In an environment of low tariffs, mass migration, and globalized capital markets, communities seek to compete for residents and investment without sacrificing their unique qualities.[3] Metropolitan regions are increasingly viewed as social and economic systems that can be more or less resilient to economic stress and natural disaster.[4] Especially on the ocean coasts, cities are coming to terms with threats associated with climate change, while also embracing strategies to reduce greenhouse gas emissions from urban housing and transportation systems.[5] And rising income inequality and the growing spatial concentration of disadvantage within metropolitan areas threaten to undermine the social sustainability of North

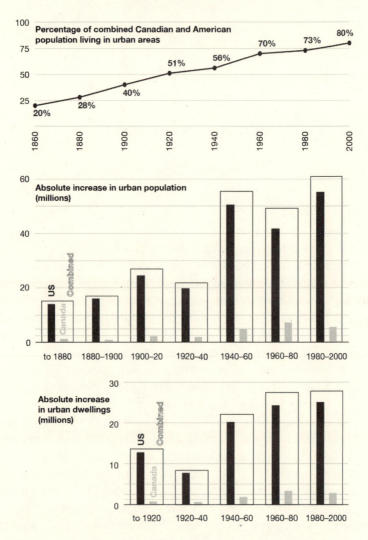

Figure 1.1 Population and housing growth, North America, 1860–2000

Note: A dramatic increase in the number of new urbanites and the amount of new urban housing occurred after the Second World War in both Canada and the United States. By virtue of the latter's much greater size, American urban population and housing growth has out-stripped Canadian in absolute terms, decade over decade. However, the proportion of each country's population living in urban settlements has been about the same over the past 150 years. The statistical definition of "urban" population has changed over time in both countries but generally refers to the population in settlements of over a thousand people. Canada did not distinguish urban from rural dwellings before 1920.

Sources: Canada and US Censuses, various years.

American cities.[6] The ongoing task of urban governance is to effectively respond to these challenges. It therefore matters whether our
inherited systems of urban governance – which were constructed to
meet the challenges of other eras – are up to the job.

This book explains why urban governance evolved differently in
the United States and Canada and how these differences have produced cities with different characteristics. Both at the national level
and through specific metropolitan case studies, this comparative
historical journey shows how both the governance of American and
Canadian cities and also their physical form are the cumulative effects
of distant choices. It reveals how, since the nineteenth century, urbanization pressures have generated lasting institutional and policy
innovations, and new patterns of intergovernmental relations, while
at the same time showing how, once created, these institutions and
relationships have structured ways in which governments have shaped
metropolitan growth. While the book's perspective is historical, it is
not just about the past. By identifying the parameters of urban governance in each national context, we can begin to chart an agenda
for shaping the metropolis of the future.

WHAT IS URBAN GOVERNANCE?

When we think about *urban* governance, we tend to think about *local*
governments and the relationships between them. American urban
politics scholars have traditionally focused on politics within, and
policies made by, municipalities. Seminal works, including Floyd
Hunter's study of the power elite in Atlanta, Robert Dahl's description
of pluralism in New Haven, and Edward Banfield's exploration of
political influence in Chicago, framed urban politics as contention
among local interests working in and through local institutions.[7]
While these accounts have focused on the agency of individuals or
groups to shape local futures, others, such as Paul Kantor, sociologists
John Logan and Harvey Molotch, and geographer David Harvey
have emphasized how the logic of the capitalist political economy
constrains local choices.[8] Clarence Stone's influential urban regime
approach finds agency within structure by conceptualizing how a
durable capacity to govern at the municipal scale may be assembled
through the pooling of resources from different sectors of the local
society.[9] In a "developmental" regime, for example, politicians mobilize institutional and political resources – regulatory support, infrastructure, and public approval – while business provides investment

capital to secure mutually desired objectives. Hank Savitch and Paul Kantor, and also Alan DiGaetano and Elisabeth Strøm, have in different ways explored how cities' distinct configurations of local institutions, political culture, and economic endowments affect their capacity to shape their own destinies in a competitive global economy.[10] Others, including Jon Pierre, have proposed more encompassing models and typologies of urban governance that are nonetheless focused on the resources, interests, and objectives of local actors working through municipal institutions.[11]

A parallel American debate has focused on increasing the efficiency and democratic responsiveness of local government in metropolitan areas. Starting in the late nineteenth century, "consolidationists" argued that merging municipalities into a single metropolitan authority would generate economies of scale, increase democratic accountability, and, by virtue of unified authority, produce more efficient economic development, infrastructure investment, and land-use outcomes, while equalizing access to services.[12] In the postwar period, "public choice" economists such as Charles Tiebout, Vincent Ostrom, and Robert Warren argued that the logic of consolidation was faulty. They proposed that greater efficiency could be achieved by encouraging competition between local governments in metropolitan areas, each of which would tailor services and tax rates to the preferences of its residents.[13] Instead of securing policy change through municipal politics, metropolitan residents could "vote with their feet" by moving to the municipality most aligned with their preferences. As I discuss later in this chapter, the public choice approach and the complex local government arrangements it justifies have been criticized for exacerbating socio-economic and racial inequality and fuelling urban sprawl.[14]

Responding to the consolidation–public choice debate, "new regionalists" have studied the potential for voluntary, bottom-up collaboration between municipalities, and the role that business and other non-governmental actors can play in building metropolitan coalitions around common economic and equity objectives.[15] Richard Feiock and his collaborators frame metropolitan governance as an "institutional collective action" problem.[16] They argue that inter-municipal cooperation is more likely if political and bureaucratic elites have shared interests and preferences, which they associate with long tenure in office and the professionally dominated council-manager form of government, and if central cities and suburbs were not divided by race. Similarly, James Visser highlights the predispositions, assumptions, and values of local officials and residents in his cultural model of interlocal cooperation.[17]

A second new regionalist approach focuses on relationships between political, social, and economic elites in metropolitan areas. Denser networks and patterns of interaction facilitate trust and reciprocity, increasing the stock of social capital that can be drawn down in pursuit of collective objectives.[18] In this spirit, Allan Wallis and David Hamilton separately emphasize the importance of "civic infrastructure" – boundary-spanning networks of non-governmental actors advocating for regional policies.[19] Similarly, Jen Nelles points to the importance of "civic capital" – a "collective sense of community based on a shared identity, set of goals, and expectations that emerges from social networks tied to a specific region or locality" – the presence of which facilitates collaborative governance.[20]

There is no shortage of more or less formalized and institutionalized interaction between local governments and non-governmental organizations across North America. Jen Nelles and David Miller have recently catalogued the existence in the United States of almost five hundred regional intergovernmental organizations, which bring local governments and sometimes third parties into collective policy-making or service delivery. Hank Savitch and Sarin Adhikari call attention to the emergence of a multiplicity of functionally differentiated "public authorities" that compensate for malcoordination in metropolitan areas. Similarly, Zachary Spicer documents cross-boundary relationships between urban municipalities and their rural neighbours in Ontario.[21] Nonetheless, voluntary collaboration has its limits, even if metropolitan identities, common values, trust ties, and racial similarity lower the cost of building coalitions across boundaries. Metropolitan-scale planning and policymaking necessarily creates winners and losers because it spatially allocates resources, costs, and benefits across space – and no local politicians are going to volunteer for their jurisdiction to become a loser.[22] As Christina Rosan puts it, "Voluntary regionalism is not superior to regulatory approaches … Metropolitan planning without authority tends to be driven more by the demands and constraints on localities rather than on a shared vision for the region."[23]

From Local Government to Multi-Level Urban Governance

By focusing on institutions, organizations, and leadership at the local level, these American perspectives – urban politics, consolidation, public choice, and new regionalism – reveal important dimensions of *local* governance in metropolitan areas, but they do not capture the full scope of *urban* governance. In particular, Americans tend to de-emphasize state government's constitutional jurisdiction over local government in favour of attention to local dynamics.[24] This is not surprising, given the states' modest direct involvement in local governance. Indeed, the federal government has at various times exerted much more influence, if indirectly, on local land-use, infrastructure, and service-delivery decisions through mandates and grant programs. Still, the fact that states' jurisdiction over local government is latent or unexploited does not mean that it does not exist. By virtue of their constitutional jurisdiction over local government and land use, American states and Canadian provinces define the authority of local governments and the resources available to them, and therefore the scope of local autonomy. They also establish the incentive structures that encourage or discourage inter-municipal collaboration. Canadian observers are perhaps more sensitive to this "vertical" dimension of urban governance because of the long history of robust provincial involvement in municipal affairs. Indeed, a comparative historical investigation of the development of American and Canadian multi-level urban governance may generate fresh conclusions about its capabilities and potential in both national contexts.

In this book, I adopt a more expansive definition of urban governance, one that resists the tendency to what Neil Brenner calls "methodological localism."[25] Here, I understand urban governance to involve governments and non-governmental actors at all levels – federal, provincial or state, and local – as they shape the development of cities. Instead of viewing national or provincial governments as forces external to the city, my approach views local government as but one type of actor in a broader field of urban governance. This approach recognizes that ostensibly "local" organized interests and policy entrepreneurs pursue objectives in diverse venues. Indeed, urban governance – and urban politics – may often not occur at the local level at all. This expansive definition resonates with Martin Horak and Robert Young's portrayal of cities as "sites of governance," as well as Jeffery Sellers's exploration of nationally specific "infrastructures of urban governance," which he associates with models of welfare capitalism.[26] Comparing Germany to the United States, Sellers demonstrates how different national patterns of intergovernmental fiscal, political, and administrative relations, as well as distinct forms

of interest aggregation, variously shape the strategies of local
While recognizing that the national distinctiveness of models c
level urban governance is rooted in specific times and spaces, Sei...
work is concerned primarily with the contemporary outcomes they
generate, not the long-term historical processes that produced and
reproduce them. By taking a long historical perspective, this book
helps us better understand why, and under what circumstances,
American and Canadian governments have mounted more or less
effective policy responses to problems associated with cities and urbanization in the past. And at the same time, history can also help us
think through the potential for more effective urban governance in
the future.

AMERICAN AND CANADIAN URBAN GOVERNANCE DIFFERENCE, AND WHY IT MATTERS

The relative environmental sustainability, social cohesion, and prosperity of Canadian cities has led some Americans to look north for
inspiration.[27] If specific Canadian or American systems of multi-level
urban governance have useful features, today or in the past, that
could be emulated, the task is to determine what they are and the
conditions of their emergence and effectiveness. First, however, I will
briefly survey differences between American and Canadian local
governance and discuss their effects on the shape of metropolitan
urban development.

Local Government Complexity

Perhaps the most visible distinction between American and Canadian
urban governance is that local government in US metropolitan areas
is more *complex*. I use "complexity" instead of the more common
"fragmentation" because the latter is freighted with negative con-
notation and typically refers narrowly to the proliferation of suburban
municipalities outside the central municipality. "Complexity" is used
here to capture a broader range of phenomena, including the degrees
to which services are delivered by independent and sometimes overlapping special-purpose bodies and to which residents live in unincorporated areas beyond the jurisdiction of general-purpose local
governments. Americans have measured local government complexity
in a variety of ways, the most sophisticated being Miller's Metropolitan

Power Diffusion Index.[28] This index cannot be calculated for Canadian cities, however, because standardized municipal fiscal data are not available.

One straightforward way of measuring local government complexity is to calculate what proportion of the metropolitan population lives in central cities versus the suburbs. Figure 1.2 shows that, in 1930, about 30 per cent of Americans and Canadians lived in central cities, a proportion that stayed more or less constant for sixty years. The proportion of Americans living in suburbs dramatically increased, from less than 15 per cent in 1930 to over 50 per cent in 2010, the suburbs overtaking core cities in about 1960. In Canada, the suburbs' share of the national population surpassed the central cities' only in the 1980s, however the central-city share later increased after several provinces encouraged or mandated the amalgamation of core cities with inner-ring suburbs in several large metropolitan areas.

Disaggregating the national statistics reveals distinct national patterns. Figure 1.3 plots two complexity indicators in 2010: central city population as a percentage of metropolitan population, and number of municipalities per 100,000 residents. While there is considerable variation in central-city dominance (the x-axis), 10 of the 17 Canadian central cities contain a higher proportion of metropolitan population than all but 4 of the 158 American cities. The second indicator (the y-axis) reveals that Canadian metropolitan areas contain fewer municipalities per capita than most American cities. One-quarter of the American regions shown contain more than 10 municipalities per 100,000 people; none of the Canadian cities have more than 4.1. As table 1.1 shows, the average central city is more populous in Canada than in the United States. Canadian metropolitan areas also have fewer and more populous suburban municipalities.

American metros are also distinguished by myriad independent special-purpose bodies. Older municipalities, typically the core cities of metropolitan areas, provide services directly, while residents of newer municipalities tend to receive services from multiple overlapping special districts. These deliver a wide range of services, including water distribution and sewer treatment, public transit, street lighting, fire protection, and solid waste management, and operate facilities such as libraries, ports, convention centres, and zoos.[29] Some levy their own property taxes and user fees, while others are funded by other governments. Independent special districts filled the governance gap in unincorporated suburban areas – territory that is urbanized

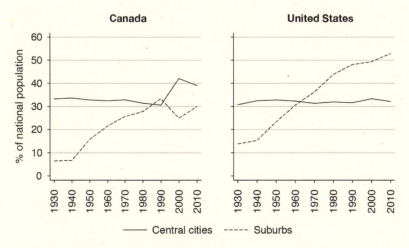

Figure 1.2 Central cities and suburbs as a proportion of the national population, 1930–2010

Note: American metropolitan statistical areas (MSAs) tend to be territorially larger than Canadian census metropolitan areas (CMAs), meaning that the American suburban share of the national population is correspondingly larger than it would be if MSAs were defined according to Statistics Canada's criteria.

Sources: United States 1930–80 from Pisarski, *Commuting in America III*, table 2–13, and 1990–2010 from source data for Figure 4-7 in Polzin and Pisarski, *Commuting in America, 2013*; Canada from Statistics Canada, Census, various years, for the thirty-six CMAs as defined in 2006.

or urbanizing, yet outside the jurisdiction of general-purpose municipal government.[30] As table 1.2 indicates, special districts proliferated during the postwar era, especially during the 1950s and 1960s, while the proportion of metropolitan residents living in unincorporated areas has remained relatively steady.

The role of local special-purpose bodies is more circumscribed in Canada. With few exceptions, they are dependent rather than independent – accountable to and often wholly funded by general-purpose local governments and in some cases also by the federal and/ or provincial governments.[31] School boards aside, the only independently elected local special district in urban Canada is the Vancouver Parks Board. Services in metropolitan suburbs are almost entirely delivered by general-purpose local governments or by multi-municipality special-purpose bodies directly accountable to the municipalities. The coverage of general-purpose local government has

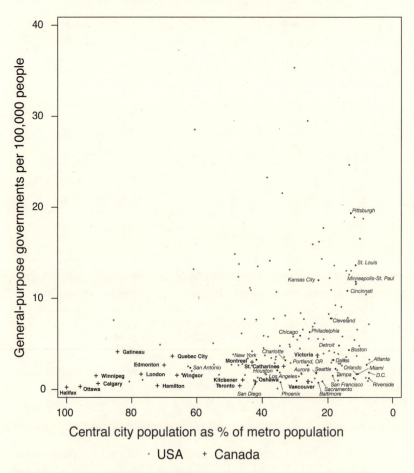

Figure 1.3 Local government complexity, 2010

Note: The proportion of the metropolitan area's population accounted for by the central city (plotted on the *x*-axis) indicates its relative weight within the region. The number of general-purpose governments (GPGs), not including counties, per 100,000 residents (*y*-axis) is another measure of government complexity. Less governmentally complex metropolitan areas are therefore found at the bottom left of the graph, while more complex cities are found at the upper right. Nationwide, the average population of metropolitan GPGs is considerably smaller in the United States, while the number of GPGs per 100,000 people is considerably higher. Excluding central cities from these measures reveals a similar relationship. For readability, only cities with more than 300,000 residents are graphed; however, the data in the graph pertain to all US metropolitan statistical areas and Canadian census metropolitan areas and census agglomerations.

Sources: Canada from Statistics Canada, Census 2011 Community Profiles; United States populations from 2010 US Census of Population and number of general-purpose municipalities in 2012 from Census of Governments.

Table 1.1
Local government complexity, 2010

	Central city-metro population ratio	All GPGs*		Suburban GPGs	
		Average population	Per 100,000 people	Average population	Per 100,000 people
Canada (n = 47)	59%	48,950	2	22,331	1.9
United States (n = 357)	38%	17,184	5.8	10,919	5.7

* GPG = general-purpose government

Note: Nationwide, the average population is considerably smaller in the United States than in Canada, while the number of GPGs per 100,000 people is considerably higher. Excluding central cities from these measures reveals a similar relationship. The calculations pertain to all US metropolitan statistical areas and Canadian census metropolitan areas and census agglomerations.

Sources: Canada from Statistics Canada, Census 2011 Community Profiles; US populations from 2010 US Census of Population; number of general-purpose governments in 2012 from Census of Governments.

increased over time, from 54 per cent of the national population in 1951 to 98 per cent in 2011.[32]

Urban Form in the United States and Canada

The physical form of American and Canadian metropolitan areas also differs.[33] Compact cities are denser and contiguously built out while sprawling cities are characterized by low-density and scattered development. To make an apples-to-apples comparison of American and Canadian cities, I calculated an indicator of metropolitan compactness called the Density Balance Index (DBI) for each decennial census year since 1970. The DBI indicates the proportion of metropolitan residents living in neighbourhoods sufficiently dense to support minimal bus service.[34] A score of 100 would indicate that all residents live in low-density neighbourhoods, while a score of zero would indicate that all residents live in higher-density ones. While there is no shortage of "sprawl" indices, they often rely on data sources that are not available or comparable across national boundaries or across time.[35] The DBI overcomes these problems because it is based on readily accessible census population data that are comparable across time and national borders.

Table 1.2
General- and special-purpose local government in the United States, 1940–2010

	Number of metros	Suburban population (millions)	SDS* per million suburban residents	Suburban GPGs** per million suburban residents	Average SDS per metro	Average GPGs per metro	% national pop. in unincor- porated areas
1940	140	15.3	72	163	8	19	n/a
1950	168	35.2	74	151	15	33	37%
1960	212	54.9	99	118	26	32	35%
1970	243	73.6	109	109	33	34	35%
1980	318	99.3	118	115	37	37	38%
1990	324	114.9	118	107	42	39	38%
2010	392	163.1	126	99	52	42	38%

*SD = special district
**GPG = general-purpose government

Note: The population and number of governments in metropolitan areas have increased in part because the territorial extents of designated metropolitan areas have been expanded and new metropolitan areas have been designated. The number of governments has been expressed in per capita terms for this reason. For convenience, the number of suburban GPGs is calculated as the total number of GPGs in metropolitan areas minus the number of metropolitan areas, although some metropolitan areas are considered to have more than one central city. SD counts do not include school districts.

Sources: Governments in metropolitan areas are from US Census Bureau, Census of Governments and National Population Estimates, various years, and Hamilton, Governing Metropolitan Areas. Metropolitan and suburban populations for 1940–90 are from table 2.13 in Pisarski, Commuting in America III. Suburban population for 2010 and population in unincorporated areas for all years are calculated from US Census Bureau, Census of Population, various years.

Figure 1.4 shows that Canadian cities, and especially larger ones, are more compact than most American cities and have become more compact over time. In the United States, by contrast, there is a clear trend toward more sprawling urban form. While there is greater variation in scores among American cities (the maximum scores are higher and minimum scores lower than those for Canadian cities), the majority of US cities score considerably higher than their Canadian counterparts – that is, are more sprawling – and the difference between the two national groups is statistically significant in all years.

Policymakers have pursued compact urban form because it is more efficient to service. Scenario modelling on both sides of the border demonstrates that compact urban form translates into lower

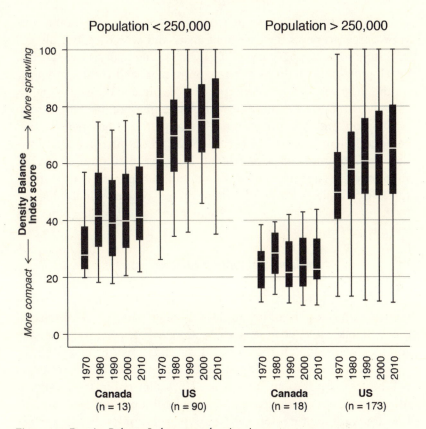

Figure 1.4 Density Balance Index scores by city size group, 1970–2010

Note: Higher Density Balance Index (DBI) scores indicate more sprawling urban form; lower scores indicate more compact urban form. This box plot shows the distribution of metropolitan DBI scores for each year within each country, separating small and large metros. The top and bottom of the solid bar indicate the metropolitan areas that are at the 25th and 75th percentile. (Half of the metro areas lie within each bar.) The white line within each bar indicates the median metro. The "whiskers" indicate the tails of the distribution. The box plots indicate that Canadian cities are generally denser than American cities, and have remained so over time, while American cities have become more sprawling over time. It also shows that large cities sprawl less than small ones.

infrastructure costs. The most comprehensive demonstration of the cost impacts of compact urban form is Burchell and collaborators' series of "costs of sprawl" studies. Their 2005 study estimates that, in the United States over twenty-five years, a compact growth scenario would save 162,000 km² of land from urbanization, $121 billion in water, sewer, and road infrastructure costs, and \$420 billion in private-sector property development costs and would reduce annual operating costs by 30 per cent.[36] Compact rather than scattered urban development also reduces impacts on natural and rural landscapes on the urban fringe, preserving their economic and amenity value, as well as the services they provide, including potable water, food production, and species habitats.[37] Finally, studies have shown that compact urban form is less energy- and carbon-intensive than low-density and scattered urban form. Density, in combination with supportive arrangements of land uses and transportation infrastructure, discourages automobile use in favour of active and collective forms of transportation, while smaller and attached dwellings use less energy per capita.[38]

Local Government Complexity and the Compact City

There is good reason to predict that local government organization influences metropolitan urban development patterns. As discussed earlier, public choice economists have argued that, in a governmentally complex metropolitan area, market discipline will bring expensive – that is, high-tax – jurisdictions into line; otherwise their residents will move to less expensive locales. Unrecognized in their original formulation is that outlying areas have a built-in cost advantage. Local government complexity spurs population and employment decentralization because outlying places tend to be more cost-competitive than central cities: they offer fewer services (and therefore levy lower taxes), impose less onerous regulatory burdens on land development, and have lower land values.[39] As a result, they attract desirable types of residential, commercial, and industrial growth away from built-out central cities and inner suburbs, while leaving behind less desirable land uses and people who cannot or will not move, generating pockets of concentrated disadvantage.[40]

From a policymaking perspective, we would also expect that greater governmental complexity would magnify the collective action problem by making it more difficult to agree on coordinated urban development policies – especially those that make spatial trade-offs in pursuit of metropolitan-scale policy objectives such as the equitable and efficient extension of infrastructure systems or affordable housing. This is not only a matter of having "too many cooks in the kitchen" wielding vetoes. The potential for metropolitan policymaking is undermined by socio-economic divisions between municipalities that establish divergent political and fiscal interests and identities – white suburbs versus black core cities, or rich outer suburbs versus poor inner suburbs, for example. The collective action problem is further magnified when suburban residents rely on a patchwork of single-purpose taxing authorities and utilities rather than general-purpose local government for services. Localized single-purpose bodies have no incentive to care about the big picture. By dividing authority over particular services across space, they make it more difficult to strategically shape urban development at the metropolitan scale through the controlled extension of water, sewer, and transportation infrastructure. The size of local governments matters. If they are small and insufficiently professionalized, they may lack the necessary fiscal and administrative capacity to make and implement urban development policies such as comprehensive plans and zoning codes. In short, the greater the local government complexity in a metropolitan area, the more difficult it is likely to be to develop and implement regional land-use and infrastructure plans.

These expectations are corroborated by the literature. Paul Lewis has found that a measure of political fragmentation correlated with measures of population and employment decentralization. Similarly, William Fulton and collaborators found a positive association between the number of local governments and the amount of low-density urban land expansion, while Ed Glaeser, Matthew Kahn, and Chenghuan Chu found that jobs were more geographically dispersed in more governmentally complex regions.[41] Analysing metropolitan areas in fourteen American states, John Carruthers and Gudmundur Úlfarsson found that, on a per capita basis, higher numbers of suburban municipalities and special districts correlate with lower metropolitan population densities, and, in subsequent work, they also found that governmental complexity was positively correlated with population growth in outlying unincorporated areas.[42] While similar research has not been done in the Canadian context, I find that the number of general-purpose governments per capita correlates positively with the DBI and travel behaviour – that is, local government complexity is associated with more decentralized urban form and longer commuting distances, controlling for metropolitan area population.[43]

Although the focus of the discussion so far has been on urban development and land-use and infrastructure planning, local government complexity has other effects. In a wide-ranging recent review of the literature, Jae Hong Kim and Nathan Jurey report that, while the evidence for fiscal and economic efficiencies is mixed, local government complexity is associated with greater social and economic inequality and racial segregation.[44] Moving beyond the typically American focus in the literature, cross-national work by researchers at the Organisation for Economic Co-operation and Development (OECD) has demonstrated strong relationships between local government complexity and a range of social and economic indicators. For example, metropolitan areas with more complex local government are shown to have lower per-capita economic growth and labour productivity, and higher levels of neighbourhood segregation by household income levels.[45]

Transcending the Local: Multi-Level Urban Governance

The structure of local government in metropolitan areas clearly matters. Nevertheless, a purely local or "horizontal" perspective captures only part of the picture. Eran Razin and Mark Rosentraub are likely correct when they suggest that less complex local government is a necessary but insufficient condition for compact metropolitan urban form.[46] At least as important, if not more so, is the "vertical" dimension of multi-level urban governance – that is, the federal and state or provincial policies and institutional arrangements that enable and constrain local government action.

Comparing vertical intergovernmental relations in Canada and the United States is no simple task. Canadians cannot easily replicate common American measures of local autonomy, such as Stephens's State Centralization Index, because the necessary data are simply not available.[47] (Fiscal data often lump together municipal and education spending, and also spending for capital and operating purposes.) It is also difficult to account for cross-national differences in the structure and functions of local government. As mentioned earlier, most Canadians are governed and receive services from general-purpose local governments, while many Americans live in unincorporated areas served by single-purpose governments and private enterprises.

Even casual observation suggests that there are substantial differences in how, and how much, national and subnational governments are involved in the governance of cities. Through conditional grants for housing and transportation projects, the US federal government has played a much larger role than the Canadian federal government in shaping cities. At the same time, Canadian provincial legal and regulatory intervention in the urban sphere is much stronger than that of American states. Perhaps the most systematic attempt to quantify the degree to which state governments direct local government land-use decision making by legal or regulatory means is the Wharton Residential Land Use Regulation project, which surveyed officials in over 2,000 municipalities regarding the restrictiveness of local land-use policies, including perceptions of the degree to which state legislatures were "involved ... in affecting residential building activities and/or growth management procedures."[48] Thirty-nine states fell within 0.5 points of the national average score of 2 (out of 5), and the highest average state score was a 3. If the large and urbanized Canadian provinces were scored on the same metric, we would likely find their enabling legislation and land-use rules to be more comprehensive and stringent, and less voluntaristic, than those of their American peers. Others report that only a handful of states have gone beyond generic enabling legislation for local comprehensive planning and zoning to enact explicit land-use policies binding on local governments.[49]

Intervention in municipal affairs by Canadian provinces is more thoroughgoing in part because there are no constitutional limits on their jurisdiction over local government. In the United States, by contrast, most states have some form of constitutional or legal "home rule," the delegation of authority to local governments to amend their own charters, and limitations on the state's ability to legislate in the municipal sphere. While home rule is by no means absolute – indeed, the National League of Cities has documented a growing trend toward the pre-emption of local authority by state governments, particularly in policing and immigration enforcement – it both legally and discursively inhibits state intervention.[50] American states also do not have departments or agencies dedicated to the active supervision of local governments. While their titles vary, all Canadian provinces have a cabinet-level "municipal affairs" department that to varying degrees regulates or oversees local government finance, municipal incorporation and boundary change, and land-use planning.

To truly comprehend urban governance, then, we must transcend the local. To be sure, local governments and inter-municipal relationships shape urban and metropolitan growth. Yet we should not forget that the organization, authority, and capacities of local governments are determined by other levels of government. Through laws, regulations, policies, and fiscal arrangements, states and provinces establish the rules and incentives that structure how local games are played.

THE PLAN OF THIS BOOK

In this brief sketch, I have shown that American and Canadian urban governance differs, both in terms of local government complexity and the relationships between different levels of government. Compared to their American counterparts, Canadian metropolitan areas contain fewer and more populous suburban municipalities, few Canadians live in unincorporated areas, and independent special-purpose bodies are virtually non-existent. Provincial governments are also more directly involved in local government organization and urban development than American states. Partially as a result, Canadian cities, and especially the larger ones, are also more compactly developed than American cities. The remainder of this book provides an historical explanation of why urban governance came to differ in Canada and the United States and concludes with a discussion of the future implications of these differences.

The Institutional Foundations of Urban Development

This book foregrounds the way institutions structure political contention and policymaking processes. To be sure, the United States and Canada share a continent, a dominant language, inherited British legal traditions, and a constitutional division of powers between federal and subnational governments. Both are typically placed in the same category in cross-national studies of welfare states and capitalist organization.[51] Canadian and American cities and their residents have also been shaped by broadly similar macroeconomic, technological, and social changes.

A central point of differentiation, however, is the internal structure of the two countries' governing institutions. In Canadian provincial Westminster systems, policymaking is led by the executive. Especially in a majority government, the premier and cabinet, who command the bureaucracy and can whip their party's caucus in the unicameral legislature, face few checks on their ability to make policy. Provinces can rapidly enact and sustain programmatic policies developed within the bureaucracy. In American state-level separated-powers systems,

policies are formed through legislative coalition-building and negotiation, often on the basis of proposals introduced by external interest
groups. Coalition building within and between legislative chambers
inhibits the enactment of programmatic policies, and adopted policies are easily undermined or overturned by opponents through
legislative amendment, the use of sunset clauses, and, especially in
western states, ballot initiative. Building on these institutional dis-
tinctions, I argue in the next chapter that Canadian Westminster and
American separated-powers government systems perform differently
in relation to changing norms and values. Provincial Westminster
institutions can be expected to be most effective when trust in government and deference to elites is high and a single party dominates
for an extended period of time, as in the early postwar period.
Separated-powers institutions can be expected to be most effective
when deference to elites is high and elites converge on programmatic
policy proposals. In short, the *institutional foundations* of government, especially at the state and provincial level, and operating within
a changing normative context, have defined the contours of multi-
level urban governance in Canada and the United States, with far-
reaching effects.

Two Countries, Four Cities

Chapter 3 applies this framework in a cross-national historical comparison of the legal and institutional development of Canadian and
American urban governance from the nineteenth century to the present. Local government was similar in the two countries in the first
half of the nineteenth century, insofar as governments did little in the
context of a rural society. However, divergent patterns of intergovernmental relations were established in the nineteenth and early twentieth century through incremental federal and state or provincial
responses to proximate pressures generated by rapid urbanization
and industrialization: public debt crises, demands for political and
administrative reform, and the Great Depression. Cumulatively, the
responses to these events established the opportunities and constraints
under which postwar actors in both countries grappled with metropolitan growth pressures. At each step, the development of urban
governance in each country was structured by the organization of
subnational – state and provincial – political institutions, which exercise legal jurisdiction over local government and land use.

Chapters 4 through 7 shift the scale of attention downwards by grounding the analysis in case studies of four metropolitan areas in their intergovernmental contexts: in Canada, Toronto and Vancouver; in the United States, Minneapolis–St. Paul and Portland, Oregon. These case histories, which draw on archival and interview research, provide what a national overview cannot: a granular perspective on how actors and interests, inside and outside government, advance policy ideas within and through political institutions amid a dynamic normative context. Although the emphasis is on rapid postwar urban growth, each case narrative begins in the nineteenth century with the original organization of local government and intergovernmental relations in the context of urban expansion.

Collectively, the chapters show that the development of Canadian and American urban governance has been structured since the beginning by the different institutional foundations of state and provincial government. While the magnitude of urban growth and the menu of policy ideas were the same on both sides of the border, Canadian provinces responded much earlier than American states, thereby subjecting a much higher proportion of postwar urbanization to programmatic policies. This occurred because of differences in the institutional foundations of government in the two countries. Especially in the early postwar period, highly centralized authority in Canadian provinces was an asset. Governing party elites and senior public servants possessed considerable decision-making autonomy in an era when trust in government and deference to elites was high and a single party dominated the electoral field. This authority was programmatically deployed to increase the capacity of the provincial and local government to respond to rapid urbanization. Centralized and closed policy-making lost legitimacy when the electorate became restive and provincial politics became more contentious and competitive during and after the 1970s. Provincial governments became less able to make and sustain policy decisions. Decentralized, legislature-centred policy-making rendered American states less able to engage in programmatic policymaking and secure durable policy settlements. A handful of state legislatures, including those in Minnesota and Oregon, enacted innovative policies in the 1960s due to the conjuncture of several factors: federal incentives, an unusual degree of consensus among civic elites, and a normative context of trust in government and deference to elites. When these conditions slipped away, so too did the potential for programmatic urban governance.

Why These Cities?

The four cities were selected on the basis of common features. Each is a relatively young city, founded in the nineteenth century. Each grew steadily before and after the Second World War, which is generally understood as the breakpoint between two general patterns of urban development – one that was relatively unplanned, dense, and supportive of collective transportation, and one that is more systematically planned, less dense, and organized around the private automobile.[52] Consistency of growth over time is important, as the focus is on the policy response to demands associated with sustained population growth and physical urban expansion, including for including new and expanded infrastructure and services, high-quality residential neighbourhoods and workplaces, amenities, and convenient transportation options to link them together.

Each has also undergone broadly similar economic and social transformations. Economically, Toronto and Minneapolis entered the twentieth century as rail-based industrial cities but avoided the economic decline of other upper Midwest and Northeastern cities by becoming centres for financial, educational, medical, and other high value-added services. Vancouver and Portland also experienced a similar trajectory of economic transformation, from natural resource extraction to post-industrial knowledge work.

While domestic and international migration has made all four cities more ethnically and racially diverse in recent decades, each was relatively ethno-linguistically homogeneous into the 1980s. African Americans made up only 1.5 per cent of the combined population of Minneapolis and St. Paul in 1950, 4 per cent in 1970, and 10.6 per cent in 1990. Similarly, Portland was 2.6 per cent black in 1950, 5.6 per cent in 1970, and 7.4 per cent in 1990. Not historically divided by race, the ethnic origin of Toronto and Vancouver residents remained overwhelmingly British and European until the 1980s.[53] Homogeneity minimizes the effect of group conflict on relations between central cities and suburban municipalities and affords a clearer vantage point on how the organization of institutions shapes urban governance.

These are not typical cities. They were chosen in part because each has at various times been recognized as an innovator in metropolitan governance reform and land-use and infrastructure planning. The Municipality of Metropolitan Toronto, created in 1954, was once hailed as the most effective government of its kind. Hitchings categorizes Portland Metro and the Twin Cities Metropolitan Council as the only "authoritative" regional governing organizations in the United States – bodies authorized to develop *and* enforce local compliance with regional plans.[54] Portland is celebrated as a "capital of good planning," and Vancouver is portrayed as a "poster child of urbanism" and a "model of contemporary city-making."[55] By closely examining ostensibly successful examples of urban governance and planning for growing metropolitan areas, we may be able to explain what may be the limit of what has been possible in each national context. Reputations are, of course, subjective. The histories of planning and governance in these particular cities have been written largely by locals who participated in the processes they describe and have a vested interest in their cities' reputations. What appears to be a success in one national context or point in time may be interpreted as a failure in others. The historical case narratives are full of stops and starts, paths not taken, and unintended consequences. Institutions and policies created for one purpose are often redirected to another. The timing and the sequence of events matter. By avoiding a short-run or "snapshot" view, and by focusing on the broader multi-level governance process rather than a single level of government or institution, it is possible to construct a more complete picture of the historical and ongoing development of urban governance in Canada and the United States.

Urban Governance, Past and Future

The case narratives are not simply of historical interest. In the final chapter, I reflect on what history can tell us about the potential for effective urban governance today. I draw two overarching conclusions. First, I conclude that we should put the institutional foundations of governance and their historical development at the centre of our analysis. This is not to argue that economic and social forces – long the focus of urban politics research – do not matter. Rather, institutional and political economy approaches are complementary, capturing different dimensions of urban politics. Without appreciating how institutions have deeply structured political contention over the making and implementation of policies in the past, we cannot begin to think through how they may enable and constrain us in the future.

Second, I conclude that provinces and states are indispensable to urban governance due to their jurisdiction over local government institutions and land use and their capacity to redistribute resources across space – something that is insufficiently recognized by those who focus on local coalition-building or federal intervention. The state and provincial levels of government deserve more attention from reformers and students of urban politics. This proposition may be controversial. As this book goes to press, a new right-populist premier of Ontario has unilaterally redrawn the City of Toronto's ward boundaries in the midst of a municipal election campaign, provoking calls from activists and editorialists for the city to secede from the province. The governor of New York state is fighting a pitched battle with the mayor of New·York City over who is responsible for the city's deteriorating subway system. President Trump is withholding authorized funding for transit projects while punishing cities that refuse to enforce federal immigration policies. Prominent commentators in both countries now routinely argue that cities can flourish only if their autonomy, authority, and resources are increased by politically, fiscally, and constitutionally decoupled from national and subnational governments. Nonetheless, urbanists and reformers should not ignore the inescapably multi-level nature of urban governance, however dysfunctional, arbitrary, politicized, or circumscribed it may be at any particular moment in time. I suggest that the performance of multi-level urban governance should be assessed in relation to how well states and provinces use their exclusive jurisdiction over local government and land use to enable and protect the productive exercise of local autonomy.

HOW TO READ THIS BOOK

This book was written with several audiences in mind. Political scientists may find it to be a useful contribution to the comparative study of political institutions and public policymaking. Urban governance and urban development in Canada and the United States is a useful case through which we can explore, and better understand, the institutional drivers of policy innovation and adaptation and, more broadly, the effectiveness of governments. Focusing on the effects of state and provincial government's specific institutional characteristics extends the mostly national-level literature on institutional performance and policy innovation to an under-studied scale.

The book is also intended to be an original contribution to the study of urban politics. As discussed, so much of the work on urban politics examines short-run and local dynamics. My analysis of multi-level urban governance over an extended period of time affords a different perspective on the urban politics of cooperation and conflict, one that has strong affinities with American and comparative political development studies that typically train their focus on the national level.[56]

Finally, the national and city historical narratives that lie at the heart of the book rely on extensive primary research that reveals and contextualizes events and actions that are not well known, even to locals. While their primary purpose is to support my broader argument about the development and performance of Canadian and American urban governance, my hope is that readers interested in the specific cities discussed will find these histories to be valuable in their own right. To this end, I have tried to avoid overburdening the reader with more explicit theory and citations than is absolutely necessary, while also providing maps and figures that make it easier to visualize the changing shape of each metropolis. The interested reader can access colour versions of the figures, and other materials, at https://ir.lib.uwo.ca/shapingthemetropolis/.

2

The Institutional Foundations of Governance

The United States and Canada have much in common. They share a border, a common majority language, close historical economic and social relations, inherited British legal traditions, and federal institutions. Both are understood to be among the most politically, fiscally, and administratively decentralized countries in the world.[1] In both countries, the physical form of industrial urbanization was shaped by the global diffusion of technological innovations: the telegraph and telephone, the railway, the macadamized roadway, the elevator, and so on, as well the diffusion of standards and practices, including zoning, building codes, and engineering techniques. Among Western countries, the United States and Canada are distinguished by the predominance of private property ownership and private investment in urban development. The sociologist Seymour Martin Lipset writes that "Canada and the United States ... resemble each other more than either resembles any other nation," while Keith Banting, George Hoberg, and Richard Simeon suggest that "the intensity of concern [regarding North American integration] may have arisen precisely because of a sense that the differences are rather small."[2]

Yet, as sketched in the previous chapter, the United States and Canada govern their cities and regulate the urbanization process differently, in ways that appear to produce distinct patterns of metropolitan development. This chapter assesses alternative potential explanations for these differences – political culture, the structure of group conflict, and the organization of governing institutions – before elaborating a theory of how the two countries' distinct institutional foundations generate policy differently.

POLITICAL CULTURE

Some observers, including Michael Goldberg and John Mercer in *The Myth of the North American City*, emphasize political culture to explain urban differences. By this argument, American local government complexity and limited or permissive land-use regulation are often explained in relation to broadly shared values forged by the two countries' different historical legacies.[3] While American political culture is ostensibly defined by individualism, localism, and privatism, as well as an enduring attachment to the Jeffersonian ideal of an agrarian republic of independent and self-regulating smallholders, Canadians are portrayed as more collectivist and deferential to authority.[4]

A closer look at the historical record complicates the divergent cultures argument. The political identity of early nineteenth-century English Canada was defined in the context of large-scale Yankee economic immigration – a population that, by the second decade of the nineteenth century, far outnumbered the United Empire Loyalists exiled from the Thirteen Colonies after the revolution.[5] Moreover, Edward Grabb and James Curtis find that radical individualism remained an elite construct in early nineteenth-century America, becoming a mass attitude only with the expansion of free public education.[6] This is consistent with Alan Ware's argument that American political conflict has been generated in part by tension between individualist liberal and collectivist republican ideologies that were crystalized in the post-Jackson party system. Rejecting Louis Hartz's thesis that American society developed from a pure liberal-individualist fragment, while Canada's ostensible collectivism is derived from liberalism's admixture with a "Tory touch," Ware points to institutions. Political conflict in the British North American colonies was submerged, and the society made governable, by the establishment and reproduction of an institutional-constitutional order that concentrated, rather than dispersed, power and authority.[7]

Moreover, counter to images of Canadian collectivism, we find evidence of a rather American attachment to local democracy and autonomy among English Canadians throughout the country's history.[8] In 1940 Kenneth Crawford, the pre-eminent scholar of Canadian municipal government, lamented the provinces' creeping pre-emption of local autonomy, stating that the municipal council "is in reality, if not constitutionally, the primary and basic unit of our democratic and representative form of government."[9] In his 1951 textbook on Canadian local government, Horace Brittain inscribed the very American sentiment that "local institutions are the bedrock and laboratories of democracy" and that the "only thing which can permanently prevent the evils resulting from the growth of the state at the expense of the citizens is the development of a large body of sturdy, aggressive and informed citizens who will scrutinize every proposal and will resist every effort to restrict unnecessarily the area of individual liberty."[10] More recently, Canadians have used the ballot box and protest to oppose provincially imposed changes to local government institutions.[11]

All of this suggests that mass and elite attitudes regarding the role of government, deference to authority, and so on, may vary within and across national boundaries, and may change over time. Norms and values no doubt shape urban governance and urbanization patterns. They are not self-executing, however. A fuller explanation must consider the governmental, social, and economic institutions through which they do their work, and how they are reproduced.

GROUP CONFLICT

A second common explanation of American and Canadian differences in urban governance and urban development is the differing structure of group conflict. No discussion of American urban politics and policy – and indeed, of American politics and society as a whole – can ignore race, yet Canadian analyses of urban governance rarely centre on ethno-linguistic difference. This is because French-speaking Canadians have always been highly concentrated in, and a majority within, a single province, Quebec, the government of which is the principal defender of French language and culture. Minority language–speakers constitute a substantial portion of the metropolitan population in only a handful of cities, including Montreal, Ottawa, and Moncton. Only in Montreal has language persistently structured urban politics.[12] Linguistic conflict is for the most part articulated through provincial politics and federal-provincial relations. Indeed, Spicer argues that the Canadian federal government's attempt to stake out a national urban policy in the 1970s collapsed in large part due to resistance from provincial governments, especially that of Quebec.[13]

Unlike French Canadians, African Americans form a majority in no state. Richard Iton argues that, as a result, racial conflict could not be politically and spatially "compartmentalized." African Americans have looked to the federal government to protect their individual rights and entitlements, regardless of where they reside.[14] As Gerard Boychuk shows in his comparative study of Canadian and American national health insurance, race profoundly inflected the development of the American residual welfare state precisely because mostly Southern whites resisted the creation of universal benefits, provided and underwritten by the federal government, that would benefit African-Americans.[15] As Ira Katznelson documents, the racial hierarchy embedded in American postwar social policy was defined by white Southern legislators during the New Deal and early postwar periods.[16]

Race took on an urban dimension due to the migration of rural southern African Americans not just into Southern central cities but also Northeastern and Midwestern ones. It is an historical irony that this occurred just as deindustrialization destabilized the cities' economic foundations, generating new urban concentrations of racialized poverty. The racial transformation of American cities was rapid. Between 1950 and 1970, in the fifty largest central cities, the proportion of African Americans increased from 14 to 24 per cent of the population (8.5 to 19.5 outside the South). At the end of the century, 52 per cent of African Americans lived in central cities, compared to only 21 per cent of non-Hispanic whites.[17]

During the 1950s and early 1960s, the dominant urban policy problem had been mounting fiscal and administrative pressures associated with metropolitan population growth and physical urban development. By the late 1960s and early 1970s, however, a discourse of "urban crisis" had taken hold, as central cities became identified with racialized poverty and disorder. Urban problems were increasingly construed as "black" problems, and federal urban policy shifted its focus from the metropolitan whole to the inner city.[18] Analogizing from Boychuk's argument about health insurance, the racial division of the American metropolis into black central cities and white suburbs by the 1970s made a universalist federal metropolitan policy politically untenable in the later postwar period.

Importantly, the initial federal, state, and local responses to postwar metropolitan growth pressures predated the racial transformation of many large non-Southern central cities and the rise to national salience of a racialized discourse of urban crisis. This is not to argue that racism and racial conflict are somehow recent phenomena in America.

To do so would be absurd, as race has indisputably structured American politics and policy since the colonial period.[19] Yet it should be recognized that, first, the racial transformation of central cities and suburbs, and the racialization of city-suburb relations, occurred at different speeds, and reached different levels, in different parts of the country. The African-American population of St. Louis, Missouri, for example, increased from 18 to 48 per cent during this period, while that of Providence, Rhode Island, increased from 3 to 15 per cent. The growth of the urban Hispanic population has also been concentrated in states on the Mexican border, but also in Chicago and the Northwest. As a result of the uneven timing and location of urban ethno-racial change, there has been considerable variation in the social basis of political coalitions and antagonisms within central cities, and between them and their suburbs.[20]

Second, the regional dimension of American political conflict – characterized by Katznelson as the "southern cage" from which national policymaking could not escape – necessarily played out differently in the smaller political worlds of the states, whose internal social composition was more homogeneous, especially outside the South. (While the average Southern state had an African-American population of 23 per cent in 1950, the corresponding figure for non-Southern states was 3 per cent. In 2010, these figures were relatively unchanged, at 22 per cent and 3 per cent, respectively.) Even as federal policymaking during and after the New Deal was structured by a regionally articulated racial order, there remained considerable potential for autonomous policy action on urban questions at the state level, especially in the earlier postwar decades – potential that was unrealized for reasons other than racial conflict in most states.

THE INSTITUTIONAL FOUNDATIONS OF POLICYMAKING

National differences in political culture and the structure of group conflict have undoubtedly shaped American and Canadian urban governance and cities, but to understand how they have done so, by how much, and when, the analysis must take careful account of how the organization of governing institutions has produced and reproduced these differences over time, and also the timing and sequence of events. To explain why urban governance and urban development differ in the United States and Canada, we must examine the historical evolution of provincial and state authority. As states and provinces are constitutionally responsible for local governments and land-use regulation, the scope of local government autonomy and the resources and administrative capacities they possess are, in effect, explicit or implicit policies of provincial and state governments. To structure this analysis, we must understand how American and Canadian political institutions make policy differently, ultimately producing different outputs, and how subnational and national governing institutions may differ. These are the *institutional foundations* of urban development.

In using the word "foundations," I do not wish to imply that other factors do not matter. Instead, I seek to foreground how institutional organization shapes policymaking processes in interaction with numerous other factors, including political culture, social makeup, technology, and the macro-economy, each of which is perennially changing. The term "institutional foundations" is borrowed from Kenneth Shepsle and Barry Weingast's "The Institutional Foundations of Committee Power," Terry Moe and Michael Caldwell's "The Institutional Foundations of Democratic Government," and John Huber and Charles Shipan's *Deliberate Discretion: The Institutional Foundations of Bureaucratic Autonomy*.[21] Each shows how institutional variation – principally between British Westminster parliamentary and American separated-powers forms of government – structures policymaking processes and outputs. Moe and Caldwell suggest that we view each system of government as a "package" of institutionalized structures, rules, and relationships whose form has "pervasive consequences for virtually all the building blocks of democratic government."[22]

How Separated-Powers and Westminster Institutions Differ

How political institutions are organized establishes the opportunities and constraints within which actors operate as they pursue policy objectives. Differently constructed institutions are therefore likely to process inputs (ideas) and generate outputs (policies) differently. Over a century ago, Walter Bagehot and Woodrow Wilson separately argued for the superiority of the Westminster over the American model.[23] Both proposed that the former's centralization of authority due to the fusion of the executive and legislative branches generated more rational, effective, coherent, and stable policy. Others have gone on to investigate the notion that the *performance* of political regimes

– which may be defined as the production of timely and effective responses to policy problems – as well as the content of policy outputs, are structured by institutional organization.[24] One of the most influential ways of characterizing deliberative processes is George Tsebelis's *veto players framework*, in which he identifies the institutionalized *veto points* at which authoritative actors – *veto players* – may slow or block policy action.[25] The more veto players and veto points, the more difficult it is to enact, or change, policy.

The American system of government is defined by its checks and balances – in essence, the institutionalization of multiple veto points. For a bill to become a law in American government, it must surmount numerous hurdles: approval by committees and by a majority in both legislative chambers, followed by approval by the executive. In the separated-powers system, the executive and legislative branches are constitutionally independent and may in fact be dominated by different parties. The authority of American state governors is weaker than that of the national president. They are constrained in their ability to initiate policy change and must rely more on rhetorical skill than institutional resources to advance their agendas. The governor's most powerful tool is reactive: the ability to veto adopted legislation. Moreover, unlike at the federal level, where the president selects the cabinet subject to Senate confirmation, most state constitutions provide for a *plural executive*, whereby major cabinet offices are directly and independently elected. Possessing independent authority and resources, the governor, the attorney general, and sometimes the treasurer and other positions, may work against each other, especially if they do not belong to the same party. One solution to executive weakness is institutional reform, and indeed there are many examples of constitutional changes to promote more programmatic state-level policymaking, including lengthening the term of office from two to four years, the line-item veto, and the reorganization of executive departments. Strengthening the executive branch's capacity, however, has often been resisted by legislators, who see no advantage in ceding their policymaking role.

Weak executive authority in American states does not necessarily mean that the legislative branch is itself strong and unified. Although state legislatures possess formal advantages over the executive, they are constrained in other ways. Historically, many state legislatures met only biennially, with the duration of sittings constitutionally limited. Especially before the 1970s, state legislators generally held office for short tenures, served part-time in addition to their primary employment, and received only token remuneration. Individual state legislators exercised considerable autonomy in relation to their party leadership yet possessed few resources to support policy development – often little more than a desk and a telephone. Large-state legislatures have become more professionalized since the 1980s.[26] Annual rather than biennial sessions are now the norm, representatives and senators are now paid full-time salaries, and party caucuses and individual legislators now have office and research budgets. At the same time, the centralization of campaign finance in party organizations and the proliferation of "litmus tests" – public endorsements of particular positions in the nomination process – have increased party leaders' ability to whip the vote and enforce ideological consistency.

Canadian provincial Westminster systems present almost the inverse condition. Provincial premiers exercise identical prerogatives to the national prime minister in their dual role as party leader and head of government. Unlike in Australia and the United Kingdom, where party leaders are selected (and removed) by their caucuses, postwar Canadian party leaders have been selected by delegated convention or direct member vote.[27] Party leaders generally leave office only when their party is defeated in a general election, or voluntarily. Government and opposition party leaders exert strong discipline over their caucuses, and premiers appoint the cabinet without caucus approval. Cohesive and disciplined majority governments therefore face few checks on their ability to unilaterally legislate (beyond concerns about future electoral performance). They may vote themselves supply and create, dissolve, or reorganize departments and agencies as they see fit. Backbench and opposition legislators possess few resources and rarely originate policy. Weaver and Rockman argue that, compared to other democratic regimes, single-party majority governments are best able to exercise autonomy from electoral pressures.[28] Canadian provincial party leaders' political independence from caucus increases the scope of this autonomy.

States and provinces also differ in another respect. Nebraska excepted, American state legislatures are bicameral, while Canadian provinces have unicameral legislatures. Inter-chamber bargaining is an important feature of the state legislative process, further increasing the cost of policy enactment. As state House and Senate seats are elected from different electoral bases, each institution may be dominated by a different party or party faction.[29] Provincial executives face no corresponding check on their ability to initiate and pass legislation.

Decisiveness and Resoluteness in the Subnational Context

Gary Cox and Matthew McCubbins distinguish between two aspects of institutional performance: *decisiveness* and *resoluteness*. "Decisiveness" refers to "the ability of a state to enact and implement policy change," while "resoluteness" refers to "the ability of a state to commit to maintaining a given policy."[30] They argue that, the greater the number of veto points, the less decisive and more resolute the system is. In separated-powers systems, the transaction costs of securing a legislative majority among multiple veto players inhibit policy change. Once enacted, however, policies are locked in by the equally high costs of securing agreement to alter them. Westminster systems, by contrast, are viewed as decisive but irresolute. With few veto points, policies are easily overturned when the executive's preferences change, principally through the electoral defeat of one party and the formation of a new government led by another.

Most studies of presidential and parliamentary systems have focused on national institutions.[31] I argue that differences in state and provincial institutions and political dynamics reverse Cox and McCubbins's expectations regarding resoluteness. Possessing limited authority, American governors are less able than presidents to countervail the legislature's centrifugal tendency. Combined with low legislative professionalization, this affords policy opponents more avenues to advance their interests, as do "sunset" clauses requiring the periodic reauthorization of laws or regulations and the constitutional availability of ballot initiative and legislative referral in several, mostly Western, states.[32]

In Canadian provinces, executive and legislative authority is highly centralized in the premier – perhaps even more so than in the national prime minister. Parliamentary sovereignty renders plebiscites and sunset clauses rare and non-binding, and so policies may be changed or overturned only by positive action.[33] Following Cox and McCubbins's logic, this should render policies more vulnerable to electoral change; however, in the context of executive-centred party government, protracted periods of single-party dominance are expected to reinforce policy stability.[34] In fact, multi-decade party "dynasties" were the norm in the larger provinces after the Second World War, especially in the 1940–80 period. The average provincial governing party tenure was 10.7 years between 1940 and 2017.[35] In Ontario, for example, the Conservatives held power from 1943 to 1985 (42 years). In Alberta, Social Credit governed from 1935 to

1971 (36 years), followed by the Conservatives from 1971 to 2015 (44 years). Social Credit governed British Columbia from 1952 to 1972 (20 years), and again from 1975 to 1991 (16 years). While governing party leadership turnover sometimes brought a change in policy direction akin to that expected with electoral change, policy continuity was the more common pattern.

Programmatic versus Particularistic Policy Outputs

Cox and McCubbins argue that the processes structured by Westminster and separated-powers institutions produce different kinds of policy. They distinguish between *public-* and *private-regarding policy*, which I will refer to as *programmatic* and *particularistic* policymaking.[36] Echoing Bagehot and Wilson, they argue that executives pursue programmatic policies (those that are general in application, internally consistent, and grounded in evidence) while individual legislators seek particularistic benefits, such as geographically specific expenditures or regulatory exemptions for the areas they represent. The type of policy produced depends on how the balance of power between the executive and legislature is institutionalized. Executive-centred policymaking in Westminster systems is more likely to produce programmatic outputs. By contrast, legislature-centred policymaking in separated-powers systems is more likely to produce particularistic outputs due to the distribution of selective benefits ("pork barrelling") required to secure a policy's enactment. This in turn may undermine the policy's internal consistency and effectiveness. To be sure, patronage and pork-barrel politics also exist in Westminster systems, but they are more often than not orchestrated centrally, by governing party leaders, to secure overall electoral advantage for the party rather than any particular legislator, and may therefore be wielded toward programmatic ends.

Policy Innovation and Permeability to External Ideas

Competition among interests has long been viewed as the engine of American politics. Robert Dahl placed the open thrust and parry among interests at the centre of his theory of pluralism. Theodore Lowi was more pessimistic in his assessment of "interest-group liberalism" as an empty politics, one in which legislatures ratify brokered settlements among interests whose legitimacy flows from due process rather than from their substance. What both perspectives presume is the relative openness of American legislative institutions to external interests and their ideas.[37] Indeed, the predominant channel through which contending policy ideas enter the legislative agenda is organized interests' lobbying of individual American state legislators, who have historically possessed considerable independence but few resources to develop policy proposals on their own. A high-profile policy problem may attract multiple potentially viable solutions, each championed by a different legislator or legislative faction. Alternatively, legislators may coalesce around a single proposal. While the separated-powers system's indecisiveness is most likely to manifest as gridlock, the brokerage of externally generated proposals may potentially lead to the innovation of new institutions and policy frameworks.

Canadian provincial Westminster institutions afford relatively limited access to external interests. Policy ideas most often enter consideration through two conduits, both of which are targets of lobbying by policy entrepreneurs: the professional public service, whose members are connected to national and transnational policy networks, and the governing party leadership. Whether the development of a policy is initiated by the political executive or the bureaucracy matters less than the closed loop of the executive-bureaucratic relationship. As Weaver and Rockman put it:

> In parliamentary systems, centralization of legislative power
> presumably decreases the alternatives open to interest groups,
> and party discipline makes appeals to individual legislators an
> almost hopeless strategy in terms of changing policy outcomes.
> The bureaucracy and cabinet ministers are the main points of
> access open to interest groups. Moreover, it is usually impossible
> to reverse a government's position (if it has a majority) once
> that position has been taken.[38]

The primary barrier to action may be a failure to generate or consider viable policy ideas in the first place. This dynamic is exemplified in Peter A. Hall's analysis of policy learning in Britain in the 1970s, where a cloistered bureaucracy proved unable to develop an effective response to economic crisis.[39] A new policy paradigm – the replacement of Keynesian demand management by monetarism – was ultimately introduced by a new governing party following an election.

Summary

In sum, the different organization of Westminster institutions in Canadian provinces and separated-powers institutions in American states systematically structures the policymaking process (see table 2.1). American state institutions are both indecisive and irresolute. While their permeability to external societal interests enables innovative policy ideas to enter consideration, the multiplicity of veto points inhibits policy enactment and rewards particularistic behaviour. At the same time, policy opponents are empowered by the openness of the legislative and judicial process, including access to the ballot initiative in some states. Canadian provincial Westminster systems, by contrast, are both decisive and resolute. Centralized, executive-centred decision making is relatively insulated from societal interests and moderated only by electoral imperatives. It is difficult for policy ideas to enter decision makers' agendas, yet those that do can be rapidly enacted, and with less need to cater to particularistic interests. As a result, Westminster systems are more decisive. They are also likely to be more resolute when a single party dominates because electoral change is minimized as a driver of policy change. Of course, much depends on the quality and feasibility of the policy ideas. A bad idea remains so whether decisively enacted by a centralized executive or generated through legislative deal-making.

THE NORMATIVE CONTEXT OF INSTITUTIONAL PERFORMANCE

Institutions, policy ideas, and interests do not exist in a vacuum. Changes in broadly held societal norms and values are, because of the legitimacy they confer, potential sources of stability and disruption for policies and the institutions that administer them. As Triadafilos Triadafilopoulos puts it, such "normative contexts ... encompass and shape domestic policy making, authorizing particular political identities, policies, and practices while discrediting others ... Shifts in normative contexts throw policies enacted under previous contexts into doubt as the grounds of legitimacy underpinning them are challenged."[40] John Campbell usefully distinguishes between *programmatic* and *paradigmatic* policy ideas. In his terms, policy programs are "elite policy prescriptions that help policy makers to chart a clear and specific course of action," while paradigms are often implicit "elite assumptions that constrain the cognitive range of useful solutions

Table 2.1
Institutional foundations and their implications

	Westminster system (Canadian provinces)	Separated-powers system (American states)
Veto points	ONE Strong executive, party discipline, unicameral legislature	MANY Weak executive, undisciplined legislators, bicameral legislature
Openness to societal interests	LOW Executive-centred policymaking; policy ideas enter through the bureaucracy and party leadership ↓	HIGH Legislature-centred policymaking; policy ideas enter through lobbying of legislators by advocacy groups ↓
Policymaking style	PROGRAMMATIC Executive and bureaucracy design policies that are rational and general in application, increasing policy coherence	PARTICULARISTIC Legislative bargaining generates a winning coalition by catering to parochial interests, undermining policy coherence
Performance	DECISIVE AND RESOLUTE Reinforced by single-party dominance	INDECISIVE AND IRRESOLUTE Reinforced by non-professionalized legislature, weak executive, sunset provisions, referenda

available."[41] Margaret Weir distinguishes *programmatic ideas* from broader *public philosophies*, the latter defined as "broad concepts that are tied to values and moral principles and that can be represented in political debate in symbols and rhetoric." She identifies a mutually supportive feedback loop between programmatic policy ideas and public philosophies, and also links the effectiveness of the former to the means of their implementation:

> Public philosophies play a central role in organizing politics, but their capacity to direct policy is limited; without ties to programmatic ideas their influence is difficult to sustain. Likewise, programmatic ideas are most influential when they are bound to a public philosophy; but these ideas must also forge links with administration. Programmatic ideas developed without reference to administration may be technically strong but are likely to be politically impotent. The influence of ideas on politics is strongest when programmatic ideas, tied to administrative

means, are joined with a public philosophy; unhinged, the influence of each becomes difficult to sustain.[42]

Similarly, Weaver and Rockman suggest that "capabilities" of government – its capacity to influence its environment – require "fit among three factors: the nature of its policy challenges, its institutional arrangements, and the conditions that facilitate and limit institutional effects," including political culture, norms, and values.[43] If alignment with the normative context lowers the cost of policy adoption and maintenance, it follows that some political institutions may perform better – that is, be more decisive and resolute – in some normative contexts than others. Before working out these relationships, however, I will first sketch out the specifics of the normative context of urban governance and urban development.

The Normative Context of Urban Governance and Urban Development

Three normative domains are especially relevant to urban governance and urban development: perceptions of the role of the state, political values, and the human relationship to the natural environment. Shifts in these domains can be periodized into three eras, which are used to interpret the case narratives. Prior to the Great Depression, it was generally accepted that people and households were individually responsible for their economic security, and that state intervention should be limited to the passive facilitation of private capital accumulation through regulation or large-scale infrastructure investment. The Depression crisis and wartime mobilization of productive capacities transformed public expectations. An atmosphere of trust in government and what might be called technocratic optimism – faith in rational and technical solutions to complex problems – prevailed in the long economic boom that followed the war. This provided a favourable context for state intervention to provide social security and promote economic development, integral to which were programs of land-use regulation and infrastructure expansion.

Technocratic optimism and trust in government receded after the 1970s. Political sociologist Ronald Inglehart views this as a result of a generalized shift in political values across the developed world. His surveys show that as affluence and education levels increase, people's political goals shift from securing material well-being or substance to "postmaterial" political objectives centred on self-expression and quality of life. At the aggregate level, this manifested as a reorientation of the axes of political contention. Writing in the early 1970s, sociologist Daniel Bell forecast the emergence of a "postindustrial" society in the West as manufacturing gave way to a knowledge-based service economy that privileged technical rationality. Samuel Huntington questioned how benign this social and economic transformation would be, arguing that political conflict would intensify as the priorities of the new service class clashed with those of the old industrial economy.[44]

These forecasts proved prescient. First, the new urban middle class rejected closed, elite-driven policymaking, demanding genuine participation. At the same time, it also challenged the legitimacy of policy outputs justified on the basis of technical criteria and expertise. The late 1960s and early 1970s featured the rise of neighbourhood opposition to disruptive urban transportation and slum-clearance megaprojects and the emergence of the historic preservation movement.[45] Centralized government came to be seen not as an instrument of collective action for the common good but as overextended and self-interested. Public suspicion of centralized government has empowered a political agenda of austerity, retrenchment, and devolution since the 1970s.[46] In this vein, Simeon, Hoberg, and Banting portray perceptions of governance failure as produced by growing incongruence between the settled worldview and social and economic conditions. For them, the post-1970s perceived crisis of ungovernability signified the end of the "social contract" established during and after the Great Depression.[47]

Of particular relevance to urban development is another manifestation of postmaterial politics: the rise of environmentalism.[48] Prior to the 1960s, the natural environment was primarily understood as subordinate to humanity, a resource or amenity to be conserved for human consumption. After the mid-1960s, this was challenged by environmentalism, which views humanity as part of nature and calls for the natural environment to be protected for its own sake.

Institutional Performance and the Normative Context

How then might these normative contexts – pre-Depression, early postwar, and later postwar – differentially support the decisiveness and resoluteness of Westminster or separated-powers policymaking? In the pre-Depression period, we would expect centralized Westminster institutions to act more programmatically to facilitate economic expansion, while action by separated-powers institutions, with their dispersed authority, would be more ad hoc and particularistic. The construction of the positive state during the Great Depression and early postwar years took place in a normative context of greater trust in government, deference to elites, and faith in technocratic progress. The Westminster system's relatively centralized, top-down, and closed decision-making process performs best in this normative context. Consensus among political, social, economic, and intellectual elites may countervail the separated-powers system's centrifugal tendencies, but only when ordinary residents are deferential to them.[49] It follows that the decisiveness of both political systems would decline during and after the 1970s as anti-government sentiment surged and deference to elites and expert knowledge waned. (See table 2.2.)

The post-1970 era also featured the transformation of party competition in both countries. In Canada, federal and provincial parties have become more ideologically distinct from one another, sharpening electoral conflict and creating the potential for substantive policy shifts following changes in government.[50] At the same time, single-party dominance eroded in the larger provinces, yielding to more competitive electoral politics. Together, these changes undermined the decisiveness and resoluteness of Canadian governments. Parties have also become more disciplined and ideologically polarized, and elections more competitive, in the American states.[51] Instead of producing greater policy coherence, however, more disciplined and rigid legislative parties – each colonized by constellations of organized interests that supply them with policy programs and that can mobilize (or demobilize) considerable electoral resources – have intensified conflicts that were previously submerged by elite-driven consensus politics.[52]

Policy Legitimacy amid Normative Change

As the normative context changes, the mass or elite coalitions that supported the creation and maintenance of policies and institutions in one era may dissolve or become antagonistic in the next. This may occur even if the policies and institutions are effective, in the sense of fulfilling their intended purpose and generating increasing returns. The challenge for defenders of established institutions and policies is to find ways to restore their legitimacy by reframing their purpose and objectives and cultivating new support coalitions.

Table 2.2
Institutional performance in a changing normative context

	Pre-Depression (pre-1930s)	Depression, early postwar period (1930s–1970s)	Later postwar period (post–1970s)
NORMATIVE CONTEXT			
Political values	• Materialist values • Nature subordinate to human needs	• Collective benefits • Deference to elites (technocratic optimism) • Trust in government	• Postmaterialist values • Environmentalism • Individual benefits • Devaluation of expert knowledge • Anti-government sentiment
Role of government	• Laissez-faire • Localism ↓	• Interventionism • Centralization ↓	• Retrenchment, deregulation • Devolution ↓
PERFORMANCE			
Separated-powers system	• More particularistic	• More decisive • More programmatic	• Less decisive • Less resolute • Less programmatic
Westminster system		• More decisive • More programmatic	• Less decisive • Less resolute • Less programmatic

Otherwise, institutions and policies risk being actively dismantled, starved of political support and resources, or displaced by new policies and institutions.[53]

Adjustment to normative change through reframing and coalition building is expected to be a central dynamic in the development of urban governance and urban development policy in the United States and Canada. However, these processes are likely to play out differently in the two countries due to the Westminster and separated-powers systems' different institutional foundations. This perspective is consistent with Simeon and Willis's argument in their comparison of "democracy and performance," as both the United States and Canada have experienced rising disaffection with government and a perceived crisis of governability in both countries since the 1970s.[54] Canada's institutional foundations have channelled emergent conflicts into federal-provincial relations, while in the United States they manifest in clashes between the executive, legislative, and judicial branches.

THE INSTITUTIONAL FOUNDATIONS OF URBAN GOVERNANCE

The framework outlined in this chapter suggests that Westminster systems in Canadian provinces and separated-powers systems in American states generate different policymaking styles defined by their decisiveness and resoluteness, and that their performance varies over time in relation to the normative context and the competitiveness of the party system. Provincial and state governments are central institutional actors in the American and Canadian fields of urban governance. They are also the primary venues for conflict among interests in relation to urbanization because they possess ultimate jurisdiction over municipal organization and land use and are major funders and providers of urban infrastructure. The policies they make directly and indirectly determine the shape of urban development. The next chapter applies this framework to the historical development of multi-level urban governance in the two countries from the nineteenth century to the present.

3

The Development of National Patterns of Urban Governance

The period from the American Civil War and Canadian Confederation in the 1860s to the Great Depression and the Second World War was politically and economically transformative in both Canada and the United States. The foundations of the positive state were laid and extended beyond the limits of what could have been imagined in the first half of nineteenth century, and the balance of authority between the national and state or provincial governments was utterly reconfigured. With some notable exceptions, most observers have concentrated on these state-building processes at the national level, while generally ignoring the construction and transformation of subnational and local governance.[1] This chapter presents a comparative historical overview of the development of urban governance in the United States and Canada. Applying the institutional performance framework introduced in the previous chapter, the focus is on the historical development of governmental authority and capacities, as well as on intergovernmental relations. In particular, the chapter shows how American state and Canadian provincial governments responded differently to similar challenges as they constructed and reformed local government institutions.

The narrative is organized into five eras, each defined by distinct policy challenges and packages of reforms and occurring in the context of broad transformations in the economy, society, and normative context.

1 *Making local governments, 1830–80.* In British North America, provinces adopted general municipal legislation that specified uniform rules and procedures for incorporation and boundary

change. This provided the basis for low-cost and consistent provincial supervision of local government. In the American states,
general legislation did not supplant ad hoc municipal charters,
opening the door to sometimes arbitrary and corrupt intervention in municipal affairs by the state legislature.

2 *Reforming local governance and intergovernmental relations,
1880–1929.* As cities expanded, local governance became more
complex, and urbanization-related policy challenges multiplied,
American and Canadian reformers advocated for greater honesty
and efficiency in local government. Building on the general legal
framework, Canadian provinces responded in part by establishing systems of administrative control over local government.
American state governments, by contrast, retreated from direct
intervention in municipal organization and finance.

3 *The Great Depression and the Second World War, 1929–45.*
The divergent paths that characterized the previous era were
reinforced during the Great Depression. Provincial policymakers
responded to municipal insolvency by expanding provincial
oversight over municipal affairs. In the United States, the federal
government pre-empted state action, further insulating local
governments from state-level control.

4 *The machinery in action: Responding to the postwar boom,
1945–75.* Rapid postwar urbanization occurred in the context
of inherited institutions and intergovernmental relations. In
Canada, provinces responded to urban growth by expanding
the oversight capacities developed in the interwar period through
the establishment of comprehensive land-use planning systems,
large investments in urban highways and other infrastructure,
and proactive reorganization of local government in metropolitan areas. As a result, urban development was largely coordinated by general-purpose local governments. South of the border,
state governments remained passive as the federal government
mandated inter-municipal collaboration as a condition of funding growth-related infrastructure projects, urban renewal, and
housing projects. Home rule, combined with legal limitations
on capital borrowing, led to the proliferation of single-purpose
districts as service providers in growing American suburbs.

5 *Normative change delegitimizes metropolitan planning, 1975–
present.* The early postwar response to rapid urbanization
occurred in a normative context of trust in government and
deference to elites. After the 1960s, however, public appetite for

state intervention declined as the economy soured and governments slid into deficit, and residents resisted the imposition of
plans and infrastructure projects justified on the basis of technical criteria rather than local community values. Governments in
both countries retrenched. In Canada, provinces became inconsistent actors in metropolitan land-use and infrastructure planning. In the United States, federal withdrawal of mandates and
fiscal support undermined metropolitan coordination of urban
development – a policy space not filled by state government.

The long-term comparative historical narrative reveals how
national responses to urbanization were deeply structured by each
country's institutional foundations – that is, by the different incentives and authority relations embedded in American separated-
powers and Canadian Westminster institutions. The cumulative effect
of these nationally distinct developmental processes in the nineteenth
and early twentieth centuries was the embedding of institutional
structures and relations that led to quite different responses to postwar urbanization.

MAKING LOCAL GOVERNMENTS, 1830–80

It has long been taken for granted that the distinguishing characteristic
of American local government is its relative autonomy from state
government. While municipalities in other countries operate under
more elaborate systems of oversight by subnational or national governments, American cities are said to enjoy "home rule," a condition
of legal autonomy from legislative interference. This was not always
the case. Home rule was an invention of the late nineteenth century,
developed to remedy a particular set of political problems associated
with industrial urbanization. Many (but not all) of the conditions
that led to the adoption of home rule were also present in Canadian
cities. Why then was constitutional or legal protection of municipal
autonomy not pursued in the Canadian context? To answer this question, we must first consider the legal foundations of local government
in each country.

Canada: Early Adoption of General Municipal Law

In what became Canada, imperial authorities had initially discouraged
municipal incorporation, taking from the American insurrection the

lesson that institutions of local self-government were the seedbed of disloyalty. Chartered in 1785, Saint John, New Brunswick, was the first and only municipal corporation in post-revolutionary British North America for almost fifty years. This changed with the liberal ascendency in the 1830s and 1840s. British authorities came to see some measure of colonial self-government as necessary for economic development and the inculcation of British political values.[2] An emerging local commercial middle class saw increasing the autonomy and self-government of villages, towns, and cities as of a piece with securing greater independence for the colony from Whitehall.[3] Colonial reformers' political objective was to transplant the Westminster system to North American soil. When the colonies of Upper and Lower Canada were unified in 1841, they were granted a form of autonomy known as responsible government, which reflected the principle that the executive resides in the legislature and is responsible to it, rather than to an appointed governor. In parallel, the larger cities in British North America were granted municipal charters: Montreal and Quebec in 1832, Toronto in 1834, Halifax in 1841, and Hamilton and Kingston in 1846.

A crucial terminological distinction must be made here between general and special legislation. General legislation applies to all objects of the law, be they individuals or corporations, while special legislation pertains to a specific object. Charters for municipal or private corporations are special acts and may be initiated by the legislature or on petition from the public. Until the mid-nineteenth century, virtually all municipal corporations in the British North American territories (including what became the United States) were chartered and regulated by special rather than general legislation. General legislation defining the structure and function of local government was introduced in the British North American colonies starting in the 1840s. In Upper Canada (later Ontario), the District Councils Act (1841) established a rudimentary system of counties and townships, leaving intact existing city, town, and police board charters.[4] This system was rationalized by the Municipal Corporations Act (1849), commonly known as the Baldwin Act, after its chief exponent, Robert Baldwin, an Upper Canadian reformer.[5] The act repealed all existing special-act charters and established three classes of urban government, defined by population size: city (greater than 15,000 people), town (3,000 to 15,000), and village (1,000 to 3,000). Larger municipalities were granted additional powers and responsibilities. The act also enumerated the structures and powers of county governments and rural townships.

After Confederation, the Ontario legislature routinely rejected petitions for incorporation if they did not meet the Baldwin Act's criteria. Review of the legislative journals and statutes at five-year intervals between 1873 and 1899 suggests that, in the 1880s and afterwards, almost as many petitions for incorporation, annexation, and change in status were refused as were granted, indicating that the legislature did not simply rubberstamp the petitions that came before it. The journals reveal two reasons for refusal: that the petition's rationale as set out in the preamble of the proposed special act "was not proven" (in other words, did not meet the criteria) or that "the general provisions of the Municipal Act are sufficient for the purposes sought" (and so change was not necessary). The rapid creation of new municipalities throughout Ontario during the railway booms of the 1850s and 1870s suggests that while incorporation was programmatically regulated by the legislature, the procedural and political barriers to doing so were not onerous. Indeed, Bloomfield, Bloomfield, and McCaskell credit the general law's early adoption with producing a larger per capita number of incorporated municipalities relative to the other Canadian provinces by the end of the nineteenth century.[6] Similar legislation was subsequently enacted in Lower Canada (Quebec), the Maritime provinces, and Newfoundland, and the system was continued after Confederation in 1867. The model was generally replicated in the new western provinces.[7] The Baldwin Act was the first legislation in the English-speaking world to consolidate in a single document a comprehensive legal framework for all forms of general-purpose local government, both urban and rural. Britain would not accomplish this until the 1880s.[8]

Ontario municipalities, large and small, urban and rural, largely went their own way within the strictures of the general law, and the principle of local autonomy became well accepted.[9] Wickett could write in 1900 that provincial intervention in local affairs was largely theoretical, because of "vigorous local spirit."[10] Weaver suggests that elites' commitment to the British principle of responsible government, transposed to the local level, animated an ideal of local government as self-governing and self-supporting.[11]

The United States: Ad hoc Municipal Organization by Special Legislation

Local government would come to rest on different foundations south of the border. While Louisiana, Indiana, Ohio, and other states adopted general municipal laws in the antebellum period, and more followed after the Civil War, they proved ineffective for several reasons.[12] Existing special-act charters were not repealed and brought under the authority of general law. The general laws also typically pertained to particular classes of municipality rather than to all municipalities. For example, an act for towns might be passed in a different year and without relation to an act governing the affairs of villages or cities. These categories were often ill defined, and existing charters were typically grandfathered rather than superseded by new general acts. Legislatures often ignored their own general municipal laws by continuing to charter municipalities by special act. The practice persisted after the Civil War and was replicated as the frontier moved west.

The fragmentation of local government law in the United States had several implications. First, the absence of a prescribed hierarchy of local government entities, and therefore a mechanism by which communities could acquire new powers as their population increased, reinforced the role of special legislation as a means of adjustment to changing circumstances. Second, the piecemeal adoption of general acts that pertained to specific classes of municipality and grandfathered existing charters only made the existing patchwork of local government law more complex. Third, the continuance of incorporation by special act meant that no uniform criteria were applied to local petitions for municipal legislation, and, as a result, the system was more permissive than a general system might have been. For example, Anderson reported that, in Minnesota, "there is little or no evidence that either the legislature or the county boards exercised restraining power of any consequence upon the petitioners."[13] Finally, the absence of a rules-based framework for regulating the establishment and modification of municipal corporations opened the door to the manipulation of the system for partisan advantage.

The Institutional Foundations of Divergent Paths

These divergent national pathways of legal development were produced by the different incentives generated by Westminster and separated-powers institutions in conjunction with evolving intergovernmental fiscal relations. American state legislatures were particularistic and irresolute: highly responsive to parochial interests and unchecked by weak executives, they had no incentive to make and sustain programmatic policies. Pre-revolutionary charters were reformed by special legislation, and new incorporations occurred mostly on a piecemeal basis. By contrast, centralized executive authorities in the British North American colonies pursued a programmatic solution: general municipal legal frameworks. These patterns were replicated in both countries as settlement moved west.

The operation of these different institutional incentive structures is illustrated by the financing of infrastructure. North of the border, British colonial authorities and, later, provincial governments used general municipal legislation to systematically promote local government formation. This distributed their debt risk while accelerating the construction of infrastructure to drive economic development.[14] When local borrowing undermined municipal solvency, provincial governments were forced to guarantee their debts and introduced general rules and oversight. By contrast, the contemporaneous American response was ad hoc. A state-level infrastructure debt crisis in the 1840s provoked the constitutionalization of state debt limits, which effectively transferred capital borrowing to the local level.[15] When municipal solvency collapsed in the decades following the Civil War, a new wave of state constitutional limitations was enacted, this time on local borrowing and tax rate increases.[16] Canadian-style programmatic municipalization and state oversight of capital borrowing would have facilitated settlement and economic development on the American frontier. Instead, fiscal devolution and municipal insolvency were the unintended consequences of efforts to restore state solvency and halt the accumulation of unfunded liabilities.

REFORMING LOCAL GOVERNANCE AND INTERGOVERNMENTAL RELATIONS, 1880–1929

The reformist wave that swept across North America starting in the 1870s brought together western agrarian populists seeking greater democratic voice, middle-class urban progressives advocating for greater efficiency and honesty in local government, and anti-monopolists decrying the power and influence of large private corporations. Diffuse in organization and sometimes conflicting in their objectives, these movements were spurred by unprecedented changes in the broader political economy: depressions and panics in the long deflationary period that followed the American Civil War, the opening of the continental interior, mass immigration to cities, and industrialization fuelled by rapid technological change.

National Differences in Reform Objectives

In the large industrial cities of the northeastern United States, moral indignation erupted in response to the excesses of boss rule – the Tweed Ring in New York and the Gas Ring in Philadelphia being the two most notorious examples. Urban population growth accelerated after 1880 as immigration increased and local economies recovered from the Panic of 1873, putting unprecedented pressure on local governments. The expansion of municipal activities multiplied opportunities for corruption and mismanagement.[17] The need to provide new infrastructure and services brought private interests and local government into close interaction. In the rapidly growing cities of the eastern seaboard and Upper Midwest, the result was a triangle of mutual influence and benefit. The new urban immigrant electorate received services as a reward for its electoral support of candidates anointed by the boss and his machine, while economic interests paid the bills in return for monopoly control of utility franchises and other favours.[18] In 1888, Lord Bryce famously wrote that "there is no denying that the government of cities is the one conspicuous failure of the United States."[19]

Local reform clubs and, after its formation in 1894, the National Municipal League were unified in their desire to improve the honesty and efficiency of local government by making its operations more businesslike – in essence, to remove the politics from civic administration. Stivers writes that "reformers saw city government not as a political mechanism for dealing with conflicting interests but as an administrative entity for finding and carrying out the best policy to deal with particular urban problems."[20] Reformers sought not to increase democracy but to secure efficiency by banishing the amateur from civic decision-making and embracing scientific principles of administration. Even if individual reform advocates were not themselves businessmen, the promotion of efficiency and economy served corporate interests as they sought to demobilize threats posed by organized labour and immigrants.[21]

Reformers initially sought to use the ballot box to replace corrupt or negligent leaders with morally upright and business-minded candidates. When this remedy proved insufficient, they demanded institutional change: non-partisan elections, the elimination of wards in favour of election at large, the strengthening of the executive, and the establishment of a merit-based professional civil service. At the same time, activities seen to be purely technical or administrative in nature, and therefore apolitical, were transferred to boards and commissions operating at arm's length from the council, thereby insulating them from petty and venal politics.[22]

Canadians observed American developments with interest and freely borrowed policy ideas and institutional models when they seemed applicable to local problems.[23] Indeed, American political scientist William Bennett Munro could write in 1929 that, "of all branches of government in Canada, the government of cities has proved the most susceptible to American influence."[24]

Copying American models, the Ontario Municipal Association was established in 1899, and a national organization, the Union of Canadian Municipalities, in 1901. Mimicking New York's Bureau of Municipal Research – a privately financed reform organization founded in 1906 – an identically named organization was established in Toronto in 1913.[25] The Canadian reformer shared the American's pro-business orientation. The motto of the People's Reform League of New York, "Municipal government is business and not politics," is virtually identical to Toronto reform alderman John Hallam's maxim that local government "should be a business concern carried out on business principles."[26] Similarly, the influential Toronto businessman reformer Samuel Morley Wickett asserted that "the municipality is regarded more as a species of joint stock company, only those contributing the capital being allowed to share in the direction of its affairs."[27]

While similarly motivated, the Canadian reform movement was not identical to its American counterpart. Having evolved within a context of provincial regulation and standardization, Canadian business largely supported government intervention, as it lowered input costs and increased the predictability of returns on investments.[28] Canada's retention of restrictive qualifications to vote and run for office also removed a crucial impetus to reform in the United States: partisan clientelism. Although the total foreign-born population was higher in Canada than in the United States between 1860 and 1930, many immigrants were excluded from voting or running for office by minimum property or income requirements in Canada. This inhibited the exchange of selective benefits for votes that underlay the American urban political machine. The restricted franchise narrowed the scope of Canadian local politics. Businessmen reformers in Toronto and other Canadian cities saw the property franchise as essential to preserving and enhancing the efficiency of municipal operations while reducing the potential electoral influence of new immigrants who, they believed, had little knowledge of or interest in civic administration. Reform was about installing more efficient governmental machinery and the right kind of people to operate it in the interest of economic growth. The result, as Weaver puts it, was "socialism for businessmen and free enterprise for workingmen," based on the precept that "civic resources should assist the endeavours of those who do the most for the material growth of the community, namely business and real estate interests."[29]

The late nineteenth-century American urban reformer desired what the Canadian city already had: local government relatively uninfected by the evils of democracy. If Canadian local government sometimes suffered from amateurism, negligence, and petty criminality, it did not experience the wholesale corruption and ethnic clientelism practised by American bosses. In 1849, Robert Baldwin had seen local government as the schoolhouse of democracy. A half-century later it would be so, but only for the right kind of people.

American Municipal Reform: Home Rule and Limits on Special Legislation

It soon became apparent in both countries that improving the efficiency and honesty of local government would require more than tinkering with municipal institutions. The constitutional fact of state and provincial authority over municipal affairs also made intergovernmental relations an object of reform. A first problem existed only in the United States: the perception that arbitrary partisan intervention by states in local affairs was widespread and undesirable. A second, found in both countries, was that of legislatures becoming overloaded by the large volume of municipal and other special legislation.

Responding to parochial interests, state legislators involved themselves in municipal incorporation and annexation; arrangements with private utility companies; the creation, abolition, and appointment of local offices; the setting of rates, salaries, and pension levels; the granting of concessions; the construction of works at local expense; and even the renaming or closing of streets.[30] Municipalities in some states lost control of their budgets when legislators arbitrarily raised the wages of firefighters and police officers and created local offices for partisan friends. So-called ripper legislation was used to prolong the terms of local partisans whose party had lost favour with the electorate.[31] Local fiscal balance was also undermined when states authorized capital expenditures on roads and utilities whose cost would be borne locally or when they preferentially awarded utility franchises. Lord Bryce reported that local delegations were often in the pockets of "sinister elements," effectively shifting "the wrongdoing from themselves to the legislature."[32] Schlesinger argued that the state legislature's legal authority over municipal affairs rendered it an important node in the network of corruption: "Because of the close control wielded by legislatures over cities, municipal bosses and their henchmen took up their residence in the state capital when the law makers were in session."[33] Teaford, however, sees partisan corruption as the exception rather the rule, arguing that state legislatures were for the most part deferential to the wishes of urban representatives carrying bills written and advanced by municipalities or other local interests.[34] In essence, the legislature was an alternative venue for local politics. What could not be secured or resolved within municipal institutions could potentially be addressed by another set of locally elected representatives – the legislative delegation.[35] Regardless, the reformer's identification of special legislation with corruption and local subjugation established a powerful and widely accepted moral argument in favour of limiting arbitrary legislative action.

The second problem was related to the first. Regardless of their content and political purpose, the sheer volume of special laws overwhelmed state legislatures, which in most states met biennially for a constitutionally limited number of days. Minnesota was typical. From the state's first session in 1858 through to 1881, the legislature enacted an average of 348 special laws, compared to 224 general laws, per biennial session. Over 60 per cent of all laws, and over two-thirds of the pages in the statute books, were devoted to special legislation during this period. The amateur legislator's primary activity was log rolling and ward heeling in pursuit of local concessions at the expense of attending to matters of statewide significance.[36] Lack of scrutiny by legislators resulted in vague and inconsistent legal wording that later proved difficult for legislators, local officials, and the courts to interpret.[37] In Teaford's words, "Harried state solons confronted by eight or nine hundred bills during a sixty-day session did not make law so much as enact it."[38]

American advocates of scientific administration sought to restrict the use of special legislation to make state government more efficient

and focused on matters of statewide application rather than the satis-
faction of parochial interests. Yet limiting special municipal legislation
meant that necessary adjustments to municipal charters would have
to occur by other means. The result was "home rule" – the ability of
municipalities to frame and amend their own city charters without
state interference or permission. In principle, enlarging the scope of
local autonomy would accomplish multiple goals. Empowering municipalities to solve problems on their own would unburden the state
legislature of the welter of special legislation.[39] At the same time,
decoupling state and local government would also eliminate the intergovernmental corruption nexus. Some also believed that home rule
would improve local morals, engender civic pride, and attract higher-
quality political leadership.[40]

The preferred mechanism was to amend state constitutions to place
particular objects beyond legislative control. In the last quarter of the
nineteenth century, state constitutional conventions adopted restrictions or prohibitions on special laws, including those pertaining to
local government. By 1895, twenty states had prohibited municipal
incorporation by special act, while seventeen also required that incorporation be permitted only through general legislation. In some states,
the constitution also restricted legislative involvement in other aspects
of internal municipal affairs, including the creation and appointment
of local offices.[41] Four states adopted constitutional home rule for
defined classes of municipalities between 1875 and 1900; by 1920
this number had grown to fourteen, and still other states expanded
municipal autonomy by legislative rather than constitutional means.[42]

Importantly, leading reformers rejected the comprehensive replacement of special-act municipal charters with universally applied general
laws. Goodnow portrayed existing American general laws as irredeem-
able failures: "The reason why they are impracticable is that in almost
all cases the powers conferred by general municipal corporations acts
… are either inadequate or are enumerated in such detail that changes
in them in the case of particular cities are absolutely necessary if
municipal government therein is to be carried on satisfactorily."[43]
Anderson agreed, stating that a detailed general law could never be
truly effective because local needs and conditions differ too much.[44]

Constitutional limitations did not resolve the problem of arbitrary
action. The existing patchwork of municipal legislation remained in
place. Legislatures also subverted general laws by crafting narrowly
defined classes of municipalities that applied to only one city, county,

village, or township.[45] Legislative gridlock and the log rolling of local bills soon re-emerged.[46]

Canadian Municipal Reform: Broadening Provincial Intervention

In Ontario, private legislation accounted for the majority of bills passed in almost all sessions in the first four decades following Confederation in 1867, and many of these were municipal in their object.[47] While legislative overload was recognized as a problem in the Canadian provinces, there was little interest in limiting legislative authority. Reformers and business interests alike saw provincial government as a positive rather than a negative force in local economic development.[48] The general municipal act was perceived as flexible and effective. Ontario's 1888 Commission on Municipal Institutions noted that its strength lay in its "simplicity, its symmetry, and, looking to the past one may fairly add, its sufficiency."[49] Echoing Anderson and Goodnow's critique of American general municipal legislation, however, the commission went on to caution against overly prescriptive general laws that would hinder local adaptation to changing circumstances. Biased toward programmatic rather than particularistic policymaking, Ontario and other provinces appear to have crafted workable general municipal legal frameworks.

Canadian reformers also found no provincial-municipal patronage nexus to break. Unconstrained by constitutional limitations and dominating the legislature, provincial premiers could dispense patronage to partisans directly, without meddling in the internal workings of municipalities. Ontario Liberal premier Oliver Mowat (1872–96), for example, could appoint a broad array of inspectors, commissioners, and other positions that worked within localities but independently of local government.[50] It is also important to note that Canadian provinces, unlike American states, lack unitary constitutional documents that can be amended independently of the legislature, by constitutional convention. Canadian reformers therefore had no extraordinary means of limiting the scope of provincial authority over local governments. Theoretically, provincial legislatures could seek amendment of the British North America Act to provide for municipal home rule, but this did not occur. Provincial politicians were not inclined to voluntarily surrender their constitutional authority.

More urbanized than the other provinces, Ontario set the pattern
of Canadian reform. The reformers' focus was not so much to reduce
the number of private bills flowing through the legislature as to find
a way to rationalize the legislature's case-by-case treatment of petitions dealing with generic concerns while maintaining the uniform
application of criteria and procedures established in general municipal
legislation.[51] Most private legislation was concerned with the financial
affairs of municipal corporations and private railway franchises.
Conflicts between municipal councils and intercity and street railway
franchises had multiplied with urban growth. The government sought
to transfer the mediation of these conflicts outside the legislature while
maintained programmatic attention to them. The first attempt was
the creation by Liberal premier George Ross of a special cabinet committee on railways in 1902. The committee was ineffective, however,
and fell into disuse after Conservative George Whitney's 1905 election
victory.[52] Whitney had earlier allied with reform advocates on the
question of public hydroelectric power generation, capitalizing on
growing suspicion of private corporate interests and a concomitant
rise in support for the regulation and public ownership of utilities.[53]
A protracted dispute between the City of Toronto and a private streetcar operator over network expansion and the provision of inter-urban
connections demanded resolution, and so in 1906 the government
introduced legislation to comprehensively regulate the activities of
intercity and street railways.

The remedy selected, the establishment of the Ontario Railway and
Municipal Board (ORMB), was a variation of a form adopted in other
North American jurisdictions: a public utilities commission – that is,
an appointed board or commission charged with regulating the provision of public services by public and private corporations.[54] Such
entities served three purposes. First, they stemmed the tide of special
legislation by removing uncontroversial yet cumbersome matters from
the legislative agenda. Second, transferring controversial issues to an
arm's-length agency insulated the government from political responsibility.[55] Third, oversight by expert appointees rather than legislators
promised more consistent and systematic treatment of matters.

Ontario and other Canadian provinces adopted this model later
than many American states. Six northeastern states had established
railroad commissions prior to 1870, and by the turn of the century
most of the rest had established similar agencies to oversee railroad,
gas, telegraph, electric, and steam companies. They could set maximum

rates; order service improvements; and review the approval of new franchises, service extensions, capital borrowing, and the sale or merger of utilities. To insulate them from political interference and corruption, these institutions were designed to exercise considerable autonomy from the executive and legislature. Constitutional or statutory guarantees of municipal home rule did not stand in their way. In Illinois and Wisconsin, for example, legislation explicitly overrode the exemptions enjoyed by cities with home rule charters.[56]

What distinguished Ontario's board from its American counterparts was that its jurisdiction over public utilities was supplemented by oversight of aspects of municipal organization and solvency. As its name suggests, the Ontario Railway and Municipal Board was concerned primarily with railroads – setting and enforcing service standards, adjudicating labour disputes, approving franchise agreements, and inquiring into problems as they emerged. The board's assumption of oversight and approval authority with respect to changes to municipal organization and certain categories of bylaws is contained in only one of the legislation's sixty-six sections, and may well have been an afterthought.[57] Municipal affairs initially accounted for only a small portion of its activities. In its capacity as a public utilities commission, the board would become a convenient repository for other objects of regulation with which the government did not want to directly burden itself: the adjudication of property-assessment disputes, the approval of land-use plans, and the regulation of other utilities and services, including local telephone systems, gasworks, and public parks, as well as the registration of motor vehicles. Similar bodies were introduced in Alberta, Manitoba, Nova Scotia, and Quebec in the following decade.[58] The incremental layering of local government oversight onto public utilities commissions was a logical extension of provincial governments' unfettered jurisdiction over municipal affairs. In the United States, by contrast, the expansion of public utilities commissions occurred largely after reformers had embedded home rule in law and public discourse, and so the purview of these commissions was not extended to include regulation of municipal affairs.

Institutional Reinforcement of Divergent Paths

The divergent national reform strategies and their outcomes were generated by the two countries' institutional foundations. In Canada, the decongestion of legislative business was secured through the delegation of authority to administrative institutions. This reinforced the programmatic regulation of the local government system as policy pressures associated with rapid urbanization mounted. American institutional development differed for two reasons. First, log rolling and local elites' pursuit of selective benefits were encouraged by the relative absence of party discipline in part-time legislatures – a centrifugal force that state executives lacked the authority to countervail. The result was particularistic and irresolute policymaking.

Second, the American extension of the electoral franchise after the 1820s generated political incentives not present in Canada. While the democratic ferment of the Jacksonian period overturned local oligarchies and expanded suffrage, it also enabled the formation of state-local party patronage machines predicated on mass electoral mobilization. These machines had an interest in maintaining a system that enabled them to confer particularistic benefits. When special municipal legislation overwhelmed state legislators and was easily exploited by partisan and parochial interests, American reformers resolved the crisis through political devolution, not administrative centralization.

THE GREAT DEPRESSION AND THE SECOND WORLD WAR, 1929–45

These separate paths of institutional development were tested and ultimately reinforced by the Great Depression. The crash of '29 was precipitous. American GDP dropped by one-third between 1929 and 1933.[59] Similarly, Canadian GNP fell by 29 per cent in the same period.[60] High tariffs were especially damaging to Canada's small, trade-dependent domestic market. (Canada's total population was less than that of the state of New York in 1931.) The American Great Plains and Canadian Prairie regions were devastated as the collapse of demand for agricultural products coincided with crop failure and drought. At the same time, urban workers suffered as domestic and international demand for industrial products declined. Canadian and American unemployment rates tracked each other closely before, during, and after the Depression years, peaking at approximately 20 per cent in 1932–33.[61] Average per capita wage income fell by almost 50 per cent in British Columbia, Ontario, and Quebec, and by even more in the three Prairie provinces.[62]

Dimensions of Local Fiscal Crisis

The Depression plunged local governments into fiscal crisis. On both sides of the border, speculators and civic boosters had taken full advantage of easy credit before and after the First World War. Bonds issued during the 1920s to finance speculative investments in urban infrastructure improvements came due when municipal fiscal health was at its nadir.[63] Debt had grown considerably faster than population. The Canadian population grew by 22 per cent during the war decade and by 18 per cent in the 1920s, while per capita local debt grew by about 45 per cent between 1913 and 1920 and another 90 per cent between 1920 and 1932. Similarly, the American population grew by about 15 per cent while debt doubled in each decade.[64] Not all debt was growth related. Municipalities also borrowed to pay for new unfunded or partially funded state and provincial mandates. In Canada, for example, provincial Boards of Health could order municipalities to provide or improve water or sewer services, yet municipalities had to finance them on their own account. Incompetent administration and lax tax collection also undermined municipalities' fiscal position, as did the toleration of annual operating deficits. By 1932, municipalities in the more urbanized Canadian provinces were worse off than their American counterparts. British Columbia's per capita municipal debt rivalled that of the most indebted states, Florida, New York, and New Jersey. Debt levels in Ontario and Quebec were both above the American and Canadian national averages, comparable to those of Michigan, Virginia, and Rhode Island. Less-urbanized provinces and states – for example, Saskatchewan, Nova Scotia, Iowa, and Arkansas – had much lower levels of per capita municipal debt.

Municipalities were the first governments to feel the Depression's impact due to their dependence on the property tax, revenue from which plummeted sharply as property values collapsed. Between 1930 and 1935, the assessed value of all property in American cities of over 100,000 residents declined by 21 per cent. In Los Angeles and Cleveland, assessment dropped by over 40 per cent.[65] Falling property values were not the only driver of revenue collapse. Mass unemployment caused property tax delinquency rates to soar.[66] In Detroit at the start of 1933, for example, 40 per cent of the previous year's taxes were in arrears, and debt servicing consumed 70 per cent of the city's budget.[67] The Canadian situation was more severe. A 1933–34 survey found that uncollected taxes topped 50 per cent of the annual levy in 245 urban municipalities.[68] Fully half of the municipal property tax levy in Ontario was in arrears in 1934.[69] By comparison, the American state with the highest proportion of uncollected and delinquent debt was Michigan, at 40.5 per cent of the annual levy in 1932–33.[70]

While municipal revenue shrank, demand for expenditure on unemployment relief, which was understood to be a local responsibility, increased. In New Jersey, for example, local relief expenditures almost tripled from 1930 to 1931.[71] Over a third of all families in Portland, Oregon, were on relief in 1933. Mass unemployment spurred long-time mayor George Baker to attempt his own New Deal. With Baker proclaiming "I'll wreck the town if it will give employment," his administration issued $845,000 in bonds to finance works projects in 1932–33.[72] Considering the City of Toronto, Riendeau notes that, "even with its stringent residence limitations [to be eligible for benefits], the metropolitan ... area still ranked among the highest in disproportionate share of the national unemployment and relief burden in 1935; it had 7.6% of the nation's population but was responsible for 12.8% of the relief recipients of the nation and 18.8% of the national relief expenditure."[73] In 1931, about one in five residents of the City of Toronto was jobless; by the start of 1933, this had risen to 30 per cent. During 1932 and early 1933, the number of families on relief in the city tripled, to over 25,000.[74] The situation was worse in the suburbs. Little East York's tax arrears topped $1.1 million by 1933, second in Ontario only to Windsor, which fell into insolvency. By February 1935, 45 per cent of East York's population was on relief, a total of 16,700 people.[75] In neighbouring North York, 40 per cent of the population, or about 6,000 people, were on the dole. At least one-third of the population was on relief in the suburban municipalities of Etobicoke, Long Branch, Mimico, New Toronto, Scarborough, and York.[76] The pattern of suburban suffering was repeated in greater Vancouver.[77] Those cities that could borrowed to fund relief costs; those that could not defaulted on their debt.

Comparing the United States and Canada, Albert Hillhouse, the director of research for the Municipal Finance Officers' Association, wrote in 1936 that "the municipal debt problem is much more acute in Canada than in the United States."[78] By his calculations, only 3 to 5 per cent of municipal debt was in default in the United States, compared with 10 to 11 per cent in Canada. By June 1935, 19.9 per

. cent of municipal debt was in default in Ontario, double the national average. Ontario's rate was the highest in the country: 13 per cent was in arrears in Manitoba, 8.6 per cent in Saskatchewan and British Columbia, 3.8 per cent in Quebec, 0.6 per cent in Alberta, and zero in the three Maritime provinces.[79] Over forty Ontario municipalities and school districts became insolvent.[80]

The geography of the fiscal crisis differed in the two countries. In Canada, the debt crisis was most acute in the suburbs of the major cities, which had borrowed heavily to finance new infrastructure and facilities. Two-thirds of suburban Ontario municipalities defaulted on their bonds, and had done so almost completely, as did the Vancouver-area suburbs of Burnaby and the City and District of North Vancouver. Detroit and Cleveland were the largest American cities to become insolvent. In the United States, most defaulters were small-to-medium-sized central cities.[81]

The American Response: Federal Intervention

Believing that the crisis was temporary and the market would bring about a "natural" solution, American governments initially saw no need to intervene. Outside of pensions, there was limited precedent for national and state government transfers to individuals. Poor relief was seen as the proper concern of local governments and charities. The larger cities launched emergency employment schemes during the devastating winter of 1932–33, but such programs were quickly abandoned as local coffers were depleted.[82] The national government viewed the deterioration of municipal finances as a state-level concern. President Hoover restricted federal action to limited expenditure on public works, persuading major firms to maintain wage rates, arranging government purchase of commodities to maintain price levels, and extending credit to large industrial and financial concerns.[83]

Federal inaction spurred state-level innovation. First New York, then New Jersey, and later Rhode Island, Wisconsin, Pennsylvania, Illinois, and North Carolina authorized the distribution of funds to local authorities for relief.[84] The 1930s were also years of administrative reform. Many states professionalized and reorganized their bureaucracies. Importantly, this did not extend to institutionalizing oversight of municipal affairs. Reflecting the naturalization of home-rule doctrine, the framers of state reorganization codes "displayed a tendency to regard the state and its local units as separate, water-tight compartments, between which only a minimum of communication was necessary."[85] No general agencies or departments concerned with municipal affairs were established, although some degree of fiscal oversight was lodged in various departments in a number of states, including the inspection of local accounts and budgets and the review of local bond issues. A more common response was for states to assume direct responsibility for select local activities, including education, roads, and some social services, thereby keeping home rule intact.

Municipalities that could not meet their obligations spent much of the Depression trapped in a sort of legal purgatory. As the "contract clause" of the federal constitution prohibits state legislatures from impairing contracts, they could not unilaterally adjust municipal debts or establish procedures for municipal bankruptcy.[86] At the same time, the doctrine of state sovereignty prevented the federal government from reaching over the states to establish a municipal debt–adjustment process of its own.[87] Only near the end of the Depression did Congress pass a municipal bankruptcy law that survived constitutional challenge. As a result, many American municipalities muddled through, negotiating piecemeal settlements with creditors inside and outside of the courts and balancing budgets through draconian expenditure reductions. In Detroit, New York, and many other cities, "financial dictators [creditors] replaced political bosses."[88] Most large cities ultimately met their debt obligations by slashing payrolls, issuing scrip in lieu of salaries and payments to suppliers, and suspending the construction of public works.[89]

Some states tried to work around constitutional and legal constraints. New Jersey and North Carolina enacted general systems of administrative receivership whereby state appointees audited accounts and negotiated with creditors but could not enforce payment plans.[90] These mechanisms avoided running afoul of the contract clause by exercising approval authority over present taxing, spending, and borrowing, rather than adjusting prior agreements. Maine, Massachusetts, Oregon, and Texas also experimented with such supervisory commissions.[91] As the contract clause did not apply to the judiciary, some states authorized the courts to appoint supervisors to sit in place of defaulting municipalities' councils and act as receivers, much as would occur in a private bankruptcy.[92] Agreements with creditors would then be approved and enforced by the court, not the state government itself.

Ultimately state-level action was unequal to the enormity of the crisis. Most states were either unwilling or fiscally unable to shoulder the burden of relief for the unemployed, and constitutional limits impeded their ability to rescue troubled local governments. Calls for federal action intensified.

The inauguration of Franklin Delano Roosevelt in March 1933 marked the end of Hoover's policy of local self-reliance and the beginning of the New Deal. That May, Congress created the Federal Emergency Relief Administration, which ultimately transferred half a billion dollars to state and local authorities for direct relief. Two-thirds of federal emergency expenditures were on employment. Congress's initial appropriation for the Public Works Administration (PWA) in 1933 amounted to almost 6 per cent of GDP; its successor, the Works Progress Administration (WPA), was allocated almost 7 per cent of GDP in 1935.[93] Infrastructure construction projects employed millions. Between 1935 and 1943, the WPA funded the construction or improvement of 123,000 bridges and tunnels, 500 water treatment plants, 1,800 pumping stations, 19,700 miles of water mains, 1,500 sewage treatment plants, and 24,000 miles of sewers and storm drains, not to mention the construction of thousands of road miles and public buildings.[94]

Expenditures on work relief and public works construction in cities, as well as farm relief, infused local economies with much-needed capital, which directly or indirectly supported the budgets of local governments.[95] The PWA and the Reconstruction Finance Corporation also bought hundreds of millions of dollars of local bonds at low interest rates and offered advances to local governments that enabled them to secure private loans and sell securities.[96]

The New Deal also generated innovation in the theory and practice of land-use, infrastructure, and economic-development planning at the national, state, and local scales. One aspect of this was promotion of rural economic development through electrification and the construction of transportation infrastructure. Mass urban unemployment would be remedied by the construction of master-planned, economically self-sufficient new towns – a state-sponsored move back to the land. Congress also authorized an executive agency charged with studying the nation's physical resources and coordinating the activities of federal and state governments in order to promote resource conservation and economic growth: the National Resources Planning

Board (NRPB).[97] Drawing on the collective expertise of academics and professionals who had earlier been associated with the Chicago Plan of 1909, the Chicago School of Sociology, the Southern Regionalists at the University of North Carolina at Chapel Hill, the 1922–29 New York Regional Plan, and the Regional Plan Association of America, the NRPB evangelized coordinated land-use and economic planning that spanned the federal, regional, state, watershed, metropolitan, and local levels. It provided funds and professional staff support to the states to establish their own planning boards, and forty-three states had done so by 1935. With considerable variation from state to state, and with varying degrees of state government support, state planning boards engaged in unprecedented study of urban and rural economic and population growth, land use, and the potential for natural resource extraction. Many promoted the formation of municipal and county planning agencies. State and local planning boards also reviewed and prioritized requests for PWA funds for local infrastructure projects.

The most far-reaching regional economic development project was the Tennessee Valley Authority (TVA). Established in 1933, the TVA was charged with redeveloping the seven-state Tennessee River basin to achieve multiple objectives: damming for flood control and hydroelectric power production for industrial development, the conservation-oriented restoration of farm and forest lands, and the promotion of local land-use planning.[98] Although, for political reasons, the TVA approach was not replicated in other American river basins, it would become an influential model of regional land-use planning and economic development.[99]

The federal government's insertion into the domain of local and regional urban and rural development policy, as well as in local infrastructure decisions, established a template for postwar intergovernmental relations: the use of conditional grants as a means of influencing state and local governments' behaviour. Those states that had embraced activist policies were subordinated by Washington and, as Ethington and Levitus put it, the New Deal "federalized the metropolis in regard to political mobilization" as local officials looked to the national capital rather than state legislatures for aid.[100] No state-level apparatus for regulating municipal affairs emerged, and the home-rule firewall separating municipal affairs and state government installed by Progressive Era reformers remained intact.

The Canadian Response: Provincial Intervention

Similar to the United States before Roosevelt's election, the initial response of Canadian authorities was to reaffirm the traditional beliefs that the locality was the most appropriate level at which to fund and administer relief and that a policy of high tariffs and fiscal probity would best enable the market to clear bad debt and restore prosperity.[101] As in the short depression of 1920–23, a federal government rooted in and committed to the agricultural economy was unwilling to break with local responsibility for unemployment relief by comprehensively aiding growing cities and their residents.[102] The federal government reluctantly intervened with ad hoc grants-in-aid. Between 1930 and 1937, Ottawa assumed 40 per cent of local relief costs nationwide.[103] Federal funding of public works projects also occurred but on a smaller scale than in the United States. These were seen as temporary measures and were authorized by annual acts of Parliament. The larger urbanized provinces initially resisted intervention, while the smaller rural ones were fiscally incapacitated. In August 1931, Ontario's Conservative premier George Henry informed a delegation of municipal officials that they "must not forget that the responsibility for relief rests primarily on them."[104]

Ontario's general municipal act and the Ontario Railway and Municipal Board had not prevented the municipal insolvency crisis. Provincial supervision of local affairs had been confined largely to the passive (and apparently ineffectual) monitoring of fiscal solvency, utilities, and borrowing. While jurisdiction over municipal affairs distinguished the Canadian boards from American public utility commissions, this jurisdiction was most often exercised in response to local initiative rather than proactively. Until the consolidation of local railway firms transferred the locus of railway regulation to the federal level, the railway work of the ORMB eclipsed its municipal activities.

This changed in 1932 following the fiscal collapse of the City of Windsor and eight neighbouring municipalities.[105] High levels of local government debt combined with the closure of the American border to Detroit-bound Canadian workers ravaged municipal finances. By 1934, 29 per cent of metropolitan Windsor's population was on relief. The official assessed value of property declined by 38 per cent from 1930 to 1935; alternative estimates surpassed 50 per cent.[106] In response, Ontario decisively replaced the ORMB with a new Ontario Municipal Board (OMB) whose primary purpose was to proactively supervise municipal finances. Unconstrained by an equivalent to the contract clause in the American constitution, the new board possessed sweeping powers to replace the elected governments of defaulting municipalities with provincially appointed supervisors authorized to exercise all powers of municipal councils and impose settlements on creditors.[107] Since 1908, the ORMB had been authorized to review and certify municipal bond issues, if requested; after 1935, all municipal bylaws initiating capital undertakings or issuing debt were to be approved by the OMB.[108] Also in 1935, the provincial government established a cabinet-level Department of Municipal Affairs to manage the oversight of municipal finances. The board, however, remained autonomous and possessed the authority to order the department to intervene directly in municipal affairs, especially in case of default.[109]

Ultimately, municipalities containing 280,000 residents – about 10 per cent of Ontario's population – came under provincial supervision during the Depression, most located in the Toronto and Windsor areas.[110] After provincial supervision failed to restore solvency in Windsor, the province appointed the Royal Commission on Border Cities Amalgamation.[111] This resulted in the forced merger of area municipalities into a new City of Windsor in 1935, a sure sign of the provincial government's growing capacity for intervention and its willingness to use it.

Other provinces had established cabinet-level departments or ministries of municipal affairs in the 1920s and early 1930s. (Ontario's late creation of a department stemmed from the success of the ORMB.) Several provinces also followed Ontario in creating arm's-length municipal boards.[112] In most provinces, departments and boards had been preceded by commissioners or inspectors of municipal activities. In British Columbia, for example, an Inspector of Municipalities created in 1914 was replaced in 1934 with a new Department of Municipal Affairs empowered to supervise local borrowing. By the Depression's end, all provinces had institutionalized new capacities to oversee municipal finances.

These changes were made possible by Westminster executive centralization. Compared to their American counterparts, provincial governments were politically, legally, and constitutionally unconstrained in their ability to decisively create, reorganize, or expand bureaucratic capacities for the oversight of municipal affairs. Importantly, the goal of provincial centralization in this period was not to undermine local self-government; rather, it was to save it. Hearing the appeal of Windsor residents opposed to municipal amalgamation, the Judicial Committee of the Privy Council (then the highest court of appeal) ruled: "It is not only the right, but it would appear to be the duty of the provincial legislature to provide the necessary remedy, so that the health of the inhabitants and the necessities of organized life in the communities should be preserved."[113]

Canadian institutional innovations did not go unnoticed in the United States. Hillhouse believed that state-level administrative machinery akin to the Ontario Municipal Board was desirable and could be made to function within the constraints imposed by the contract clause. Still, the model was not adopted. He blamed this on the symbolic potency of home rule:

> An over-emphasis on the doctrine of home rule in debt policies also accounts in part for the absence of proper restrictive legislation. Farsighted state governments might, a decade ago, have set up the type of local government board now functioning in the major Canadian provinces if cities had not made a shibboleth of home rule and had not strongly resisted state supervision of both borrowing and debt retirement.[114]

The British legal principle of community self-government was inherited by both Canada and the United States, yet it found very different expression in the two countries' laws related to municipal incorporation and intergovernmental relations.

The Divergent Normative Contexts of Early Postwar Planning

The Depression and wartime experience transformed public expectations of government. A new generation of technocrats, many associated with earlier good-government advocacy, believed that the state could use scientific planning to create a more secure and stable social and economic order. This desire coalesced around projects of postwar reconstruction. Still, differences in the timing and substance of the two countries' responses to the Depression crisis produced different patterns of politics during the war years and immediately afterward.

In the United States, public acceptance of New Deal intervention diminished as the 1930s wore on. The emergency atmosphere of 1932–33 having faded, a 1936 Gallup poll found that two-thirds of Americans wanted Roosevelt to reduce public expenditure.[115] The court-packing episode, the Roosevelt Recession, and other actions enabled Republicans to articulate a counter-message emphasizing local and personal autonomy and self-reliance, the creativity and vitality of the free-enterprise system, and a market-led rather than state-led path to recovery and growth. The revitalized Republican Party's message embraced the New Deal's optimism and progressive rhetoric, and some of its policy content, while repudiating its statism.[116] The GOP doubled its representation in the House and elected eight new Senators in the 1938 midterm elections. Congressional Republicans and conservative Democrats could now block Roosevelt's proposals. The New Deal effectively ended as Republican governors were elected in a dozen states. After the United States entered the war in 1941, Roosevelt's economic managers shifted their focus from combatting depression to mobilizing war production and planning for the postwar future. Akin to the Beveridge Report in Britain, the NRPB prepared a blueprint for a comprehensive welfare state, but the normative context was not conducive to such far-reaching intervention.[117] Congress declined to reauthorize the NRPB in mid-1943. It, and the state and local planning activities it sponsored, disappeared.

In Canada, federal reluctance and provincial inability to mount a direct response to the economic crisis, combined with a positive perception of the American New Deal, had created new political opportunities on the left. The principal beneficiary of this shift in normative context during the war years was the Co-operative Commonwealth Federation (CCF), a socialist party founded in 1932 that merged agrarian cooperative populism with industrial labour support.[118] Its intellectual engine, a group of academics working as the League for Social Reconstruction, called for comprehensive economic and social planning by the state.[119] Electoral success followed. The CCF won power in Saskatchewan in 1944 and surged to become the official opposition in British Columbia in 1941, Ontario in 1943, and Manitoba in 1945. Nationally and in the provinces, the Liberal and Conservative Parties retained their electoral duopoly by stoking anticommunist sentiment and tacking to the left. The governing federal Liberals under Mackenzie King commissioned the far-reaching Royal Commission on Dominion-Provincial Relations in 1937. It proposed, among other recommendations, a national system of income redis-tribution.[120] Many feared that postwar demobilization would lead to a return to high unemployment. Influenced by the American New Deal and contemporaneous British efforts, the federal and provincial governments turned to postwar planning, establishing study commissions and departments charged with planning for reconstruction, including a comprehensive system of social security underpinned by fiscal centralization.[121]

This comparison reveals the importance of timing in the interaction between the evolution of national and subnational government capacities and the changing normative context. In the United States, federal New Deal intervention between 1932 and 1938 pre-empted innovation by the states; in Canada, federal non-intervention spurred provincial innovation that built on existing policy legacies. As the provinces lacked the fiscal means to confront economic depression directly, they responded by asserting greater regulatory control over matters within their jurisdiction, including local government structure and finance. Even before the war, Americans had tired of state intervention and rewarded New Deal opponents – free-enterprise Republicans and southern Democrats. Washington's capacity for intervention remained intact, however, and would be expanded in the 1950s and 1960s as political circumstances allowed, but state governments remained subordinate and reactive. In Canada, by contrast, elites and citizens had come to support state intervention and rewarded the Liberal and Conservative Parties' "left turn" at both the federal and provincial levels. The politics of the early postwar years were therefore more conducive to programmatic state intervention in Canada than in the United States.

THE MACHINERY IN ACTION: RESPONDING TO THE POSTWAR BOOM, 1945–75

Canadian and American governments responded to the postwar boom using the legal and administrative machinery inherited from earlier times. Building on the general municipal law, Canadian provincial governments had responded to the Great Depression by institutionalizing new capacities to oversee local government activities. These were readily expanded and extended in the postwar period. In Canadian provinces, executive-centred decision making coupled with single-party dominance enabled governments to be both decisive and resolute

– able to enact programmatic policies and adhere to them for extended periods of time. This was a facilitated by a normative context of deference to political, intellectual, and economic elites. American states, by contrast, entered the postwar period overshadowed by the federal government, often constitutionally limited from intervening in local governance, and with meagre administrative capacities. Captive to parochial interests, state legislatures were passive and inconsistent makers and implementers of policy. Action in this sphere was incremental rather than programmatic and was often induced by federal mandates and fiscal incentives rather than motivated by problem solving. Where created, new policies and institutions remained vulnerable to political challenge as antagonistic interests pressed their case in the legislature. The great irony of the early postwar period is that American policy ideas regarding the planning and governing of the growing metropolis were adopted more completely in Canada than in the United States.

Reforming Local Government Complexity

During this period, American reformers, many of them associated with the National Municipal League or the League of Women Voters, strenuously advocated for local government restructuring in metropolitan areas as a means of realizing service delivery efficiencies and aligning the scale of political representation with the scale of metropolitan economic and social relations.[122] These efforts met with little success. Home rule and constitutional restrictions on special legislation precluded unilateral legislative action, and, even if they did not, the states had developed no administrative capacity to oversee municipal incorporation and boundary change. Where state law required affirmative votes of residents in both the annexed and annexing territory, suburbanites could readily veto central-city annexation.

During the 1950s and 1960s, reformers pursued a parallel programmatic objective in Alaska, California, Minnesota, Oregon, and Wisconsin: the creation of state-level commissions to exercise criteria-based oversight of local government incorporation and annexation, and to promote general-purpose over special-purpose local government formation. These bodies bore some resemblance to the Ontario Municipal Board and, at least in the Alaska, Minnesota, and Oregon cases, were partially inspired by it (see further discussion in chapters 5 and 7). Their authority was eroded, however, as lobbyists for municipalities and special districts exerted pressure on the legislature. State legislatures' structural incentive to reward particularistic interests led to the accommodation, if not the encouragement, of special district formation and suburban municipal incorporation.[123]

A quite different chain of events played out north of the border. Previously, provinces had used their oversight authority with respect to local government organization to discourage the creation of new general- and special-purpose local governments. In the postwar period, provincial governments of all stripes became more proactive. For the large cities, the provinces sought to create metropolitan authorities capable of planning and servicing suburban growth. More generally, provinces also sought to increase the fiscal and administrative capacities of local governments so they could take on greater responsibilities, including planning and infrastructure management. In this sense, provincial governments saw restructuring as a means of enhancing local autonomy, democratic accountability, and fiscal and administrative capacity, rather than limiting it.

No province went further than Ontario, where several rounds of municipal and school board restructuring reduced the number of local government units by more than half. First in Toronto in 1954 and then in other urban centres, consolidation of lower-tier municipalities was paired with the empowerment of counties, whereby infrastructure and other services benefiting from economies of scale were transferred to upper-tier municipal governments.[124] Manitoba and Quebec emulated the Metropolitan Toronto model. Greater Winnipeg was reorganized into a two-tier arrangement in 1960 and then consolidated into a single-tier government in 1971. Quebec established two-tier governments for the island of Montreal, Quebec City, and Hull in 1970, and facilitated the amalgamation of rural municipalities elsewhere in the province. In British Columbia, existing inter-municipal infrastructure and service districts across the provinces were consolidated into multipurpose "regional districts" in the late 1960s and early 1970s. In Vancouver and Victoria, these became de facto metropolitan governments. Alberta comprehensively reorganized rural local government in 1951 while promoting the ongoing annexation of urbanizing fringe areas by Calgary and Edmonton. Provincial governments in the slow-growth Atlantic provinces also brokered or imposed annexation and consolidation, the comprehensive reform of rural government in New Brunswick in the 1960s being the most far-reaching example. These decisive programmatic actions were made possible by the confluence of four factors: the relative insulation of executive-centred Westminster decision-making from societal interests; sustained single-party domin-ance; the prior existence of administrative oversight of local govern-ment organization; and a normative context of technocratic optimism and deference to elites.

The United States:
Federal Promotion of Intergovernmental Coordination

In the United States, state governments' limited response to rapid urban growth led to federal action. During the 1950s and 1960s, Washington built on Depression-era precedent by legislating new intergovernmental fiscal-transfer frameworks that imposed mandates in exchange for funding.[125] Section 701 of the 1954 National Housing Act – legislation directed primarily at slum clearance and mortgage finance – established a Comprehensive Planning Assistance Program under which state and local governments could apply for federal grants to "facilitate urban planning for smaller communities lacking adequate planning resources."[126] For one of its architects, the 701 program was nothing less than the realization of what the National Resources Planning Board and the state planning boards might have achieved had they not been abolished a decade earlier.[127] To access funds, individual cities of less than 25,000 people or metropolitan areas (as defined by the Census Bureau) were required to form advisory planning commissions. In Scott's assessment, "the urban planning assistance program ... encouraged states to pay more attention to local planning and to increase their support of local planning and development agencies" in high-growth areas.[128] In this it was success-ful – 139 advisory metropolitan planning commissions were formed by 1964. Most were established with state involvement, if not always legislative sanction, as minimally resourced organizations with no binding authority over municipal decisions. As result, their effective-ness was limited.

The land-use planning-coordination mandate soon paralleled another for urban transportation infrastructure. By the early 1960s, the network of federally funded inter-city highways was largely com-plete. What remained was their interconnection within the cities themselves in the form of beltways and downtown-access corridors. The 1962 the Federal-Aid Highway Act required that all transporta-tion projects in urban areas of over 50,000 residents be based on an ongoing, collaborative state-local planning process. By July 1965, all 224 designated urbanized areas had established intergovernmental transportation-planning processes. Sometimes these were connected to the planning commissions established to meet the requirements of the earlier Housing Act, but in most cases highway-oriented state transportation departments took the lead.

Lyndon Johnson's landslide victory in the 1964 presidential election, coupled with liberal Democratic hegemony in Congress, aligned political conditions for a dramatic expansion of federal intervention in state and local welfare, health, and education services. The economy continued to grow rapidly, but the problems of urban racialized poverty and inadequate urban infrastructure climbed the public agenda. Under the rubrics of the Great Society and the War on Poverty, Johnson worked with Congress to, among other things, appropriate billions of dollars for expanded conditional grants-in-aid to state and local governments, with a metropolitan focus. Influenced by the Advisory Commission on Intergovernmental Relations, the Housing and Urban Development Act (1965) required the formation of "councils of governments" (COGs) composed of elected representatives of local governments (as opposed to staff) as recipients of federal planning assistance.[129] A year later, section 204 of the Demonstration Cities and Metropolitan Development Act required that all local applications for federal water and sewer infrastructure and urban renewal funds be reviewed by COGs in order to ensure proper coordination of action. It soon became apparent that these reviews occurred too late in the process to meaningfully influence outcomes, so Congress passed the Intergovernmental Cooperation Act (1968) and its implementing regulation, the Bureau of the Budget's Circular A-95, which required each state to designate planning bodies at the state and metropolitan levels to review and comment on all proposals for federal aid in relation to local, regional, and state land-use and infrastructure plans. COGs were strengthened by the 1973 Highway Act. Reflecting the influence of urban legislators who saw state highway department dominance of metropolitan transportation planning as insensitive to urban conditions and needs, the act allocated funds for the creation of "metropolitan planning organizations" (MPOs) made up of local officials and enabled federal highway grants to be used for transit projects.[130] In many cases, COGs became the designated MPOs, establishing an opportunity for the metropolitan coordination of land-use and multi-modal transportation planning.

Between 1970 and 1975, Washington State US Senator Henry Jackson championed the National Land Use Policy Act, which in its various permutations would have provided grants-in-aid to state governments to undertake ongoing statewide land-use planning.[131] Existing federal support for metropolitan and local planning would nest within state planning. This paralleled the release of successive drafts of the American Law Institute's *Model Land Development Code*, which called for states to establish two agencies: one to collect and disseminate information, establish rules, and supervise local planning, and the other to adjudicate disputes on appeal – in essence, something akin to a Canadian provincial Ministry of Municipal Affairs and Ontario's municipal board.[132] While President Richard Nixon had assumed office in 1969 seeking to make signature moves in both "urban" (*qua* housing and social welfare) and environmental protection policy, Jackson's proposal ultimately fell victim to a turf war between urban-focused policymakers of the Department of Housing and Urban Development and the environmental protection agenda of the Environmental Protection Agency.[133] Nonetheless, Jackson's proposal reflected broader interest in the states taking on new roles in urban and rural land-use planning, either directly, through the formulation of plans and policies, or through comprehensive revision of enabling legislation for planning by municipal, county, and metropolitan authorities, much of which had been little altered since the 1920s.[134] Only a handful of states ultimately adopted legislation and policies that recognized the state's interest in land use in this period.

Canada: Promoting Metropolitan Planning through Metropolitan Governance

Importantly, the creation of two- or single-tier metropolitan governments in Canada's large cities occurred after the early postwar reform of land-use planning legislation in most provinces. Indeed, planning was viewed as a basic purpose of new metropolitan institutions. First Ontario in 1946, then other provinces, passed new general planning laws that drew on contemporaneous American policy ideas.[135] These reforms reflected the technocratic optimism of the postwar reconstruction moment.

For the first two decades following its creation in 1954, Metropolitan Toronto used subdivision review and infrastructure extension to encourage a policy of contiguous, fully serviced suburban expansion. Metropolitan Winnipeg exercised similar authority after 1961.[136] Alberta created inter-municipal regional planning commissions for Calgary and Edmonton in the early 1950s and encouraged progressive annexation by the central cities.[137] In each case, land-use regulation was linked to infrastructure provision, enabling the construction of a contiguous, fully serviced urban form. British Columbia authorized advisory inter-municipal planning boards in 1949 that provided planning assistance to rural local governments and evangelized a land-use concept premised, again, on contiguity and comprehensive provision of urban services. With many false starts, regional planning came later to Quebec and the Montreal region.[138] The island-wide upper-tier Montreal Urban Community assumed some authority over land-use planning and infrastructure planning and operations in 1972.

Unlike in the United States, the Canadian federal government's involvement in urban affairs was modest at best. While Ottawa funded housing, central-city redevelopment, and transportation projects, it did not use its spending power to programmatically influence provincial and municipal actions in relation to urban development. It did, however, play a small but formative role in the planning profession's early postwar revival. The newly created Central Mortgage and Housing Corporation (CMHC) sponsored the formation of professional schools of planning in universities across the country, disseminated policy ideas, and funded the activities of the Community Planning Association of Canada (CPAC), a focal point for amateur and professional advocates of land-use planning. Yet provincial governments, not the federal level, remained the locus of urban development policymaking. The only federal attempt to develop an explicit urban policy in the early postwar period – the short-lived Ministry of State for Urban Affairs, established in 1971 – was abandoned due to friction with mainline departments and opposition from the provinces.

NORMATIVE CHANGE DELEGITIMIZES METROPOLITAN PLANNING, 1975 TO THE PRESENT

Elite-driven and technocratic institutions and policies crafted in the early postwar period were delegitimized in both countries as the normative context changed in the late 1960s and early 1970s. Economic malaise undermined the acceptability of state intervention, generating a new appetite for austerity, deregulation, and devolution.

A new urban middle class demanded direct participation in policy-making, while voicing suspicion of government overreach. This led Canadian and American governments to retreat from metropolitan governance and planning.

The United States: Federal Disengagement

By the mid-1970s, COGs and MPOs possessed potentially far-reaching powers to shape urban development, but their capacity to act was increasingly bogged down by disputes over representation. The typical one-government, one-vote arrangement was challenged by large municipalities, which desired influence in proportion to their share of the population. Local interests challenged COGs' legitimacy, viewing them as undemocratic and unaccountable. These factors inhibited COGs' ability to stake out strong positions and enforce compliance to adopted policies. Only rarely did regional bodies use A-95 review to criticize local government policies, and municipalities could deviate from advisory metropolitan plans with little consequence.[139]

At the same time, many central cities in the South, Northeast, and Midwest were racially transformed during the 1960s, as African Americans sought urban industrial jobs and economically mobile whites departed for the suburbs. Growing racial disparities between central cities and suburbs, and the distinct place-based interests they generated, undermined the potential for inter-municipal agreement on metropolitan plans and policies. This was magnified by racial conflict in some central cities, which undermined their economic and fiscal health while accelerating "white flight" to the suburbs. The 1968 report of Otto Kerner's National Advisory Commission on Civil Disorders portrayed a future in which central cities would become ghettoes of racialized poverty.[140] The parallel Douglas National Commission on Urban Problems had been charged to study problems associated with metropolitan growth and change – housing quality, blight, and land-use regulation. Instead, it was seized with the corrosive effects of socio-economic segregation. The large central city was described as a "slum," its disproportionately black and poor population as "imprisoned ... by the white suburban noose."[141] The growing central-city minority population found electoral expression. The first African-American big-city mayor was elected in Cleveland in 1967 and was soon followed by others. Core-suburban racial division undermined metropolitan policymaking, partially because white suburbanites saw little benefit in sharing resources with minority-dominated central cities, and also because new minority political elites in central cities had little interest in diluting their newfound control over municipal institutions.[142]

The racial transformation also altered the political incentives for federal and state governments. The Douglas Commission had presciently stated that "the characteristic phenomenon of American politics in the 1960's will someday be seen as the emergence of the city as a political issue."[143] But instead of spurring a coordinated federal and state policy response, the diagnosis of urban crisis was followed by federal disengagement from urban problems, as anti-government sentiment and party polarization increased, the balance of metropolitan electoral power shifted away from the central cities toward the suburbs, and electoral politics became geographically polarized between Democrat-leaning (and increasingly non-white) cities and Republican-leaning (and overwhelmingly white) rural areas.[144]

Personifying the new context and elected by a coalition anchored by suburban and rural white voters unsympathetic to "urban" problems and government intervention to address them, Ronald Reagan assumed the presidency in 1981 with a mandate to reduce public expenditure, devolve authority, and disentangle intergovernmental relations. Between 1979 and 1984, thirty-eight of thirty-nine federal mandates for metropolitan planning or coordination were eliminated, including A-95 review. MPOs remained, but their oversight was left to the states, whose interest varied.[145] As a result, many councils of governments lost influence, and coordination waned for lack of political support from state and local governments. Yet the effectiveness of COGs and MPOs during the 1970s should not be overstated: only a few developed beyond being advisory "talking shops."

Regional transportation planning by and through MPOs was later revived by the 1991 Intermodal Surface Transportation and Efficiency Act (ISTEA), the 1998 Transportation Equity Act for the 21st Century (TEA-21), and successor legislation. These authorized federal funds for MPO operations and transportation capital projects, subject to an array of conditions related to congestion mitigation, environmental and social impacts, public safety, and goods movement. Unlike before, MPOs were given the authority not merely to study, advise, and recommend, but also to make infrastructure-planning and -spending decisions.[146] Federal mandates for metropolitan transportation planning by MPOs are not paired with equivalent incentives for the metropolitan-scale coordination of land-use and other infrastructure planning, however. Policy concern about environmental impacts, including on air quality, as well as about the economic costs of traffic congestion, has often led state and local transportation policymakers back to land-use questions, yet the crafting and implementation of metropolitan land-use visions has remained elusive.[147] Few states have established state-level planning agencies and state-level land-use policies to programmatically guide local decision-making, or modernized local planning enabling legislation.[148]

Canada: From Provincial Devolution to Re-engagement

Growing discomfort with activist government amid economic malaise put a stop to unilateral local government restructuring in the 1970s. (Quebec is the exception. The reformist Parti Québécois government restructured the county system in the late 1970s and early 1980s.) Municipal restructuring returned in the 1990s, however, this time in the service of small-government orthodoxy. Motivated by a desire to reduce governmental overlap and duplication, provincial governments in Ontario, Quebec, and Nova Scotia collapsed many existing two-tier systems into single-tier municipalities.[149] As the outer boundaries of the units remained unchanged, these restructurings had little or no impact on metropolitan governance. While the objectives of municipal restructuring have changed over time, its continuation indicates that provincial authority remains decisive, constrained only by electoral imperatives.

The 1970s signalled a decline in provincial interest in local and regional planning. In the 1980s, populist right-wing governments in Alberta and British Columbia abolished or defunded regional planning, arguing it was an unnecessary duplication of local planning and placed unnecessary burdens on business.[150] In Ontario and Quebec, provincial governments removed themselves from day-to-day supervision of municipal planning, arguing that it was the job of newly empowered upper-tier local governments to supervise lower-tier planning decisions. Across the country, cash-strapped provincial governments reduced their funding of infrastructure expansion. As a result, urban transportation infrastructure expansion virtually ceased. While municipal land-use planning regulation had become highly developed in Canada's metropolitan areas, inter-municipal coordination was lacking.

By the 1990s, growing transportation congestion and the rise of anti-sprawl discourse made regional planning and infrastructure an electorally salient issue. There was little appetite to restructure local governments along metropolitan lines. Instead, provincial governments saw electoral benefit in encouraging inter-municipal coordination through regulation or new institutional frameworks. Ontario enacted increasingly stringent policy statements to guide local planning. British Columbia restored the regional planning authority of the inter-municipal regional districts. Quebec created new "metropolitan communities" for Montreal and Quebec City, inter-municipal federations akin to earlier American COGs with limited authority over land-use and infrastructure planning.[151] Similarly, Alberta created inter-municipal partnership organizations for Calgary and Edmonton, both more recently replaced by more authoritative agencies.[152] Provincial governments also transferred regional public-transit planning, and in some cases operations, to regional bodies in Montreal, Toronto, and Vancouver. These have been relatively low-cost solutions for the provinces, which have effectively transferred the political costs of urban development policymaking to municipalities without assuming much in the way of new expenditures. Local implementation may restore the legitimacy of metropolitan planning and policymaking in some contexts, but its long-term success hinges on the provision of supportive physical infrastructure whose cost is beyond the reach of local tax bases. Contemporary "thin" inter-municipal coordinating arrangements lack the close integration of regulatory land-use planning and infrastructure provision that was so central to the effectiveness of the restructured metropolitan local governments of the 1950s and 1960s, and provincial governments have frequently pursued projects at odds with adopted regional planning objectives.

Federal involvement in urban affairs has been indirect at best. Created by a Liberal government in 2004, the short-lived Ministry of State for Infrastructure and Communities did not survive the transition to Conservative government in 2006. Federal infrastructure money, including as part of economic stimulus packages during the post-2008 recession, has generally flowed through provincial governments or to politically desirable projects, and has been widely dispersed to achieve the greatest electoral impact. Other federal spending initiatives have focused on social problems that are concentrated in cities – homelessness, injection drug use, urban Indigenous poverty – and have given provincial and municipal governments broad discretion in how to spend federal money.[153] After winning the 2015 federal election, the Liberal Party has expanded federal fiscal support for urban transportation and housing projects, as well as support for urban economic cluster development.[154] Nevertheless, compared to the provinces, the federal government remains a secondary player in urban development.

SUMMARY AND NEXT STEPS

This chapter presented a holistic comparison of the long-term political development of urban governance in the United States and Canada. It demonstrated that the weak executives and undisciplined bicameral legislatures found in American states encourage particularistic policymaking, whereas centralized executive authority in Canadian provinces encourages universal policies. These differences shaped the legal foundations of local government during the first three-quarters of the nineteenth century.

The critical difference between the two countries in the second half of the nineteenth century was not that local affairs in Canada were centrally directed while American localities were left to themselves. In fact, communities enjoyed broad autonomy on both sides of the border. Rather, it was whether local initiative was channelled through a general set of rules as opposed to ad hoc, parochial measures. In the American states, legislators responded to political pressures with special legislation, undermining the potential for state oversight of local government formation and boundary change. In what became Canada, executives enacted general municipal legislation because it enabled low-cost and consistent provincial supervision of local government organization and finance.

As urbanization put increasing pressure on legislatures in the late nineteenth century, reformers in the two countries pursued different objectives. In the United States, they worked to increase municipal autonomy by erecting a firewall between local and state government through home rule and the constitutional limitation of municipal special legislation. In Canada, the solution to the growing volume of municipal business was to delegate authority to new administrative bodies charged with oversight of aspects of municipal affairs. By the First World War, American state governments had retreated from direct intervention in municipal organization and finance, while Canadian provinces had established the rudiments of a system of bureaucratic control over local government.

While the focus of reform had been on improving city government, neither country was yet truly urban. Rural residents would not become a minority in both countries until the 1920s. It was in the boom of the 1920s and the bust of the 1930s that relations between municipalities and senior governments entered a new phase. The fiscal crisis of the Great Depression converted provinces' unconstrained but latent authority over local government into an institutionalized function of the provincial administrative state. In the United States, by contrast, states were constitutionally restrained in their ability to respond, not only by home rule and the multiple veto points of the separated-powers system, but also by the contract clause in the federal constitution. State intervention was also pre-empted by the federal New Deal, and so states did not develop additional administrative capacity to oversee municipal public finance, organization, and boundary change.

It was in these distinct national institutional and normative contexts that rapid urban population growth generated unprecedented demands for infrastructure and services in the early postwar period. Canadian provinces were institutionally equipped to respond to urbanization-related challenges, while American states were not. This was reinforced by a subtle difference in the timing of change in the normative context. In Canada, governments' failure to grapple with the Depression mobilized party-movements of the left, generating a public appetite for state intervention in the wartime and postwar reconstruction periods. In the United States, the New Deal interventionism of the 1930s was followed by a political counter-reaction on the right that emphasized limited government and local autonomy.

Inspired by American planning ideas, provincial governing parties established comprehensive land-use planning systems, led highway and infrastructure development, and proactively reorganized local government in metropolitan areas. In the United States during the 1950s, the federal government reached over the states with fiscal incentives to induce inter-municipal collaboration, particularly in relation to transportation planning. Regulatory land-use planning by municipalities and counties remained underdeveloped, however, hampered by growing local government complexity and unreformed state enabling legislation. Metropolitan urban form was influenced only indirectly, by review of infrastructure-system extension in relation to policies, rather than directly, through land-use regulation. As a result of their divergent paths, the urban development of the larger and faster-growing Canadian metropolitan areas was shaped by policy earlier, and to a greater extent, than their American counterparts.

The 1970s brought a changed normative context. Across the continent, public appetite for state intervention declined as the economy soured and governments slid into deficit, and residents resisted the imposition of plans and infrastructure projects justified on the basis of technical criteria rather than local community values. Governments in both countries retrenched. In Canada, provinces became inconsistent actors in metropolitan land-use and infrastructure planning. While reformed local governments became sophisticated planners and regulators of urban development, inter-municipal coordination within metropolitan areas ebbed. Traffic congestion surged as local governments lacked the funds and institutional means to expand regional transportation infrastructure networks, and senior governments did not come to their aid. In the United States, federal withdrawal of mandates and fiscal support eroded metropolitan coordination. Since the 1980s, only a handful of states have articulated a programmatic interest in urban development or empowered or supported existing regional planning agencies.

At a high level of abstraction, this chapter has periodized and identified critical junctures in the development of urban governance and intergovernmental relations. Less visible at the "macro" level, however, are the circulation of policy ideas and the evolving patterns of contention among local interests. To further reveal how Westminster and separated-powers institutions structured policy development and the participation of societal actors, we must increase the level of magnification. The next four chapters shift the focus to the development and functioning of multi-level urban governance in four cities: Toronto, Minneapolis–St. Paul, Vancouver, and Portland.

4

Toronto

Toronto's international reputation as an exemplar of honest and efficient government – "New York run by the Swiss" – was made in the 1950s and 1960s. The creation of the Municipality of Metropolitan Toronto in 1954 has often been invoked, especially by Americans, as the quintessential metropolitan government reform. As we shall see in later chapters, policy entrepreneurs and policymakers in Minneapolis–St. Paul, Vancouver, and Portland studied Metro Toronto closely as they debated local reforms. Travel back to the Toronto of 1910 or 1930, however, and one would be hard pressed to identify portents of future innovation. Compared to Montreal and upper midwestern and northeastern American cities, Toronto was a provincial backwater whose Anglo-Protestant political and business leaders were, for the most part, cautious and unimaginative. How, in only a generation, did Toronto go from being a highly unlikely context for the germination and implementation of radical reform to become what was perhaps the most elaborate system of metropolitan governance and planning arrangements on the continent? And why, by the 1980s and 1990s, did Toronto-region urban governance seem to have lost its way?

The answer to these questions lies at the provincial rather than the local level. As discussed in the previous chapter, Ontario was the first jurisdiction in the British common-law world to adopt, universally apply, and consistently maintain general municipal legislation. As urbanization generated new demands before the Second World War, Ontario responded by constructing new institutions to supervise local government organization, finance, and utilities. This apparatus was readily extended in the years after the war to respond to intensifying

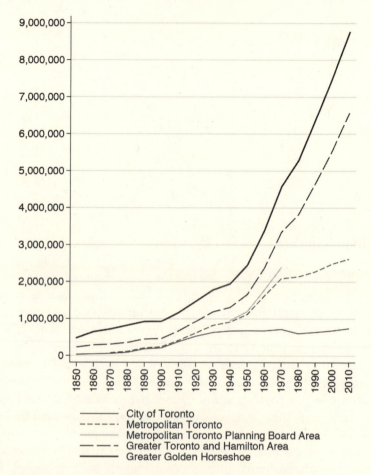

9,000,000
8,000,000
7,000,000
6,000,000
5,000,000
4,000,000
3,000,000
2,000,000
1,000,000
0

1850 1860 1870 1880 1890 1900 1910 1920 1930 1940 1950 1960 1970 1980 1990 2000 2010

——————— City of Toronto
– – – – – · Metropolitan Toronto
——————— Metropolitan Toronto Planning Board Area
— — – Greater Toronto and Hamilton Area
——————— Greater Golden Horseshoe

Figure 4.1 Toronto population by zone, 1850–2010

Note: Most growth in the Toronto region occurred within the City of
Toronto itself until the 1920s. The creation in 1954 of Metropolitan
Toronto and its planning board (the MTPB), which exercised extraterritorial jurisdiction over an area twice the size of Metro itself, contained most
growth into the 1970s. From the MTPB's dissolution in 1974 to the province's enactment of the Growth Plan for the Greater Golden Horseshoe
in 2006, virtually all population growth occurred outside Metro Toronto
(after 1997, the amalgamated City of Toronto) in the rest of the Greater
Toronto and Hamilton Area, and also in the surrounding outer ring of
counties and regional municipalities that make up the Greater Golden
Horseshoe.

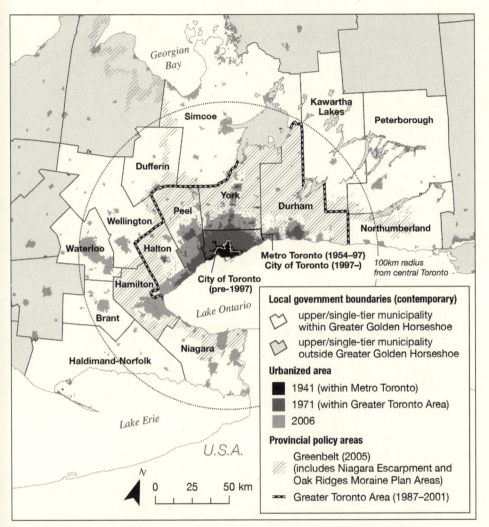

Figure 4.2 Administrative boundaries, urbanization, and policy areas in Toronto

Sources: Municipal boundaries adapted from Statistics Canada cartographic
boundary files. Urbanized area for 1941 adapted from Harris and Luymes, "The
Growth of Toronto"; 1971 from Canada Land Use Monitoring Program, Natural
Resources Canada; and 2006 from Ontario, *Built Boundary;* Greenbelt boundary
from Ontario, *Greenbelt Plan, 2005.*

pressures associated with urban growth. Perhaps the most sophisticated land-use planning legislation on the continent was adopted
in the 1940s, its municipal implementation supervised by the province.

Throughout the 1950s and 1960s, the province also became directly involved in the planning, financing, and construction of water, sewer, and transportation infrastructure. And, first in Toronto and then across the province, the provincial government unilaterally reorganized local governments to enhance their capacity to plan, finance infrastructure, and provide services.

These programmatic provincial actions were enabled by the Westminster system's institutional foundations: decisive executive-centred policymaking, unicameralism, and strong party discipline. This programmatic action was supported in the early postwar period by a normative context of technocratic optimism, trust in government, and deference to elites, and was reinforced by the sustained electoral dominance of the Conservative Party in Ontario politics. When these conditions came undone during the 1970s, so too did the provincial glue that held the Toronto region's governance together. Since then, the provincial government has been an inconsistent actor in the governance of the Toronto region.

BECOMING METROPOLITAN, 1834-1945

In 1909, good-government reformer and Toronto's transportation commissioner Samuel Morley Wickett drafted a memorandum advocating "early action" in the metropolitan sphere.[1] Arguing against annexation, and citing the London County Council and metropolitan service districts in Boston and Chicago, he called for the creation of a council of local representatives representing a vast area – the "thirty or forty" municipalities stretching from Brampton to Aurora to Port Union – that would be charged with addressing the provision of roads, electricity, inter-urban railways, water, and sewers. Although never adopted, this proposal prefigured future debates between advocates of annexation, local autonomy, and narrow conceptions of the region with those favouring a two-tier arrangement, central control, and broad conceptions of the region. It also exemplified progressive reformers' linkage of long-term planning to metropolitan government reform.

Incorporated in 1834 – three years before Chicago – Toronto grew slowly during the nineteenth century. Only in the 1880s did urbanization spill beyond its original boundaries. Several adjacent villages had already incorporated by this point – Yorkville in 1853, Parkdale in 1879, and Brockton in 1880 (see figure 4.3). The City of Toronto annexed incorporated and unincorporated urbanizing areas between 1883 and 1912. Both Toronto and its urbanizing fringe found annexation to be mutually advantageous. Toronto benefited by converting free-riding commuters into taxpayers. Urban residents of mostly rural York Township supported annexation to obtain urban services for which their rural neighbours were unwilling to pay.[2] Urban villages such as Yorkville and Parkdale pursued annexation to gain access to urban services and relieve unsupportable debt burdens.[3] Annexation of villages was eased by the fact that the law required only the approval of council, not a vote of residents.

Unlike in the United States, where cities are integral to counties, and city residents directly elect both municipal councillors and county boards, Ontario adopted the British doctrine that rural and urban areas should be independently governed. Toronto and other urban municipalities were administratively separated from their counties and took on county functions within their boundaries.[4] The problem of overcoming the City of Toronto's institutional separation from York County would be the fulcrum on which later metropolitan solutions would turn.

The End of Annexation and the Rise of the Suburbs

Annexation stopped because the incentives that made it desirable to both city and suburb faded. The City of Toronto undertook its last major annexation, of North Toronto, in 1912, and formally ruled out further expansion in 1914 because it did not wish to absorb growing suburban debts for water, sewer, and road infrastructure.[5] Growth spilled beyond the city's boundaries in the 1920s. Separately incorporated urban municipalities were soon carved out of neighbouring rural townships. York and Etobicoke Townships were subdivided by a series of town and village incorporations: Mimico in 1911, New Toronto and Leaside in 1913, North York in 1922, Forest Hill in 1923, East York in 1924, Swansea in 1926, and Long Branch in 1930 (figure 4.4). The secession of North York left a rump York Township composed of two discontiguous segments. The eastern portion separated to form East York two years later. In some cases, including North York, secession represented a defensive strategy on the part of rural voters to prevent eventual absorption into the city. In other cases, such as Forest Hill and Swansea, urban and urbanizing parts of rural townships seceded in order to improve school and other

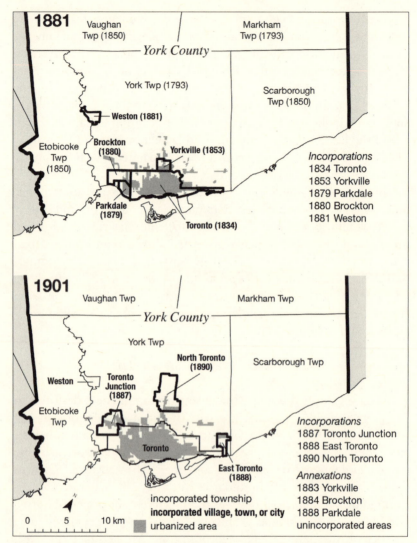

Figure 4.3 Urbanization and boundary change in southern York County, 1834–1901

Sources: Municipal boundaries adapted from Statistics Canada cartographic boundary files (1996) and the Canadian Century Research Infrastructure Project (1911–51). Urbanized areas adapted from Harris and Luymes, "The Growth of Toronto."

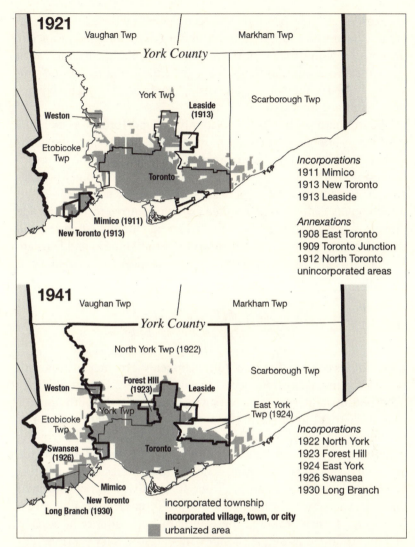

Figure 4.4 Urbanization and boundary change in southern York County, 1911–41

Sources: Municipal boundaries adapted from Statistics Canada cartographic boundary files (1996) and the Canadian Century Research Infrastructure Project (1911–51). Urbanized areas adapted from Harris and Luymes, "The Growth of Toronto."

services.[6] Had their petitions not been denied by the provincial leg-islature, well-to-do suburban neighbourhoods in York and Etobicoke Townships would have followed their example.[7] Still others – in particular York and East York – sought annexation to Toronto but were rebuffed. Of the original townships, only Scarborough's bound-aries remained intact.

The southern portion of York County beyond Toronto's city limits doubled in population in the 1920s, from 88,000 to 190,000, grew slowly during the 1930s, and almost doubled again in the 1940s, to 440,000 in 1950. The city's share of southern York County popula-tion dropped from over 90 per cent in 1911 to 75 per cent in 1931, and to 60 per cent in 1950. Limited growth occurred in areas outside Toronto's orbit, including Peel, Ontario, and Durham Counties, and the northern portion of York County. (Most of Ontario and Durham Counties would become part of the new Regional Municipality of Durham in 1974.)

Sharing the Costs of Growth: Minister Henry's Metropolitan District

It was in this context that East York member of Provincial Parliament (MPP) and minister of public works and highways George S. Henry proposed in January 1924 the establishment of a Toronto "metro-politan district" to promote the orderly and equitable extension of urban infrastructure and services in suburban areas.[8] Rapidly growing fringe municipalities lacking an industrial tax base could not provide urban-style services, including schools, to their residents, most of whom worked in the city proper, while Toronto, with its rich industrial tax base, contributed little to York County's coffers. With annexation foreclosed, Henry proposed that southern York County be severed and incorporated as a new county with extraordinary powers.[9] His draft bill contained four innovations. First, the metropolitan district would exercise authority over major roadways, water and sewer services, street railways, policing, town planning, and disposal of garbage. Second, the City of Toronto would cease to be a separated city. But, although Toronto was to be part of the new district council and the primary contributor to its budget, the draft bill did not require it to transfer its existing assets and services to the district; the enumer-ated services were to be delivered only beyond the city's borders. Third, the district was to be deemed to constitute a single board of education, operating all schools within the area, including those within the City of Toronto. Finally, recognizing that about 80 per cent of the metropolitan area's population resided within Toronto, the council's structure departed from the traditional county formula of equal representation by unit. Instead, the City of Toronto would have twelve seats, York three, East York two, and the other six municipalities one each, for a total of twenty-three seats, and a warden would be appointed by the province. (In Ontario, the heads of township councils are called reeves and the heads of county councils wardens.) Toronto would retain a permanent "floor" of half of the seats, should new incorporations necessitate the council's expansion.

Despite Henry's status as a senior cabinet minister and a close friend and loyal lieutenant of the premier, his proposal received only lukewarm support from fellow Conservative legislators. It was also opposed by municipal and school board leaders and newspaper editorialists, who condemned it as a raid on central-city ratepayers and an invitation to suburban land speculation.[10] Mayor Janes of the Village of New Toronto, which possessed a significant industrial tax base and had previously constructed its own sewer and water works, demanded that any metropolitan scheme credit municipalities for infrastructure investments already made.[11] While the proposal was not adopted, it established a template for future reform. Calls to harness Toronto's rich industrial tax base to finance suburban growth would resurface in subsequent decades, as would advocacy of equitable service levels for all metropolitan residents. Rather than introducing special-purpose bodies in parallel to existing municipalities, reform would entail the erasure of Toronto's separated-city status and the empowerment of a county-like body – the metropolitan district – as an incorporated, general-purpose local government.

Sharing the Burden of Fiscal Crisis

The Great Depression devastated Toronto's growing suburbs. Ten of the twelve suburban municipalities became insolvent as residential property values collapsed and poor relief expenditures sharply increased. Only wealthy Forest Hill and Swansea were spared the indignity of provincial supervision – that is, the replacement of elected local officials by appointed supervisors charged with cutting costs and renegotiating debt payments. Township leaders in York County's rural north had no interest in aiding insolvent villages and towns in the urban south.[12] For its part, Forest Hill sought to avoid subsidizing its neighbours by becoming a separated city.

To confront the problem, York County Council formed a Metropolitan Area Committee, chaired by county warden and North York reeve A.J.B. Gray, in June 1932. George Henry, by then premier, deemed it sufficiently important to attend the first meeting of the committee.[13] Its January 1934 *Interim Report* recommended dissolving the "illogical union" of the county's urban south with the rural north. The urban zone would then be governed by a two-tier metropolitan county akin to Henry's 1924 plan. Stepping beyond the Henry proposal, however, it also recommended that the City of Toronto participate fully in metropolitan services rather than acting only as paymaster to the suburbs.[14]

Partially in response to the York County effort, the premier appointed a legislative special committee, chaired by Minister of Lands and Resources William Finlayson, to study metropolitan problems across the province. The 1931 census (the first to follow the US Census Bureau's practice of defining metropolitan districts) revealed substantial urban growth outside of central municipalities in Ottawa, Hamilton, and Windsor, and hence local government reorganization might be required in all of the province's larger urban areas. The committee was well aware of alternative models. Early in 1934, it submitted a brief to the minister describing metropolitan governance and service delivery arrangements in Boston, Chicago, New York, Montreal, Windsor, Vancouver, and Winnipeg.[15] Predictably, a survey of area municipalities found that metropolitan integration was opposed by those that had already financed and constructed infrastructure.[16] The committee would operate for only a few months: Henry's Conservatives lost the June 1934 election to Mitch Hepburn's resurgent Liberals, which transcended their rural base to win sixty-nine of ninety seats.[17]

While Hepburn did not continue the special committee, he moved quickly to establish a new Department of Municipal Affairs, with former Windsor mayor David Croll as minister, and a royal commission to study the amalgamation of insolvent local governments in greater Windsor. Overruling a local referendum that opposed annexation, Croll moved to consolidate Windsor with its suburbs and contemplated the same solution for the Toronto region. That same year, he commissioned a study on metropolitan government by University of Toronto political scientist Arthur Plumptre. His report, which the

government deemed too controversial to publish, rejected the metropolitan county option, recommending instead a provincially imposed
amalgamation of all existing urban areas into one municipality
followed by a policy of incremental annexation as urbanization
expanded.[18] Despite holding a majority of the seats in both the City
of Toronto and York County, the Liberals could not ignore the opposition of the city and its businessmen, including the influential editor
of the Liberal *Toronto Daily Star*, Joseph Atkinson. Having remained
solvent during the Depression, the city had little interest in assuming
the debts of its bankrupt suburbs. Croll postponed introduction of
an amalgamation bill in the hope that improvement in the fringe
municipalities' fiscal condition would make annexation more palatable.[19] Before the issue could be taken up again, however, Croll
resigned from cabinet to protest Hepburn's repression of the General
Motors strike in Oshawa, which had been fomented by the radical
Congress of Industrial Organizations (CIO).[20] He was replaced by
Eric Cross of rural Haldimand-Norfolk, who until his election in
1937 had been chair of the Ontario Municipal Board (OMB).

Toronto's suburbs continued to seek independent destinies. The
OMB refused petitions from Forest Hill and York Township to separate from York County. In response, the province established another
Metropolitan Committee led by A.J.B. Gray, who was, by then, the
deputy minister of municipal affairs.[21] In parallel, the Municipal Act
was amended to permit the OMB to study and impose annexation,
subject to legislative approval, on request of the minister or on petition from a municipal council or residents.[22] Hearing records reveal
almost universal opposition to annexation of the suburbs by the city.[23]
Under great fiscal strain, the suburban municipalities had addressed
their most pressing infrastructural deficits through construction of
their own pipes, plants, and buildings, through bilateral contracts
with the city and each other. The position of Reeve Warren of East
York is representative:

> Insofar as the metropolitan idea is concerned, we must point out
> that in our opinion it is about ten years too late. We have built
> our main trunk sewers and disposal plants, costing many hundreds
> of thousands of dollars. We have our own system of trunk water-
> mains leasing to the Township of Scarborough and schools situ-
> ated adjacent to city schools. All this no doubt would have been
> entirely different had a metropolitan idea been applied years ago

and, after building these services, we are at a loss to see just how a metropolitan area could benefit us to any great degree.[24]

Toronto Mayor Ralph Day publicly sparred with Cross for months, characterizing unwanted annexation as "legalized piracy" that would raise city taxes. Cross countered that administrative efficiencies would reduce the cost of government. Indeed, his primary concern appears to have been increasing efficiency rather than reducing intra-metropolitan inequities.[25] Toronto responded that the province should increase its support for education, relief, and hospital services, thereby lifting the most onerous fiscal burdens from the region's shoulders, and that only after doing so should some form of metropolitan integration be considered. Condemning the Gray committee's lack of an official representative from the city, Toronto's council resolved to place annexation on the ballot in the 1940 municipal election, the outcome of which would almost certainly be negative.[26] Cross disbanded the committee when war was declared in September 1939 as it prepared to recommend a metropolitan county on the Henry model.[27]

Normative Change and Political Re-alignment: From Laissez-faire to Postwar Reconstruction

Public frustration with the provincial and federal governments' laissez-faire response to the Depression, combined with a positive perception of the American New Deal, had established an appetite for government intervention. At the same time, government organization of war production had demonstrated the efficacy of the positive state. This fuelled support for the socialist Co-operative Commonwealth Federation (which became the New Democratic Party in 1961), which won a majority of Toronto-area seats in the 1943 and 1948 provincial elections. In opposition, Ontario's rebranded Progressive Conservative Party saw opportunity in a left turn. Under George Drew, the PCs narrowly beat the CCF in 1943 by promising (but not delivering) a universal public health care service.[28] A Conservative majority government was achieved in June 1945 by painting the CCF as a tool of international communism. While the Conservatives' turn toward statism was perhaps driven by electoral opportunism, it outlived the CCF's surge in popularity. In the context of postwar reconstruction, both parties agreed that government action was required to absorb demobilized troops into the home economy.[29] Moreover, Premier Drew was optimistic about the province's future – he believed that the war years had unleashed new productive energies and that peacetime heralded unprecedented economic expansion.[30] But, unlike the British Labour government elected in July 1945, which sought to secure full employment by nationalizing industrial production and the right to improve land, reformers in Drew's circle believed that the private sector would remain the primary source of investment. White sums up the Tory image of postwar reconstruction:

> [The] government stepped in energetically to create the infrastructure necessary for a modern economy ... Activist this certainly was, but not interventionist. The prevailing social goal for the two decades after the War was fostering strong economic growth. The provincial government ... saw its role as providing the facilities necessary to encourage economic development, but not to direct or regulate it.[31]

The province's instrument was to be planning, broadly construed. With all-party support, the government established a Department of Planning and Development under minister Dana Porter in 1944. The department was given a broad mandate to formulate "plans to create, assist, develop, and maintain productive employment" through inter-ministerial coordination and collaboration with municipal governments and sectoral associations. Over the next two years, the department would establish two durable legislative frameworks and corresponding institutions with implications for Toronto's regional governance.

The first was a new Planning Act (1946), which consolidated existing laws governing zoning, land subdivision, and the preparation of comprehensive land-use plans.[32] Municipal planning remained voluntary rather than mandatory (as had been advocated by the CCF). New to the act was oversight of local planning and development control by a Community Planning Branch within the new department. Municipal comprehensive plans would now be made "official" on approval of the minister rather than the OMB. Although few municipalities had adopted such plans, this provision signalled a shift from a reactive to a proactive stance. In principle, municipal planning would be actively encouraged by the provincial executive and supervised in relation to the province's interests. The act also replaced the earlier practice of extraterritorial subdivision control by central cities with the provision for "planning areas" defined by the minister, which could include part or all of a municipality, multiple municipalities, or parts thereof.[33] Planning boards would be appointed by the designated municipal council, which was typically the largest city of a multi-municipality area. Plans would be adopted by the designated municipal council before seeking approval from the minister. The new Planning Act embodied American ideas. Planning's advocates were well versed in current American proposals, including the desirability of linking local development control to metropolitan planning. Consultant A.E.K. Bunnell, who strongly influenced the act's content, maintained close ties to the American Society of Planning Officials (ASPO).[34]

The second initiative was the creation of the Conservation Branch in the new department and the establishment of watershed-management bodies, which were called "conservation authorities." During the 1930s, amateur naturalists, rural municipal leaders, and farmers' groups in Ontario had criticized the government's laissez-faire approach to natural resource management. They advocated a comprehensive program of "conservation" in the form of reforestation and woodlot management, control of agricultural water pollution, and the improvement of soil quality.[35] As the war drew to a close, the perceived success of American New Deal conservation-oriented employment programs spurred Ontario policymakers to study how postwar employment could be stabilized by similar projects.[36] Minister Porter made a weeklong visit to examine the Tennessee Valley Authority in 1944. The trip impressed on the minister the need for a holistic system of natural resource management.[37] Conservation would sustain finite resources while yielding economic dividends. On these bases, conservation was incorporated into the broader postwar reconstruction project. The Conservation Authorities Act (1946) provided for the creation, on petition of area municipalities, of special-purpose bodies with the power to make plans for watershed areas concerning flood control, land use, forestry, wildlife, and recreation. To implement the plans, the authorities were empowered to borrow funds, construct works, and expropriate land and property. Conservation authorities would later become involved in dam building and floodplain management, the acquisition of lands for recreational facilities inside and outside urban areas, and the preservation of woodlots and other natural features. Four were established in the Toronto area.[38]

The reconstitution of the Ontario Municipal Board, the imposition of the Windsor amalgamation, the creation of the Departments of Municipal Affairs and Planning and Development, and the adoption of the planning and conservation legislation signalled a transformation in the provincial government's involvement in municipal and metropolitan matters. The emergence of a normative context supportive of state intervention, and of economic, social, and environmental planning in particular, created new opportunities for parties in power to decisively enact programmatic policies, not only in response to urbanization pressures but also in other domains.

Crucially, the new general statutory planning and conservation systems were grafted onto the new administrative capacities established in response to the Depression crisis, which in turn represented an extension of the legislature's programmatic exercise jurisdiction over local government. The new land-use planning regime would not have been possible without the prior creation of the Ontario Municipal Board and the Department of Municipal Affairs. Yet despite these ostensibly centralizing moves on the part of the province, belief in the necessity of local autonomy remained intact. In speech after speech, Premier Drew railed against the dangers of centralization.[39] Speaking in Stratford on 20 June 1946, for example, he compared centralization to Soviet communism, stating that "the reason behind our solid development is our continued belief that authority should remain vested in the government closest to the people."[40] There was all-party consensus that the provincial government had a legitimate interest in local economic development and in public health. It could pursue this interest by enabling, promoting, and monitoring local planning, but would intervene directly in local affairs only as a last resort.[41]

MAKING METROPOLITAN TORONTO, 1945–65

Sustained postwar growth promised a rising tide that would raise all boats. The St. Lawrence Seaway, which would enable deep-water cargo ships to enter the Great Lakes, was expected to spark an industrial boom in Toronto. As the metropolitan population surpassed one million in 1949, the Toronto and York Planning Board forecast that the regional population would grow by a further 300,000 to 500,000

people by 1970 and suggested that "Greater Toronto has an opportunity that staggers the imagination and is a challenge to courage and
foresight."[42] Beverley Matthews, the chair of the Toronto Board of
Trade, was closer to the mark when he predicted a broader regional
population of five million by the millennium.[43] To accommodate
expected growth, the region's infrastructure and governance would
have to be modernized. The reorganization of local government came
to be seen as necessary for the orderly expansion of infrastructure
systems and rational land-use planning on a metropolitan basis.
Accomplishing this would test the political limits of the provincial
government's capacity to be decisive.

Planning for Efficiency and Equity:
Responding to the Metropolitan Infrastructure Crisis

The region's uneven patchwork of infrastructure and service agreements buckled as the combined population of North York, Etobicoke,
and Scarborough Townships tripled to almost 200,000 residents
during the 1940s.[44] Schools and other community facilities were in
short supply. The narrow dirt roads in some communities were unable
to accommodate exploding automobile use as suburban workers
commuted to city jobs. Between 1947 and 1950 alone, the number
of cars and trucks registered in the region increased by 40 per cent.[45]
By the early 1950s, suburbs were forced to raise property taxes
dramatically to keep pace with growth, much of it for the construction and operation of schools, which consumed almost half of the
suburban levy.[46]

A shortage of quality housing spurred unregulated shacktown
construction lacking adequate water and sewer services. Even when
expanded, the city's main sewage-treatment plant lacked sufficient
capacity to serve the growing regional population, and smaller plants
located on suburban rivers and tributaries were also overloaded.[47]
Major suburban water shortages occurred in the summer of 1951.
Engineers Gore and Storrie reported that 6,000 of landlocked North
York's 10,000 dwellings were served by septic tanks situated in unsuit-
able clay soils, and 2,100 had no means of sewage disposal at all.[48]
Forest Hill Reeve Frederick Gardiner told the *Toronto Star* that "we
are sitting at the edge of a volcano in permitting them ... The leakage
from these cesspools could easy be responsible for a major epidemic"
if groundwater became contaminated.[49] While North York officials

disputed the danger to public health, it was generally accepted that inadequate infrastructure put the region's economic growth at risk.[50]

The debate was not only about efficiency and public health. It was also about ensuring equitable access to services. During the Depression the "metropolitan problem" had been framed as a zero-sum game in which the suburbs' success would come at the expense of the central city. Now it appeared that both could share in the benefits, and therefore the burdens, of a rapidly growing economy. The perception of growth's inevitability brought opponents of government intervention on side. This combination of efficiency and equity discourses was visible in the editorial positions of Toronto's three daily newspapers – the Liberal *Star* and the Conservative *Globe and Mail* and *Telegram* – all of which supported the merger of Toronto and its suburbs. Even the right-wing *Telegram* could refer to municipal boundaries as "artificial" and call for "the present and potential advantages and obligations [of growth to be] shared equally and equitably by all citizens of a single community."[51] The *Globe*'s business-friendly editors saw planning as the "basis" of metropolitan reform:

> The one irrefutable factor, which the opponents of amalgamation have consistently evaded, is the necessity for metropolitan planning. The bane of the area is the haphazard development which has taken place. There has been no attempt to correlate and balance [residential and industrial land uses]. Moreover, the worst errors of Toronto's unplanned growth during the last century have been reproduced in the surrounding municipalities.[52]

The editors also wrote that "it is neither fair nor sensible that some residents should be so much better off than others, in terms of school standards and civic services. These inequities can only be corrected by making the tax revenue of the whole area available to the whole area."[53] The most liberal (and Liberal) of the three newspapers, the *Star*, was also the most cautious, stating that, while amalgamation would equalize access to services and buttress the suburbs from a possible return to depression, the additional cost to city taxpayers should not be ignored. The *Star* called for voluntary incremental annexation as a more digestible solution.[54] In the context of the anticommunist hysteria of the late 1940s, it is no small irony that comprehensive metropolitan land-use and infrastructure planning and consolidated public ownership of local utilities and works were

embraced by conservative elites who traditionally favoured incrementalism over radical change, local control over centralization, and
private enterprise over state intervention.[55]

Local Disagreement Spurs Provincial Engagement

While growth-related problems were manifest, there was little agreement on how to proceed. The two leading metropolitan governance-
reform proposals from before the war – amalgamation coupled with
incremental annexation, and the creation of two-tier metropolitan
government severed from York County – were revived.

Taking advantage of the new Planning Act, a Toronto and Suburban
Planning Board was designated in 1946. It moved quickly to com-
mission reports on water, sewer, and transportation infrastructure.[56]
Chaired by the head of the City of Toronto's planning board, Tracy
Le May, the board also included Frederick Gardiner, the influential
Conservative reeve of wealthy Forest Hill and one-time warden of
York County. A dedicated defender of local autonomy and opponent
of regionalization during the 1930s, Gardiner came to believe in the
need for radical reform to meet the infrastructural challenges posed
by rapid growth. When the suburbs refused to contribute funds for
the board's operation in 1947, Gardiner used his party connections
to have it reconstituted as the Toronto and York Planning Board, with
the county rather than the individual lower-tier municipalities serving
as the city's interlocutor.[57] This did not resolve the problem – the
county also refused to fund its share of implementing the board's
proposal for a greenbelt, and there was little agreement on the funding of transportation projects.

The industrial suburb of Mimico had applied to the OMB in 1947
to establish an "inter-urban administrative area" – in essence, a metropolitan special-purpose body – for the urbanized and urbanizing
areas of southern York County. Such a body would coexist with
current municipal and county governments, managing education, fire
and police protection, administration of justice, health and welfare,
sewage disposal, and public utilities, including transportation and
major highways.[58]

After becoming the Toronto and York Planning Board's chair,
Gardiner pushed for a more radical solution: amalgamation. In late
1949, the board recommended the amalgamation of the eight municipalities between the Humber River and Scarborough Township,

with the proviso that the three lakeshore municipalities to the west – Mimico, New Toronto, and Long Branch – would be brought into the scheme at a later date. Gardiner rejected the notion of a joint services board or a metropolitan county, arguing that the ongoing necessity of inter-municipal collaboration under a two-tier arrangement would impede the creation of efficient area-wide systems.[59] York County and its rural municipalities rejected this proposal because it would deprive the county of most of its tax base, effectively doubling northern residents' tax burden.[60] (This was a reversal. Only a decade earlier, the county had endorsed the separation of its insolvent southern constituent units.)

Reversing its long-standing opposition to annexation, the City of Toronto endorsed the report and applied to the Ontario Municipal Board in February 1950 for the staged amalgamation of the thirteen metropolitan municipalities, leaving aside the rural corners of Etobicoke and Scarborough.[61] The city appears to have had mixed motives. Some believed that amalgamation would provide more efficient government and enable Toronto to capture the fruits of suburban growth. The prestige of overtaking Montreal as the country's most populous municipality was no doubt also attractive.[62]

Faced with a deadlock between three contradictory positions – the city's insistence on total amalgamation, the urbanizing municipalities' desire for continued existence with or without some form of metropolitan organization, and York County's fear of having its fiscal base cut out from under it – Drew's successor as premier, Leslie Frost, personally convened a Toronto Area Committee of southern York County mayors and reeves in January 1950 in the hope that they would work out a mutually acceptable accord. His selection of engineer A.E.K. Bunnell as chair may have signaled his preferred option. Bunnell, who had played a key role in drafting the new Planning Act, had argued forcefully to the premier the previous year for complete amalgamation of the area spanning from Port Credit in the west, Highway 7 in the north, and the outer border of Scarborough in the east.[63] At the group's first meeting, Frost invoked the spirit of George Henry's two-tier metropolitan district proposal of twenty-five years earlier.[64] This may have been strategic: in correspondence with Gardiner, who had supplied his speaking notes, Frost argued for downplaying amalgamation to avoid antagonizing opposed municipalities.[65]

Frost had good political reasons to punt the issue back to the municipalities. The electoral cost of unilaterally legislating a solution, or permitting the OMB to impose one without legislative approval, was uncertain.[66] Provincial politics were in flux. While the Conservatives had a commanding majority in the legislative assembly (fifty-three of ninety seats), Frost had not faced the electorate since succeeding Drew as party leader and premier in 1949. Despite Drew's redbaiting, the CCF had more than doubled its seat count in the 1948 election, increased its share of the popular vote, and defeated Drew in his own Toronto seat.[67] Indeed, the CCF held seven of thirteen City of Toronto seats and three of the four York County seats. Representing rural Victoria County, Frost had won the party leadership on a wave of antipathy to the metropolis, defeating three Toronto-based contenders.[68] He would have to tread carefully if he was to blunt the CCF's urban incursion without alienating the rest of Ontario, which, due to rural over-representation, accounted for 80 per cent of all seats and 90 per cent of the Tory caucus.

Although Frost gently threatened that the province would unilaterally impose a solution if no consensus were reached, the municipalities remained deadlocked.[69] Two reports were submitted at the end of March 1950. A majority report called for a two-tier solution. The separated City of Toronto would be integrated with an empowered York County.[70] This new "metropolitan county" would be authorized to plan, construct, and operate water and sewer facilities, major roads and highways, public transportation, and waste disposal. Toronto and Mimico's minority report called for the amalgamation into a new single-tier unit of all southern York County municipalities with the exception of the rural corners of Etobicoke and Scarborough Townships.[71]

With opinion divided along familiar lines, the way was cleared for the OMB to hear Toronto's and Mimico's earlier applications. During sixty-seven days of hearings between June 1950 and May 1951, a three-member OMB panel chaired by Lorne Cumming received over three hundred exhibits, and over two million words of testimony were transcribed. The established municipal positions were vigorously rehearsed. In July 1950, Cumming intimated that an interim joint water and sewer board could be created in advance of the board's decision on amalgamation.[72] Toronto's opposition to a two-tier system was complicated by Mayor Hiram McCallum's defeat by Allan Lamport in December 1951. While a member of the city's Board of Control, Lamport had opposed McCallum's amalgamation stance. On becoming mayor, he quickly called a meeting with the suburbs with the intent of heading off a potential OMB decision in favour of amalgamation. Facing a pro-amalgamation council, however, Lamport's initiative failed.[73]

Negotiations continued on the side. Spurred by Cumming, the City of Toronto and York County engaged in talks in early 1951. Etobicoke and the three Lakeshore municipalities proposed a single-tier, two-city solution, one comprising the four municipalities west of the Humber River, the other those east of the Humber, including Toronto. Although it was acknowledged that this would reduce the complexity of government, the proposal foundered on its failure to provide for metropolitan planning. As with Toronto's merger plan, planning's advocates argued that these areas were too small to accommodate expected growth. Perhaps to mollify the city's opposition to county empowerment, York County proposed a quasi-independent countywide service district to manage water and sewer infrastructure, garbage disposal, arterial roads, transportation, and land-use planning. Its board would be composed of three provincial appointees, the mayor of Toronto, the warden of York County, one representative of each suburban municipality, and an equal number of Toronto councillors. It would have the power to borrow to finance works and would levy operating funds from municipalities in proportion to their property assessment. Toronto condemned the plan for creating additional administrative burdens and plundering its resources without adequate representation. Mimico opposed it for not going further to include education, health, and welfare.[74]

The OMB also heard from organized interests. The city's principal business organization, the Board of Trade, argued for amalgamation of a broader territory along the lines advocated by the Civic Advisory Council, a city-appointed panel of business, professional, and academic leaders. The council had earlier defined the region as including not only southern York County, but also ten additional municipalities in York and Peel Counties.[75] The Toronto Metropolitan Homebuilders' Association also argued in favour of amalgamation, suggesting that housing construction was limited by overly restrictive suburban bylaws and a failure to comprehensively service new development.[76] Business- and government-backed advocacy groups such as the Community Planning Association of Canada, the Toronto Bureau of Municipal Research and its national counterpart, the Citizens Research Institute of Canada, all strongly endorsed metropolitan-scale planning.[77] These groups and their leaders paid close attention to American metropolitan governance and planning ideas.

Testimony in the hearings revealed a basic dispute over fiscal impacts. Without a common property assessment for the region, experts could not agree on the probable impact of amalgamation on tax rates. (While Toronto had reassessed all property within its boundaries in 1948, suburban property valuations were an inconsistent patchwork.) Using available data, A.J.B. Gray, the city's assessment commissioner, presented an analysis in September 1950 that suggested that all suburbs would benefit from amalgamation with Toronto.[78] This finding was disputed by suburban municipalities, and especially York Township, the city's most populous neighbour.[79] The tax issue was magnified by tight capital markets. Canadian municipalities, including North York, reported difficulty floating bonds.[80] Without borrowing, growing suburban municipalities would have to pay for capital works out of current revenues, which would necessitate substantial property tax hikes. To break the logjam, the province commissioned, at its own expense, a reassessment using common standards for all suburban properties.[81] While the reassessment was hailed as essential when the process began in 1951, its findings were not released until after the OMB published its recommendations two years later.

Creating Metropolitan Toronto

Frost's political position improved in the November 1951 election, when the Conservatives won seventy-nine of ninety seats, including all but two seats in Toronto and York County. The Conservatives could now claim a mandate from all parts of the Toronto region – city, suburb, and rural hinterland – and from the province as a whole. Frost became less constrained by the opposition of the area's Conservative politicians to one or another of the reform options and the rest of the province's concerns about special treatment for Toronto.[82] It had become clear to Frost that the OMB could not simply choose between the proposals in the applications before it: Toronto's amalgamation plan and Mimico's inter-municipal service board. The two-tier metropolitan county model had strong proponents, but they were not party to the hearing. To minimize political controversy but also be durable and effective, the solution would have to bridge the various positions and be tolerable to all parties.

The OMB's January 1953 final report charted its own course, recommending a new metropolitan county in southern York County, the Municipality of Metropolitan Toronto (Metro). Amalgamation was rejected on the basis that efficiency benefits would be outweighed by the negative effect on community responsiveness.[83] At the same time, the OMB argued that voluntary inter-municipal cooperation was unlikely to move quickly enough to address the growing urban infrastructure gap.[84] Including Toronto in an empowered county arrangement would resolve many vexing issues: the unevenness of municipal tax rates and debt levels, the corresponding unevenness of infrastructure and service quality, and the suburbs' difficulty accessing financing for capital works. The plan drew on previous proposals. Indeed, the OMB case file contains a copy of Henry's 1924 draft act, suggesting that Cumming was aware of it.[85] Local water and sewer systems would be transferred to the new metropolitan government, which would also manage property assessment and capital borrowing for all local projects, health and welfare services, and the administration of justice. Metro would become the exclusive operator of transit services, assuming the assets of the city's transportation commission and several private suburban bus companies. It would also control the planning, construction, and maintenance of highways and major arterial roads. Jurisdiction over public housing and parks would be shared. Finally, to remedy disparities in education, the many area school boards would be reorganized into a parallel two-tier arrangement, with the metropolitan board managing capital expenditures.[86]

Metro would possess land-use planning authority. Accepting the argument that the long-term planning of urban growth would require unified authority over the rural hinterland, the OMB recommended replacing the Toronto and York Planning Board with a new Metropolitan Toronto Planning Board (MTPB) responsible to Metro Council. The OMB did not specify its jurisdiction, but the minister would later designate a vast, 1,865 km² area: Metro plus the adjacent thirteen villages, towns, and townships in Peel, York, and Ontario Counties.[87] Importantly, the MTPB would not replace local planning boards. Instead, their official plans, zoning bylaws, and public works would be required to conform to the MTPB's official plan, once adopted. The MTPB would also comment on all applications to the province for rural land subdivision.

Metro's council would not be directly elected. As in existing Ontario counties, its membership would be delegated from local councils. Each of the suburban reeves would sit on the council, as would the senior member of each of Toronto's nine two-member wards, the mayor, and two members of the Board of Control. The province would appoint the chair in the first year, and he or she would be selected by the council thereafter. As in Henry's metropolitan district proposal thirty years before, the council would balance city and suburban representation. Metro's territorial jurisdiction would also expand in step with urbanization.[88]

The OMB's recommendations received a mixed reception. Toronto's council (excluding Mayor Lamport) continued to beat the drum for annexation.[89] One councillor referred to it as "the greatest act of confiscation since the expulsion of the Acadians."[90] The *Globe and Mail* assailed the plan as creating a distant power and condemned it as an undemocratic infringement on local autonomy.[91] While pleased to avoid annexation, suburban municipalities opposed Toronto's dominance of Metro Council.[92] The opposition Liberals renewed their call for incremental annexation.[93] Non-governmental organized interests also disapproved. The Toronto District Labour Council called on the legislature to pursue amalgamation instead, calling Cumming's plan "totally unrealistic, not in accord with recognized democratic principles, and ... unduly cumbersome and unnecessarily expensive."[94]

Having the proposal come from the OMB gave Frost political cover, but the proposal was very much a product of the provincial government. Secure in its new electoral majority, the government was unswayed by opposition. While the OMB was in principle an arm's-length body, Frost, Cumming, and A.E.K. Bunnell had been in regular contact throughout. Bunnell had consulted his colleagues in the American Society of Planning Officials (ASPO) for the latest American thinking on metropolitan government reform and regional planning. Indeed, he had discussed extraterritorial planning jurisdiction at the previous year's ASPO conference and urged Cumming to pursue the idea.[95] A bill was introduced in the legislature within weeks.[96] Frost's personal interest was evidenced by his decision to introduce the bill himself, a task that would ordinarily have fallen to his municipal affairs minister. The legislation was passed after only modest debate.[97] Metro commenced operation on 1 January 1954 with Frederick Gardiner appointed as its first chairman.

Neither the OMB nor the province directly addressed the role of conservation authorities. It would take the devastating impact of Hurricane Hazel in October 1954 to align the region's conservation authorities with the structures of the new metropolitan government. After ravaging Haiti, the hurricane made landfall in the Carolinas and cut a path of destruction northwards through Virginia, Pennsylvania, and New York. Merging with a cold front, it gained strength before stalling over central Toronto. All told, eighty-one people died and over four thousand were left homeless when flash floods inundated settled floodplains. Afterwards, in 1957, the province combined the four Toronto-area conservation authorities into a new Metro Toronto and Region Conservation Authority (MTRCA) whose boundaries roughly corresponded with the MTPB's planning area. Metro Council would appoint members of the MTRCA's board and provide much of its funds. Through its integration with Metro, the MTRCA had the resources to embark on an extensive program of damming and property acquisition to improve flood control, while at the same time establishing new parks and recreational spaces in concert with Metro's land-use and infrastructure planning.[98] (See figure 4.5 for a comparison of the boundaries of Metro Toronto, the extraterritorial jurisdiction of its planning board, and the conservation authority.)

Metro Delivers on Its Promise

Metro achieved much during its first fifteen years, rapidly expanding the scope of urban infrastructure and services. It pursued two planning objectives.[99] First, the patchwork of existing water and sewer systems, wells, and septic tanks would be replaced by a fully lake-based delivery and treatment system. Water would be drawn from Lake Ontario, used, treated, and returned to the lake. By the end of Metro's first decade, virtually the entire urbanized area had been converted from well and septic systems to centralized water and sewage treatment, and fears of groundwater contamination disappeared.[100] To ensure the efficient provision of water and sewer infrastructure, the MTPB's planners used subdivision review to enforce contiguous urban growth. Second, Metro constructed a transportation system that balanced automobile and transit use. Metro viewed the major arterial roads under its jurisdiction as conduits for the movement of people in both private cars and transit vehicles, and a program of arterial road widening supported the Toronto Transit Commission (TTC) as it extended bus service into the emerging suburban hinterland.

Metro's infrastructure extensions quickly opened up large tracts of rural Etobicoke, North York, and Scarborough to urban development. Metro-wide, 141,000 dwellings were constructed between 1954 and

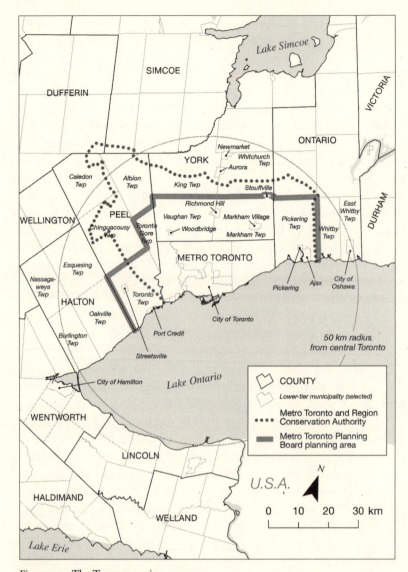

Figure 4.5 The Toronto region, 1954

Note: Only selected lower-tier municipalities are represented and labelled. The planning area of the Metropolitan Toronto Planning Board encompassed an area approximately double that of Metro Toronto itself, in Peel, York, and Ontario Counties. With the exception of the western half of Toronto Township in York County, the jurisdiction of the Metropolitan Toronto and Region Conservation Authority (MTRCA, established in 1957) included all of this area and also the headwaters of the Humber, Don, and Rouge Rivers to the north.

Sources: Municipal boundaries from Canadian Century Research Infrastructure Project; MTRCA boundary from Conservation Authority Administration Delineation 2004, Ministry of Natural Resources.

1961.[101] As expected, urban growth increased land values, which in turn helped to fund growth-related infrastructure and services. Metro's taxable property assessment grew by 80 per cent between 1954 and 1964 – double the increase in population. The City of Toronto's share of assessed value decreased from 62 to 44 per cent, while Etobicoke, North York, and Scarborough's combined share doubled from 19.7 to 41 per cent.[102] The scale of the land development and construction industries was correspondingly enlarged to meet demand for housing and employment land, and to function within Metro's system of large-scale subdivision master planning. Before Metro, no developer produced more than 100 dwellings per year; by the end of the 1950s this figure was commonplace, and some were constructing between 250 and 500.[103] Land development firms supported Metro's land-use and infrastructure planning because it ensured predictable returns on their speculative land investments.

Although Metro's creation was in large part motivated by the perceived need to plan the future pattern of urban development and supportive infrastructure systems, the preparation of an official plan took a back seat to physical infrastructure construction.[104] A draft plan released in 1959 and revised in 1966 was never formally adopted, in large part because local councils resisted incursion on their autonomy and did not want to be bound by growth targets. Still, MTPB planners Eli Comay and Hans Blumenfeld – both non-Canadians with substantial American and, in the latter case, European experience – articulated core planning principles that were largely observed as infrastructure was constructed and subdivision applications were reviewed: the maintenance of a contiguous urban form to enable efficient lake-based water and sewer servicing and a transportation system that balanced the personal automobile with public transit. By 1965, twenty-two of the twenty-six municipalities in the MTPB planning area had planning boards, and eighteen had adopted official plans. Many of these were prepared with the aid of MTPB staff and so reflected Metro's land-use concept.[105] Contiguity of development was also ensured through the planning board's review of subdivision applications.[106] Those violating the planning principles were refused. Between 1954 and 1957, only 42 per cent of 116,000 proposed residential lots were approved.[107] During the 1950s, Metro Toronto captured 80 per cent of population growth in the six-county area, and other 12 per cent occurred in the MTPB's extraterritorial planning area. Only 8 per cent of the region's population growth occurred beyond the MTPB's jurisdiction.

Metro's creation came at no apparent political cost to the Conservatives, which in the 1955 election took seventeen of eighteen seats in Metro and three of the four adjoining districts over which the MTPB exercised partial jurisdiction. Metro was sustained in its early years by Gardiner's muscular leadership. He did not simply preside over the council as chair. As chief executive with direct access to Metro's growing bureaucracy and the information it produced, he actively promoted his own point of view.[108] Using carrots and sticks, he persuaded Metro council to vote with him most of the time, making sure to balance city and suburban interests.[109] It was clear that Gardiner had the full support of the provincial government that had appointed him. His personal authority and prestige as a powerbroker in the provincial and federal Conservative Parties, combined with his close friendship with Premier Frost, ensured that Metro never acted with less than the full support of the provincial government and that the province rarely acted in ways contrary to Gardiner's preferences. Frost himself credited Gardiner with Metro's very existence.[110]

The province's unilateral imposition of Metro and support for its activities in its critical first decade exemplify the decisiveness and resoluteness of executive-centred Westminster governance in the context of a conducive normative context and single-party dominance. While its constitutional authority to remake the local government system was unfettered, Frost's government carefully managed the politics of unilateral action by creating opportunities for the municipalities to arrive at their own solution, and by allowing the OMB's ostensibly independent consideration of Toronto's and Mimico's applications to play out. To be sure, the creation of new metropolitan institutions represented a deep incursion into local autonomy. Nonetheless, the approach was consistent with the government's desire to empower local governments within provincial enabling frameworks so that they could address their own problems. A new era would begin after Frost and Gardiner left the political scene in 1961, one in which the province assumed increasing direct responsibility for metropolitan policymaking.

PROVINCIAL OVERREACH LEADS TO POLICY DRIFT, 1965–87

Ontario politics and society were transformed during the 1960s. The provincial population increased by a quarter, to almost eight million. The growth and diversification of the population and the economy increased demands on the state, which was radically expanded. During the 1960s, the Ontario Public Service doubled to 65,000 employees, nominal provincial expenditure quintupled to $5 billion, and legislative office became a full-time job.[111] Presiding over this transformation was John Robarts, who was premier from 1961 to 1971. Bequeathed a strong majority and divided opposition in the provincial legislature, Robarts's Conservatives won the 1963 election decisively and the 1967 election with a reduced majority. The party's support remained broad, both within Metro Toronto and across the province.

Robarts's government pursued an activist agenda that reached deeply into communities. The informal and personalist politics of earlier times gave way to more strategic and programmatic governance. This was driven by a new generation of politicians and public servants who viewed government as an instrument for the resolution of social and economic problems. Their approach was rationalist and technocratic. For the most part they were young, having come of age in the optimistic early postwar atmosphere. In the words of one participant, one could "believe, truly, that anything was possible" during the first half of the 1960s.[112] Robarts himself was only forty-four when he took office in 1961. His minister of economics and development, Robert Macauley, aged forty, immediately launched a reorganization of the government's economic departments and, with Robarts's full support, laid the groundwork for proactive economic management.[113] In 1965, thirty-five-year-old academic Ian Macdonald was recruited to be chief economist with a mandate to break down departmental silos and reform fiscal management. Budget making would no longer entail simply balancing expenditures with anticipated revenues. Spending would be coordinated to achieve broader strategic objectives.[114] In 1966, Robarts promoted to cabinet Darcy McKeough, then thirty-three, first as minister without portfolio and then as minister of municipal affairs. Under Premier Bill Davis (1971–85), McKeough would later serve as a kind of economic super-minister, serving as treasurer and minister of economics and intergovernmental affairs in 1971–72 and 1975–78. Senior public servant Nigel Richardson would later describe him as "unequivocally ... the dominant figure, indeed the very symbol, of the times."[115]

The Ontario state's modernization mirrored developments elsewhere on the continent. American state expenditure more than doubled between 1960 and 1969, and the number of state-level employees increased by almost 60 per cent.[116] As in Robarts's Ontario, American states sought to improve coordination across departments and embraced new managerial innovations such as multi-year program budgeting. Reformers also sought to improve policy coordination by empowering the governor, and to improve the quality of legislation by reorganizing committee systems, lengthening the legislative session, and increasing staff support. The scope of government intervention and administrative modernization was greater in Ontario than in any American state, however, because there are no constitutional limits on the ability of a Westminster majority government to enact legislation, set spending priorities, and reorganize the internal structure of provincial departments and agencies.

This political, normative, and institutional context underlay five parallel, but ultimately related, policy initiatives that inserted the provincial government into local and metropolitan governance and planning in new ways. The first was a review of Metro Toronto's internal structures and boundaries. This paralleled the work of the Smith Committee, a comprehensive review of provincial and municipal public finance and intergovernmental fiscal relations. That committee's work led to Local Government Review, a program of local government reorganization on the premise that larger municipal units would be more financially viable and able to provide services more efficiently and equitably. The fourth initiative was the Metropolitan Toronto and Region Transportation Study, a forecast of future transportation infrastructure demand. The fifth was Design for Development, a comprehensive regional economic development strategy designed to channel growth to underperforming regions of the province.

Taken together, these ambitious projects shared an acceptance of the "region" (however defined) as a spatial framework for the resolution of policy problems. This was more than a discursive shift from "metropolitan" Toronto. It also expanded the range of issues implicated in regional governance and planning and assigned the province a direct role in addressing them. The broader region centred on Toronto was also understood to be differentiated not only from other parts of the province but also within itself – a polycentric zone comprising a core and hinterland. The question was not whether this new region should be governed, but how, and by whom.

Choosing Not to Expand Metro: The Goldenberg Commission

An increasing proportion of urban growth began to spill beyond the boundaries of Metro and its planning board during the 1960s. If

metropolitan growth were to be managed by a single authority, either
Metro, or its planning area, or both, would have to have to be
expanded – as its architects had originally intended. To study Metro,
in 1963 Robarts appointed a royal commission in the person of
Montreal labour lawyer Carl Goldenberg, who had extensive experience with municipal issues. The impetus was disagreement over
municipal representation on Metro Council. The city renewed its push
for amalgamation of the thirteen municipalities while the suburbs
demanded representation on Metro Council in proportion to their
growing populations.[117] Communities outside Metro but within the
MTPB's jurisdiction repeatedly asked for seats on the Metro-appointed
planning board but were denied.

While Goldenberg's recommendations were concerned predominantly with the representation question, service consolidation, and the
amalgamation of municipalities within Metro – the thirteen municipalities were ultimately reduced to six – many participants in the
public hearings argued for the expansion of Metro or its planning
area. Goldenberg opposed outright amalgamation, arguing that a
two-tier system was more territorially flexible.[118] With amalgamation
off the table, the City of Toronto endorsed Metro's extension eastwards to include urbanizing parts of Pickering Township and west-
wards to include southern Peel County. Other municipalities within
Metro came forth with a variety of proposals to expand the jurisdiction of Metro into the neighbouring counties. York County and its
southern tier of municipalities opposed inclusion in Metro, arguing
that the existence of the planning board, combined with provincial
assistance for the construction of water and sewer infrastructure,
made change to Metro's northern boundary unnecessary.[119]

Seeking to manage the orderly staging and servicing of new development, the Metro Toronto Planning Board called for the province to
add rapidly growing Brampton and Bramalea to its jurisdiction, as
did the Ontario Water Resources Commission (OWRC).[120] Starting
in 1957, the British firm Bramalea Consolidated Developments assembled 24 km² of land just outside of the MTPB's jurisdiction in Peel
County with the intention of building a free-standing new town – a
direct contravention of the MTPB's planning principles.[121] The county
and the rural townships lacked the fiscal capacity and expertise to
construct a comprehensive servicing scheme for Bramalea and other
proposed master-planned communities. Testifying on his own behalf
before the Goldenberg Commission, MTPB planning commissioner
Eli Comay illustrated the pressure at Metro's edges and made the case

for a broader planning perspective: "By 1970 or 1975, many of the things that Metro has achieved within its boundaries will be needed outside. We must recognize that the situation on Metro's fringe is rapidly becoming analogous to the situation here before Metro was formed."[122] Comay opposed the creation of a "second Metro" in Peel County, arguing that the division of planning authority would undermine the rational organization of urban development. Extension of the planning board's jurisdiction was endorsed by the Urban Development Institute (the main lobby group for residential, industrial, and commercial property developers), the Metro Toronto Board of Trade, and the Community Planning Association of Canada.

Goldenberg ultimately recommended expanding Metro and its planning area only if the province chose not to restructure local government in the adjacent counties.[123] Provincial legislation to implement his recommendations regarding the internal reorganization of Metro made no provision for boundary extension. However, the *Globe* quoted an unnamed senior provincial official who stated that the government planned to expand Metro to the north and east in stages as growth warranted. In words of the journalist, "The province [opposes amalgamation because it] sees the federation as the proper instrument to handle and control a flexible number of local municipal units."[124] There is also evidence that a group of MPPs privately endorsed the northern extension of Metro, as did Frederick Gardiner, who later argued that the Goldenberg report's principal defect was its failure to expand Metro's northern boundary.[125] This line of thinking appears to have been shut down by former OMB chair Cumming, who had become deputy minister of municipal affairs.[126] Moreover, the new minister of municipal affairs, Darcy McKeough, saw Metro expansion as parochial empire-building, later recalling that advocates wanted to "expand it to the Arctic Circle."[127] Although advocates continued to call for the territorial enlargement of Metro into the 1970s, this never occurred.[128]

Local Government Review:
Regionalization as County Empowerment

The Toronto-region boundary-reform question was soon subsumed by a province-wide program of local government reorganization intended to increase municipal fiscal and administrative capacity. Metro became but one piece of a province-wide puzzle rather than the exclusive manager of Toronto-area urbanization. Of Ontario's 940 municipalities in 1964, 276 had fewer than a thousand residents.[129] While the Frost government had overhauled provincial-municipal grants a decade earlier, small municipalities continued to find themselves unable to meet their obligations.[130] A legislative Select Committee on the Municipal and Related Acts, chaired by East York MPP Hollis Beckett, concluded that local governments would have to become bigger if local own-source revenues were to be matched to growing municipal responsibilities.

The perceived failure of county government was an important factor in Beckett's conclusion. The territory and tax-assessment base of urbanizing counties had been chipped away by annexations to separated cities across the province since the 1950s. In 1960, seventeen counties submitted a brief to cabinet arguing that annexation was a symptom of the counties' failure to effectively accommodate growth. The Association of Ontario Counties (AOC) was founded that same year to lobby for reform, and by 1965 it was arguing for counties to take on service-delivery roles.[131] The AOC communicated regularly with its US counterpart, the National Association of Counties (NACO), which advocated vigorously for county empowerment. In a 1964 address to the AOC, the executive director of NACO outlined the new role for urban counties in the United States as "regional cities" or "city-states," performing tasks that were previously the preserve of lower-tier units.[132] Metro Toronto was a compelling local example of what county-based reform could accomplish. Beckett's 1965 final report recommended duplicating the Metro Toronto model across the province.[133] Municipal restructuring and the incorporation of separated cities into empowered counties was endorsed by major interest groups and municipal associations: the Urban Development Institute, the Ontario Municipal Association (Town and Village Section), the Association of Ontario Counties, and the Community Planning Association of Canada.[134]

Municipal Affairs Minister J.W. Spooner agreed that county government's usefulness had diminished and that either abolition or strengthening was necessary.[135] He held back, however, pending the recommendations of the Ontario Committee on Taxation, chaired by Lancelot Smith.[136] Smith's 1967 final report went beyond Beckett's, calling for a sweeping reorganization of local government in southern Ontario into twenty-two large "regional" units whose boundaries would be drawn from scratch to reflect modern needs as well as shared historical, economic, social, and geographical conditions.

The government rejected Smith's wholesale reorganization as "overly theoretical and politically unmanageable."[137] Even senior bureaucrats who believed that Beckett's county-based units were too small felt that Smith's were too large.[138] Nonetheless, there was a general consensus within the government that reform was necessary. In 1964–65, the province launched the Local Government Review program, a series of commissions of inquiry to make recommendations on restructuring almost all major city-county areas in the province, both to improve local governments' fiscal and administrative capacity and to enable the devolution of provincial service delivery.[139] The review commissions generally supported county-based restructuring. Recommendations that deviated from county boundaries, as in Ottawa–Carleton County and Peel-Halton, were generally rejected in favour of Metro Toronto–style two-tier arrangements incorporating previously separated cities.[140] Pragmatism trumped Smith's planning and efficiency rationales for the more radical reorganization. Lionel Feldman, who served as secretary and research director of the Halton-Peel study, suggests that the retention of existing boundaries was a pragmatic move – it was politically and administratively easier to transfer powers between existing levels of government than to abolish or redraw their boundaries.[141] At the same time, the government's positive perception of Metro, as well as Cumming's influence over the review process, steered it toward replicating the Metro model within existing county boundaries.[142] Politically, county empowerment converged with urban counties' desire for greater authority.

The conversion of traditional counties into Metro Toronto–like bodies called "regional municipalities" was repeated across the province between 1969 and 1974. In the Toronto region, York County was converted in 1971. Reform came to Metro's east flank in 1974 with the merger of Durham and Ontario Counties into a new Regional Municipality of Durham, and to the west with the creation of Peel and Halton Regional Municipalities that same year.[143]

Local Restructuring in the Service of Local Autonomy

From Beckett to Smith to Local Government Review, the drive to "regionalize" local government should not be interpreted as a centralizing move on the part of the province. While local government restructuring was viewed as necessary to improve the efficiency of local administration and promote economic development, its advocates also believed that it would rescue local democracy from modernizing pressures that threatened to overwhelm it. Smith's seemingly contradictory prescription – the destruction of existing local governments in order to preserve local autonomy – is worth recapitulating in full:

> The measures we have suggested ... would have far-reaching effects on Ontario's time-honoured municipal structure ... Local autonomy has ever been a cornerstone of municipal institutions in this province. We consider ourselves second to none in our espousal of this principle which has served so long and so well in promoting democratic values within a framework of decentralization. But if local autonomy is to remain a reality, the institutions it fosters must be worthy of its challenge. Local autonomy, precisely because it stresses the importance of strong municipal institutions, is not a haven for municipalities and school boards so small and weakly organized that they cannot discharge their functions in acceptable fashion. Again local autonomy, which is a bastion of responsive and responsible government, cannot condone the multiplication of *ad hoc* special service authorities removed from the immediate arena of the political process. Through the medium of a rationalized regional government system, we believe we offer a dynamic opportunity for the material advancement of local autonomy throughout Ontario. We look to provincial action that will augment, not curtail, local initiative.[144]

The notion of enhancing local autonomy through local government restructuring was expressed inside and outside of government by Robarts and McKeough, and also by the advisory Ontario Economic Council.[145] It was also paralleled in the reform of school boards. One of the most contentious issues of Robarts's tenure was the amalgamation of small and often fiscally troubled school districts – 1,012 boards were reduced to only 230.[146] The reconciliation of the traditional faith in local autonomy with the technocratic reorganization of the provincial and local government represented continuity rather than rupture, an extension of the Conservatives' fusion of progressive rationalism and localism in the 1946 Planning Act.

Toward Provincial Planning for a Greater Toronto Region

Local government restructuring in the Toronto region and across the province was only part of the 1960s story. The government launched two parallel initiatives in the same period: the Metropolitan Toronto and Region Transportation Study (MTARTS) and a province-wide regional economic development program called Design for Development.[147] While initially unrelated, these efforts would merge, culminating, at least in principle, in a provincial plan for the broader Toronto region. By the mid-1970s, however, the whole enterprise collapsed, undone by political and economic change, as well as by unresolved contradictions within the policy itself.

Inspired by federally mandated metropolitan transportation-planning exercises in the United States, the provincial Department of Highways launched the Metropolitan Toronto and Region Transportation Study in 1962. Its scope was much larger than Metro and its planning area, considering a region stretching from Hamilton in the west, north to Barrie on the shore of Lake Simcoe, and to east of Oshawa, containing eighty-five municipalities, 8,260 km², and 2.73 million people.[148] With striking accuracy, the study forecast a population of 6.43 million in 2000.[149] What began as a conventional transportation analysis typical of contemporary American practice was soon broadened in scope. A regional development subcommittee was struck to consider growth trends and compare the implications of four alternative regional land-use patterns, called "goals plans" in the final report, through to the turn of the millennium. The subcommittee accepted the MTPB's core planning principles: contiguous urban growth fully serviced with lake-based water and sewer services and a transportation system that balanced automobile use and transit for local and long-distance trips. A multi-purpose service corridor called the Parkway Belt would run parallel to the lake north of Metro Toronto, separating two tiers of more or less self-contained urban settlements, which in the future would contain Highway 407.[150]

Only the province could orchestrate such a scheme. The final report – printed in November 1967 but released to the public only in June 1968 after another Conservative election victory – called for the province to develop a "specific plan ... to guide public and private decisions and investment" in the region.[151] The plan would coordinate local official plans and could be administered by either a "single regional administration" or a "special agency."[152] Following the reformist Darcy McKeough's accession to minister, the Community Planning Branch of the Department of Municipal Affairs began consulting stakeholders in 1968–69.

MTARTS paralleled the growing interest in regional economic development. Two provincial government–sponsored international conferences were held in 1965.[153] The same year, newly installed provincial chief economist Ian Macdonald recruited a cadre of regional science and economic geography experts, including Queen's University geography professor Richard Thoman as director of a new Regional Development Branch.[154] In a policy statement, penned by Macdonald, called *Design for Development*, Premier Robarts outlined a new role for the province in "guiding, encouraging, and assisting the orderly and regional development of the province."[155] The province would not simply accommodate economic and physical growth, as in the past, but would direct it using infrastructure investment and land-use planning in order to "smooth out … conspicuous regional economic inequalities."[156] Ontario's ten multi-county regional development *associations*, which had been established in the 1950s as talking shops for area municipalities and businesses, were re-created as compulsory regional development *councils*, for which the government would define regional development plans. Ontario was the first subnational jurisdiction in North American to embark on such a program.[157]

Robarts initially stated that the promotion and coordination of economic development within and across regions was unrelated to local government restructuring, but reversed himself following the Smith Committee's report.[158] Speaking to the legislature, he stated that Design for Development's aims could be achieved only in partnership with stronger, restructured local governments.

By 1968, Design for Development had expanded beyond its original economic objectives to become an umbrella for the Robarts government's pursuit of programmatic, joined-up, and regionalized governance. Cabinet approved staff recommendations to incorporate environmental policy as well as land-use and transportation planning goals into regional economic development policies. In early 1969, responsibility for developing the post-MTARTS regional land-use and transportation plan was moved from the Department of Municipal Affairs to the Regional Development Branch in the Department of Treasury and Economics. While MTARTS had been concerned with securing the efficient provision of growth-related transportation and other infrastructure by constructing a supportive settlement pattern (one that was contiguous and relied on lake-based services), these objectives were altered when folded into the regional economic development agenda. The *Design for Development: The Toronto-Centred Region* policy statement (TCR) released in May 1970 added a new feature: the redistribution of population and economic growth *within* the region.[159] Growth would be channelled away from Zone 1, the "lakeshore urbanized area" that stretched from Hamilton to Toronto to Oshawa, and toward Zone 3, which contained slow-growth towns beyond the Toronto commutershed. Separating them, Zone 2 would be preserved for agricultural and recreational activities. The Parkway Belt was retained as an infrastructure corridor and "urban separator" between two tiers of urban development along the lakeshore. While Metro Toronto lay at the core of the "Toronto-centred" region, the development concept was not centralizing; in fact, the goal was the opposite (see figure 4.6).

Also incorporated into the TCR was a plan to protect the Niagara Escarpment, a linear natural feature stretching 725 km from the tip of the Bruce Peninsula to Hamilton and then into Niagara. Its gravel deposits were the basis of a multi-million-dollar extraction industry, and in Niagara the escarpment provided a conducive microclimate for fruit growing. Naturalists prized it as a recreational amenity of rare beauty, and a new cadre of environmentalists argued for the protection of its vulnerable ecosystems and habitats from resource extraction.[160] In 1968, Regional Development Branch planner Leonard Gertler recommended legislating a provincial plan to which municipalities would be required to conform. A permanent, provincially appointed Niagara Escarpment Commission was created in 1973 to review development proposals and prepare the plan.

Conflict brewed throughout this period between the Department of Municipal Affairs' Local Government Review and land-use planning programs, on the one hand, and the work of the Regional Development Branch within the Department of Treasury and Economics, on the other.[161] A chicken-and-egg dilemma emerged. Was local government reorganization a necessary precursor of regional planning, as Municipal Affairs Minister Darcy McKeough believed?[162] Or, should local government boundary reform be dictated by the Regional Development Branch's economic criteria? After a battle in which the regional development mandarins were persuaded to integrate their work with local government restructuring, it was agreed that the Regional Development Branch would produce general "goals

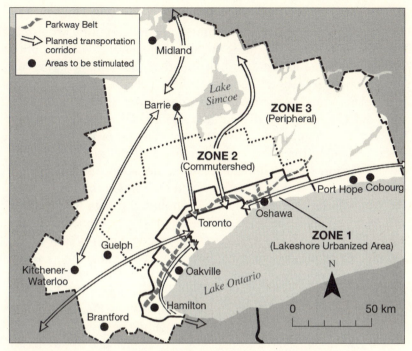

Figure 4.6 The Toronto-Centred Region development concept, 1970

Note: The Toronto-Centred Region scheme divided the Toronto region into three numbered zones: (1) the "lakeshore urbanized area," including Metro; (2) the "commutershed," to be preserved for recreational and agricultural uses; and (3) the "peripheral zone," to which economic activity would be directed. The Parkway Belt crosscuts Zone 1.

Source: Redrawn from Thoman, *Design for Development in Ontario*, 80.

plans" for each of the province's ten multi-county economic regions. The province would support the plans through its infrastructure investments.[163] Local official plans would conform to the official plans of the reformed "regional municipalities" as they came into existence, which would in turn be aligned with the province's regional goals plans, much as the plans of the lower-tier municipalities in Toronto were required to conform to Metro's official plan.[164]

While, in principle, the province would coordinate local land-use planning at the regional scale, several practicalities remained unresolved. Despite the conceptual elegance of this hierarchy of nested plans, it would be years before the components would be in place. The problem began at the hierarchy's apex. The TCR regional development "concept" remained vague and lacked legal status. The land-development industry demanded greater certainty, protesting that the gap between lofty ideas and institutional reality was disrupting land markets and impeding urban growth.[165] Second, there was still disagreement regarding the scale at which the province's regional goals plans would be defined. The Toronto-Centred Region's boundaries did not align with those of the regional development councils – in fact, it overlapped with five of them. Third, as of 1970 the counties surrounding Toronto remained unreformed and so it would likely be years before future regional municipalities adopted official plans.

To resolve these contradictions, Bill Davis, who had succeeded Roberts as premier in March 1971, announced Design for Development's "third phase" in 1972.[166] The regional development councils were dissolved as the government announced that it would devise regional plans on its own in consultation with local actors. The ten economic development regions were reduced to five "planning regions," one of which, slightly expanded, would be the Toronto-Centred Region.[167] (This name change completed the discursive fusion of *regional economic development* and *regional planning*.) Although the local government reviews had mostly recommended county-based reforms, Davis also announced the government's intention to reopen the process. In some cases, the premier stated, the "present counties may not provide a suitable base for local government [and so] it is now time to broaden the basis on which studies are undertaken."

From Activist Government to Policy Drift in a Changing Normative and Political Context

Unified under the control of a powerful minister and a group of senior public servants, the many moving parts of Design for Development appeared to be proceeding toward greater coherence. Yet the 1972 Phase Three announcement was the beginning of the end for Design for Development and province-led regional planning for greater Toronto. Despite continuing work to refine the TCR development scheme within the bureaucracy, no provincial plans for the five planning regions were ever produced.[168] Without its keystone, the arch could not stand.

The government's activist and modernizing impulses were revealed to be out of step with public opinion by the early 1970s. The technocratic optimism of the 1960s, symbolized by the charismatic Roberts and his young cabinet, faded. While rural residents were suspicious of rising taxes, encroachments on local autonomy, and statism more generally, the new urban middle class opposed environmental degradation, governmental paternalism, and the imposition of large-scale infrastructure projects on their neighbourhoods. This dissatisfaction empowered both rural Liberals and urban New Democrats. The Conservatives adapted to changing public expectations by retreating from large-scale and intrusive initiatives.[169] Only three months after taking office, Davis cancelled the Spadina Expressway, which would have cut a broad swath through central Toronto. Local Government Review was not reopened; instead, it was halted in 1974 following a bellwether by-election defeat in 1973.[170] If there was a moment at which the grand policymaking of the *ancien régime* symbolically ended, it was the 1975 election, in which the Conservatives were reduced to a minority. In an increasingly competitive three-party system, Davis would maintain Conservative hegemony in Ontario until 1985 only by scrupulously avoiding initiatives that would put the government ahead of public opinion.

While parallel provincial reviews of the Planning Act and of Metro Toronto recommended the creation of a coordinating body for greater Toronto in 1977, the 1979 White Paper on planning reform recommended that coordination remain informal.[171] Creating a new level of government was politically untenable in the new normative context. Although the regional municipalities' land-use planning role would not mature until the 1980s and 1990s, Local Government Review ultimately produced local governments in urbanizing areas that were more territorially extensive and possessed greater fiscal and administrative capacity than before. A comprehensive revision of the Planning Act in 1983 devolved land-use planning authority to municipalities and removed the province from day-to-day land-use approvals. Although the new act provided for the government to issue "provincial policy statements" binding on local governments, none were immediately issued.

In the absence of provincial policies or coordinating institutions for the greater region, Metro Toronto and its neighbours each went their own way. Metro's focus turned inward as it became fully built out and the creation of the new regional municipalities eliminated the extraterritorial jurisdiction of the MTPB. Only two of the regional municipalities – Durham and Halton – produced official plans by the mandated deadline, and these reflected the preferences of lower-tier municipalities rather than a region-wide interest.[172] Metro Toronto and the other regional municipalities would not enact official plans until the 1990s. If certain principles continued to be observed – full servicing and a prohibition on new free-standing settlements in favour of contiguous urban expansion – it was because they had become embedded in professional practice and general provincial policies. The result is a remarkable uniformity in the appearance of urban development, not just in Toronto but across southern Ontario.

The grand promise of integrated and programmatic policymaking remained unrealized. Metro's consolidated control over metropolitan infrastructure systems was lost. The province encouraged suburban municipalities to establish bus systems independent from the TTC, and municipal transit bodies' integration with the emergent GO Transit regional rail and bus system was minimal.[173] The province also directly designed, financed, and constructed urban water and sewer systems in fringe areas, reducing the incentive for the suburbanizing munici-palities in surrounding countries to collaborate with Metro.[174] By the early 1980s, according to one senior public servant, "Ontario's 'plan' for its primate metropolitan region consist[ed] of seven different 'regional' official plans scotch-taped together at the edges, virtually a reversion to the early 'fifties on a grander scale."[175] Even this por-trayal was somewhat optimistic, given planning's slow development in the regional municipalities.

ELECTORAL CHANGE UNDERMINES POLICY DURABILITY, 1987–2002

The Toronto region grew briskly between 1970 and 2000. Most of the growth occurred outside of Metro Toronto, which had little remaining undeveloped land. The population of the four surrounding regional municipalities tripled to 2.6 million between 1970 and 2000, surpassing Metro's 2.5 million residents. Despite this extraordinary growth, little new highway or transit infrastructure had been con-structed since the 1970s. By the mid-1980s, traffic volume was growing by 6 per cent per year and was forecast to triple by 2011. The region's main east-west artery, Highway 401, was already 25 per cent over its designed capacity. A second issue was the looming problem of solid waste management: the region's sanitary landfill capacity was expected to be depleted by 1992.[176] Although problems associated with met-ropolitan urbanization were multiplying, the Conservative government appeared powerless to address them.

Planning the Greater Toronto Area

The Conservatives' forty-two-year electoral hegemony came to an end in 1985, when David Peterson's rejuvenated Liberal Party formed a minority government with the support of the New Democratic Party (NDP). While initially not inclined to become involved in municipal governance and planning, the Liberals promised action to address growing concerns about traffic congestion and "sprawl" after securing a parliamentary majority in 1987.[177] That October, Peterson convened a Greater Toronto Coordinating Committee (GTCC), composed of municipal officials and, in parallel, an internal committee of eleven ministers. A year later the government created a small Office for the Greater Toronto Area (OGTA) reporting to the finance minister.[178] The creation of a small "office" rather than a ministerial "branch" or a free-standing agency is suggestive of the province's disengagement from municipal affairs since the 1970s. Publicly and privately, the government took pains to stress that the OGTA was not, and could not become, a new level of government. Indeed, any suggestion of the entity's purpose was deliberately eliminated from its name.[179] Its goal was to promote collaboration, not to tell municipalities what to do. Perhaps to head off complaints about special treatment for Greater Toronto, its mandate stated that growth in the Greater Toronto Area (GTA) – comprising Metro Toronto and the regional municipalities of Durham, Halton, Peel, and York – must pay for itself and not be subsidized by residents located elsewhere in the province.[180] While the OGTA's deputy minister Gardner Church frequently lamented insufficient resources and support from other ministries and municipalities, it conducted important foundational work during the Peterson period.[181] Region-wide forecasts of population and employment growth revealed individual municipal forecasts to be more aspirational than realistic.[182] Municipalities often assumed that they would capture a greater proportion of regional growth than was warranted, resulting in over-investment in local infrastructure and overly optimistic expectations of future property tax revenue. The OGTA also commissioned an "urban concepts study" illustrating the infrastructure costs associated with different patterns of urban development.[183] These were the first regional studies since the MTARTS and TCR research two decades earlier.

The 1990 election brought Bob Rae's NDP to power. The OGTA was placed under Ruth Grier, minister of the environment and minister responsible for the GTA. This did not necessarily signal an increase in political support, however. Grier's primary interest was in the environment portfolio. As she became engaged with the Toronto file, she shifted the OGTA's focus from infrastructure and the economy toward livability and environmental quality.[184] Reflecting these new priorities, a vision statement for the region was articulated in 1991 and fleshed out in early 1992.[185] In the fall of 1991, the government appointed six provincial-municipal working groups on social issues, economic development, urban form, the countryside, infrastructure needs, and infrastructure financing. These were composed of public servants; no politicians or non-governmental participants served on them. The working groups' findings were summarized in a discussion paper, *Shaping Growth in the GTA*, which signalled the government's intention to produce a "strategic action plan" for the region.[186] Internal background reports prepared in late 1993 and early 1994 presented options for such a plan, which would be implemented through the existing planning system in the form of a GTA-specific provincial policy statement under the Planning Act.[187]

Facing declining popularity amid the deepest recession since the Great Depression, Rae shuffled his cabinet in 1993. The OGTA was transferred to the Ministry of Municipal Affairs, which had begun revising the Planning Act and associated provincial policies to speed up housing approvals, increase environmental protection, and promote housing affordability. The GTA policy statement was never integrated with this process, however, and was ultimately shelved.[188] The OGTA's work was nonetheless significant because it entrenched the Greater Toronto Area as a publicly accepted territorial unit of policymaking, produced a body of up-to-date research, and established new lines of communication and collaboration within and between provincial ministries and municipalities. It also identified a set of policy issues that provincial and municipal planners and public servants accepted could be resolved only at the regional scale: transportation, waste management, and economic development. Local politicians increasingly took these ideas seriously. As a counterpart to the GTCC, long-time Mississauga mayor Hazel McCallion convened regular meetings of GTA mayors and chairs to discuss shared problems.

A Final Opportunity for the Metro Model: The Greater Toronto Area Task Force

The idea of reforming Toronto-area governance resurfaced late in the NDP's term. Pressure was building for the province to address metropolitan competitiveness. A growing differential in non-residential property tax rates between Metro and surrounding municipalities was credited with hollowing out the core and undermining the region's global economic competitiveness.[189] This was exacerbated by the Canada-US Free Trade Agreement's ravaging of Toronto's manufacturing base.[190] In 1994 the *Toronto Star* began to call attention to the lack of regional coordination for land-use planning and economic development, and to criticize the Rae government for not doing enough for Toronto.[191] At the same time, the previous government's 1988 decision to make Metro Toronto council directly elected had increased rather than reduced City-Metro conflict, and business interests began agitating for amalgamation into a single-tier entity.

In February 1995, only months before an expected election, Premier Rae announced the creation of a Greater Toronto Area Task Force.[192] Led by United Way of Greater Toronto chair Anne Golden, the task force's primary mandate was to study and recommend ways of improving economic competitiveness. In particular, Golden was asked to examine the property tax differential and to recommend options for the GTA-wide sharing of certain expenditures borne exclusively by Metro – principally for social services and facilities of regional importance. The task force was influenced by new popular and academic ideas regarding the competitiveness of "city-regions." The GTA was Canada's largest urban economy, yet it lacked a unified voice and policymaking capacity. Economic competitiveness was linked to the long-standing issues of infrastructure and service provision, and also to environmental issues, by the precept that business investment decisions are driven not only by costs but also by quality of life.[193] The economic, social, and environmental determinants of competitiveness were viewed as metropolitan, rather than provincial or local, in scope.

While the task force did not begin with preconceived notions regarding changes to government structures, it soon became convinced that institutional reform was needed.[194] Four options emerged. The first was for the province to take on the coordinating role for itself – in essence a revival of the approach first envisioned by the authors of the MTARTS final report and elaborated through the Design for Development and Toronto-Centred Region exercises, and revived by the OGTA's regional provincial policy statement project. This was rejected on the grounds that the provincial government, representing a much broader constituency, would be unable to focus on and advocate for the region's specific needs.

The second option was to encourage inter-municipal cooperation through bilateral agreements. This was rejected as impracticable – if the municipalities had proven unable to collaborate on infrastructure planning and service provision thus far, there was no reason to believe that they would do so in the future. A third option, advocated by Metro Toronto, North York, and former MTPB chief planner Eli Comay, was to expand Metro to include the entire contiguous urban zone and its urbanizing fringe. The task force saw this directly elected "supercity" as too centralized and remote from residents, while being too territorially small to deter leapfrog development to outlying rural areas. Finally, the task force considered a "consensual model" along the lines of the Greater Vancouver Regional District (see chapter 6). This was rejected for being too incrementalist, given the urgency of Toronto's problems, and incompatible with Ontario's long postwar experience with authoritative, hierarchical relationships as embedded in the planning and two-tier local government systems.

The Task Force concluded that the most effective solution would be to replace Metro and the four surrounding regional municipalities with a new region-wide Greater Toronto Council. The lower-tier municipalities would remain intact and, consistent with the subsidiarity principle, would take on greater responsibilities. The regional council would do less than Metro, assuming responsibility for regional planning, economic development, management of regional assets (such as conference, cultural, and recreational facilities), and highways. It would be indirectly responsible for transit, police, conservation and environmental protection, solid waste management, and water and sewer services through a series of flexible service districts. Local control would be maintained, as regional councillors would be appointed by the municipal councils rather than directly elected. In essence, the Task Force's proposal transposed the original Metro model to a broader territory. Much as in 1953, the objective was to achieve regional coordination while preserving local autonomy and disentangling the province from direct involvement in local and regional affairs.

The Conservative Counter-Reformation

The unpopular NDP was decimated in the June 1995 election. With affinities to the American New Right, the Conservatives under Mike Harris mounted a populist attack on the government activism of the

Peterson and Rae years. On taking office, the Conservatives moved quickly to deregulate, shrink the size of the public service, devolve powers and responsibilities to municipalities, and cut taxes. The NDP's newly enacted land-use planning policies were replaced by a streamlined guideline aimed at facilitating development. The GTA Task Force was also instructed to report earlier than originally planned, in January 1996.

Although the Task Force's report was received favourably by Minister of Municipal Affairs Al Leach, municipal opposition soon emerged.[195] The chairs of the regional municipalities lobbied to retain their independent existence, while the mayors of Toronto, North York, Mississauga, and Oshawa jointly argued for greater autonomy. Echoing Margaret Thatcher's abolition of the Greater London Council a decade earlier, a Conservative Party task force on Metro chaired by MPP and former Scarborough mayor Joyce Trimmer advocated for Metro's elimination, portraying the two-tier system as wasteful duplication of government. Metro dropped its two-tier GTA "supercity" proposal, instead advocating its consolidation into a single-tier unit. At the same time, the province appointed former City of Toronto mayor and prominent Conservative David Crombie in May 1996 to recommend options for disentangling provincial and local governance and finance. It recommended a GTA-wide body similar to that proposed by Golden.[196]

Mindful of their suburban electoral base – the Conservatives had won sixteen of twenty-nine seats in Metro, but almost all of them outside the City of Toronto, and every seat in the surrounding regional municipalities – and ideologically committed to reducing the size of government, the creation of a new GTA-wide government was a bridge too far. At the same time, simply abolishing Metro, as Trimmer had recommended, risked undermining the solvency of the smaller Metro municipalities as the government proceeded with a province-wide overhaul of property tax assessment and "local services realignment" – that is, the transfer of numerous provincial responsibilities to municipalities in exchange for the partial "uploading" of education financing.[197] The government introduced a hybrid solution at the end of 1996. Metro Toronto would be amalgamated into a single-tier city at the beginning of 1998. The regional municipalities would remain intact. Formalizing Mayor McCallion's mayors and chairs group, a new GTA-wide entity called the Greater Toronto Services Board (GTSB) was created later the same year. While given authority over the provincial regional rail and bus transit system, it was not empowered to develop and impose policies and plans on municipalities.

Decisive Yet Irresolute Urban Governance

The 1987–2002 period is one of stunning electoral and policy reversals. The decades-long era of Conservative hegemony collapsed, inaugurating a fully competitive three-party system typified by growing policy polarization. The Liberal and New Democratic Parties increasingly battled for progressive urban support while the Conservatives became a more socially and economically conservative party of the right. All parties sought to construct a winning coalition by marrying their base to the growing suburban electorate. Three different parties won majority governments and used their control of the legislative process to pursue different policy priorities in a rapidly changing economic context. Facing a public that was sceptical of state intervention but nonetheless demanded that government "do something," the provincial government had become a decisive yet irresolute actor in the multi-level urban governance system, as much a source of disruption as of sustained support for local initiative.

THE REBIRTH OF PROVINCE-LED REGIONALISM SINCE 2002

As the century ended, the interlinked region-scaled issues identified by the OGTA and the GTA Task Force – traffic congestion, solid waste management, the financing of growth-related infrastructure, environmental protection, and global economic competitiveness – remained unresolved. Considerable provincial effort had been put into restructuring local government, and not just in Metro. The number of municipalities was reduced from 884 to 447 province-wide between 1995 and 2002.[198] Affecting less than half of the GTA's population, however, the amalgamation of Metro into a single-tier municipality did nothing to create new governing capacity at the regional scale. Neither the province nor the local governments that funded it showed much interest in the GTSB, which was abolished in 2001.

The Conservatives Discover "Smart Growth"

The political costs of inaction mounted in the Conservatives' second term (1999–2003), especially in the rapidly growing GTA suburbs that formed a crucial portion of their electoral base.[199] A critique of "urban sprawl" gained currency as the region continued to attract 100,000 new residents per year. A crucial dimension of this critique was aesthetic: while generally applicable provincial land-use and infrastructure policies had encouraged relatively compact development by North American standards, the new suburban landscape was viewed as monotonous and undifferentiated. Urban development on the Oak Ridges Moraine – long recognized as a scenic landscape and the location of the headwaters of numerous rivers – became a hot-button issue in York Region.[200] Traffic congestion multiplied as transportation infrastructure expansion failed to keep pace with population growth.

In a bid to retain its suburban electoral base, the Conservatives established a land-use plan for the moraine and appointed "Smart Growth" study panels for different regions of the province.[201] In both policymaking processes, the government reached beyond the provincial bureaucracy and municipal leaders to involve a broad range of extra-governmental stakeholders. The objective was to reach consensus on the prioritization of provincial infrastructure investments. While inclusion brought environmentalists, developers, farmer groups, and other organized interests tentatively on side, it was not enough to rescue the Conservatives from defeat in the October 2003 election.

From Smart Growth to Province-Led Regional Planning

The Liberals led by Dalton McGuinty won a majority in the fall of 2003 with strong electoral support in the amalgamated City of Toronto and its northern and western suburbs. The party's "strong communities" platform was informed by its close relationship with environmental organizations that had been radicalized by their exclusion from policymaking during the Conservatives' first term (1995–99).[202] The Liberals received strong support from urbanites who had opposed municipal amalgamations in Toronto and elsewhere. Building on the earlier provincial plans for the Niagara Escarpment and Oak Ridges Moraine areas, the Liberals established a Greenbelt of "protected countryside" around the Toronto region in 2005.[203] The Conservatives' Smart Growth agenda was redirected from infrastructure prioritization to the development of a regional regulatory land-use planning framework. A "Growth Plan for the Greater Golden Horseshoe" was enacted in 2006 – in essence, a provincial policy plan to which local governments had to conform.[204] This represented the fruition of the never-enacted Design for Development scheme forty years earlier: a provincial plan for the region that is binding on, and administered by, municipalities. In addition, a transportation planning and service coordination authority for the GTA and Hamilton called Metrolinx was established in 2006. (While the consolidation of all local transit service into a single regional operating body was considered, the region's many municipal providers, and especially the Toronto Transit Commission, which carries most of the riders, resisted it.) Through Metrolinx, the Liberal government undertook the largest transportation infrastructure expansion since the 1960s. Together, these initiatives constitute an integrated and programmatic system of province-led regional planning, one that addresses the redevelopment of established urban areas, "greenfield" suburban growth, protections for agricultural and environmentally sensitive lands threatened by urbanization, and transportation infrastructure.

The implementation of province-led regional planning has not been smooth. Bringing official plans and zoning bylaws into conformity with the Growth Plan took years longer than anticipated. Many municipalities were given extensions after missing the 2009 deadline. A 2013 review found that only about half of the region's upper- and single-tier municipalities had revised official plans in full effect, and only 60 per cent of lower-tier municipalities had amended their plans to bring themselves into conformity with upper-tier plans.[205] Conformity was largely achieved only in time for comprehensive revisions to the four provincial plans in 2017, which initiated a new conformity clock. This delayed implementation makes it difficult to assess the physical impact of the Growth Plan more than a decade after its adoption.

Separate from the provincial regulatory hierarchy, there has been considerable debate over transit expansion priorities. While the Liberal government increased the frequency of service on regional commuter rail routes and committed billions to light-rail and subway projects in the Toronto region, some of its routing and station-location decisions have been criticized for following political logic rather than a sound business case based on forecast ridership. The TTC's six-station Line 1 subway extension, for example, passes through York University's campus before terminating in the suburban municipality of Vaughan – an area represented at the time of its approval by then-premier Dalton McGuinty's chief lieutenant, Greg Sorbara.[206] While designated as an "urban growth centre" in the Growth Plan, the Vaughan station area remains only partially developed, and ridership north of the university is expected to be modest. The City of Toronto's cancellation of its adopted light-rail network plan for Scarborough in favour of a $3.35-billion three-stop subway extension (later reduced to one stop) has been widely criticized as a crass appeal for suburban votes. (The province endorsed the subway scheme in advance of a critical 2013 by-election, ultimately won by the Liberal candidate.[207]) Provincial and municipal politicians of all stripes have fuelled a narrative that the suburbs "deserve" the same subway service as core-area residents, despite ridership forecasts more in line with express bus or light-rail service.[208]

Re-elected to a majority government in 2007, a minority in 2011, and a majority 2014, the Liberals were virtually wiped out by a resurgent Conservative Party in 2018. The Conservatives carried almost every rural seat in the province, plus many seats in the GTA's postwar suburbs, while the NDP displaced the Liberals in their urban base. The province's electoral geography has never been so polarized. As the Conservatives ran on vague populist themes rather than a concrete platform, it is difficult at the time of writing to predict their intentions for Toronto's metropolitan governance and planning. The statutory and regulatory framework for regional planning created by the Liberals fifteen years ago is now deeply entrenched in planning practice, but the coalition that supported its original development has eroded. While environmentalists applaud restrictive growth controls, the residential property development industry blames them for rising housing prices, and municipalities argue that they lack the own-source revenues to meet growth-related capital needs. Will electoral change bring about land-use deregulation and the reordering of infrastructure spending priorities to reward non-metropolitan electoral constituencies, or even a halt to large-scale infrastructure planning and construction in the name of fiscal prudence or local autonomy? Or will the government keep the policy framework in place but decline to actively enforce it?

CONCLUSION

For 150 years, provincial and local governments in Ontario have wrestled with the same economic, social, and environmental problems associated with urbanization as in other North American jurisdictions, and their responses drew on the same, mostly American, planning and governance ideas. Ontario, however, embarked on a more thoroughgoing path of institutional reform and policy innovation than elsewhere in North America. In only a generation, Ontario and Toronto went from being a highly unlikely context for the germination and implementation of radical reform to produce what was perhaps the most elaborate system of metropolitan governance and planning arrangements on the continent.

This path was enabled by Ontario's institutional foundations. In the nineteenth century, executive-centred party government facilitated programmatic supervision of local government incorporation and boundary change by the legislature within a general legal framework. The administration of this function was taken over and expanded by the Ontario Municipal Board and the Department of Municipal Affairs in response to the Great Depression. As the normative context shifted in favour of state intervention during the 1940s, Ontario established general, statutory frameworks for land-use and conservation planning. The province's amalgamation of insolvent Windsor in 1935 anticipated its later unilateral restructuring of local government in growing metropolitan areas – first Metro Toronto in 1951–53, then the regional municipalities between 1967 and 1974. Backed by parliamentary majorities with strong urban and rural support and supported by a normative context favourable to state intervention, successive Conservative governments and the professional bureaucracy were unfettered in their ability to set the terms of multi-level urban governance.

The Ontario government's capacity for decisive, programmatic, and resolute policymaking diminished after the 1970s. The normative context of trust in government and deference to political, economic, and intellectual elites faded. The Conservative Party's long hegemony was displaced by increasingly polarized three-party electoral competition. The Westminster system's potential for decisiveness remains – hence the Harris Conservative government's province-wide municipal restructurings in the late 1990s, including the amalgamation of Metro Toronto, and the Liberal government's adoption of the Toronto-region planning framework in the mid-2000s – but the provincial government's capacity to sustain programs over time is diminished. In a highly competitive electoral environment, provincial governing parties have every incentive to engage in particularistic policymaking to win specific seats. And when parties become ideologically polarized, disruptive policy reversals after elections is to be expected.

We can draw two overarching findings from this historical narrative. First, the provincial government has been perennially involved in Toronto's multi-level urban governance. Since the very beginning, it has more or less programmatically used legislation, regulation, and policy to define the rules and incentives within which local governments operate. At times, it has intervened more directly, by restructuring municipal institutions – though always with the aim of increasing the administrative and fiscal capacity necessary for self-governance by enlarging its scale. It is hard to imagine what the Toronto region would look like in the absence of 150 years of provincial intervention.

Second, the narrative reveals both the potential and pitfalls of the Westminster system's institutional foundations for the effectiveness of Toronto's multi-level urban governance. Under some conditions – a conducive normative context and single-party dominance – the provincial government rapidly produced highly coherent programmatic policy interventions. When these conditions changed, however, the government's problem-solving capacity became inconsistent. It may be that Toronto's relative social, environmental, and economic advantages established in the early postwar period are thanks to an idiosyncratic conjuncture of inherited institutional legacies and political and normative context that cannot be repeated. Or, it may be that effective multi-level urban governance for the twenty-first century can be achieved through a new conjuncture whose contours have yet to be discovered. I shall return to this theme in the concluding chapter. First, however, we must journey to other American and Canadian cities to understand how different institutional foundations have shaped multi-level urban governance and, ultimately, the shape of the metropolis.

5

Minneapolis–St. Paul

The Twin Cities and Toronto had much in common in the first two decades after the Second World War. Both faced rapid population growth, a burgeoning water and sewer crisis due to unregulated development, and the challenge of how to adapt a rail-based economy and transit-oriented urban form to an era of mass automobile ownership and roads-based goods movement. In both, there was considerable political disagreement over how to coordinate development and pay for its servicing, culminating in the creation of new metropolitan institutions: Metropolitan Toronto and its associated bodies in 1954, and the Twin Cities Metropolitan Council in 1967. This is where the similarities end. While Metro Toronto was crafted *intra mures* by provincial political and administrative elites, the Met Council was designed by the Citizens League, a self-appointed group of business, media, and intellectual elites. While Metro Toronto was to operate under provincial supervision within established and expanding general legal frameworks of local government and land-use planning, the Met Council was created by a factionalized legislature only reluctantly, after a decade of debate, and at the cost of limiting its influence over land-use and capital infrastructure. Although the Met Council governs a vast territory and is potentially powerful, it has never found legitimacy either as an instrument of state government or as a form of local government. It has failed to reconcile the intergovernmental politics of urban development in an increasingly hostile normative context. Metro Toronto became obsolete when urbanization overwhelmed its boundaries; in the post-Metro era, effective regional governance for Toronto has depended on the ebb and flow of programmatic provincial intervention. These different trajectories of metropolitan governance are the products of the policy styles generated by the institutional foundations of the Westminster and separated-powers systems and their changing performance in a dynamic normative context. Charting Minnesota's grappling with urbanization pressures since the nineteenth century, we can see the costs and benefits of the separated-powers system: its capacity for policy innovation in extraordinary times of crisis and societal consensus, and also its tendency toward indecision, incrementalism, particularism, and irresoluteness.

GROWING TOGETHER, 1848–1945

The Twin Cities has always been a polycentric region. The three urban settlements that had emerged in the mid-nineteenth century were assigned different public institutions: Minneapolis, the land-grant university; St. Paul, the capital; and Stillwater, the prison. The Minnesota legislature initially played an active role in organizing local government. St. Paul and Minneapolis were incorporated in 1854 and 1858, respectively. The legislature reincorporated Minneapolis as a city in 1867 and merged it with the neighboring Village of St. Anthony in 1872 (see figure 5.3). Legislative intervention came to an end with two state constitutional amendments: a prohibition on special municipal legislation in 1881 and the permission of home rule in 1891. Annexation by Minneapolis and St. Paul in step with outward urbanization halted, and residents on the metropolitan fringe soon incorporated their own local governments: Crystal, Robbinsdale, Golden Valley, St. Louis Park, and Edina on Minneapolis's west flank, and Mendota, New Brighton, North St. Paul, South St. Paul, and West St. Paul around St. Paul (see figure 5.4). Accelerated by the extension of inter-urban electrified streetcar service after the 1870s, semi-urban settlement also occurred at a remove from the urban cores, on the many scenic lakes and rivers (see figure 5.5). The unregulated patchwork of small incorporations on the core cities' fringe and rural hinterland defined the geographical division of local government authority within which later urbanization would occur.

Separated in the south by the Mississippi River, Minneapolis and St. Paul are divided in the north by the industrial Midway district, which, before the opening of Panama Canal in 1915, was one of the world's largest entrepôts, connecting eastern and Pacific railroad

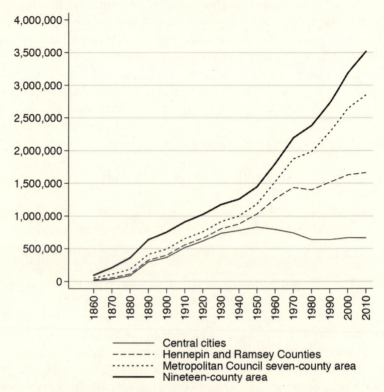

Figure 5.1 Twin Cities population by zone, 1860–2010

Note: A long-term chart of population growth in concentric zones of the region –
the central cities, the remainder of Hennepin and Ramsey Counties, the outer five
counties of the seven-county region, and the twelve contiguous "collar counties" in
Minnesota and Wisconsin – shows that the central cities captures the vast majority
of population growth through the 1930s. Their population declined from the
1950s through the 1980s, marginally increasing in the early 2000s. The 1940s were
a point of inflection – thereafter, all population growth occurred outside the central
cities in the extremities of Hennepin and Ramsey, and also in Anoka, Carver,
Dakota, Scott, and Washington Counties. After the 1970s, population growth has
accelerated in the Minnesota and Wisconsin collar counties as well.

networks. The separate origins and physical separation of the two
cities found institutional expression: each had its own daily newspapers, civic and business associations and clubs, utilities, and airport.
Minneapolis and St. Paul were knit together by rapid growth, their
combined population increasing by 100,000 in the second decade of

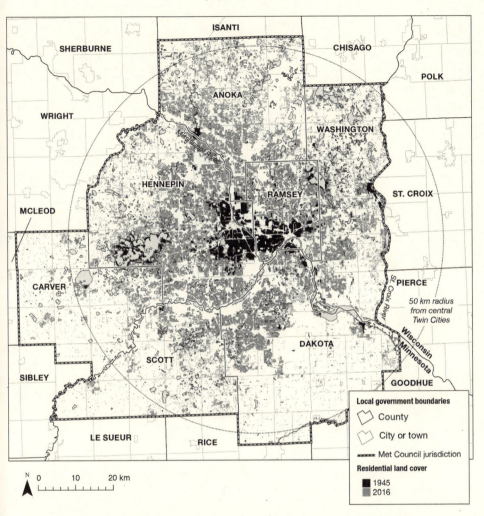

Figure 5.2 Administrative boundaries and residential urbanization in the Twin Cities

Note: Historical land use data for the seven-county Twin Cities region are consistently available only for residential land. While radiating out from the centre, the pattern of fringe urban development has been discontinuous.

the twentieth century and another 121,000 in the 1920s. An increasing share of growth spilled beyond the cities' boundaries as they became built out. While the central cities captured 94 per cent of population growth in the seven-county area between 1900 and 1920,

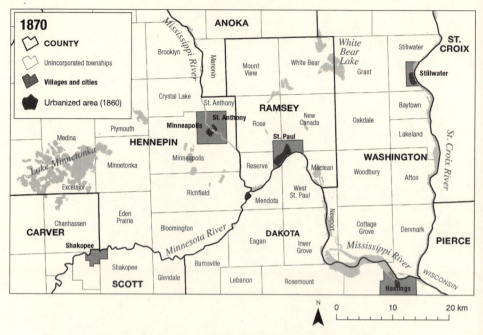

Figure 5.3 Municipal organization and urbanization in the Twin Cities, 1870

Note: Only large lakes are shown. The northern portion of Dakota County was annexed to St. Paul in 1874, becoming part of Ramsey County in the process.

Sources: Historical municipal boundaries adapted from Gilhousen, *A Brief History of Municipal Incorporations*; schematic urbanized areas redrawn from *The Challenge of Metropolitan Growth*.

this declined to 81 per cent during the 1920s, and only 43 per cent during the 1930s.

The Metropolitan District Association

Local elites saw the uncoordinated development of the central cities as an urgent problem. In June 1923, the northwest section of the American Society of Engineers, of which St. Paul planning engineer G.H. Herrold was president, recommended the formation of a metropolitan organization to manage a joint sewage system, the planning of parkways connecting the two cities, and the joint regulation and interconnection of the cities' separate telephone and electricity utilities and bus and streetcar systems. Herrold's Minneapolis counterpart A.C. Godward publicly endorsed the scheme, arguing that the region's

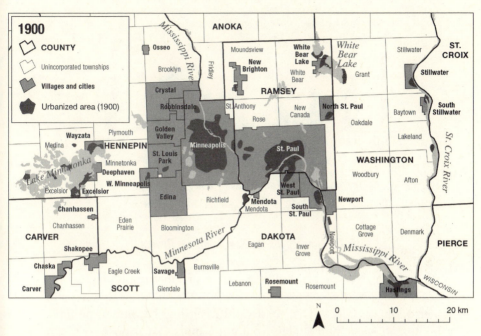

Figure 5.4 Municipal organization and urbanization in the Twin Cities, 1900

Note: Only large lakes are shown.

Sources: Historical municipal boundaries adapted from Gilhousen, *A Brief History of Municipal Incorporations in the Twin Cities Metropolitan Area*; schematic urbanized areas redrawn from *The Challenge of Metropolitan Growth*.

growth was hampered by a lack of coordination.[1] This led to the formation of an informal "metropolitan district association" composed of leading businessmen and chaired by prominent Minneapolis architect Edwin Hewitt to seek state legislation to form a commission empowered to prepare studies and, ultimately, a regional plan that would be implemented by municipalities and privately owned utilities.[2] The group agreed that the district should include all or part of Anoka, Carver, Dakota, Hennepin, Ramsey, Scott, Washington, and Wright Counties within a 40 km radius of the cities' centre – a vast area of almost 5,000 km².[3] Their pursuit of a legislative foundation for the plan set them apart from business-led advocacy in other cities.[4] They may have believed that only the state's sanction could overcome rivalry between the two cities; however, the scheme ultimately foundered on legislative indifference and the coming of the Great Depression.[5]

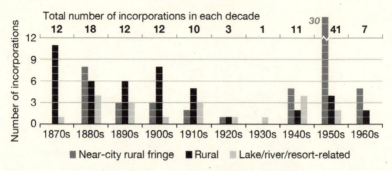

Figure 5.5 New municipal incorporations by type, 1870–1970
Source: Gilhousen, *A Brief History of Municipal Incorporations*.

The Minneapolis–St. Paul Sanitation District

While the legislature resisted the creation of a metropolitan planning agency, it would soon intervene to resolve a public health crisis of metropolitan scope.[6] The Mississippi River had become so polluted by human waste and sludge from grain mills that it posed a major public health risk. In 1923 the state Board of Health wrote to the Minneapolis and St. Paul city councils requesting joint action, but the cities could not agree on a solution. The legislature appointed a Metropolitan Drainage Commission in 1927, which recommended establishing a special-purpose body empowered to issue bonds to construct and manage a unified sewage system.[7] This proposal went nowhere in the 1929 legislative session but was revived in 1931. Once again, the commission recommended a metropolitan sanitary district covering Minneapolis, St. Paul, and South St. Paul that would construct a new sewage disposal plant. Municipal disagreement over the allocation of costs spilled onto the floor of the state House, which enacted a funding plan that benefited well-organized South St. Paul meatpacking interests at the expense of Minneapolis, provoking the governor's veto.[8]

The disagreement was resolved in the 1933 session only by dropping South St. Paul from the plan. The board of the new Minneapolis–St. Paul Sanitation District (MSSD) was composed of three members from each city plus a gubernatorial appointee to break ties. Funded by bonds and federal grants, a new interceptor sewer system and central treatment plant was constructed between 1934 and 1938. The MSSD was the first public body to deliver infrastructure across the cities' boundaries and therefore represented the first concrete step toward regionalization. (The regional streetcar company was a privately owned franchise.) Adjacent municipalities, including Richfield, Lauderdale, and St. Louis Park contracted with the M S S D as they urbanized, although without board representation.

The Metropolitan District Association and the M S S D episodes illustrate how American state government is highly sensitive to parochial interests, and how the barriers to legislative enactment were high. Local governments opposed ceding autonomy to authorities beyond their control, the central cities distrusted each other, and suburban interests resisted the perceived imperial designs of the central cities.

Toward the State as "Guiding Hand":
The Rise and Fall of New Deal Planning

The Great Depression provoked a reordering of American federalism. The implosion of private markets in 1929 engendered, at least temporarily, acceptance of unprecedented government intervention in economic and social relations. Minnesota exemplified this phenomenon and its limits in the American context. Politically dominated in the interwar period by the most successful third party in American history, the socialist Farmer-Labor Party, Minnesota was perhaps better positioned than anywhere else in the United States to institute a more regulated state-level response to metropolitan growth.

Emerging from the ashes of pre–First World War Progressivism and urban socialism, the Minnesota Farmer-Labor Party was an electoral coalition of urban trade unionists and rural opponents of national economic policies that benefited eastern industrial interests. Akin to party-movements in neighbouring Iowa, Wisconsin, and North Dakota, the party exemplified what Valelly calls "state-level radicalism."[9] Midwestern radical parties sought power at the state level because the Republican-Democratic duopoly was less entrenched at that level and because earlier Progressives had instituted reforms – the direct election of plural executive offices and the officially non-partisan legislature – that frustrated the development of highly organized party machines and lowered the barriers to entry by third parties. (From 1913 to 1972, candidates for the Minnesota legislature ran without party label. On taking office, however, they sat in left- and right-leaning caucuses. The liberal caucus in this period was composed

largely of Farmer-Labor and Democratic legislators, while the somewhat less cohesive conservative caucus was loosely identified with
the Republican Party. The result is what Mitau calls the "non-partisan
partisan legislature.")[10]

With the election of Floyd B. Olson as governor in 1930, Farmer-
Labor successfully challenged the Republican Party's post–Civil War
dominance in Minnesota. Olson aligned himself with the New Deal.
In return, President Roosevelt discouraged the already weak
Minnesota Democratic Party. Olson's agenda was initially frustrated
by conservative caucus domination of both legislative chambers,
but a Farmer-Labor majority in the House in 1932–34 temporarily
freed his hand.[11] Olson secured the enactment of a moratorium on
rural mortgage foreclosures, a progressive income tax, property tax
reductions for farmers, spending on relief, and the creation of an
old-age pension system.[12] In 1934 he leveraged federal funding to
establish the Minnesota State Planning Board (MSPB) and its thirteen
subcommittees to make a comprehensive inventory of the state's
economic, physical, and social development. In particular, the
Taxation Committee, the Committee on Administrative Units, and
the Metropolitan Committee sought to reshape the relationship
between the state and local government.[13]

The Taxation Committee, chaired by eminent authority Roy G.
Blakey, and the Committee on Administrative Units, chaired by lawyer
and influential Democrat John F.D. Meighen, both acknowledged the
influence of University of Minnesota political scientist William
Anderson, a nationally recognized exponent of progressive municipal
reform. The Taxation Committee argued that, as the state was ultimately responsible for the debts of insolvent local governments, it had
a material interest in ensuring local fiscal health. The committee
recommended state supervision of local debt, including the approval
of bond issues in high-debt counties by the Minnesota Tax Commission,
a state agency.[14]

The recommendations of the Committee on Administrative Units
were more radical. Arguing that the rural insolvency crisis was exacerbated by the small size of county and local units, and that fiscal
retrenchment and limited supervision could not solve the problem on
their own, the committee called for a "quite drastic reorganization in
the interest of both economy and efficiency."[15] The committee proposed a permanent commission to recommend changes to municipal
and school board boundaries, the final decision to be made by the

legislature, and for the transfer of some or all local authority over law enforcement, education, health, relief and welfare, road building, and property tax assessment from municipalities to the county or state level.

The Metropolitan Committee, chaired by St. Paul planning engineer G.H. Herrold, revived the Metropolitan District Association's call for a Twin Cities planning authority. The committee's vision of the "ideal city" was both efficient and attractive:

> The city which will attract population will be the one that is consistently planned, is honestly built, and gives the most in service – that has the most spacious, convenient and purposefully designed street thoroughfares; the most attractive parkways, parks and public squares; the finest recreation system; the most satisfying community life; where taxes are made less burdensome by long-term financial budgets; and where obsolescence and disintegration are treated more scientifically than heretofore.[16]

The committee made several recommendations. First, the legislature should enable the formation of multi-county metropolitan agencies to undertake comprehensive planning, zoning, and subdivision control. Second, general enabling legislation should be passed for comprehensive planning as distinct from zoning, a power that heretofore had been granted to municipalities through one-off charter revisions.[17] Noting the problem of premature subdivision – thousands of approved lots remained unbuilt – as well as the uneven provision of suburban infrastructure, the committee also called for the metropolitan planning authority to control suburban land subdivision. Importantly, local and metropolitan planning and land-use regulation would operate under the "guiding hand" of state government: "As the first premise it will be assumed that there will be a State Planning Agency. Thereafter the position of local, county, area or regional planning in the general state planning scheme must be considered. It is obvious that the coordination of planning from the top to the bottom is the thing ultimately desired."[18]

Separately, Herrold wrote that a suitably empowered state planning board "will of course make a state master plan ... [that] will give proper direction to all smaller governmental units ... City planning and county planning are simply the planning of smaller units of the state, in which the local groups should have the most to say and in which they can do the best work, the state planning board exercising a guiding hand."[19] This vision of a hierarchy of scientific plans supervised by state government reflected the professional orthodoxy of the day.[20]

The findings and recommendations of these and other committees were consolidated into a "digest and interpretations" report for consideration by the legislature in 1935. It concluded with recommendations for immediate action, including "enabling legislation for city and regional planning" and "reorganization of local political units."[21] Governor Olson signalled his intention to press the legislature for approval of a permanent state planning board. Dominated by the conservative caucus, however, the legislature did not take up the governor's and the board's requests.

Olson unexpectedly died of stomach cancer while running for a fourth two-year term in 1936. His replacement, Elmer Benson, won handily, and Farmer-Labor regained control of the House and Senate.[22] The MSPB transmitted revised recommendations following the election. The municipal reorganization plan proposed by the Committee on Administrative Units was dropped entirely, as was the earlier call for enabling legislation for regional planning. The board once again asked to be made permanent but stated that its role would be to collect and analyse information, not to prepare a plan: "in no case should [such a board] make administrative decisions or execute adopted plans."[23] Governor Benson called for the same in his January 1937 inaugural message. Despite the party's dominance of the executive and legislature between 1936 and 1938, and the scaling back of the board's agenda, the Senate scuttled a House bill to make the board permanent. Without legislative sanction, Benson reconstituted the State Planning Board in late 1937, this time composed entirely of business and municipal leaders.[24]

The Farmer-Labor Party's underlying coalition came undone after 1936 due to Benson's incompetence, a generalized decline in support for government intervention, and a schism in the labour movement. Benson's Farmer-Labor Party was deserted for a revived Republican Party in the 1938 election by Twin Cities business leaders, conservative rural voters, and urban moderates alike, signalling a sea change in state politics.[25] Riven by factionalism, the Farmer-Labor Party was absorbed by the Democratic Party in 1944, which recast progressive populism in anti-communist terms. The establishment of a new Democratic Farmer Labor Party (DFL) integral to the national Democratic coalition ended state-level radicalism in Minnesota.

The embodiment of the Republican reaction in Minnesota was a dynamic thirty-one-year-old lawyer named Harold Stassen – the youngest governor ever elected in any state.[26] Stassen argued forcefully against the corrosive influence of socialism and government expansion. In the keynote speech to the 1940 Republican National Convention, which established him as a national figure and prospective presidential candidate, Stassen fulminated against government's growth during the New Deal:

We must recognize that in a free economy, government, in meeting the need of its people who are unemployed, is not solving a problem, but is only temporarily easing the consequences of an unsolved problem. We must recognize that the answer to all of our problems of a domestic nature is not to shrug our shoulders and say "Let the government do it." The role of government must be that of an aid to private enterprise, and not of a substitute for it … [Inefficiency, red tape, and intergovernmental conflict:] these are the things by which Lilliputians are restraining the slumbering giant of democracy and free enterprise and making him ineffective. The inefficiency of our government is a travesty in a land that has developed such magnificent efficiency in private endeavor.[27]

This statement reflected the post–New Deal normative context in Minnesota and across the country, one that valued individualism, localism, and free enterprise as the motor of American democracy and economic growth. Anticipating Congress's disbanding of the National Resources Planning Board in 1943, Stassen discontinued the MSPB and transferred its staff to a rural economic development committee. Efforts to promote postwar "reconversion" of production to support civilian employment emphasized private-sector and local initiative rather than state planning, broadly construed.[28]

Inhibited by the legislative process's multiple veto points and delegitimized by the national shift in normative context away from activist government, the opportunity to legislate a general framework of state supervision of municipal organization and planning ended. Had the MSPB's initial recommendations been adopted, the legislature would have established for Minnesota and the Twin Cities something like Ontario's Department of Municipal Affairs and the Metropolitan Toronto Planning Board. Instead, the state would provide little support to local governments as they responded to rapid urbanization following the war.

THE METROPOLITAN PROBLEM, CIVIC ELITES, AND THE STATE, 1945-67

Much as in Toronto, population growth exploded beyond the central cities' boundaries after 1945 (see figure 5.1). The seven-county area had added only 87,000 people during the 1930s, but 185,000 in the 1940s and 340,000 in the 1950s – an increase of 29 per cent in the latter decade alone. The housing stock increased by a third during the 1950s, mostly detached houses on large lots serviced by well water and septic tanks.[29] Meanwhile, the central cities' population peaked in 1950 and declined thereafter.

Federally funded highway construction fuelled suburbanization.[30] Ridership on the private transit franchise collapsed as automobile commute times diminished.[31] Jobs decentralized in tandem with population. General Mills, for example, moved 800 employees from central Minneapolis to suburban Golden Valley in 1955. The suburbanization of employment undermined the central cities' tax bases and created a powerful incentive for employees to move closer to their jobs. A transformative event was the Dayton Company's then-risky decision to develop Southdale, arguably the continent's first enclosed shopping centre, in suburban Edina in 1956. (Dayton's, the precursor of Target Corporation, was Minneapolis's dominant department store.) Austrian socialist architect Victor Gruen sold Dayton on the notion of the integrated shopping centre as the hub of the new society: "I hope it becomes the crystallizing force for this sprawling suburban area ... This is the town square that has been lost since the coming of the automobile. It should become the center of this civilization."[32] Southdale's success led Dayton to develop other shopping centres in the Twin Cities, and the model was soon replicated across North America.

Rapid population growth spurred unregulated suburban municipal incorporation. The northern townships contiguous to Minneapolis and St. Paul organized into five cities during the 1940s. Forty-one municipalities incorporated in the seven-county area in the following decade, most of them to the north in Anoka and Ramsey Counties and in western Hennepin County. (See figure 5.6.) Half of the new municipalities had a population of less than 1,000 at their creation. Pine Springs in Ramsey County had only 124 residents, and Landfall – a trailer park – was only 24 ha in size. Eighteen were essentially neighbourhood enclaves of less than 24 km².[33] Small incorporations led to perverse outcomes, including "island" municipalities completely surrounded by others, such as Hilltop (another trailer park on the site of a former dairy farm in Columbia Heights, just north of Minneapolis), and municipalities composed of multiple discontiguous parts, such as Orono and White Bear Lake. Others, such as Minnetonka, Plymouth, and Blaine, were of entire townships with no alteration of boundaries (see figure 5.6). The most dramatic example of the rush to control the lucrative non-residential tax base and forestall annexation was the incorporation of Maplewood on St. Paul's eastern flank. When the Minnesota Mining and Manufacturing Corporation (now known as 3M) announced that it would move to a location on I-94 in the unincorporated township of New Canada, on an inverted L-shaped area located just north and east of St. Paul's city limits, St. Paul petitioned to annex the one-mile-wide strip of land. The township, however, had already registered to incorporate as Maplewood, and so 3M eluded St. Paul's grasp (see figures 5.4 and 5.6).[34]

Joe Robbie and the Minnesota Municipal Commission

During the 1940s and 1950s, Twin Cities elites joined the national consensus that reorganizing municipal boundaries was essential to effective metropolitan planning and infrastructure provision. The League of Minnesota Municipalities (LMM), which represented incorporated areas, had advocated unsuccessfully for reform of annexation and incorporation laws since 1947. Only in 1957 did the legislature establish an interim commission on municipal annexation and consolidation.[35] This may have been an attempt to bury the issue. Created late in the legislative session and composed mostly of minor legislators, it confronted low expectations.[36] The turning point was the hiring of lawyer and DFL heavyweight Joe Robbie, an abrasive but talented dealmaker who gave the commission intellectual substance and political firepower. His personal interest was not simply to facilitate the creation of larger municipal units that would be better able to finance and provide urban services. He also saw the potential for a state

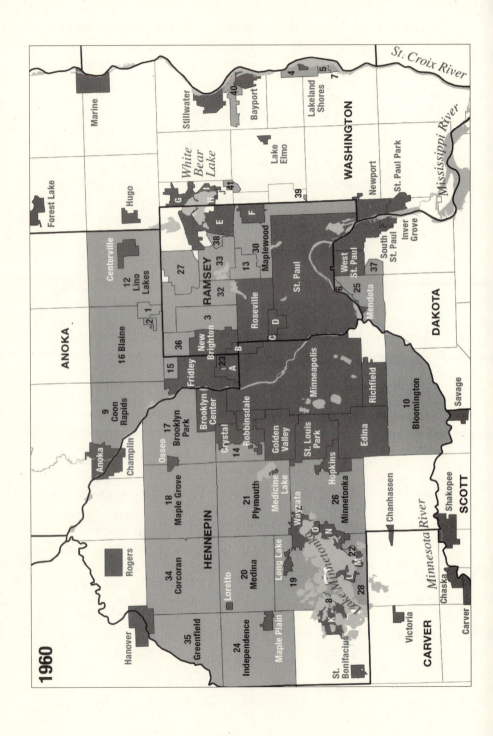

1960

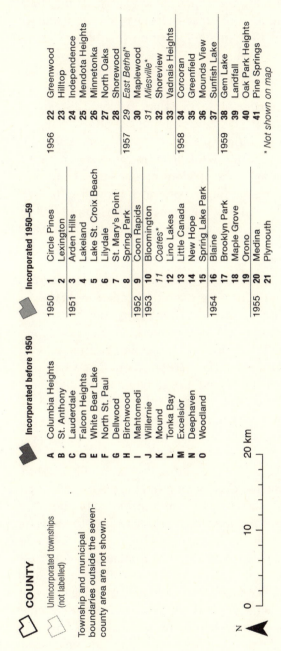

COUNTY

Unincorporated townships
(not labelled)

Township and municipal
boundaries outside the seven-
county area are not shown.

Incorporated before 1950

A Columbia Heights
B St. Anthony
C Lauderdale
D Falcon Heights
E White Bear Lake
F North St. Paul
G Dellwood
H Birchwood
I Mahtomedi
J Willernie
K Mound
L Tonka Bay
M Excelsior
N Deephaven
O Woodland

Incorporated 1950–59

1950
1 Circle Pines
2 Lexington

1951
3 Arden Hills
4 Lakeland
5 Lake St. Croix Beach
6 Lilydale
7 St. Mary's Point
8 Spring Park

1952
9 Coon Rapids

1953
10 Bloomington
11 Coates*
12 Lino Lakes
13 Little Canada
14 New Hope
15 Spring Lake Park

1954
16 Blaine
17 Brooklyn Park
18 Maple Grove
19 Orono

1955
20 Medina
21 Plymouth

1956
22 Greenwood
23 Hilltop
24 Independence
25 Mendota Heights
26 Minnetonka
27 North Oaks
28 Shorewood

1957
29 East Bethel*
30 Maplewood
31 Miesville*
32 Shoreview
33 Vadnais Heights

1958
34 Corcoran
35 Greenfield
36 Mounds View
37 Sunfish Lake

1959
38 Gem Lake
39 Landfall
40 Oak Park Heights
41 Pine Springs

* Not shown on map

N

0   10   20 km

Figure 5.6 New municipal incorporations in the Twin Cities, 1950–59

Note: Forty-one municipalities were incorporated between 1950 and 1959, spurring the creation of the Minnesota Municipal Commission.

Source: Gilhousen, *A Brief History of Municipal Incorporations.*

agency to encourage and integrate comprehensive land-use and infra-structure planning, especially in the metropolitan area. At that time, the state government had no such capacity. Its involvement in munici-pal affairs was limited to a single "community advisor" in the Department of Business Development.[37]

The commission made study trips to Los Angeles, Miami, San Francisco, Seattle, and Toronto. Robbie was particularly impressed with Metro Toronto and the Ontario Municipal Board's general jurisdiction over municipal incorporation and boundary change.[38] The commission's report to the 1959 legislative session recommended replicating the Ontario model.[39] While new restraints on municipal incorporation could not undo the previous decade's proliferation of units, they could influence the future pattern of growth – the five-county area's population was forecast to increase by 50 per cent by 1980.[40] Robbie saw state supervision of municipal organization as a precondition of effective metropolitan planning:

> Sound annexation policy is one of the most important tools for the future planning of the urban growth of the metropolitan area and Minnesota's other growing cities. The planners can only fight a war of attrition unless their work on the drafting board is accompanied by a realistic public policy relating to annexation, consolidation and the incorporation of new cities and villages. The problems of land use, zoning, sewage disposal, police and fire protection, and the many other vital municipal services can only be further complicated unless annexation and incorporation practices are brought up to date.[41]

After intense lobbying by Robbie and the LMM, a bill establish-ing the Minnesota Municipal Commission (MMC) passed only three days before the session's end. Like the Ontario Municipal Board, it would function as a tribunal, conducting hearings on applications for municipal reorganization. It was the first such body established in the United States and was hailed nationally.[42] As Robbie had hoped, the MMC arrested the subdivision of townships into smaller incorporated units, but it soon came under attack from legislators carrying briefs for parochial interests. While the original statute permitted the commis-sion to unilaterally order the annexation of unincorporated areas to a city (an idea promoted nationally by the Advisory Commission on Intergovernmental Relations), this was changed in 1963 to require the approval of a majority in the affected area to give effect to decisions on incorporations, mergers, and the annexation of one municipality to another.[43] A creature of the legislature with little support from the governor, the MMC could bring limited political capital to bear and endured only by avoiding controversy. The state government would not proactively use the MMC as a policy instrument to proactively shape the pattern of urban growth, as Robbie had recommended.[44]

C.C. Ludwig's "Practical Opportunity": The Metropolitan Planning Commission

The MMC's creation paralleled the establishment of the Twin Cities Metropolitan Planning Commission (MPC).[45] Its architect was Clarence C. Ludwig, a University of Minnesota political science professor who had served as the LMM's executive secretary since 1935 and was head of the Municipal Reference Bureau (MRB), an urban-reform organization dating back to the Progressive Era. He was well versed in the issues and was trusted by municipal leaders and legislators alike.[46] His multifarious role in Minnesota local government affairs stems from the university's origins as a public land-grant college that offered extension programs to teach farmers modern agricultural techniques. An outgrowth of this mission was assistance in the organization and management of rural local government, which in turn led to the formation of a statewide municipal association (the LMM) and information clearinghouse (the MRB), both headquartered at the university. University affiliation involved scholars of national stature, including political scientist William Anderson and geographer John Borchert, in the LMM's and MRB's activities. Ludwig leveraged this institutional base to promote metropolitan municipal reorganization and planning.

Ludwig organized three LMM-sponsored conferences on regional planning at the university in 1953 and 1954. He was aware that the Twin Cities would have to create a regional body of some kind to take advantage of the new federal metropolitan planning-assistance grants in the 1954 National Housing Act. The challenge was to build constituency among local actors for a body with the appropriate powers and resources to effectively address the Twin Cities' problems. Widely attended by government officials and interested citizens, the conferences produced a consensus that voluntary inter-municipal agreement would be insufficient to resolve metropolitan problems, and that only an agency authorized in state legislation and with independent revenues could overcome parochialism.

The LMM prepared a bill for the 1955 legislature to establish an advisory planning commission for the census-designated five-county metropolitan area – consisting of Anoka, Dakota, Hennepin, Ramsey, and Washington Counties – financed by a 1/5 mill property tax levy and with representation from the central cities, counties, suburban municipalities, school boards, townships, and private citizens. The governor would appoint the private citizen representatives, including the board's chair. Although the bill was supported by influential state senator and future Republican governor Elmer L. Andersen and endorsed by several suburban newspapers, it faced opposition from Minneapolis, which argued that its tax base should not pay for suburban planning, and suburbs that feared central-city domination.[47]

Ludwig regrouped after the bill's failure. A revised bill reflected a carefully crafted municipal consensus, the LMM having called on county and local councils to adopt favourable resolutions in advance of its introduction in the 1957 legislature. Ludwig and his deputy at the LMM, Orville Peterson, also evangelized the bill in the media and to the League of Women Voters and other good-government groups. This time, the bill passed the House unanimously with bipartisan support from Senator Andersen and the newly elected DFL governor Orville Freeman. The Metropolitan Planning Commission was granted a small, 1/10 mill share of the property tax, and membership was made compulsory. In 1959 and 1960 its jurisdiction expanded to include Carver and Scott Counties – the former on application, the latter by invitation.

Ludwig was appointed the MPC's first chair, and Joe Robbie served on the board. Robbie believed that the MPC was the prototype of a future metropolitan government. Unlike Robbie, however, Ludwig had little interest in what he saw as utopian reforms to municipal governments and their boundaries. Responding to critics who argued that a metropolitan government must precede metropolitan planning and policymaking, he later wrote that, "to me this is a theoretical counsel of perfection which is unrealistic in a situation with a strong home rule and local autonomy tradition as we have here … I believe we should minimize talk about metropolitan government now and that we should emphasize the practical opportunity we have to work helpfully with our existing governments on a voluntary consent and partnership basis." It was in this spirit that

Ludwig pursued a pragmatic agenda of inter-municipal coordination and information sharing:

> [The MPC's] role, briefly, is to be a friendly collaborator with a multitude of diverse governments and private interests. There are so many diverse and incongruous pieces in our metropolitan pattern, but the commission can "oil the machinery" and help to smooth operations, reconcile differences, minimize conflicts. This role of the commission will not be dramatic and glorifying but it can be statesmanlike nevertheless.[48]

Toward a Regional Plan: The Joint Program

A three-phase, ten-year work program for the MPC was agreed to in 1958. It would begin with basic research, followed by the development and implementation of a metropolitan plan. The MPC produced an extensive array of reports between 1958 and 1960 on demographics; parks; industrial, commercial, and retail location; water and sewer infrastructure; transportation; and best practices in local planning. These framed local problems in metropolitan terms and promoted public acceptance of planning. The plan development phase was pursued in collaboration with the state highways department, county and central city staff, and the university. The majority of the $2 million budget of what came to be known as the Joint Program for Land Use and Transportation Planning was funded by federal grants. Yet even with federal money, resources remained constrained. The MPC lobbied for a tax levy increase, which the legislature authorized in 1963 and 1965.[49] Viewed in national perspective, Minnesota's MPC was rare in that it was established by state legislation and was granted a dedicated tax levy, and membership was made compulsory.

The Joint Program's objective was to produce a metropolitan "guide plan," or "development guide," by 1965. Its prospectus emphasized that, as the MPC was purely advisory and exercised no direct control over land use or infrastructure, the Joint Program's primary goal was "to develop understanding and acceptance of a plan for the Area through continuous involvement of those who will have the responsibility and authority for implementing the plan's recommendation."[50] The MPC consulted widely in order to ensure the acceptability of its recommendations. Three advisory committees were established, one of elected officials from each of the more than three hundred local governments in the area, one of more than a hundred business leaders and citizens, and one of technical experts. These groups met several times in 1965 to comment on the MPC's proposals.[51] A draft development guide was completed in 1966–67, the content of which is discussed below.

As work progressed, it became clear that even those local governments that wished to be "guided" might lack the administrative capacity and legal authority to fulfil the plan's objectives. Unlike Ontario, Minnesota had not adopted modernized enabling legislation for comprehensive planning and zoning. The laws on the books had barely changed since the 1920s.[52] Very few municipalities had enacted even rudimentary zoning ordinances, subdivision regulations, and comprehensive plans, and fewer still employed professional planners.[53] In smaller townships, development approval occurred through open vote at citizen meetings. To increase the consistency of regulation over broader geographic areas, the MPC first proposed adopting Detroit's approach, whereby municipalities would establish "development districts" to exercise delegated planning authority under the Joint Powers Act. When municipalities opposed this proposal, the MPC advocated for a greater county role in planning.[54] Uploading subdivision review to a county or metropolitan authority and legally subordinating zoning bylaws to a comprehensive plan were political non-starters. However arbitrary, under-resourced, and disjointed it was in practice, land-use regulation remained a municipal function, and the MPC an advisory body. The questions of how local land-use policies could be harmonized across local boundaries and of how the meagre administrative capacities of the region's many small local government units could be expanded remained unresolved.

Urban Growth and the Suburban Groundwater Crisis

The MPC jolted complacent residents in 1964 with a widely publicized regional population forecast entitled *4,000,000 by 2000!* (The seven-county population was a little over 1.5 million according to the 1960 census.) Presenting a dystopian vision of a congested "big-city" future, the MPC exhorted citizens to "face facts" and take control of metropolitan growth: "Change is inevitable only because human beings constantly make decisions that accumulate or conflict to cause change. What the changes are depends on what the decisions are ... Decisions can be haphazard or they can be made with a purpose in mind."[55]

Concern about future growth was concretized by an immediate crisis: groundwater pollution due to inadequately and haphazardly serviced suburban areas and the undercapacity of the MSSD's sewage treatment system.[56] In 1959 the state health department determined that half of all wells in rapidly growing suburban communities were contaminated by sewage runoff. Tens of thousands of households were at risk of disease. The problem was especially severe in the northern suburbs, where the clay soil was ill suited to septic tanks, but trouble also appeared in rapidly growing Bloomington to the south.[57] The negative consequences of a lack of local land-use planning, or at least a linkage between subdivision control and infrastructure provision, were becoming clear.[58] The Federal Housing Administration had also announced more stringent water provision, sewage treatment, and drainage requirements, which meant that local practices would have to change. The water and sewer crisis dominated the agendas of the MPC and Robbie's 1959 Interim Commission on Municipal Laws. While Robbie preferred creating an open-ended multi-purpose body that could assume other functions with local consent, the commission limited itself to the sewer question. It recommended that the MSSD be expanded to cover a broader area, cautioned against the emergence of a patchwork of independent suburban water and sewer districts, and proposed that annexation of unincorporated areas occur without popular ratification.[59]

The reconstitution of the MSSD as a metropolitan agency was endorsed by successive governors of both parties, the MPC, the LMM, Bloomington, and suburban mayors. Still, the legislature did not act in the 1959 and 1961 sessions. In 1962 a further study committee also recommended the creation of a single metropolitan agency to design, construct, and operate all sewer systems in the five-county area, yet no bill was passed in the 1963 and 1965 sessions.[60] As in the 1930s, the central cities had no desire to subsidize suburban infrastructure, the suburbs feared a loss of autonomy, and both were suspicious that this was the leading edge of a general metropolitan government that would diminish their authority. These opposing perspectives were carried into the legislature by the region's urban and suburban delegations, while the rural-dominated conservative caucus's committee leadership blocked intervention in metropolitan affairs.

In the meantime, suburban municipalities continued to contract with the MSSD (often at wholesale rates higher than those paid by central-city customers), and service gaps were eased by the installation of secondary treatment facilities.[61] Unwilling to wait for legislative action, groups of municipalities formed their own sanitary districts under the Joint Powers Act. A North Suburban Sanitary District covering parts of Anoka County upstream from the central cities was organized in 1962.[62] Reform advocates argued that treatment facilities for all communities drawing from the Mississippi River should be accommodated through expansion of the MSSD's downstream Pig's Eye plant, but they failed to mobilize a supportive majority in the legislature.[63]

The Institutional Foundations of Indecision and Incrementalism

The postwar story through to 1967 is one of legislative indecision and incrementalism generated by the institutional foundations of the state-level separated-powers system. The new scale of population growth, its impact on the landscape, and its servicing needs were manifest by the early 1950s. Time and again, sympathetic members carried externally generated proposals into the state House, and yet sufficient support for the passage of legislation remained elusive as veto players exercised their prerogatives. Rural over-representation in the legislature magnified the difficulty of articulating a metropolitan policy. Despite gubernatorial prompting and bipartisan coalition-building by committed policy entrepreneurs, the rural-dominated legislature acted on the creation of the Metropolitan Planning Commission largely to take advantage of federal grants, and on the Municipal Commission only after intense lobbying by Democratic Party insider Joe Robbie and with the inside support of legislators who had served on the interim committee that developed the proposal. Legislative indecisiveness, with well-developed proposals being adopted multiple biennial sessions after their introduction, meant that Minnesota's response to rapid growth in the Twin Cities was more reactive than proactive.

The impasse was temporarily broken, at least in part, by the conjuncture of four factors: the reapportionment of the legislature, which increased metropolitan representation in the legislature and brought in a new generation of reformist members; gubernatorial efforts to increase executive policymaking capacity; the imposition of new federal mandates; and the emergence of a new bipartisan network of civic elites.

Political and Normative Change

As in other states during the 1950s and 1960s, federal courts ordered the state legislature to provide for equal representation. Minnesota's legislature had not been reapportioned since 1913, leading to rural over-representation.[64] The new electoral map produced by the legislature in 1959 was challenged after the release of the 1960 census. The battle intensified after the US Supreme Court's 1962 *Baker v. Carr* decision, which declared redistricting subject to judicial review, and later decisions that mandated absolute population equality by district. After two earlier bills were vetoed by Governor Karl Rolvaag, a special session of the legislature in 1966 transferred eleven House seats from outstate areas to the growing Twin Cities suburbs.

The election of a new generation of urban and suburban legislators intent on modernizing government to solve social and economic problems launched an era of bipartisan policy activism. In 1966, all of the new seats were won by affiliates of the conservative caucus, cementing its control of the legislature, including majorities of rural, central city, and suburban seats. The new urban conservatives differed, however, from the rural faction that had controlled the legislature in most sessions since the 1930s. While the old guard was loosely aligned with the Republican Party nationally and in gubernatorial elections, it generally eschewed overt partisanship, and members understood themselves primarily as community representatives.[65] The state's GOP organization began to recruit candidates for legislative elections after 1962. While the progressive Republican "Young Turks" did not numerically dominate the conservative caucus, they injected new energy and policy ideas into legislative debate and worked closely with sympathetic Republican governor Harold LeVander following his election in 1966.

Reapportionment paralleled efforts to expand the capacities of state government to address new and more complex policy challenges. LeVander and his DFL predecessor, Karl Rolvaag – the first to serve after the chief executive's term was extended from two to four years in 1962 – presided over government expansion. The number of state employees increased by 69 per cent during the 1960s.[66] A State Planning Agency (SPA) was established in 1965 to collect data and conduct research on pressing issues. An Office of Local and Urban Affairs housed within the SPA was created in 1967, charged with providing technical assistance to local governments and coordinating their relations with state and federal funding programs. Influenced by policy ideas from the Advisory Commission on Intergovernmental Relations (ACIR), the Council of State Governments, and other national organizations, Minnesota also joined a majority of states (and Ontario, as seen in the previous chapter) in creating multi-county regional economic development agencies.[67] The state's eighty-seven counties were grouped first into seven regional development commissions in 1967 and then eleven in 1969, each of which was to coordinate state activities and service delivery and promote local cooperation on economic development and federal grant applications under the SPA's supervision.

New Federal Mandates Spur State Action

New federal policies also induced state-level institutional change.[68] The 1965 Housing and Urban Development Act mandated the transformation of advisory MPCs into broadly representative "councils of governments" (COGs) with the power to review local applications for federal funds in relation to metropolitan plans. Minnesotans viewed the new federal mandates with suspicion. In an April 1965 speech to the local chapter of the League of Women Voters, influential *Minneapolis Tribune* journalist Ted Kolderie highlighted the potential dark side of the new federally mandated metropolitan reviews, stating that they "may become, then, either a major new tool in the hands of local leaders or a device for far greater direct federal control over metropolitan development."[69] With the MPC's support, civic leaders called on the legislature to create a new metropolitan institution before 1 July 1967, when the 1966 Demonstration Cities and Metropolitan Development Act would come into effect. If they did not, the new federal mandates would transform the unelected MPC into a policy-making body – an unacceptable outcome in the context of the bruising reapportionment battle. As early as 1964, the MPC had argued that, much as a city planning board reports to a city council, an elected metropolitan council could usefully serve as a focal point of community response to the Joint Program's emerging planning proposal.[70] What was missing was a democratically accountable body.

Civic Elites Set the Policy Agenda

The new crop of activist state legislators found that they possessed few resources to engage in policy innovation.[71] Legislative service was considered a part-time job into the 1970s, and legislators had no offices, administrative support, research assistance, or dedicated staff. Often they voted without having seen' the text of bills and amendments. As a result, they were poorly equipped to develop legislation on their own. Most substantive policy ideas were developed by pressure groups and good-government advocates and championed by entrepreneurial legislators. As a consensus emerged during the early 1960s that the growth-related problems faced by the Twin Cities required a regional solution, solutions were generated not within the state bureaucracy or the legislature but through public debate among urban civic elites working through an overlapping network of good-government and sectoral groups.[72] The groups to which these elites belonged had overlapping memberships that linked media, intellectual, professional, and business leaders, and also crossed party lines. They paid close attention to policy ideas generated by intergovernmental and professional associations and federal task forces, including the ACIR, the Institute of Public Administration, and the Council of State Governments.[73] The Municipal Reference Bureau and League of Minnesota Municipalities, which remained linked through their affiliation with the University of Minnesota, served as conduits for the dissemination of these ideas.

As the menu of options narrowed, "metropolitan government" ceased to be a dirty word. "By 1965," Harrigan and Johnson would later write, "the serious debate was not on whether there should be a regional agency, but on what kind of agency it should be."[74] In April 1966, the *Minneapolis Star*'s editorial board wrote that the surprise was not that particular proposals were subject to criticism; rather, it was "the acceptance throughout the Twin Cities area of the idea of more metropolitan co-operation."[75]

The organization that did more than any other to shape the debate was the Citizens League.[76] Founded in Minneapolis in 1951, its initial focus was city charter reform, but its advocacy and membership soon expanded into Hennepin County and then to the broader metropolitan area. By the mid-1960s it had more than three thousand dues-paying individual and corporate members. Officially non-partisan, the group's membership and leadership were composed of business and professional elites, and while both DFLers and Republicans were involved, the league was dominated by progressive Republicans.[77] Its operations were financially supported by large home-grown enterprises, including 3M, Pillsbury, General Mills, Control Data (now Ceridian), food processor Cargill, and Dayton's. Senior executives, who more often than not were locals with strong ties to the city and the state, served on study groups that deliberated on pressing policy issues selected by the membership, each ultimately producing a detailed background report and set of policy proposals. Members obeyed a strict ground rule: that partisan and personal interests be checked at the door. Once the board of directors accepted a report that recommended legislation, a sympathetic legislator would be found to introduce a bill. League leaders frequently made presentations to legislative committees and in other public venues. Such was the group's prestige that its policy proposals were automatically perceived as credible and were widely publicized. In 1966 the league struck a Metropolitan Affairs Committee to study the regional governance question. Through its work, it collected and synthesized the ideas of other civic and municipal elites into a detailed legislative proposal, the contents of which are discussed below. While the Citizens League was the most influential non-governmental actor, the issue was also taken up by the League of Women Voters.[78]

The region's four daily broadsheets – the Minneapolis *Tribune* and *Star* and the St. Paul *Dispatch* and *Pioneer Press* – were also important opinion leaders, not simply through reportage of events, but also through the active engagement of their staff in civic discourse. Ted Kolderie, a city hall reporter and later editorialist for the *Star* and *Tribune*, and his counterpart Peter Vanderpoel at the *Pioneer Press*, separately became interested in metropolitan issues in the late 1950s and informally participated in Citizen League discussions as private citizens in the early 1960s.[79]

Kolderie was particularly instrumental in shaping debate through his writing and activism. He was influenced by the prominent public administration authority Luther Gulick, who in *The Metropolitan Problem and American Ideas* (1962) argued that local government consolidation in metropolitan areas was not only unlikely due to institutionalized home rule and localist sentiment, but also undesirable insofar as it undermined the vitality of community self-government. The objective, then, should be to properly assign responsibilities to the appropriate order of government in the federal system, recognizing that no one government or order could meet the metropolitan challenge alone.[80] Kolderie sketched out the parameters of such a settlement in two agenda-setting five-part series published in the *Star* in October 1965 and January 1967, both of which were reprinted for stand-alone distribution.[81] He emphasized the indivisibility of the metropolitan area as an economic and social unit, stating that only if unified could the region prosper under increasing national competition for public and private investment. At the same time, he argued for the ongoing necessity of democratic local self-government. As he saw it, the challenge was to "develop area-wide arrangements which will provide the local units with an incentive to work together and with a mechanism through which they can act."[82] This would not mean an area-wide municipality or municipal federation, or the consolidation of counties, as some had advocated. He rejected federation as impracticable because of the large number (almost three hundred) and disparate population sizes of the region's local governments, and undesirable because it would put government at a greater remove from citizens. Instead, he proposed a metropolitan council that would be made up of citizens appointed by the legislative delegation of each of the seven-county area's thirty or so state senatorial districts.[83] Its role would be technical rather than political – a non-partisan body, liberated from municipal parochialism and responsible to the people through the legislature. Its purpose would be to "handle genuinely area-wide problems – sewage disposal, water supply, transit, major roads, air pollution, planning, mosquito control, airports, and perhaps regional parks."[84]

Business elites – and especially the leaders of large local enterprises – also embraced the metropolitan idea. Participation in a forum on "modernizing local government" hosted in the Twin Cities in 1966 by the Committee for Economic Development (CED), a national business policy leadership group, rendered metropolitan reform respectable for local business elites.[85] Later that year the Upper Midwest Research and Development Council sponsored a seminar for over a hundred business leaders at St. Thomas College on metropolitan problems. The seminar was funded by the Dayton Company, whose president, Donald Dayton, was active in the Citizens League, a trustee of the CED, and a vocal supporter of metropolitan reform.[86] A backgrounder written by Ted Kolderie synthesized options for debate.[87] The choice was either creating a new metropolitan agency that would consolidate the existing special-purpose bodies and directly carry out their functions, or creating an agency empowered to coordinate their existing activities. (A third option, strengthening voluntary intergovernmental coordination, was something of a straw man.) The group endorsed a directly elected operating body.[88] While leaders of large enterprises participated in the Citizens League, small business developed proposals through a joint effort of the central cities' and suburban chambers of commerce, the Urban Study and Action Committee. (Large corporations generally eschewed the chambers.) The committee's proposal aligned with the emerging consensus, calling for a directly elected metropolitan area services council with representation by senatorial district.[89]

The LMM and mayors of the central cities and western inner suburbs supported the agenda. DFL Minneapolis mayor Art Naftalin (1960–69), a University of Minnesota political scientist who had served on the ACIR, was supportive of a directly elected multi-purpose metropolitan agency, as were his St. Paul counterparts George Vavoulis (1960–66) and Tom Byrne (1966–70). Byrne saw a metropolitan agency as a means of achieving some degree of equalization of benefits and burdens as cross-municipal disparity in tax capacity increased.[90] New Hope mayor Milton Honsey, the chairman of the Hennepin County League of Cities and a former MPC member, returned from a June 1964 trip to Toronto with the opinion that that city's governance provided the best model for the Twin Cities. He was especially impressed with Metro Toronto's ability to finance and construct infrastructure in both established areas and the developing fringe, and he suggested the creation of a Metro Toronto–style council made up of delegates of municipal councils.[91] (Metro Toronto was effectively a reform of two-tier county government. What Honsey thought would happen to the seven existing Twin Cities counties was unclear.) Other mayors of inner and outer suburbs – Stanley Olson of Richfield, Bruce Nawrocki of Columbia Heights, Kenneth Wolfe of Saint Louis Park, and Wheelock Whitney of Wayzata – also supported some form of metropolitan authority, while leaders in Bloomington, Robbinsdale, and Edina questioned the need for what they saw as an expensive new level of government.

Finally, both parties' candidates for governor in the 1966 election ran on platforms to create a metropolitan body. Incumbent DFL governor Karl Rolvaag proposed the creation of an elected multi-purpose district to operate area-wide services in place of single-purpose districts, and promised to establish five issue-based task forces and call a governor's conference on metropolitan problems if re-elected.[92] Republican nominee Harold LeVander's platform was virtually identical, and directly addressed the fear of federal pre-emption: "The State must recognize its responsibility to set up a proper structure for urban functions or there is a danger that the national government will undertake to dictate a structural form for the state."[93]

The only visible dissent was in the suburbs. The director of the Bloomington Chamber of Commerce refused an invitation to participate in the joint Urban Study and Action Committee established by the central cities' and some suburban chambers of commerce, arguing that "the suburbs are a rebirth of the American dream ... [I am not afraid of] 300, 500, or 1,000 special districts because if you have one government, you might as well move to Russia."[94] While the urban broadsheets championed reform, several independently owned regional chains of small suburban newspapers editorialized against it, seeing it as the thin edge of the wedge for imposing "urban" problems on their communities and ultimately the displacement of local self-government by a "metro monster."[95] Suburban opponents offered no compelling counterproposal of their own, however, and lacked sufficient influence with Citizens League–aligned civic elites to alter their direction.

As a group, property developers and builders were largely absent from the debate due to their lack of organization. Minneapolis and St. Paul each had separate builders' associations (they merged only in 1992), and neither was an effective lobby during this period.[96] Until the 1980s, virtually all residential development was undertaken by a multiplicity of small independent builders, the largest of which might complete only a few hundred dwellings in any given year.

Agenda setting by civic elites was untrammelled by demands for involvement by residents' groups and other non-elites. It is difficult to ascertain where ordinary voters stood. As both gubernatorial candidates supported a metropolitan council, electoral support cannot be used as a proxy for support for a metropolitan council. Newspaper polls suggested general support for metropolitan coordination, but little consensus on whether a metropolitan council should be a directly elected local government or a state agency, or if it should take over infrastructure operations.[97]

To summarize, elite opinion coalesced around a coherent proposal between 1964 and 1967: a multi-purpose, seven-county district that would consolidate the functions of existing special-purpose bodies and perhaps take on other functions, including transit. The new entity would not simply advise or passively coordinate but would actively make policy. On the heels of the reapportionment debate, it was

universally accepted that representation be based on the equal representation of residents, with senatorial districts seen as a convenient
basis. By 1967 most groups favoured direct election. The notion of
delegated representation from municipalities was dismissed out of
hand, not simply because there were so many but because it was
generally believed that local officials could not be trusted to set aside
parochial concerns and adopt a metropolitan perspective. While
democratic accountability and equal representation were viewed as
important aspects of the body's design, and it was expected to make
authoritative decisions in the interest of efficiency, its role was viewed
as more technical than political. There was little apparent concern
that it might become a partisan body or a venue for conflict.

The Legislature Acts

The Citizens League synthesized the elite consensus, releasing a comprehensive proposal in February 1967.[98] Civic elites had reached
agreement, but only the state legislature could enact a solution. The
venue now shifted to the state capitol. Four separate bills were introduced by members of the majority conservative caucus, two in the
House and two in the Senate.[99]

Representative Harmon Ogdahl's and Senator William Frenzel's
bills were similar, and ultimately merged to become the Ogdahl-Frenzel
bill. Both were Republican Young Turks from Hennepin County,
Ogdahl from Minneapolis and Frenzel from inner suburban Golden
Valley. Their proposal, which mirrored the elite consensus, was for
an elected, multi-purpose metropolitan service district that would
assume and operate existing and future metropolitan functions: planning, sewers, transit, and potentially also water treatment and supply.
The integration of existing service delivery districts was seen as essential to effective planning and coordination. The new council would
assume the MPC's federally mandated review authority. The district's
council would initially be appointed but would become directly elected
within three years. Its operations would be financed by a vehicle
registration tax (for transit) and a property tax levy (for everything
else). It would also be empowered to issue bonds without referendum.
This proposal found strong support in the liberal caucus and among
new-guard central-city and inner-suburban conservatives.

The second proposal, introduced by Arden Hills senator Robert
Ashbach and suburban White Bear Lake representative Thomas

Newcome, was for a council appointed by the governor and confirmed by the Senate. Members would serve at large. The council would not operate systems or provide services. Instead, it would coordinate the existing special-purpose districts in accordance with the MPC's development guide. It could indefinitely suspend local plans if they conflicted with the development guide, with major disputes settled by the state legislature. No dedicated revenue source was included. The Ashbach and Newcome bills were backed by the conservative caucus leadership – the master of the Senate Gordon Rosenmeier from outstate Little Falls, and Stillwater Representative and House Metropolitan and Urban Affairs Committee chairman Howard Albertson – and found broad support among rural and outstate conservative members. (Despite its sponsors, it soon became publicly known as the Rosenmeier-Albertson bill.)

The dilemma was this: Should metropolitan problems be addressed by a new, free-standing, metropolitan-scaled local government operating in parallel to existing municipalities and counties? Or should they be addressed by an agency of state government? Rosenmeier favoured an appointed council because he saw in a directly elected council a rival power base, a "state within a state" that would institutionalize divisions between growing urban and declining rural areas to the detriment of the latter. Characterizing metropolitan institutions as "parochial and provincial," he argued that, since the metropolitan area accounted for half the state's population, the legislature was obliged to take direct ownership of the matter. An elected council would generate conflict with state government, while an unelected metropolitan service operator would create a dangerous accountability gap. Twin Cities politicians responded by characterizing metropolitan government as a form of local government. Mayor Honsey of New Hope, the enthusiast of a Toronto-style federation, stated that "we oppose Rosenmeier coming down here from Little Falls and attempting to tell us in the metropolitan area just how we are to run our local government." Minneapolis Mayor Naftalin argued that "one of the basic essentials of metro government is that it be essentially local in character – the object is to strengthen, not to weaken, local government."[100]

Ultimately, the Ogdahl-Frenzel bill fell prey to procedural manoeuvres in the legislature. Rosenmeier was the chair of the Senate's Civil Administration Committee, the approval of which was necessary for any bill affecting local government to proceed. To make an

end-run around Rosenmeier, Ogdahl tried to have his Metropolitan
Problems subcommittee elevated to full committee status. This failed,
as most members of the subcommittee preferred the Rosenmeier-
Albertson bill. In the House, a majority on Albertson's Metropolitan
and Urban Affairs Committee favoured the Ogdahl-Frenzel bill, leading him to hold back its consideration. A flurry of amendments were
advanced to bring the two sides closer together, but these were mostly
rejected by both. Ultimately, the relevant House and Senate committees rejected the Ogdahl-Frenzel bill, and the Rosenmeier-Albertson
proposal advanced to the full legislature. The only major concession
was that the fourteen governor-appointed councillors would represent
districts of equal population rather than serve at large.

Amendments to restore direct election by 1970 failed. The Senate
vote was tied, 33 to 33, and the measure lost on a revote. In the
House, direct election was defeated 66 to 62. The cleavage was geographical rather than partisan. While metropolitan-area representatives of both parties overwhelmingly favoured election, they were
outnumbered by rural and outstate representatives. After the failure
of the election motion, both chambers passed the Rosenmeier-
Albertson bill by large majorities.

To enact a special law for the Twin Cities metropolitan area, the
legislature had to circumvent the state constitution's prohibition on
special legislation except in cases where it affected governing bodies
or where voters approved – a principle called "local consent" – or
where provided for by a general law.[101] The legislature took advantage
of the latter loophole to exempt the metropolitan council bill from
local consent. That the state constitution could be set aside so easily
is indicative of the legislature's power when its will was unified.

Governor LeVander signed the bill into law on 25 May 1967, and
the Twin Cities Metropolitan Council became operational in August
of that year. The governor appointed as chair James Hetland, a progressive Republican University of Minnesota law professor and
Citizens League member who had written the metropolitan governance plank of LeVander's platform.[102] He also appointed metropolitan advocate and business leader Donald Dayton to serve on the
first council.

The legislature's decisiveness during the 1965–67 period stands in
stark contrast to the previous two decades. This action was the product
of a conjuncture. Reapportionment brought new voices into the legislature, federal deadlines incentivized state-level action, and the

gubernatorial candidates of both parties converged on a policy agenda.
Most important, however, was the emergence of the Citizens League
as the hub of a bipartisan civic elite network that spanned business,
the media, and academe. Such was its influence that all alternative
agendas were foreclosed. Nonetheless, Rosenmeier steered the state
legislature to reshape the Citizens League's proposal. Constituted as
an appointed state agency, the new Metropolitan Council was, at least
potentially, the institutional expression of the state's distinct interest
in the Twin Cities region. The question for the next decade was how
the state would use it.

THE STATE SUPPORTS REGIONAL GOVERNANCE, 1967–76

The new decade brought new political winds of change. In 1970,
Minnesotans elected as governor Wendell Anderson, an energetic
thirty-seven-year-old DFL state senator and former Olympic hockey
player. Activist government was reinforced when DFL-aligned liberal
legislators overturned two generations of conservative dominance by
winning the House and Senate in the 1972, 1974, and 1976 elections.
With Anderson's support, a bipartisan legislative coalition pursued
an agenda of comprehensive tax and education finance reform, as
well as expanding and empowering the Twin Cities' new regional
governance institutions. At the state level, as nationally, the DFL's
fortunes were buoyed by the collapse of Richard Nixon's presidency,
which temporarily delegitimized the Republican Party.

Sharing the Costs and Benefits of Growth:
The Fiscal Disparities Act

Suburbanization's erosion of the central cities' property tax base
was manifest by the mid-1960s. In 1969, the Citizens League proposed pooling a portion of the metropolitan property tax base so that
municipalities who were de facto "losers" in the location game would
share in the benefits of regional business investment.[103] The concept
was naturally controversial among suburban "winner" municipalities,
especially Bloomington and Richfield, and was viewed with suspicion
by outstate conservatives who saw it as a socialistic affirmation of
"regionalism."[104] Anoka conservative representative Charles R.
Weaver unsuccessfully championed a Citizens League–drafted bill
in 1969. A similar bill passed in 1971 with support from rural and

central-city representatives, but almost universal suburban opposition. Still in effect today, the Metropolitan Fiscal Disparities Act requires all municipalities in the seven metropolitan counties to pool 40 per cent of incremental commercial and industrial property tax revenues after the base year 1971.[105]

Consolidating Systems Coordination under the Metropolitan Council

The Metropolitan Council's framers expected that the primary mechanism for influencing urban development patterns would be review of the functional plans and capital projects of the independent service districts. Proposals it found to be inconsistent with its development guide could be indefinitely suspended. The limits of *post hoc* review soon became apparent. Occurring only after the special districts had put considerable money and effort into preparing their plans and projects, the political and fiscal cost of exercising the veto was high, and the council's ability to influence outcomes correspondingly small. Legislative changes in the 1969, 1971, and 1973–74 sessions aimed to make the council more effective as a coordinating agency and sought to address emerging conflicts between it and the special districts.[106]

The first step was the long-debated consolidation of wastewater governance. The council's enabling legislation had mandated a study of sewer and water governance reform. While more stringent regulations and conditional infrastructure funding from the federal and state governments had induced the MSSD, local authorities, and suburban sewer districts to address the problem of groundwater pollution, sewer governance remained disjointed. Rising federal environmental standards meant that twenty-nine of the thirty-three existing treatment plants were deemed inadequate, and upgrades would be costly.[107] The Met Council recommended that the legislature consolidate all sewage treatment facilities into a single operating body.[108] The 1969 legislature accepted the recommendation and established the Metropolitan Sewer Board (renamed the Metropolitan Waste Control Commission in 1974). Within two years the board assumed the assets of the MSSD and the two recently created suburban sewer districts.

This consolidation occurred only after almost a decade of elite advocacy for two reasons. First, new federal conditional grants to meet higher water quality standards created a powerful incentive to centralize infrastructure planning. Indeed, the federal government paid 75 per cent of the cost of reconstructing the region's wastewater collection and treatment system, and the state about half of the remainder. Second, the Met Council's prior creation neutralized the primary municipal objection to regional sewerage consolidation: fear that it would be a steppingstone to the creation of a general-purpose metropolitan government. The legislature's acceptance of the council's sewerage proposal boosted the council's legitimacy.[109] Building on this success, the 1969 legislature granted the council supervisory authority over county planning for sanitary landfills, the siting of a new state zoo, and the acquisition of parks and open space.

A second issue was airport planning. Established in 1943 on the template of the MSSD, the Metropolitan Airports Commission (MAC) had been created to resolve conflict between Minneapolis and St. Paul over the location of a regional airfield.[110] By 1967 the international airport located south of the two cities had exceeded its designed capacity and the MAC began to study locations for a second facility. The MAC submitted proposals to the Met Council in 1969 and 1970 for a new airport to be built in Anoka County at Ham Lake. Both were vetoed by the council on environmental grounds. This provoked a public battle between the two agencies, won by the Met Council, further cementing its legitimacy.[111]

In parallel to the Met Council, the 1967 legislature had created a permanent Metropolitan Transit Commission (MTC). The private Twin City Lines franchise had almost collapsed, as annual ridership declined from 201 million in 1946 to only 60 million in 1964. The streetcar system had been dismantled by the mid-1950s, but the bus network was not expanded in step with suburban growth. Some suburbs were served by an uncoordinated patchwork of seven private bus operators that accounted for a small fraction of total ridership. The MTC was charged with two responsibilities: to develop a comprehensive plan for a "complete" transit system "in cooperation with" the Met Council and to "improve" service.[112] To these ends, the MTC was empowered to issue bonds and expropriate private transit providers. The assets of the virtually bankrupt Twin City Lines were acquired in 1970.

The MTC's creation was supported by the Citizens League, which endorsed the notion of a regional transportation system that balanced the automobile with some form of mass transit.[113] What form this system would take was the subject of debate, and competing plans would put the MTC on a collision course with the Met Council. Initially, the council supported the MTC, providing it with planning grants and collaborating on the slow development of the transportation chapter of the development guide. After three years of study, and MTC recommended the construction of a 92-km, $1.3 billion subway system patterned on the recently constructed Metro in Washington DC and San Francisco's Bay Area Rapid Transit.[114] The Citizens League opposed a hybrid rail and bus trunk-and-feeder system on the basis of high cost, route inflexibility, and the belief that Twin Cities residents would find changing vehicles inconvenient.[115] The Met Council accepted this logic and shelved the MTC report. Which would prevail – the council's statutory authority to plan and coordinate the development of the region, or the MTC's statutory authority to plan and operate a transportation system – remained unclear, and so the issue was taken up by the legislature in 1973–74. While the House approved the MTC's plan, the bill died in the Senate.[116] Instead, the Senate appropriated $500,000 to study a third option: Boeing's "personal rapid transit" (PRT) technology, in which users would call up car-sized pods that would travel from point to point on electrified elevated rails.[117] This study too went nowhere. Fearing that the magnitude of capital expenditure required to build rapid transit risked the future fiscal health of the metropolitan area and even of the state, legislators brokered a deal to support the council's bus-only option.[118]

The immediate consequence of the conflict between the MTC and the Met Council was the passage in 1974 of the Metropolitan Reorganization Act, which expressly subordinated the MTC and the Sewer Board to the Met Council, which would now appoint their members and review their plans in relation to "policy plans" in the development guide. The council would also henceforth approve the MAC's capital expenditures. All municipalities and counties would be required to submit their comprehensive land-use and infrastructure plans to the council for comment. A further amendment in 1976 mandated the council to set regulations and guidelines for the determination of whether "any proposed matter" was of "metropolitan significance." If such a matter were found to be inconsistent with the development guide, the council could suspend it for one year.

The legislature authorized the council to designate, plan, and issue bonds for the acquisition of regional parks and open space, which would in turn be managed by local governments.[119] A bill to create a metropolitan parks commission had been passed in 1969 but declared unconstitutional because it was adopted too late in the legislative session. After a similar bill failed in 1971, in part because of strong opposition from the counties, the council appointed an Open Space Advisory Board chaired by former governor LeVander's chief of staff, the future US senator David Durenberger, and made up of municipal and county officials and interested citizens. This intergovernmental collaboration led to the legislature's adoption of the Metropolitan Parks Act, 1974, which established a Metropolitan Parks and Open Space Commission appointed by the Met Council, and which was required to conform to a general parks policy plan in the development guide.

These legislative actions affirmed the vision of the council as a coordinating rather than an operating body, but at the same time they subtly transformed its role. At least in principle, the council would no longer simply *coordinate*, in the sense of resolving conflicts between the plans of the autonomous single-purpose districts. Instead, it would proactively make policies to which the metropolitan districts and local governments would conform, and against which local applications for federal and state project grants would be assessed. The council's new powers were formidable, yet their political acceptability remained untested.

Clarifying the Meaning of Metropolitan Planning

The development guide was to be the focal point of the Met Council's policymaking, yet its content remained in question. The MPC's final act had been to adopt a development guide as the culmination of the Joint Program.[120] Reflecting the ideas of lead planner Robert Einsweiler, the MPC had envisioned planning as a process through which local governments and metropolitan agencies would negotiate a metropolitan vision and associated trade-offs.[121] Having "bought in," each would presumably work to fulfil the vision without coercion. No normative land-use concept – in other words, what the region *should* look like – was mapped. Ultimately, the MPC advanced a vision of the region as a "constellation" of mixed-use "diversified centres." Concentrating retail and institutions into centres would provide an economic and cultural focus to undifferentiated residential suburbs and minimize long-distance automobile travel by placing amenities in proximity to homes. The formation and development of the centres and employment areas would be influenced not by direct land-use regulation (which lay outside the MPC's and the Met Council's jurisdiction) but by the strategic location of "shaping elements" or "levers": public institutions, open space, transportation facilities, and water and sewer services.[122]

Council chair James Hetland was persuaded by the policy-planning approach. When asked by the editors of the Suburban Newspapers chain whether the council should assume control over zoning, Hetland responded that regional land-use regulation would be unnecessary if inter-municipal competition for commercial and industrial property assessment was reduced and if the location and timing of transportation and sewer infrastructure was strategically planned.[123] While the council did not formally adopt the MPC's development guide – as discussed, the council's first five years were consumed by clarifying its relations with the operating districts – its actions were informed by the process-oriented approach.

The council's land-use objectives resembled those of the Metro Toronto Planning Board: its directives to the metropolitan districts called for an urban development pattern that was contiguous and fully serviced, minimized impacts on environmentally sensitive areas, and maximized existing infrastructure systems. The practical limits of indirect influence soon became apparent, however. A 1973 review revealed that these principles were inconsistently applied because each implementing body relied on different time horizons and forecasts of population growth and land need. The independently designated service areas for sewer, water, highway, transit, and protective services differed dramatically, and each exceeded the current extent of urbanization. Moreover, no systematic criteria were established against which to evaluate service extensions and impingement on natural features.[124] This "slack in the system" undermined service extension as a means of shaping urban form.

At the same time, few suburban and rural local governments possessed the expertise and administrative machinery to meaningfully plan and evaluate private development proposals on their own.[125] Comprehensive planning, zoning, and subdivision control for cities and villages had evolved on a piecemeal basis since the 1940s through a bewildering array of general and special legislation. Only in 1965 was a general enabling law for municipal comprehensive planning and zoning adopted, yet planning remained optional and there was no requirement that zoning bylaws conform to adopted comprehensive plans. In 1972, only 65 of 191 cities and townships in the seven-county area had adopted or were preparing comprehensive plans, and only 10 employed professional planners.[126] If municipalities were to implement the council's policies through their plans, they would need to be equipped with sufficient legal authority and resources and the incentive to use them.

Governor Anderson's first council chair, Al Hofstede, pushed the creation of a "development framework" to the front burner, seeing it not as one chapter among many in the development guide, but as the master chapter that would guide the rest. Chaired by lawyer and former Bloomington councillor Robert Hoffman, the council's Planning and Development Committee began work on a new policy in the latter half of 1972 to strengthen coordination among the special districts and define a spatial vision for future urban development. Its cornerstone was the division of the region into urban and rural service areas.[127] Contiguous, fully serviced development at densities sufficient to ensure the economical provision of services would be limited to a mapped urban service area, which would be expanded only when need arose. To strengthen the council's influence over municipal planning, all municipalities and school boards within the seven-county area would be required to submit comprehensive plans for review. Any modifications the council recommended would be binding.

Small developer-builders attacked these proposals. Working through the newly created Minnesota Housing Institute, they argued that the urban service area would create rather than reduce sprawl by raising land and housing prices within it, displacing development to the "collar counties" beyond the Met Council's jurisdiction.[128] The council responded with a study that found that land values were increasing across the region, and that coordinated public infrastructure investment would reduce overall housing costs. Compared to a "continuing trends" scenario, a "guided growth" scenario would result in 2,072 fewer square kilometres of urban development and a savings of $2 billion by 1990.[129] Urban municipalities, including the central cities, were generally supportive, as restricting fringe-area development might steer investment back to declining core areas. Farmers in rural areas also welcomed the reduction of development pressure. Public hearings and stakeholder consultations found general support for managed growth, but the proposal to mandate municipal planning put the council on a collision course with urbanizing fringe municipalities. Drawing the urban service area boundary would create winners and losers, and all municipalities wanted to be winners. Hoffman and the council tried to neutralize opposition by emphasizing collaboration. They proposed that municipalities, not the council, would delineate the urban service area boundary, albeit in conformity with council policies, thereby maintaining local autonomy.[130]

When Hofstede resigned to run for mayor of Minneapolis in 1973, Governor Anderson appointed former state representative John Boland to succeed him. He immediately embarked on a charm offensive, interacting frequently and directly with municipal officials, and also the Association of Metropolitan Municipalities and the Metropolitan Inter-County Council. The Met Council adopted a development framework in March 1975 that schematically mapped the metropolitan urban service area (MUSA) and proposed additions to accommodate growth to 1980 and 1990.[131] It was, however, mostly toothless in the absence of mandatory local planning and a statutory plan review process as Hoffman had originally proposed.[132] With the endorsement of the Association of Metropolitan Municipalities, Boland asked the legislature to pass further legislation, the Metropolitan Land Planning Act, to implement the Hoffman committee's proposals.

The bill failed following concerted lobbying by the Minnesota Housing Institute, which persuaded legislators that an economic recession was no time to drive up the cost of housing and undermine the real estate sector's contribution to the regional economy. At the same time, local officials in rural Dakota County publicly revolted against the bill and the legitimacy of the council. After negotiations with local governments, a revised bill passed the 1976 legislature. To provide predictability, the new law required the council to submit "metropolitan systems statements" to the seven-county area's 195 municipalities and 49 school districts by July 1977. These would provide all necessary data and guidance for local governments to develop fifteen-year comprehensive plans, including defining their urban service areas. Local governments would have until July 1980 to submit their plans for review; if they departed from metropolitan policies, the council could order alterations.

The State and the Metropolitan Interest

The Met Council was successful during its first decade insofar as the state executive and legislature gave it active political support and expanded its authority in the face of other institutional actors. The state government was able to sustain its interest in the council and, through it, in metropolitan problems, due to the conjuncture of three factors: the ascendency of a new generation of urban reformist legisla- tors in both parties, the continued activity and coherence of the bipar- tisan elite support coalition centred on the Citizens League, and a normative context of trust in government and deference to elites. This conjuncture was not to last.

THE STATE LOSES INTEREST, 1976-90

Incremental expansion of the council's powers came to an end with the passage of the Metropolitan Land Planning Act in 1976. The council appeared to have consolidated its policymaking and coordi- nating authority and was poised for implementation. Yet its influence declined over the next two decades as the normative context changed, the influence of the civic elite network waned, and consensus politics gave way to partisan polarization.

Bipartisan consensus and civic elite activism began to unravel in the early 1970s. If the dominant cleavage in the legislature during the early postwar period had been between metropolitan and outstate districts, regardless of party affiliation, it was now between DFLers and Republicans. (Indeed, for the first time since 1913, party labels appeared on the ballot for House election in 1972 and Senate elec- tion in 1974.) In internal organization, campaign machinery, and ideology, the state parties were now fully integrated into the increas- ingly polarized national party system. State parties were drawn along as their national counterparts recast their appeal in relation to civil rights, Watergate, and the Vietnam conflict, and also in response to new demands for more open and accountable government and less state intervention.

"Sunshine" laws and other efforts to increase government transpar- ency and public participation disrupted the elite-led policy develop- ment of the 1950s and 1960s. The visibility and influence of the Citizens League and other reform advocates diminished as individual citizens' participation in, and scrutiny of, government came to be seen as more legitimate. As homegrown companies became regional and national players or were acquired by firms headquartered elsewhere, locally rooted business elites were gradually superseded by nationally oriented executives who were less interested in volunteer collective reform activity.[133] The legislature's tendency toward indecision and particularistic policymaking was no longer countervailed by external elite consensus. The University of Minnesota also became less important as node in the circulation of policy ideas and personnel between the university, state government, the League of Minnesota Municipalities, and the Met Council after the LMM was severed from the university's extension service in 1974.[134]

Republicans were the primary political beneficiaries of the economic malaise of the 1970s, projecting a message of limited government, devolution, and individual responsibility. In Minnesota as nationally, activist Great Society Democrats were seen to have overreached as deficits mounted and the public mood turned against state intervention. In 1978, Republican Al Quie won the governorship, and the DFL lost thirty-two House seats in what became known as the "Minnesota Massacre."[135] Neither the new crop of legislators nor the new governor, who had served for two decades in the federal House, had participated in the debates that had led to the council's creation. Quie's appointee as Met Council chair was sitting council member and the architect of the Fiscal Disparities Act, Charles Weaver. Despite Weaver's experience, his relationship with the legislature deteriorated, even as the development guide's implementation generated friction with municipalities.[136]

The focus of state-level political conflict also shifted away from urban and metropolitan questions. Pressure on infrastructure and transportation systems declined as population growth slowed, providing breathing room for metropolitan institutions to catch up to demand. Both legislative chambers abolished the special committees on metropolitan affairs created in the early 1970s. The Minnesota Municipal Commission – viewed in the 1950s as an essential tool for shaping urban development – was dismantled under municipal pressure. The biggest challenge, however, was fiscal crisis. In the 1982–83 session, Quie faced a budget deficit of 17 per cent of total expenditure and was forced to craft an unpopular budget-balancing compromise with the DFL legislative leadership. He declined to run for a second term.

Quie's two-term DFL successor, Rudy Perpich (1983–91), was a colourful booster from northern Minnesota's Iron Range region. His focus was on statewide economic growth through investment attraction and megaproject development. He appointed St. Paul developer Gerald Isaacs to chair the Met Council with a mandate to redirect it to economic development. At the same time, Perpich pursued pet projects of metropolitan significance without involving the Met Council. Isaacs's successors, Sandra Gardebring (1984–86) and Steve Keefe (1986–91), refocused on the council's existing mandates and strengths, but its influence diminished.

In sum, the 1978–90 period represented a shift away from active and consistent support from the state legislature and governor, and toward benign neglect and even subversion. This mirrored a broader shift in the normative context away from trust in government and deference to elites. The decline of the Citizens League's prestige and influence, and also legislative turnover, denied the Met Council its original support coalition, removing the principal countervailing force against the fragmentation of state government authority. These shifts undermined the council's legitimacy and therefore its capacity to implement the development framework, renew the public transit system, and respond to megaproject proposals.

Undermining Regional Planning

The metropolitan urban service area introduced in the 1974 development guide and given legal foundation by the 1976 Land Planning Act was to be defined piece by piece as municipalities submitted comprehensive plans to the council for review. While framed as a technical task, review became a political flashpoint as municipalities jockeyed for urban development and infrastructure projects. The protracted intergovernmental bargaining process, coupled with the continuing underdevelopment of municipal planning capacity, meant that the first MUSA was not fully defined until 1984, almost a decade after the development framework chapter's adoption.[137]

The MUSA's piecemeal definition and application demonstrated the limits of the Met Council's influence. Some municipalities permitted scattered urban development beyond the MUSA in direct contravention of the density thresholds and other council policies. As the council did not directly regulate specific land uses, the MUSA could not stop urban development from occurring. Builders could construct urban housing outside it by assuming the full cost of sewer infrastructure. Mostly they did not have to, as the negotiation process led to a "loose" MUSA with abundant undeveloped land within its boundaries.

Developers and suburbanizing municipalities also undermined the MUSA's intent through litigation and lobbying. The courts found that local zoning ordinances superseded council-approved comprehensive plans. The legislature did not work to reverse this finding; in fact, it amended the Metropolitan Land Planning Act in 1985 to allow such ordinances.[138] In 1987, the legislature created a de facto subsidy for outer suburban development when it mandated a flat cost-sharing formula for sewer infrastructure expansion.[139] Previously, built-out and fully serviced areas paid less than suburbanizing areas, encouraging more compact development.

Finally, much of the council's leverage over municipal planning was lost when the federal government rolled back conditional grant programs and eliminated requirements for area-wide review in the early 1980s.[140] Council reviews of municipal applications were limited and non-binding. It ceased reviewing applications for federal mortgage insurance altogether in 1992 because the federal Department of Housing and Urban Development and municipalities simply ignored negative recommendations.[141]

Even within these limitations, the council narrowly construed its authority, refusing applications rarely and only when a high threshold was surpassed – that is, when a local plan was likely to have a "substantial" impact on, or constitute a departure from, a metropolitan system.[142] Since the Land Planning Act's passage in 1976, the council has reviewed 2,099 local plans and amendments, turning back only 25. A generous interpretation of this low proportion is that most problems have been resolved informally.[143] A more likely explanation is that the council has avoided conflict by adopting a permissive stance.

Megaprojects Test the Council's Influence

In principle, the council possessed sweeping authority over projects of "regional significance." Of its own initiative, the council could assess the impacts of major public and private developments in relation to the development guide and functional agency plans. Yet the state legislature either circumvented the council in pursuit of large-scale megaprojects or the council played a weak hand.[144] The first such project was the siting of a new domed stadium to house the region's major-league football and baseball teams. Minneapolis, St. Paul, Bloomington, and several other municipalities vied to host the old stadium's replacement. To resolve the conflict, the legislature in 1977 established a new special-purpose body, the Metropolitan Sports Facilities Commission, to evaluate proposals and select a site and to finance construction. Despite the undeniable regional economic, transportation, and land-use impacts of a 50,000-seat stadium, the Met Council played no role in the process.

The council was later called upon to review other megaprojects – a new convention centre in Minneapolis; a world trade centre in St. Paul (personally championed by Governor Perpich); the Mall of America in Bloomington (at its construction the world's largest enclosed shopping centre); a horse-racing track ultimately located in exurban Shakopee; the Target Centre basketball arena in downtown Minneapolis; a velodrome; and numerous industrial parks. The council remained passive in each case. In Harrigan's words:

> There is no way to know how a strong, resourceful Metropolitan Council would have ruled on any of these developments, because the Council did not try to impose its will on any of them. The more important the project was to big development interests, the less the Council seemed to affect the decisions. The result is that the siting of most of these projects resulted from the traditional politics of land use rather than from a guided land use policy directed by the Development Framework.[145]

The council's weak involvement in the siting of major projects fell short of the earlier MPC planners' vision of guiding development through the manipulation of "shaping elements," including major employment centres and other large-scale traffic generators. Most striking, however, is state government's deliberate circumvention of the very agency it had established to express its interest in metropolitan affairs.

Transit: The Legislature and Counties Muscle In

After the legislature's clarification of the relationship between the council and the MTC in 1974, the latter leveraged its seven-county property tax base and federal and state funding to renew the bus fleet and plan for suburban expansion. The state- and national-level Republican ascendency sharply curtailed transit funding, however: the combined federal and state contribution to the MTC's budget declined from 45 to 17 per cent between 1978 and 1983.[146] At the same time, low suburban densities and discontinuous street networks inhibited cost-effective provision of neighbourhood bus service. While core-area bus trips required a 50 per cent operating subsidy, suburban fares covered only one-third of the cost. In this context, the Citizens League lobbied for partial transit privatization, and in 1981 the legislature enabled municipalities to opt out the MTC on condition that they provide their own service. Ultimately twelve prosperous and growing municipalities on the central cities' south and west flanks contracted with private operators to provide suburb-to-downtown rush-hour express service. Their departure undermined the potential for a comprehensive and integrated regional transit network and denied the MTC a lucrative portion of the property tax levy.

The legislature further muddied the waters by assigning the counties a role in transit planning. The counties, which had expanded their role in recreation and social policy since the 1960s, could draw on a source of legitimacy unavailable to the council: their boards were directly elected. Some counties had acquired decommissioned rail rights-of-way starting in the late 1970s in order to preserve them for future transportation or recreational use. Lobbied by light-rail advocates who sought to neutralize the council's opposition to rail, the legislature authorized county "regional railroad authorities" to plan and levy taxes for service on the acquired corridors independently of the council and the MTC. To square the circle, the legislature created a new policymaking body in 1984, the Regional Transit Board, tasked with developing a capital projects "implementation plan" in relation to the council's broad-strokes long-term transportation policy plan.[147] Under the new arrangement, the MTC would focus entirely on transit operations. Despite this clarification, relations between the three agencies remained strained.

CRISIS, REFORM, AND BEYOND: THE STATE AND METROPOLITAN GOVERNANCE SINCE 1990

By the early 1990s the council was politically adrift. Its intended role as a coordinator of functional plans and a defender of the regional interest in local land-use and infrastructure planning had been transformed in the early 1970s as the legislature assigned it a more directive policymaking role. But even as its formal powers increased, the bipartisan coalition of civic and legislative leaders that had created and nurtured it in its early years faded. The council came to be seen primarily as an executive agency by virtue of the governor's appointment power.[148] Neither successive governors not legislators have consistently recognized the council as the state's primary means of programmatically exerting its interest in the social, economic, and environmental performance of the state's metropolis. Without the state's political backing and lacking an alternative source of legitimacy, the appointed council members adopted a strategy of conflict avoidance. In 1989, retiring St. Paul mayor George Latimer publicly accused the Met Council of "receding leadership" and blamed Perpich for failing to understand the council's role. In reply, council vice chair Joan Campbell admitted to complacency in the context of legislative turnover: "For years we had the luxury of having friends in the Legislature who had been involved in our development. Perhaps we have been a little remiss in being over there to explain things."[149]

The Gathering Storm

The 1990 election brought to the fore two entrepreneurial politicians who would reinvigorate debate over the council's role. The new Republican governor, Arne Carlson, who had previously served in the legislature and as state auditor, was pragmatic and somewhat independent from his increasingly right-leaning party. He lambasted the council for its passivity and lack of policy leadership and gave it two years to reform itself or be abolished.[150] In giving his council appointees a strong mandate for reform, he signalled that all options were on the table.

Law professor Myron Orfield, who represented Minneapolis's poorest district in the Minnesota House of Representatives, was energized by concern for the environment and social equity – the widening gap between have and have-not municipalities and residents, including the emergence of racialized poverty in the central cities.[151] Inspired by Portland Metro and the Oregon land-use system (see chapter 7), he believed that the legislature could restore the council's legitimacy and leadership by making it directly elected and strengthening its control over suburban land development and farmland protection. At the same time, he sponsored legislation to reduce the concentration of public housing in the central cities while promoting housing affordability in the suburbs, to increase financial support for transit over highways, and to direct more state funding to less-well-off communities.[152] He believed that reducing implicit subsidies of suburban development would benefit distressed established urban areas. He built a coalition of the central cities and declining northern inner suburbs – organized as the North Metro Mayors Association – on affordable housing and other issues, but most of his proposals were either vetoed by the governor or failed to pass the legislature. (Governor Carlson had a combative relationship with the DFL-dominated legislature, vetoing more bills than all other postwar governors combined during his two terms.) Counties, homebuilder organizations, and the prosperous "fertile crescent" of southwestern suburbs actively lobbied against these initiatives.[153] Still, Orfield energized policy debate in the context of Carlson's ultimatum.

Despite Carlson's challenge, the council did little to renew itself or exercise greater policy leadership. The affordable housing file exemplified the council's inability to pursue a consistent policy position under pressure from outside interests. Although it first supported Orfield's proposal for municipalities to commit to affordable housing targets in exchange for federal and state financial aid, it then flip-flopped under pressure from the governor, Republican legislators, and wealthy suburbs.[154] A *Star-Tribune* editorial was scathing: "Thus does the Council again live up to its reputation for timidity and unpreparedness on the very issues in which it is supposed to be bold and far-reaching."[155]

The straw that broke the camel's back was the near collapse of the MTC's Metro Mobility para-transit service for seniors and disabled residents. Contracted to a new private provider in 1993, the system rapidly deteriorated to the point that the governor mobilized the National Guard to drive vehicles. The crisis revealed the costs of muddled accountability and bureaucratic autonomy in transit governance. The MTC (itself appointed by the Regional Transit Board, which was appointed by the Met Council, which in turn was appointed by the governor) appeared incompetent and unaccountable.[156] Institutional reform was inevitable, although its form remained unclear.

The Metropolitan Reorganization Act

The legislature appointed a special study committee in 1993 to resolve the accountability crisis and respond to Carlson. It recommended merging the independent sewer and transit agencies with the Met Council and creating a "regional administrator" – a professional chief executive officer with broad discretion to hire and fire staff, set administrative rules, and define corporate strategy. Council reorganization bills introduced by Orfield in the House and Carol Flynn in the Senate picked up these recommendations. Orfield argued forcefully for direct election to improve accountability and transparency. Carlson promised to veto, and an elected council bill failed by only one vote in the House. When election was removed, the bill passed 118 to 11.[157] With election off the table, many legislators saw strengthening the council's relationship to the governor as the best means of enhancing political accountability. Councillors had served staggered fixed terms since 1967. Now they would serve at the pleasure of the governor.

The bill's initial focus was transit: resolving the conditions that had produced the Metro Mobility fiasco, arresting declining ridership, and reconciling the divergent policy agendas of light-rail transit and bus advocates. The Metropolitan Waste Control Commission was included in the merger only late in the bill's evolution. The Metropolitan Airports, Sports Facilities, and Parks and Open Space Commissions remained independent.

Overnight, the Met Council turned from a relatively small body dominated by planning staff to a sprawling multi-division entity with a budget of over $700 million and several thousand employees. The intense and rapid legislative bargaining that produced the merger had occurred with little consultation with councillors and staff. The transition was virtually immediate, occurring less than two months after the bill's passage. The new regional administrator – long-time public servant James Solem – was forced to navigate a complex array of competing interests.[158] The governor and legislature believed the merger would reduce costs, and they demanded visible savings. Employees and their unions strongly resisted the harmonization of work rules. (Indeed, Solem believes that the merger could not have occurred under a DFL governor, due to union opposition.) The Metropolitan Waste Control Commission resisted losing its independence, while staff inherited from the three transit bodies remained openly hostile to one another. While these administrative and operational challenges were largely overcome by the decade's end, the merger did little to increase the council's influence over the shape of urban development.

"Bus and Flush" Trumps Regional Planning

Although the council's formal influence over urban development weakened following the rollback of federal review mandates in the early 1980s, its hand was strengthened by legislative and judicial actions. After a decade in which the legal status of council review of municipal plans was in question, the legislature affirmed the primacy of municipal comprehensive plans over zoning bylaws and development controls in 1995, and further clarified requirements for conformity with the council's development framework and regional systems plans.[159] When largely rural Lake Elmo refused to accept growth in proportion to its infrastructure capacity, the state Supreme Court sided with the council in 2004, finding that the town's actions constituted a substantial impact on its adopted systems plans.[160] Forays into providing incentives for brownfield redevelopment and affordable housing construction have no doubt influenced the shape of development, although the council has been criticized for its permissiveness.[161]

Since taking them over in 1994, the council has emphasized sewer and transit operations over its older regional land-use planning and coordinating function. Although the council was willing to confront Lake Elmo for opposing growth, 2003–10 chair Peter Bell has said that the council never opposed a suburb that wanted growth.[162] The council has had little appetite to take a hard line with municipalities. No local plans have been turned back since the Lake Elmo decision. The principal policy instrument, the Metropolitan Urban Service Area, is kept loose in order to avoid conflict with municipalities and developers, and to avoid speculative land acquisition.[163] As a result, population has grown faster in percentage terms outside the MUSA than within it, and spatial analysis has shown that half of all land urbanized between 1986 and 2002 was located outside the MUSA.[164]

By the early 1990s, fifteen years' experience with the Metropolitan Land Planning Act and associated policies, combined with the mainstreaming of environmentalist discourse, led critics to call for the council to exercise more muscular planning controls. Inspired by the Portland example, Representative Orfield unsuccessfully championed a proposal in 1993 to transform the MUSA into a more restrictive regulatory instrument – in effect, an urban growth boundary. His bill to this effect, the Metropolitan Land Use Planning Act, was drafted by the Land Stewardship Project, an environmentalist organization.[165]

As initially advanced by developers back in the 1970s, the strongest argument against exercising more restrictive land-use controls is that growth would simply leapfrog to the twelve adjacent "collar counties" in Minnesota and Wisconsin beyond the council's jurisdiction. Indeed, population growth in this zone began in the 1970s and has accelerated since the 1990s (see figure 5.1). The legislature has never considered internalizing this growth by expanding the council's territorial jurisdiction. A more logical solution would be the adoption of statewide planning policies binding on local governments that would set minimum standards for development. In 1997, the then DFL-dominated legislature passed an act that articulated statewide planning goals, incentivized voluntary land-use regulation by cities elsewhere in the state, and required the State Planning Agency to review and comment on local plans. (An initial proposal to mimic Oregon by mandating municipal planning and establishing growth boundaries for all urban settlements was dropped.) Responding to opposition from local governments and the Minnesota Association of Counties, House Republicans successfully repealed most of the act and in 2003 abolished the State Planning Agency altogether.[166] This was the closest Minnesota came to articulating a programmatic interest in the shape of urban development.

The State: An Inconsistent Master

The Metropolitan Council's legitimacy and effectiveness have continued to be undermined by Minnesota's growing political polarization since 2000. Tying the council more closely to the governor has increased its vulnerability to the ebb and flow of governors' priorities, attention spans, and political fortunes. Carlson's successor, former professional wrestler and suburban Brooklyn Park mayor Jesse Ventura (1999–2003), was elected on the populist Reform Party ticket and pledged a kind of post-partisan pragmatism in contrast to the rancorous DFL-Republican battles of the Carlson years. He actively supported the council, treating its chair, Ted Mondale, as equivalent to a member of cabinet.[167] Republican Tim Pawlenty (2003–10), by contrast, took little interest in the council as he pursued a small-government agenda. His council chair, Peter Bell, presided over transit and parks expansion, as well as ongoing modernization of the sewer system, only by minimizing controversy and carefully tending executive relations. Bell later recalled that "my view was never to embarrass the governor and to realize that it was my job to get along with him, not the other way around. I didn't go to him very often, maybe five or six times [in eight years] ... My agency was never a major priority [for the governor]."[168] While Pawlenty opposed light-rail transit, he did not stop projects started under his predecessor. Elected in 2010, DFL governor Mark Dayton has supported the council during his two terms, advocating for increasing its own-source revenues to fund transit expansion and supporting it in conflicts with municipalities over the necessity and alignment of new higher-order transit corridors. Despite coming from opposite ends of the political spectrum, both Pawlenty and Dayton defended their prerogatives by vetoing bills that would have restored staggered terms for council members.[169]

The council remains caught in partisan crossfire in the legislature. Republican candidates for governor in 2010, 2014, and 2018 have campaigned on the Met Council's abolition or the radical diminution of its powers.[170] The legislature's Republican leadership has advanced bills (vetoed by Dayton) that would eliminate gubernatorial appointment in favour of local government representatives or increase the representation of outer suburban and rural areas.[171] State funding of council transit operations has also been politically contentious, pitting successive governors against legislative majorities of the opposing party.[172] To patch the fiscal hole, area counties entered into a joint-powers arrangement to raise a 0.25 cent sales tax in 2008, but this unravelled with the departure of Dakota County in 2017.[173] The legislature has also undermined the council's role in reviewing regionally significant facilities. New stadiums for the region's professional baseball and football teams were both explicitly exempted from council review.

There is little reason to believe that the legislature will choose to "own" the council and its work. In 2017, the legislature overrode the council by inserting the reclassification of a parcel of land in rural Anoka County into a budget bill. In 2018, legislators went further by amending a bonding bill, now passed, to enable local governments to appeal council policies regardless of the process that led to their adoption, while also giving the small city of Nowthen a veto over the council's land-use policies.[174] These moves amount to the active subversion of the council's authority by the legislature.

CONCLUSION

The Twin Cities story features iconoclastic policy entrepreneurs, powerful interests, and shifting social forces battling over the form and purpose of institutions designed to respond to the consequences of urbanization. The historical narrative shows that the state legislature has always been the central venue of conflict, for it is the state that establishes the legal framework governing local government organization and land-use planning. And the state has only rarely pursued programmatic policymaking in the metropolitan domain. This reflects the institutional foundations of state government. At each point, decisive programmatic legislative action was inhibited by the multiple veto players and dispersed authority inherent in the separated-powers system. Even policy agendas generated by broad extra-governmental coalitions failed to advance or were watered down as they traversed the multiple veto points embedded in the legislative process. While governors such as Olson, LeVander, Anderson, and Ventura have occasionally offset the legislature's tendency to particularism, the executive's role has generally been reactive and defensive rather than proactive and programmatic.

These dynamics have been evident almost from the state's founding. The legislature could not articulate an interest in managing urbanization by establishing durable executive oversight of municipal organization, both statewide but especially in the Twin Cities, where urbanization was most advanced. The Great Depression provided an early opportunity for state government to overcome this reluctance, but attempts at doing so were frustrated by legislative opposition and ultimately foreclosed by a shift in the normative context. The legislature's establishment of the Sanitation District in 1933, the Minnesota Municipal Commission and Metropolitan Planning Commission in 1959, the Metropolitan Council and the Transit Commission in 1967, and the Sewer Board in 1969 occurred only after bills had failed in several legislative sessions, and only after the construction of a bipartisan elite consensus outside the legislature. In the MMC's case, the legislature's indecisiveness led to action only after the horses had escaped the barn, and subsequent lobbying led to legislative erosion of its authority and ultimately its abolition. Similarly, the legislature was late to adopt general enabling legislation for municipal and county land-use planning and to encourage its use. As a result, local land-use regulation matured only after the Twin Cities region's urban development pattern was largely set.

The programmatic legislative actions of the 1960s and early 1970s were the product of a conjuncture. The emergent civic elite network centred on the Citizens League played an integrating role, temporarily overcoming state government's centrifugal nature. It could do so in part because of a supportive normative context. While genuine political disagreements existed, the public had faith in government and deferred to political, economic, intellectual, and media elites. The relative social homogeneity of these elites, as well as of the general population, also minimized conflict. Federal mandates and fiscal inducements also compelled the legislature to act. On the one hand, legislators and local elites sought to head off federal incursion into metropolitan affairs; on the other, they wanted to take advantage of federal grants for infrastructure and housing. The institutional and organizational landscape was also relatively uncluttered. The property development industry was not yet organized. Counties were still backwaters with few operating responsibilities. Outside the central cities, few of the region's many small local governments engaged in land-use and infrastructure planning.

By the end of the 1970s, the bipartisan civic elite network was eclipsed by conventional interest group lobbying in an increasingly party-polarized environment. This deprived the network's greatest triumph, the Metropolitan Council, of its initial support coalition, and no durable alternative source of legitimacy emerged to take its place. Frequently debated, direct election was never adopted. Moreover, the council never established a direct relationship with residents through broad-based outreach and consultation. Instead, it increasingly relied on the governor, who appoints its members, for legitimacy and authority. Its conversion into an operating body consolidated this relationship, yet successive governors have made inconsistent use of the council to advance the state's interest in metropolitan affairs. Instead, it has become a pawn in Minnesota's increasingly polarized political game.

6

Vancouver

Vancouver is a young metropolis. About three-quarters of the region's population growth has occurred since 1950, a similar proportion to American sunbelt metropolises. Subject to the same social, economic, and technological pressures as other North American cities – rapid regional population and economic growth, mass adoption of the automobile, and the resultant dispersal of residential, commercial, and industrial activity to the suburbs – Vancouver entered the automobile age with a small urban core that was soon dwarfed by low-density residential suburbanization. Politically, the Lower Mainland region and British Columbia as a whole have long been cleaved by class and regional divisions that pit business against labour and metropolis against hinterland. Given these trends, Vancouver and British Columbia might be unlikely candidates for the emergence of durable and effective regional governance and planning policies.

Today Vancouver is recognized internationally as a "poster child of urbanism" and a "model of contemporary city-making" that routinely tops global lists of the most desirable cities in which to live.[1] American observers have taken note of British Columbia's distinctive regional governance institution, the regional district.[2] More than in any other North American city – and perhaps more than any other city in a democratic society – policymakers have aggressively promoted rural land preservation, urban intensification, and a polycentric pattern of residential and commercial development. The cumulative impacts of these policies are evident. Greater Vancouver is the only North American region in which the rate of rural land conversion to urban uses is less than that of population growth and the single-detached housing stock has declined in absolute terms.[3] It is also among a

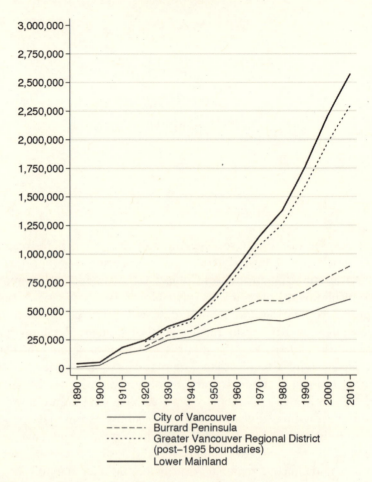

Figure 6.1 Vancouver population by zone, 1890–2010

Note: Until the 1940s, virtually all growth in the Lower Mainland occurred in the City of Vancouver, after which growth dramatically accelerated in surrounding communities. While most has occurred in the western end of the Lower Mainland – on Burrard Peninsula and elsewhere within the jurisdiction of the Greater Vancouver Regional District – better transportation accessibility has facilitated growth to the east.

rarified group of North American centres in which the populations of the metropolitan area, the central city (without annexation), and the central business district have all increased over the past forty years.[4]

This chapter describes how Vancouver's metropolitan governance and planning regimes were constructed beginning in the nineteenth

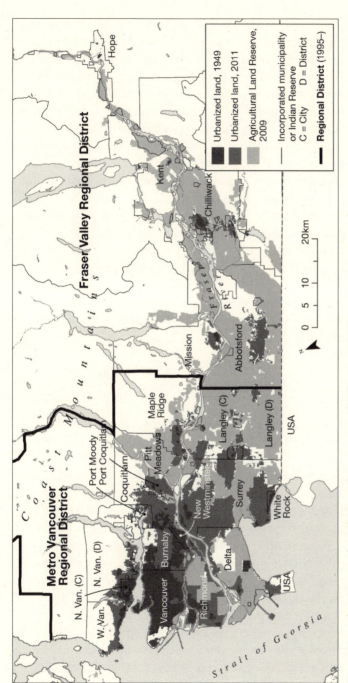

Figure 6.2 Administrative boundaries, urbanization, and policy areas in Vancouver

Note: Since 1995 the Lower Mainland has been divided into two regional districts. The Agricultural Land Reserve (ALR), established in 1973, prohibits urban development in much of the region. Urban development has been largely contiguous and compact, forming discrete settlements in the ALR's "holes."

Sources: 1949 urbanization redrawn from *The Way Ahead*; 2011 redrawn from Z. Taylor, Burchfield, and Kramer, "Alberta Cities at the Crossroads."

century. The provincial government has long been the essential actor in the development of Vancouver's regional governance and planning, as it has decisively, if not always overtly, intervened to promote inter-municipal cooperation and discourage conflict. As in Ontario, executive-centred government, especially when combined with sustained periods of single-party dominance, facilitated decisive and programmatic policymaking in the early postwar period. While the province remained active during and after the 1970s, its support for regional agendas ebbed as the normative context changed and party politics became increasingly competitive and polarized. In contrast to the Toronto and Minneapolis cases, in Vancouver local actors with long experience working within regional institutions actively defended them, and their policies, against provincial threats. Today, the Vancouver region's governance system is singularly successful at managing inter-municipal conflict, even if provincial support for its activities has not always been consistent. The case also points to the how institutions can regulate conflicts and facilitate reciprocity by establishing incentives for actors, and can also generate collective identities.

LOCAL GOVERNMENT AND METROPOLITAN INFRASTRUCTURE, 1858-1929

To understand how this system emerged, we must begin with the provincial government's development of a local government system in the Lower Mainland with distinct characteristics and properties. The region's local governments were established before significant urbanization occurred. New Westminster – the original colonial capital – and Vancouver were chartered in 1858 and 1886, respectively. Crucially, British Columbia (and Alberta, Saskatchewan, and Manitoba, but unlike all other North American states and provinces) did not adopt the county system. Two-tier local government was deemed unnecessary in a vast and sparsely populated territory. Instead, the legislature encouraged the formation, on local initiative, of "district municipalities," a minimalist form of local government akin to the rural townships found in other parts of North America, yet more territorially extensive.[5] By the beginning of the twentieth century the Lower Mainland's 50,000 residents were almost completely organized into incorporated local governments, with few living in unincorporated areas (see figure 6.3). Relatively strict procedural barriers put

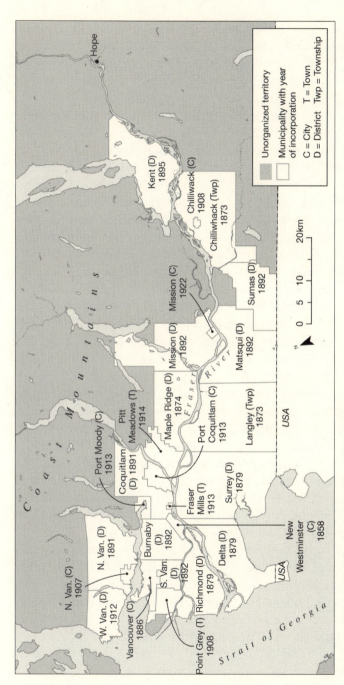

Figure 6.3 Lower Mainland municipal boundaries, 1929

Note: Municipal boundaries shown are those immediately prior to the amalgamation of Vancouver, South Vancouver, and Point Grey and the incorporation of Hope in 1929.

a brake on arbitrary incorporation. Incorporation and annexation occurred only on local petition to the legislature for special legislation or, following the passage of a general municipal law, cabinet approval.[6]

During the first third of the twentieth century, the general pattern of municipal reorganization was of freestanding urban settlements seceding from previously incorporated rural district municipalities: the City of North Vancouver from the surrounding District of the same name; Point Grey from South Vancouver; Fraser Mills, Port Coquitlam, and Port Moody from Coquitlam District; and the City of Chilliwack from its surrounding township. Defensive incorporations, whereby urbanizing areas beyond city limits incorporated to avoid annexation by the central city, were rare because most territory was already municipally organized. In fact, only one annexation to the City of Vancouver occurred between 1886 and 1929: a small portion of already incorporated South Vancouver and Burnaby in 1911. The city's voluntary merger with South Vancouver and Point Grey in 1929 was the exception that proves the rule, motivated not by the need to organize urban development and servicing but by the boosterish desire to surpass Winnipeg as the primate city of western Canada.[7]

The City of Vancouver grew rapidly, from a town of 13,700 people in 1891 to a burgeoning city of 246,600 in 1931. Rapid growth strained infrastructure systems, and the problem of how to finance and provide water and sewer services rose on the public agenda.[8] After serious disease outbreaks, the city installed a trunk sewer system in 1888, but by 1911 beaches were closed as the water bodies could no longer assimilate the outflow. Recognizing that watersheds and shorelines crosscut municipal boundaries, the councils of Vancouver, Point Grey, South Vancouver, and Burnaby formed a Burrard Peninsula Joint Sewerage Committee, which retained internationally recognized engineer R.S. Lea of Montreal to study the problem.[9]

Lea's 1913 report contained both an engineering scheme to meet anticipated needs for forty years and a governance model that adapted elements from several British, American, and Australian federative special-purpose bodies. He proposed an inter-municipal board, authorized to raise capital on bond markets, that would be responsible for designing and constructing trunk infrastructure. As with Melbourne's Metropolitan Board of Works, its board would be composed of delegates from municipal councils. Capital borrowing and operating costs would be divided among the municipalities in proportion to the benefits received, a proxy for which would be the assessed value of the area drained in each municipality. Forecasting that the central city's share of the regional population would decline from two-thirds to less than half by 1950, he recommended that municipal voting strength and fiscal contribution be periodically revised.

Chartered by the province on the municipalities' request, the Vancouver and Districts Joint Sewerage and Drainage Board followed Lea's design.[10] The legislation provided for a board composed of the mayors of Vancouver and New Westminster; the reeves of Burnaby, Point Grey, and South Vancouver; and a chair appointed by the provincial cabinet. (The new City of Vancouver Council appointed three members after the 1929 amalgamation.) As Lea had recommended, operating and borrowing costs were apportioned by the assessed value of the area drained in each municipality. The governance model was consistent with the depoliticizing objectives of the turn-of-the-century urban reform movement. Invisible to ratepayers, the sewer board wholesaled services to municipal utilities, not residents. Operationally, elected officials delegated decision making to professional staff. Bureaucratic management was not contested as long as services were efficiently delivered.

The proportional governance and financing model was copied when a Greater Vancouver Water District for Vancouver, South Vancouver, and Point Grey was established in 1924. The water district sold water to each municipality at a uniform price per gallon. Although separately chartered, comprising different memberships at different times, and financed according to slightly different formulas, the water and sewer boards were administratively unified under a single commissioner. Burnaby joined in 1927, the District of North Vancouver in 1928, West Vancouver in 1929, and Fraser Mills, New Westminster, Richmond, Coquitlam, and Port Coquitlam in 1931. Delta's application was rebuffed in 1927 on the grounds that the district's location south of the Fraser River was too distant. By 1935, 46 per cent of the provincial population lay within the Water District's jurisdiction.[11]

Single-tier municipal organization across the metropolitan area meant that spillover issues would be resolved primarily through horizontal inter-municipal cooperation. Existing municipal delivery of basic sewer and water services to households, coupled with mutual recognition of cross-boundary watershed and drainage basins, gave municipalities a political interest in remedying infrastructure failures without involving the province. This had the side effect of forestalling more muscular involvement by the province. The governance model incentivized participation by equitably apportioning costs, benefits, and representation, and in a way that could be readjusted over time as the balance of municipal populations shifted. By offering the same terms to new members as existing ones, suburbs could access professional expertise and realize economies of scale without facing onerous costs. This contrasted with many other North American metropolitan areas, where central-city or core-area utilities imposed higher wholesale rates on growing suburbs without representation on decision-making bodies, thereby leading suburbs to create separate infrastructure systems.[12] This flexible and proportional model was the template for later metropolitan reforms.

INSTITUTIONALIZING REGIONAL PLANNING FOR THE LOWER MAINLAND, 1926–75

The regulation of land use at the regional scale emerged through the interplay of two reform projects. In Vancouver, a small group of reformist elites became convinced of the need for metropolitan-scale planning of urban growth. While the sewer and water districts rationalized existing infrastructure systems and responded to service demand within the narrow technical logic of pollution mitigation, they were not designed to engage in the long-term integrated planning of residential, industrial, and agricultural land uses. At the same time, political party leaders at the provincial level came to believe that government-led regional economic development planning was necessary for postwar reconstruction. The local reformers piggybacked on this provincial agenda, working through provincial party elites to secure enabling legislation for regional planning boards. This resulted in the creation in 1949 of a Lower Mainland Regional Planning Board, patterned on the water and sewer boards, which would develop a land-use policy informed by American New Deal regional planning ideas.

From City Planning to Regional Planning

Perhaps influenced by experience with the infrastructure boards, local officials recognized the need for inter-municipal coordination as the population grew. Vancouver and Point Grey's advisory town planning commissions jointly hired leading American consultant Harland Bartholomew to prepare a comprehensive plan in 1926.[13] Recognizing that growth would soon spread beyond city limits, Bartholomew acknowledged an even broader geographical context. While his zoning scheme pertained only to the post-1929 City of Vancouver, the plan's sections on streets, public transit, parks and recreation, and transportation also covered New Westminster and still-rural Burnaby. The Vancouver Town Planning Commission (TPC) built on this foundation during the Depression and war years, convening a Regional Planning Association of eleven Lower Mainland municipalities that met six times between December 1937 and its dissolution at the start of the Second World War.[14] The TPC's chair, H.V. Jackson, and its long-time engineer-secretary, J. Alexander Walker, were both strong advocates of planning, and the latter closely observed the work of state planning boards in the Pacific Northwest.

The TPC again retained the Bartholomew firm as the war came to an end. While his revised city plan had never been adopted, his background study on regional planning – *A Preliminary Report upon Decentralization and City Planning* – made a public case for the regional coordination of urban development. He recommended slum clearance, urban renewal, and road improvements to reinforce the central city's primacy in the face of market-led decentralization. In rural and suburbanizing areas, strict control of subdivision would be required to halt speculative building and ensure sufficient density and contiguity of settlement to permit the economical extension of infrastructure and services. Industrial development would be planned at the metropolitan scale to avoid destructive inter-municipal competition. To accomplish these objectives, he proposed a regional agency for the entire Lower Mainland empowered to draft plans for highways, major parks, river navigation, flood protection, and electrical power generation, and to encourage municipal comprehensive planning and zoning and craft plans and zoning bylaws for unorganized areas. While the proposed regional institution covered a much larger geographical area, its structure resembled that of the water and sewer boards: representation by population, with costs apportioned in relation to benefits received. It is unknown whether Bartholomew's recommendations regarding the region's boundaries and the organization of the planning board were his own or if they were inserted at the behest of planning's advocates on the TPC. Certainly the endorsement of an internationally respected expert conferred legitimacy on the notion of regional planning by a regional agency.

Planning and British Columbia's Postwar New Deal

Local advocacy of metropolitan planning in Vancouver paralleled an emergent regional economic development agenda at the provincial level. British Columbia's resource-based export economy was hit especially hard by the Depression, multiplying demands on the state for relief, both for the unemployed and for insolvent municipal governments. In 1933, the provincial Liberals, led by pugnacious progressive Duff Patullo, won a landslide victory over the incumbent Conservatives under the genteel Simon Fraser Tolmie, which had responded to the crisis with spending cuts and tax increases. Much like Floyd B. Olson in Minnesota, Patullo called for a kind of "socialized capitalism" that would eliminate the abuses of the unconstrained market while preserving private initiative.[15] His government combatted the Depression with public works projects, economic development in the vast and sparsely settled northern regions of the province, and direct aid to the unemployed and insolvent local governments. Patullo's "little New Deal" remained a provincial project, as the federal government resisted deficit spending and viewed social welfare as a provincial and local concern.[16]

As in Toronto, the residential suburbs were hardest hit. Overwhelmed by relief expenditures, Burnaby and the City and District of North Vancouver defaulted during the winter of 1932–33. Under new legislation, the province appointed commissioners to assume control of local administration from elected councils, renegotiate debts, and ultimately restore control to elected officials.[17] This led to the establishment of a new Ministry of Municipal Affairs in 1934, which was charged with supervising municipal borrowing. As in Ontario, the province's objective was not to restore, not usurp, local autonomy. There was no talk of reorganizing financially embarrassed municipalities, on the part of either the provincial government or the municipalities themselves.

Premier Patullo's reformism faded under fiscal pressure by the end of the 1930s. The socialist Co-operative Commonwealth Federation (CCF) won the popular vote in the 1941 election but received only the second-highest number of seats. After Patullo's caucus forced him to resign, his finance minister, John Hart, joined with Conservative leader Royal Maitland to form a self-styled "free-enterprise" coalition government to combat the socialist threat. In office, the coalition tacked left to blunt the CCF's appeal, but not so far as to alienate big business.

The coalition government was constrained fiscally by federal war-time emergency powers over industrial production and taxation, and politically by divisive policy debates. Its first year in office was dominated by the passage of a controversial law, opposed by the CCF and the marginalized Patullo, to open up northern oil fields to private exploration.[18] In part to mollify the left, which favoured public control, Hart appointed Education Minister Harry Perry in 1942 to chair an all-party Post-War Rehabilitation Council (PWRC) of legislators. This was not simply a sop: national and subnational governments throughout the British Empire and in the United States were consumed with postwar reconstruction planning. The council's objective was to avoid postwar depression by opening up the productive capacities of the province's undeveloped interior. Its twelve members included CCF leader and Burnaby legislator Harold Winch; J.A. Paton, a Conservative planning enthusiast who had earlier served as Point Grey reeve and had been an inaugural board member of the Water District; and the maverick Conservative legislator and future premier W.A.C. Bennett.[19] Hailed as a harbinger of a post-partisan age, the PWRC embraced "planning," broadly construed.[20] What this meant in practice, however, remained unclear.

On the basis of extensive consultation with municipalities, which provided lists of potential postwar infrastructure projects, the PWRC released two reports in 1943–44 that threw the province's backward-ness into sharp relief. Outside of the larger urban areas, road access was poor and electricity service limited. In many ways, British Columbia resembled the American hinterland before the New Deal: isolated, impoverished, and underserviced. The report recommended massive investment in rail and highway infrastructure to connect the coast to the interior, the creation of a steel industry, the development of forest and mining resources, and the nationalization of hydroelectric power production. It also called for mandatory municipal comprehensive land-use planning and the creation of a provincial Department of Planning and Reconstruction that would define regional planning areas, develop plans for them, and mobilize resources at all levels of government to carry them out. The PWRC's articulation of regional planning bore the imprint of New Deal regional economic development ideas. Its interim report, tabled in February 1943, makes direct reference to the Tennessee Valley Authority. Echoing the discourse of the American National Resources Planning Board, and citing Lewis Mumford, the Perry report imagined a future in which the development of the province's economic regions was equalized, and regional economies were internally balanced.[21]

At least in part, the PWRC's endorsement of regional planning reflected the lobbying of Vancouver's planning enthusiasts. In June 1942, TPC members H.V. Jackson and F.E. Buck appeared before the PWRC to advocate for the creation of regional planning boards that would operate under the supervision of a provincial planning commission. With Perry's personal encouragement, they drafted and submitted a draft bill to this effect.[22] The government did not immediately adopt these recommendations, despite continued advocacy from municipalities and planning advocates.[23] A Bureau of Post-War Rehabilitation and Reconstruction responsible to the provincial cabinet was created in 1944, and a Regional Planning Division was established within it at the start of 1945. Its first task was to divide the province into ten study regions, the first being the Lower Mainland – a 4,600 km² area spanning twenty-three municipalities and comprising the majority of the province's population. The following year, the division published its *Preliminary Report,* which summarized studies of agriculture; the diking of the Fraser River; natural resource extraction; transportation, water, and sewer infrastructure; parks and recreation; education; health and social services; and community planning. While unprecedented in scope, these descriptive studies were not in themselves a plan. As for how to create one, the division commented favourably on Winnipeg's recent formation of an inter-municipal body to prepare a regional plan.[24]

By 1946, then, there were two overlapping currents of interest in planning. Vancouver-based enthusiasts sought a metropolitan-scale land-use planning capacity to manage anticipated postwar urban growth, while provincial governing party elites, influenced by the American New Deal, sought to stimulate economic development in the province's laggard regions. The two agendas converged in the Lower Mainland, where the growing metropolis coexisted with a rural hinterland whose economy was based on agriculture and forestry. It remained unclear, however, if the province was inclined to institutionalize supra- or inter-municipal planning agencies, as envisioned by the Vancouver group, or if it would pursue its economic development objectives directly.

A political opening emerged with the unsettling of the coalition government. In 1946 and 1947, Hart and Maitland were succeeded by Liberal premier Byron Johnson and Conservative deputy premier

Herbert Anscomb. Although both lacked the full support of their parties, and their relationship was soon strained by policy differences, all-party support for province-led regional economic development planning held.[25] It was in this context that the local advocates made their move. Anscomb's party leadership campaign had been organized by former party president and insurance man Tom McDonald, a committed amateur proponent of town planning. As a reward for his efforts, McDonald prevailed on Anscomb for an amendment to the Town Planning Act that would permit the establishment of regional planning boards on petition from municipalities. It no doubt helped that Anscomb had previously served as minister of municipal affairs and had installed an ally in that role on becoming deputy premier.[26] The new minister, former heavyweight wrestler R.C. MacDonald, had led Coquitlam for eighteen years, participated in the Lower Mainland Regional Planning Association in 1937–39, and served as president of the Union of British Columbia Municipalities, the provincial local government lobby group. With the dissolution of the Bureau of Post-War Rehabilitation and Reconstruction in 1947, the Regional Planning Division reported directly to the minister of municipal affairs.

The Vancouver planning advocates were also aided by new federal financial and organizational resources. The 1944 National Housing Act established a public corporation to finance public housing and insure mortgages, the Central Mortgage and Housing Corporation (CMHC). A minor section of the act gave the CMHC responsibility for encouraging public interest in planning. Following a successful conference attended by interested amateurs and professionals, it was agreed that the CMHC would establish and fund the Community Planning Association of Canada (CPAC) as a means of furthering this objective.[27] The Vancouver group immediately formed provincial and Greater Vancouver chapters. CPAC lent resources and legitimacy to pro-planning advocacy by establishing an institutional focus outside of local government. It was under this banner that McDonald lobbied Anscomb to authorize regional planning in 1948, and it was through CPAC that local advocates worked to secure sufficient municipal support for a Lower Mainland board.[28] Any lingering doubts about the need for regional coordination were dispelled by the catastrophic 1948 Fraser River flood, which inundated 200 km² of land and displaced 16,000 people. The enabling legislation provided for the establishment, on petition from area municipalities, of boards made up of municipal representatives, each appointing one member, with municipal engineers serving *ex officio*. These boards would serve as forums for inter-municipal planning discussion, conduct surveys and research on regional planning issues, and provide planning services on a contract basis to small municipalities and unorganized areas. The minister established a Lower Mainland Regional Planning Board (LMRPB) in June 1949.

The Liberal-Conservative coalition's developmental agenda, including regionalism, was sustained even after the coalition's collapse in 1951. The electoral beneficiary was to be the Post-War Rehabilitation Council's most fervent exponent of province-led regional economic development, W.A.C. Bennett, who had left the Conservative Party after unsuccessfully challenging Anscomb for the leadership. The Liberals and Conservatives were decimated in the June 1952 election. A newly adopted preferential ballot voting system designed to thwart the CCF ended up working against the two mainline parties.[29] After the ballots were tallied, a new party-movement called the Social Credit League had secured enough second-choice support to win nineteen of forty-eight seats – one seat more than the CCF, albeit with 28,000 fewer votes. Social Credit's appeal lay in its populist rhetoric and recruitment of candidates among local elites in the interior, yet it lacked a leader and had little in the way of a coherent program. Bennett had run as a "Socred" candidate and, as by far the most politically experienced member of its caucus, quickly secured the leadership, and therefore the premiership, at a post-election convention. Inheriting the Liberal-Conservative coalition's "free enterprise" base, he would remain premier for twenty years by vigorously championing the Perry Report's objective of infrastructure investment in the service of market-led economic expansion.

Institutional Foundations and Postwar Reconstruction

In sum, from the province's early years to the end of the Second World War, the provincial government had incrementally established the rudiments of a system of multi-level urban governance in the Lower Mainland region: general municipal legislation that facilitated early "wall-to-wall" municipal incorporation, flexible service districts providing water and sewer services in Greater Vancouver, a Ministry of Municipal Affairs, and a statutory system of regional planning. As in Ontario, these early interventions and their maintenance were enabled by the institutional foundations of the province's Westminster system of government. Unconstrained by home rule and facing few checks, the provincial executive could unilaterally act in the local government sphere. Again, similar to Ontario but not Minnesota, the province reorganized itself to expand its capacity to make and implement programmatic policies to confront the Depression crisis. A programmatic response to underdevelopment – British Columbia's own New Deal – would come only after the war. While partisan conflict was bitter, the 1940s brought an all-party consensus in favour of proactive and programmatic state intervention to modernize infrastructure and facilitate economic development. Efficient service delivery and effective planning for urban growth in the Lower Mainland were but one piece of this province-wide agenda. As in Ontario, the provincial government modernized legislative frameworks for local and regional planning immediately after the war, in the process creating the Lower Mainland Regional Planning Board. Planning was championed by local elites and provincial party activists and leaders from across the political spectrum as part of the broader postwar reconstruction project.

The Lower Mainland Regional Planning Board and American Regional Planning Ideas

The Lower Mainland Regional Planning Board commenced operation at a time of rapid growth, especially in the outer suburbs. Indeed, Surrey and Richmond doubled their population in each decade between 1930 and 1960. Fifteen municipalities participated at the board's inception. Its first chair was D.J. McGugan, the chief engineer of the Fraser Valley Diking Authority, and Vancouver planning advocate Tom McDonald served as secretary. A startup fund of $7,500 was provided by CPAC. Thereafter, the board was funded by a provincial subvention and an annual per capita grant from member municipalities.[30] It remained an empty vessel, however. While the TPC/CPAC group was enthusiastic about "planning" in principle, there was little consensus on the objectives of regional planning and how it should relate to municipal and provincial activities.

The vessel would be filled with the ideas of two men recruited from the east: H. Peter Oberlander and James Wood Wilson. Both had absorbed American regional planning ideas. Oberlander had studied at Harvard with Catherine Bauer, the co-author of the 1937 National Housing Act, close associate of urbanist Lewis Mumford and architect-planner Clarence Stein, and onetime secretary of the Regional Plan Association of America.[31] On returning to Canada in 1948, Oberlander went to work for Humphrey Carver, the British-born architect-planner responsible for CMHC's research and education activities, including CPAC. Carver seconded Oberlander to start a new planning course at the University of British Columbia in 1950.[32] On the basis of his university appointment and planning training, the LMRPB retained Oberlander to devise a program of work and to recruit a professional staff.[33] His first act was to hire as director Wilson, a Scottish civil engineer who had studied regional planning at the newly organized city- and regional-planning program at the University of North Carolina in Chapel Hill. Wilson had worked on a Tennessee Valley Authority research project on the potential for planning by small cities and had observed the TVA's planning-assistance program up close.[34] His thesis, a regional plan for the Chapel Hill–Carrboro area, is notable for its pragmatic attention to local implementation.[35] When Wilson arrived in Vancouver in June 1951, he saw along the Fraser River something akin to the Tennessee Valley: a river basin rich in natural beauty and productive potential yet held back by underdeveloped infrastructure and the absence of land-use regulation. It was agreed that the LMRPB's first task would be to undertake a comprehensive regional survey and then build municipal support for a regional plan.[36] Wilson was ideally placed to take up this challenge.

As a consultant to the LMRPB, Oberlander produced a land-use vision that reflected the influence of the American regional planning tradition and contemporaneous British thinking on urban containment and New Town development.[37] In his view, the central planning challenge was to balance the Vancouver conurbation's growth with the health of the agricultural base, which was threatened by scattered subdivision and fragmented "ribbon" development along roadways. He proposed that planned industrial development be used to strategically concentrate population growth in self-sufficient towns connected by limited-access highways. At the same time, compact urban development would be assured by the comprehensive protection of productive agricultural and wilderness lands.

Constructing an Economic Argument against Sprawl

While "planning" was the board's putative purpose, the 1949 legislation provided little guidance as to what a regional plan should include.
The board had no legal authority over local government. During the
1950s and early 1960s, however, it marshalled evidence in support
of Oberlander's land-use concept and, in the process, produced a
sophisticated critique of prevailing urban development patterns.[38]

The board was perhaps the first public agency to use the term
"urban sprawl." Its widely disseminated report *Urban Sprawl* appeared
two years before sociologist William H. Whyte popularized the term
in a canonical *Fortune* magazine article.[39] While the characterization
of "sprawl" was colourful – haphazard ribbon development along
country roads was compared to termites eating through wood – its
critique was primarily economic. Almost two decades before the
Anthony Downs's landmark *Costs of Sprawl* study, the LMRPB empir-
ically demonstrated that the per capita cost of public works decreased
with density, that service costs were highest and revenues lowest in
low-density areas, and that actively farmed rural areas paid their
own way.[40] It also found that servicing was inconsistent in haphazardly developed areas. Compared to Metropolitan Toronto and
Calgary, where subdivision control was linked to servicing, and
residential connection to trunk sewer systems was already almost
universal, only 68 per cent of dwellings in the Vancouver area, and
only 36 per cent in fringe areas, were hooked up to trunk services
in 1961.[41] If trends continued, newly urbanized areas would lack
adequate sewer and water services, let alone sufficient levels of street
paving and lighting, fire protection, schools, parks, and bus transit.[42]
In addition, Wilson's staff demonstrated that interspersing residential
development in rural areas undermined the agricultural economy,
which accounted for one in five jobs in the Lower Mainland.[43] A
case was also made on the basis of food security: as the urban population expanded, the region would increasingly depend on imported
food. To protect farmland from fragmentation and urbanization, the
board recommended designating half of the Lower Mainland's usable
land area for exclusive farm use.

These planning ideas were incubated in and reproduced through
local institutions and networks. Oberlander's planning course at UBC
would send its best graduates to work for the board, while Wilson

and his staff taught in the planning program. This group was the nucleus of the province's nascent planning profession. The Planning Institute of British Columbia (PIBC) was founded in 1958 with eight members, including Wilson.[44]

Increasing the Authority and Legitimacy of Regional Planning

The LMRPB's precarious status as a voluntary inter-municipal body inhibited progress toward developing a regional plan. Wilson publicly characterized the board as "an unattached brain seeking to attach itself to twenty-six different bodies which are willing to a greater or less extent to accept its advice."[45] As municipal interest in the board's work waxed and waned, Wilson and his staff routinely travelled to the municipalities to beg councils for continued payment of annual contributions to its budget. Some municipalities refused to participate altogether.[46]

Wilson repeatedly pressed the Ministry of Municipal Affairs to mandate municipal membership and make the board's plans legally binding. Passed after the 1956 election that consolidated Social Credit's hold on government, a new Municipal Act clarified the regional plan adoption process and specified that local plans and undertakings had to conform to adopted regional plans. An Official Regional Plan (ORP) would take legal effect if adopted by two-thirds of member municipalities and approved by the minister of municipal affairs. The new act also required that regional planning boards be composed of elected municipal councillors. (Heretofore members were appointed by councils but were not required to be councillors.) These changes bound municipal councils more closely to the board's decision making and increased the incentive to participate. The new act also formalized fee-for-service planning assistance, which intensified relationships with the smaller municipalities. In time, the LMRPB prepared comprehensive plans for at least eight member municipalities, as well as numerous studies and model bylaws. These projects articulated the regional land-use concept at a more granular level, while tailoring its implementation to local conditions. Wilson later characterized the planning-assistance program as a "Trojan Horse" strategy through which the board built support for planning and the regional concept.[47]

Although municipal councils appointed delegates annually, continuity of personnel was high. During its twenty-year existence, 55 of the board's 183 individual members served four years or more.[48] After collectively puzzling through issues, long-serving members brought a regional perspective back to their local councils. In this way, the board provided for the rural valley municipalities what the water district had in the metropolitan core: a venue for routinized cross-boundary interaction between municipal politicians, and between public servants, which in turn engendered support for a binding regional plan. Collaboration also facilitated the acceptance of planning and the diffusion of planning ideas across the region. In 1949, only the City of Vancouver employed full-time planners. By 1960, eight Lower Mainland municipalities had planning departments, while the rest used the board's planning-assistance program.[49]

While the board built trust and facilitated shared understandings through outreach and collaboration, it could not impose a consensus. The City of Vancouver saw little immediate benefit from its services. It resented paying its share of the budget and the fact that it appointed but one board member. The small rural municipalities that benefited from planning assistance were quick to complain when they believed the board had usurped their autonomy. Conflict increased as the board drafted a binding official regional plan.

Adopting the Official Regional Plan

The first step in generating a binding regional plan was the articulation in 1963 of a "development concept," *Chance and Challenge*, which reiterated Oberlander's original principles: that the region is "a unity" and that the goal of regional planning is to balance the needs of, and demands for, urban, agricultural, recreational, and wilderness lands.[50] To protect farmland, haphazard valley development would be redirected to urban settlements defined by exclusive rural zoning – "cities in a sea of green." To efficiently serve the valley towns and promote a higher-density and more contiguous urban form, the board proposed extending the jurisdiction of Vancouver's water and sewer districts to the entire Lower Mainland – an idea publicly endorsed by the water board.[51]

While service on the LMRPB nurtured a cadre of regionally minded municipal officials and increased the legitimacy of the board and land-use regulation more generally, many local politicians remained suspicious. Consultation on *Chance and Challenge* elicited favourable responses from business, labour, and community groups, as well as professional associations, but municipalities were divided.[52] Most approved of minimum standards for new urban development, but, especially in the Fraser Valley, municipalities viewed the plan's legal imposition as infringing on local self-government and private property rights.[53] Langley District councillor Bill Blair argued that it sacrificed democratic accountability to a remote technical logic. As paraphrased in a newspaper account of a public meeting, "The council ... is elected by the residents of today and not by future generations, and must give consideration to the wishes of those who elected them."[54] Reeve Simpson of Chilliwhack Township was more direct: "All we want is to be left alone, but you won't let us."[55] In the metropolitan area, North Vancouver and New Westminster argued that the regional plan should apply only to the rural valley because local planning was already mature in built-out urban municipalities.[56]

The draft ORP circulated at the end of 1965 was essentially a broad-brush zoning plan. The region was divided into five general categories: urban, rural, industrial, park, and "reserve" (which included major linear infrastructure and institutional uses), each subject to specific policies (see figure 6.4). Established and developing urban areas, for example, were required to be fully serviced by water and sewer systems. Conversion to urban use of agricultural and park areas, the former covering half the usable land in the Lower Mainland, was prohibited. Industrial lands and highway and rail connections would ensure that each urban centre would share in economic growth.[57] Municipal plans and zoning bylaws would flesh out neighbourhood- and site-level policies and designations within these broad categories. Importantly, the plan grandfathered existing municipal regulations – only future municipal plans and zoning bylaws would have to conform to the ORP.

As the plan moved closer to adoption, the most fundamental objection was that exclusive agricultural zoning amounted to the confiscation of property values. Following a public presentation by board staff, Surrey councillor Ted Kuhn pithily summed up the argument: "How can we have a regional plan that tells the land owner what he can and cannot do with his land for the next fifteen years if there is no compensation to a man whose lands are frozen?"[58] The characterization of the plan as a land "freeze" was repeated in public statements and suburban newspaper editorials as potentially affected property-owners demanded compensation.[59] In this view, exclusive agricultural zoning would unjustly harm farmers who hoped to pocket the uplift in land values by selling to residential developers when they

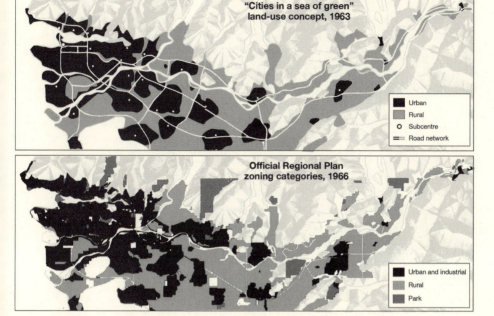

Figure 6.4 The Lower Mainland Regional Planning Board's evolving land-use concept, 1963–66

Note: The schematic "cities in a sea of green" land-use concept in the 1963 *Chance and Challenge* report (top) was the basis of the zoning in the 1966 *Official Regional Plan* (bottom).

Sources: Redrawn from *Chance and Challenge* and *Official Regional Plan*.

retired. (Of course, the justification for exclusive agricultural zoning was to avoid such uplift, which risked pricing active farmers out of the market.)

Municipal approval of the ORP was not assured. In a memorandum dated only eighteen days before its adoption on 23 June 1966 by the LMPRB, the province's regional planning director, Don South, cited communication from LMRPB executive director Victor Parker (who had succeeded Wilson in 1964) stating that twenty-one of twenty-eight municipal councils had voted in favour and that, of the remainder, only three or four were "really against the plan." Suggesting that the board's outreach had been successful, Parker reported that "by and large, all of them approve of the Plan really, but do not want to lose face because they have not been in favour in the past."[60] Quiet provincial suasion encouraged municipal approval. Deputy Minister

James Everett Brown advised the reformist minister of municipal affairs Dan Campbell to mollify defectors.[61] Campbell's personal support was apparently sufficient to overcome opposition in caucus and cabinet despite evidence that other ministries refused to work constructively with the board.[62] In the end, only Langley District withheld its endorsement, but it was still bound by the plan under the two-thirds approval formula.[63] Minister Campbell congratulated Parker in a telegram. He recognized the tension between regional and local interests, stating that "I am sure that your work will be long remembered as the success of the idea that a couple of dozen municipalities can in fact work together in a regional context and still maintain community identity."[64] Parker and his planners recognized that ratification was the beginning, not the end, of the process. Even with provincial support, implementation would require sustained cooperation from municipal politicians and planners. The achievement of land-use regulation's potential would also require more direct integration with infrastructure planning and operation.

Provincializing Agricultural Land Protection: The Agricultural Land Reserve

While agricultural land protection was a cornerstone of the Official Regional Plan, scattered exurban subdivision and urban development continued because nonconforming land uses and existing local land-use regulations were grandfathered. Only new comprehensive plans and zoning bylaws had to conform to the new designations. In addition, municipalities permissively evaluated applications for zoning changes. While estimates of rural land conversion during this period differ, the ORP was amended dozens of times, cumulatively redesignating thousands of hectares from agricultural to urban or industrial use.[65]

Such was its salience that all parties campaigned on some form of farmland protection in the 1972 election. The surprise victory of Dave Barrett's New Democratic Party over the Bennett Socreds provided an opening for non-incremental policy change.[66] In its first year in office, the NDP issued a province-wide regulatory freeze on the subdivision of agricultural land. Henceforth, all farmland within a provincially defined Agricultural Land Reserve (ALR) could be subdivided or converted to non-farm use only on application to a provincially appointed commission. The Agricultural Land Commission Act resolved the ORP's "grandfather" problem. Municipalities and regional planning boards were now required to ensure that all adopted bylaws and plans were consistent with the ALR and the regulations of the Agricultural Land Commission (ALC).

The province defined the ALR's boundaries using the federal Canada Land Inventory, which classifies the capability of farmland, in consultation with regional authorities and provincial ministries. The Lower Mainland ALR was based largely on the agricultural zoning in the 1966 Official Regional Plan (see figure 6.4).[67] This reflected strong personal relationships between the Vancouver regional planners and the NDP government. The architects of the regulatory approach to farmland protection were Minister of Lands, Forests, and Water Resources Robert Williams, a man regarded as Barrett's most powerful minister, and his adviser Norman Pearson. Both had worked at the LMRPB and taught in the UBC planning school, and they were committed to the regionalist perspective and ORP's policy principles.

The 1972–75 NDP government's creation of the ALR represented the province-wide extension of the LMRPB's core planning idea – agricultural land protection not simply to secure the economic productivity of farming, but as a means of constraining urban growth. While the NDP government was short-lived – it would lose the 1975 election to a resurgent Social Credit Party led by W.A.C. Bennett's son Bill – it represented continuity insofar as it pursued internally developed technocratic objectives. The "uploading" of farmland protection to the provincial level affected the region's long-term development in two ways. First, as the ALR was a much stronger instrument than the ORP's agricultural zoning, it promised to "lock in" the ultimate limits of urban growth in the Lower Mainland. Second, by shifting the venue of contention to the provincial level, the regulation of the urban land supply became hitched to provincial political exigencies. As long as the province remained programmatically committed to supporting agricultural land protection and inter-municipal governance of regions, the land-use vision would hold. With the LMRPB's plan and the ALR in place, the vision was poised for implementation.

Provincial Support and Social Learning

In principle the ORP was the voluntary creation of the board's member municipalities, yet the board faced considerable local resistance from these municipalities and their residents. It is unlikely that the plan would have been adopted without sustained quiet support from the provincial government. The province did not leave the board and municipalities to their own devices after 1949; rather, successive ministers repeatedly lent the board political support, increased its statutory authority, and encouraged the participation of recalcitrant municipalities. The province's resolute support for the board and its work was enabled by the institutional foundations of the Westminster system, which insulated the executive from local and parochial interests, and by the Social Credit government's sustained electoral dominance during the 1950s and 1960s. Although the Lower Mainland remained under-represented in the rural-dominated legislature, and long-serving ministers of municipal affairs Wesley Black and Dan Campbell did not represent Lower Mainland districts, the executive remained committed to local and regional land-use planning as long as the plans were consistent with its broader economic development objectives.[68]

Like other North Americans in the early postwar period, British Columbians endorsed an interventionist state at the ballot box in the service of economic development but would not countenance the usurpation of local government autonomy and individual property rights. The provincial government saw its responsibility as encouraging the robust exercise of local autonomy. Although British Columbia did not develop as extensive and centralized a municipal affairs bureaucracy as did Ontario, it facilitated inter-municipal collaboration by providing supportive legal frameworks and through the careful nudging of resistant local officials.

While essential, provincial support is only half the story. The board also achieved its objectives through strategic constructive engagement with its members. In this it drew on Wilson's observation of the TVA's planning-assistance program, which had demonstrated how a regional body could work in concert with local elected officials to develop a coherent scheme of physical and economic development at the regional scale. The board's collective deliberations, buttressed by the give-and-take of the planning-assistance program, were the crucible for social learning by municipal leaders. This, in tandem with the strong relationship with UBC's planning school and the emerging planning profession, reproduced and legitimized land-use planning and the regional land-use concept.

CONSOLIDATING METROPOLITAN GOVERNANCE
IN GREATER VANCOUVER, 1950-75

The consolidation of Lower Mainland regional planning paralleled a related debate over how best to govern and service the growing Vancouver conurbation. During the 1940s, the region's population increased by almost 200,000 people, or 45 per cent, straining existing infrastructure systems. Metropolitan government rose on the agenda of Vancouver elites for several reasons: an emerging public health crisis as the region outgrew Lea's earlier sewer system, the contemporaneous creation of Metro Toronto in 1953-54, and a campaign by the LMRPB for greater authority to implement its plan. The provincial government's solution, a province-wide system of "regional districts" – flexible, semi-voluntary inter-municipal service bodies patterned on Vancouver's water and sewer boards – ultimately reinforced the inter-municipal collaboration model.

The Province Induces Sewer System Expansion

While the Water District had expanded as urbanization spread outwards – by 1950, it had fourteen members – the Joint Sewerage and Drainage Board covered only the Burrard Peninsula. After the war, coastal pollution re-emerged as a public health threat. Even in the City of Vancouver, one in four households relied on septic tanks rather than on sanitary sewers, leading to outbreaks of disease.[69] To study the situation, in 1950 the sewer board, with provincial support, appointed a three-member panel of engineers consisting of that board's long-time chairman, E.A. Cleveland, and two internationally recognized authorities on sanitation engineering, retired University of California professor Gilman Hyde and A.M. Rawn, the chief engineer and general manager of the County Sanitation Districts of Los Angeles County. After exhaustive surveys and study, the panel recommended the expansion of the sewer board's jurisdiction to include the entire Greater Vancouver Area, which it defined as the City and District of North Vancouver, West Vancouver, Coquitlam, Port Coquitlam, Port Moody, Fraser Mills, and Richmond – an area containing over 500,000 people, or 80 per cent of the Lower Mainland population.[70] It forecast that the metropolitan population would reach 1.4 million by 2000 (overshooting by only 80,000) and recommended an expensive long-term borrowing program to finance, among other works, a new sewage treatment plant at Iona Island in Richmond. The report also endorsed the existing principles of equitable distribution of financial burdens in proportion to benefits received and the addition of new members on the same terms.

Viewing its task as purely technical in nature, the commission had consulted neither municipalities nor the public.[71] While hailed by newspaper editorialists, the report was attacked by New Westminster, North Vancouver, and Richmond, which felt the plans were needlessly extravagant.[72] Lea's 1913 scheme had relied on the ocean to assimilate outflow, and so sewage was released untreated. The construction of a treatment plant was criticized as an expensive and perhaps unnecessary activity, regardless of the expert panel's recommendations. Only Vancouver and Burnaby accepted the recommendations.

Minister of Municipal Affairs Wesley Black, a dour schoolteacher from Nelson, in the province's interior, was an astute pragmatist with little desire to court conflict by overriding municipal objections. He adopted a back-door strategy that publicly respected municipal autonomy while using other means to influence their behaviour. He abandoned a draft bill, introduced in 1954, that would have made sewer board membership compulsory. Two years later he reconstituted the existing board, still with only Vancouver and Burnaby as members, as a new Greater Vancouver Sewerage and Drainage District (GVSDD) with the mandate to implement the engineers' plan. At the same time, Black created a provincial Pollution Control Board (PCB) to enforce minimum pollution standards in the Fraser estuary and Burrard Inlet drainage area. This, he hoped, would induce participation in the new GVSDD.[73] In the context of beach closures by public health officials, the PCB overrode Richmond's objection to the Iona treatment plant in 1958. Reinforced by rising public concern about water pollution, Black's strategy was a long-term success. As municipalities could no longer escape minimum pollution standards, seven joined the GVSDD over the following decade.[74] By the mid-1960s, the dozen or so metropolitan municipalities were administratively and infrastructurally bound together.

Ruling Out Toronto-Style Metropolitan Government

Even as municipalities squabbled over infrastructure, others advocated for a two-tier government patterned on Metropolitan Toronto. In

1952, the LMRPB recommended the creation of a regional body to coordinate the future ORP with infrastructure planning – a Lower Mainland council or, failing that, separate councils for the metropolitan area and valley.[75] Two years later, in a report entitled *The Greater Vancouver Metropolitan Community*, the board called for an inquiry into forming a metropolitan government for the eleven urban and urbanizing municipalities centred on Vancouver. The authors looked to Metro Toronto, noting that "what Toronto is today Greater Vancouver will be tomorrow."[76] Acknowledging the area's increasing polycentricity, the LMRPB forecast that the City of Vancouver's share of the population would decline as the suburbs grew, and made a compelling empirical case that the area constituted a single market for labour and goods. In a communication to the minister, Jim Wilson proposed that the LMRPB become the planning arm of any future metropolitan government, much as the Metro Toronto Planning Board was responsible to Metro Toronto's council.[77] Also inspired by the Toronto example, the Vancouver Board of Trade struck a committee in early 1954 to study metropolitan planning and administration.[78] A CPAC-convened committee of mayors and reeves on metropolitan issues revealed their ambivalence to deeper integration, however.[79] Nonetheless, ideas about metropolitan government found their way into law. The 1957 Municipal Act, which gave legal authority to official regional plans, also enabled the minister to establish "joint committees" of municipal councillors to study the formation of "metropolitan authorities." If a committee recommended consolidating services, it would be put to a vote of the people.

The minister established a Vancouver metropolitan joint committee in 1957. Officially, the committee was appointed at the eleven municipalities' unanimous request, but Black had quietly indicated that he would appoint one anyway if they dissembled.[80] As in the sewerage governance controversy, the provincial imposition of a metropolitan government on unwilling municipalities was politically untenable in the British Columbia context. Publicly, Black emphasized that he wanted to avoid politicizing what he framed as a technical matter and that there was more to be gained from "selling rather than enforcing the idea."[81] Still, the minister used the Ontario government's imposition of Metro Toronto in 1953 as a stick to encourage municipal cooperation. He told the group at its first meeting that he would not intrude on its deliberations but "would be very sorry if conditions carried on without a solution until some future government would be forced to take action in the manner which occurred in Toronto."[82]

The committee's chair was charismatic lawyer Hugo Ray, who had previously served as West Vancouver reeve, a director of CPAC, and a member of the Vancouver Board of Trade.[83] The committee recruited a full-time staff led by former Bank of Canada research director J.E. Howes and embarked on a two-year program of study, commissioning reports on land use, infrastructure, government organization, and specific services. Ray and his committee travelled extensively in 1958 and 1959, attending conferences and visiting metropolitan agencies in San Francisco, Boston, Colorado Springs, London (England), Miami, Minneapolis, Toronto, and Tokyo.[84] In its final report, the committee recommended a two-tier arrangement similar to Metro Toronto, consolidating jurisdiction over all of the policy areas listed in its terms of reference into a single metropolitan agency.[85] As with the existing regional institutions, municipal councils would appoint board members. Ray's affinity for Metro Toronto was in evidence from the start, as he pronounced that, "if the voters in the metropolitan area of the Lower Mainland of British Columbia do decide that they want metropolitan government, its form will be similar to that of Toronto."[86] The report was approved by all committee members except for New Westminster's delegation, which agreed only to the consolidation of parks planning. Some argued for an even more encompassing entity. Without support from his council, Richmond's Robert McMath, a convinced regionalist who would serve fourteen years on the LMRPB, argued for a unified Lower Mainland government. The committee ultimately endorsed the Fraser Valley municipalities' inclusion on any future metropolitan board.[87]

Municipal leaders voiced opposition even before the final report was transmitted, and some councils repudiated committee recommendations endorsed by their own delegates. New Westminster, the City of North Vancouver, Port Coquitlam, and later Richmond rejected the formation of a metropolitan board on familiar grounds: that it would impose new costs and a new layer of unaccountable administration on residents.[88] While Burnaby's current reeve supported the plan, the district's former reeve presented a brief on behalf of the Burnaby Board of Trade, arguing that if municipalities lost control of zoning, they would lose control of economic development policy.[89] Recognizing that a referendum would likely fail, and noting that none had been required to create Metro Toronto, Ray called for a five-year trial period before putting metropolitan government to a vote.[90] Municipal opposition intensified after the Vancouver Board of Trade, with the support of the City of Vancouver's mayor, demanded that the province impose a metropolitan government without a referendum. City of North Vancouver mayor Bill Angus said the proposal smacked of Soviet Russia, and that he would "bring out the shotgun" if metro government was imposed.[91]

The premature death of Hugo Ray in 1960 deprived the proposal of its champion, and one-third of the committee's members were defeated in municipal elections later that year.[92] Although supportive of metropolitan coordination, Black had little political incentive to impose it. While retaining a strong majority in the legislature, the Socreds had lost seven seats in the 1960 election, six of them in the Lower Mainland. He formally abandoned the proposal in March 1962.[93] The result was a stalemate. The LMRPB and central-city civic elites had forcefully argued for reform, and Wesley Black had been persuaded by his staff that the consolidation of functions was needed to effectively respond to rapid metropolitan population growth. Yet suburban and valley business interests and municipalities strongly opposed any reform that would undermine local autonomy or risk the City of Vancouver dominating their affairs.

Crafting the Regional District System

While two-tier metropolitan government was off the table, some municipalities pursued voluntary collaboration. Building on the metropolitan joint committee's recommendations and with the support of the LMRPB, Burnaby, the City and District of North Vancouver, Richmond, Vancouver, and West Vancouver in 1966 formed a metropolitan parks district patterned on the water and sewer boards. They also jointly asked the minister of health to assign responsibility for air pollution to the existing water and sewer boards.[94] Still, the minister, the LMRPB, and some municipal leaders believed that a more integrated approach was needed to solve the region's problems, although a politically acceptable means of achieving it remained elusive.[95]

A solution to the conundrum was crafted by Deputy Minister James Everett Brown and his staff and enthusiastically championed by the new minister of municipal affairs, Dan Campbell. In 1964 Brown's staff quietly started work on a province-wide reform proposal that they hoped would resolve three separate technical and political problems: the coordination of planning and services in rapidly urbanizing Greater Vancouver and Victoria, disjointed and inefficient service delivery in the sparsely populated interior, and the decentralization of provincial administration from Victoria, the provincial capital. Few settlements were municipally organized outside of the Lower Mainland and southern Vancouver Island. Approximately 20 per cent of British Columbia's two million residents lived in unorganized territory, where, in the absence of counties, services were provided either directly by the province or through multiple single-purpose bodies. Province-wide, the number of such bodies providing water, fire protection, street lighting, irrigation, and other services had increased from sixty-six in 1945 to three hundred by the mid-1960s.[96] At the same time, the province sought to decentralize hospital financing and administration. Brown also contemplated devolving a variety of other provincial responsibilities to local governments, including the administration of justice and rural policing.

The proposal that emerged in 1965 was to divide the province into multi-purpose regional districts – that is, federations of municipalities and unincorporated areas whose territorial building blocks would be the province's seventy-four school districts, which the province had comprehensively reformed in the late 1940s. As the previous decade's events made clear, the political challenge was to avoid provoking resistance from municipalities protective of their autonomy and from mostly rural residents who opposed new layers of government. The province also wanted to avoid the political minefield of public ratification at all costs, and so the program was designed to avoid needing the approval of the legislature, municipalities, or residents to establish regional districts. Instead, the enabling legislation authorized the minister to act unilaterally by issuing letters patent.[97] To render this politically palatable, the districts were designed to enter life with no fixed responsibilities. Joint provision of services through the regional district would occur only at municipal initiative.[98] Even this was not an all-or-nothing proposition. Individual municipalities (or groups of electors in unorganized territories) could opt out of participation in particular services. While regional districts' territorial jurisdictions were fixed, their service areas could differ. As the minister later put it in a communication to municipalities, "It's up to you to decide how much gas you put in this vehicle – the member municipalities and areas are in the driver's seat."[99]

Following the Vancouver water and sewer board model, municipalities would finance services proportionally. Municipal representation and voting strength would be defined using a formula to ensure rough proportionality to population. Each regional district's letters patent defined its "voting unit." Each municipality's number of votes was calculated by dividing its population by the voting unit. The number of seats on the board was calculated by dividing the number of votes by five. No constituent unit could have less than one vote and one seat. The standard formula resolved a conflict in areas (especially the Lower Mainland) where substantial variation in the population size of units led large municipalities to challenge the principle of equal representation on district boards. The formula assigned large units more seats and votes than smaller units, but since the multitude of smaller units could not have fractional seats and votes, they diluted the representation of their larger peers.

As a result of these design features, the regional district model met with little controversy. With no prescribed purpose and pitched as an inter-municipal framework for collective action, the model was difficult to characterize as the imposition of a new bureaucracy or a new "level" of government. Moreover, it sufficiently resembled the format of existing special-purpose bodies that it did not appear foreign to local elites.

With provincial encouragement, twenty-eight regional districts were created between 1965 and 1969 covering virtually the entire province.[100] The government moved slowly to establish regional districts in the Lower Mainland, however. Even after the legislation was passed in 1965, it was unclear whether there would be a single regional district for the entire Lower Mainland and whether the water, sewer, and planning boards would be absorbed into it. The LMRPB's staff had advocated for a Lower Mainland–wide regional district, but municipal officials saw little use in consolidating existing regional institutions because they already functioned well. In June 1967, Minister Campbell divided the Lower Mainland into four districts corresponding to the boundaries of separately established hospital finance bodies.[101] The boundaries of the Vancouver-centred regional district aligned with those of the existing water and sewer districts. It was designated the Fraser-Burrard Regional District, as including "Vancouver" in its name would have signalled the city's dominance, which was politically insupportable. (Nonetheless, it was soon renamed the Greater Vancouver Regional District because foreign lenders were unwilling to buy bonds from a body whose name did not correspond to a recognizable place.) The remainder of the Lower Mainland was divided into three units: north of the Fraser, the Dewdney-Alouette Regional District (DARD) stretched from Pitt Meadows to Mission; south of the Fraser, the Central Fraser Valley Regional District (CFVRD) included Langley, Matsqui, Abbotsford, and Sumas; the eastern end of the Lower Mainland, from Chilliwack to Hope, was incorporated into the Fraser-Cheam Regional District (see figure 6.5). This scheme mollified Fraser Valley residents' fears of metropolitan domination while giving each rural population centre its own sphere of influence.[102] While the LMRPB would continue to advocate for the Lower Mainland's essential unity, this was overwhelmed by the logic of integrating the existing metropolitan special-purpose bodies.

Empowering the Regional Districts

The fledgling Fraser-Burrard Regional District began operating in 1967, but with an uncertain future. The water, sewer and drainage, and parks districts remained independent and actively resisted integration, while the Lower Mainland Regional Planning Board publicly and privately defended its autonomy in order to protect the integrity of its plan, the territorial scope of which overlapped with four regional districts. Over the next five years, however, all of these functions and more would be assumed by the renamed Greater Vancouver Regional District (GVRD) as the province quietly but forcefully encouraged the incremental consolidation of existing inter-municipal special-purpose bodies into the regional districts.

The existing hospital district was immediately absorbed by the new regional district. By 1972 the existing water, sewer and drainage, and parks boards were brought in as well, overcoming the resistance of their officials. The flexibility of the regional district model was evidenced by the extra-territorial participation of municipalities in particular functions. By 1973, for example, Maple Ridge and Pitt Meadows, both members of the Dewdney-Alouette Regional District, participated in the GVRD's water function, while the City of Langley, a member of the Central Fraser Valley Regional District, belonged to the Greater Vancouver Sewer and Drainage Board. The City and Township of Langley, Matsqui, and Maple Ridge participated in the GVRD's parks function. The boards' different memberships and

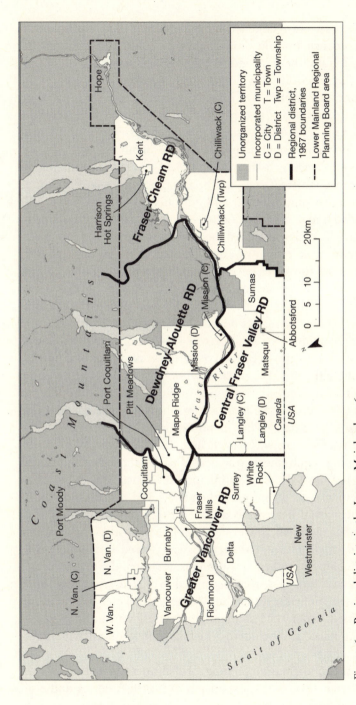

Figure 6.5 Regional districts in the Lower Mainland, 1967

Note: The provincial government divided the Lower Mainland into four regional districts in 1967. They assumed joint authority over the Official Regional Plan when the Regional Planning Board was dissolved in 1969.

The following labels appear on the map:

Legend:
Unorganized territory
Incorporated municipality
C = City   T = Town
D = District   Twp = Township
Regional district, 1967 boundaries
Lower Mainland Regional Planning Board area

Hope
Kent
Fraser-Cheam RD
Harrison Hot Springs
Chilliwack (C)
Chilliwack (Twp)
Mission (C)
Sumas
Dewdney-Alouette RD
Mission (D)
Central Fraser Valley RD
Abbotsford
Port Coquitlam
Pitt Meadows
Maple Ridge
Fraser River
Matsqui
Langley (C)
Langley (D)
Canada
USA
Coast Mountains
Coquitlam
Port Moody
Fraser Mills
Surrey
White Rock
Port Moody
N. Van. (D)
Greater Vancouver RD
Burnaby
Delta
New Westminster
USA
N. Van. (C)
W. Van.
Vancouver
Richmond
Strait of Georgia

20km
0   5   10
N

statutory bases were reconciled by maintaining the legal fiction of their independence. In reality, the GVRD functioned as a single administrative entity, and the same municipal delegates served on all boards governing the functions in which they participated.

These functions were soon joined by others: capital borrowing (1969), labour relations and public housing (1971), air pollution control (1972), and solid waste management (1974). Not all such integration occurred unanimously, and some members required provincial suasion. Concerned about the centrifugal tendency inherent in the opt-out mechanism, the GVRD board appointed a subcommittee to study its emerging political and administrative structures.[103] It recommended that certain functions become mandatory for all members. The province then amended the Municipal Act in 1970 to effectively eliminate municipal opt-outs. Thereafter the public housing, water, and sewer functions became mandatory for all municipalities if a simple majority of board members, with a majority of votes under the statutory formula, agreed. (This overcame resistance to the integration of the water and sewer boards.) Moreover, any other function would become mandatory on approval of two-thirds of board members possessing two-thirds of the votes, and if two-thirds of participating municipal councils consented. Tennant and Zirnhelt see this change as instrumental: the province initially permitted opting out in order to allay the fears of local leaders; however, the minister was prepared to eliminate it when it posed problems.[104] By then, the regional district system was entrenched, and the majority or supermajority voting requirements transferred political conflict and risk to the municipal level. If some municipalities mustered the votes to impose their will on a minority, then they, and not the provincial government, would bear the consequences. Such conflict remained more potential than real, however. Much like the collaborative water and sewer districts before it, the GVRD was viewed as a limited technical partnership of municipal sovereigns. Regional districts were not designed to have, nor were they permitted to evolve, strong executive or independent political leadership. As a result, the regional district boards gained experience at managing functions but were rarely compelled to make authoritative decisions that might alienate municipalities or the province.

Viewed in the normative context of technocratic optimism that fuelled postwar government expansion in North America and elsewhere, the regional districts' establishment represents the same rationalist impulse exemplified by Ontario's Local Government Review, Minnesota's creation of the Met Council, and the empowerment of counties and councils of governments across the United States. Campbell and Brown were directly influenced by prevailing consolidationist public administration ideas, in particular the desire to bring metropolitan governing structures in line with the "real" city to increase efficiency and improve democratic accountability.[105] The effort was more effective in Great Vancouver than in other North American jurisdictions because inter-municipal decision-making processes were already deeply institutionalized and the single-tier local government system meant that there were no challengers, such as counties, for the same role.

Integrating Land-Use and Infrastructure Planning

At first it seemed that the province's four regional planning boards, including the LMRPB, might co-exist with the regional districts. At the end of 1967, Minister Campbell told the LMRPB that he expected it to continue.[106] In 1969, however, he dissolved the boards and transferred their authority to the corresponding regional districts. In the Lower Mainland, a Review Panel of mayors and reeves was established to maintain the Official Regional Plan and coordinate the planning activities of the regional districts.[107] This move was roundly criticized by Vancouver's planning advocates, who believed that the board's dissolution was retribution for its public opposition to the province's expropriation of 1,620 hectares of land in Delta, which had been zoned in the ORP for exclusive agricultural use, to build a new port facility (the Roberts Bank Superport) and associated rail links.[108] The opposition NDP vigorously attacked the government in the legislature, characterizing the LMRPB's dissolution as a "hatchet job" designed to eliminate planning altogether.[109] The decision was also opposed by several suburban and valley municipalities, the Greater Vancouver Real Estate Board, the Associated Chambers of Commerce of the Lower Mainland, and the Matsqui-Sumas-Abbotsford ratepayers.[110] Minister Campbell denied that the board's dissolution was connected to the superport controversy – indeed, he asserted that his decision to dissolve the planning board predated it. He publicly emphasized the necessity of regional planning, provided that it was accountable to local governments, and he expressed full confidence in the ability of the regional districts to collectively maintain the regional plan.[111] Still, he made it clear that the province was prepared to override regional land-use plans and regulations should they conflict with its own policy agenda.

There was an undeniable logic to transferring regional planning authority to the regional districts, whose basic purpose was to integrate policymaking with service delivery. The ORP's legal status was unchanged. Its administration by a general-purpose regional district had the potential to more directly integrate land-use planning with infrastructure systems while reducing the visibility of planning expenditures. Moreover, the regional district's proportional representation and weighted voting system met the City of Vancouver's demand for greater influence over the planning board.[112]

Local Autonomy and the Calculus of Provincial Intervention

The provincial executive had the legal authority, and, by virtue of sustained single-party dominance, the political autonomy, to unilaterally intervene in the region's governance and planning. It chose, however, to achieve its objectives through means that were less visible and disruptive: incentives, regulation, and quiet suasion. British Columbia did not seek to comprehensively reorganize local government in the Lower Mainland during the 1960s because wall-to-wall single-tier local government was both less complex and more flexible than Ontario's inherited patchwork of counties and separated cities. The long-standing water and sewer districts, as well as the regional planning board, were the templates for the new regional districts. With each institutional development, the principles of inter-municipal voluntarism, proportionality, and delegated municipal representation were maintained. This approach not only preserved the image of local autonomy, but it also ensured that the local level remained the primary venue of political conflict over urban development. Nevertheless, the province could impose its priorities when it saw fit, as exemplified by the Roberts Bank Superport project.

THE PROVINCE AND THE REGION SINCE 1975

The defeat of W.A.C. Bennett's Social Credit government in 1972 signalled a profound shift in British Columbia's body politic and reflected the emergence of a new normative context. The developmental agenda that had governed the province since the end of the

Second World War no longer captured the imagination of urban citizens, whose political expression increasingly turned on matters of identity and lifestyle. With the founding of Greenpeace in 1972, Vancouver emerged as an important node in global environmental movement networks. The progressive consensus in favour of efficient urbanization came under fire as human settlement itself was increasingly seen as a threat to fragile ecosystems. The new urban middle class became interested in the city as a living space, mobilizing against expressway projects and neighbourhood redevelopment, which they saw as compromising quality of life.[113] Residents and neighbourhood associations demanded not merely to be informed and consulted, but to be directly involved in policymaking. As in other North American cities, the election of reform mayors and councils was symptomatic of growing public scepticism of expert knowledge, elite consensus, and economic rationality. The election of Vancouver Mayor Art Phillips and his progressive council slate in 1973 ended the long dominance of the business-friendly Non-Partisan Association on city council and inaugurated a new focus on neighbourhood livability. As a result of this political and normative shift, the relationship between the province and regional districts and local governments became increasingly adversarial following Social Credit's return to power in 1975.

Re-legitimizing Planning amid Normative Change: The Livable Region Program

The changing normative context and a deteriorating economy might have delegitimized planning altogether. This did not occur for two reasons. First, as discussed, the exemplar of early postwar planning, the LMRPB, was dissolved and its jurisdiction transferred to a new institution – a planning department of the GVRD – whose public image and authority had not yet been fixed. In this fluid context, the new planning director, a genial easterner named Harry Lash, adapted the LMRPB's regional planning objectives and land-use concept to changing times.[114] Second, the rise of a new generation of planners allowed new relationships to be forged. Disillusioned, most members of the LMRPB's staff had moved on after its abolition in 1969. The GVRD embarked on an unprecedented program of consultation not only with municipal officials, professionals, and interest groups, but also with the general public. Lash and his team believed that the GVRD's plan should be developed in accordance with what "the people" wanted.

A contemporary of Oberlander's at McGill, Lash had worked for public planning agencies in Edmonton, Toronto, and Montreal, and had come to the conclusion that orthodox land-use planning methods – technical research by professionals leading to the preparation of official zoning maps and associated policies – were a dead end. In his view, planning's core task was goal setting, a process that was political, not technical. Only with public support and full political engagement could planning be effective. Two public engagement processes commenced. The Public Program, run in-house by UBC social work professor Leonard Minsky, consisted of a series of public meetings. An Urban Futures Project mounted by UBC geography professor and Vancouver city councillor Walter Hardwick surveyed the attitudes of 1,500 residents on a range of economic, social, and environmental issues.

On this basis, the GVRD adopted a vision statement, *Livable Region 1976/1986*, in 1975. While often referred to as a "plan," it was not a traditional regulatory instrument. Rather, it was considered by Lash and his staff to be a set of continuously evolving proposals to guide ongoing policymaking. The overarching goal was livability. This was a qualitative shift from the LMRPB's earlier economic focus on conservation and efficiency and may be read as a mirror to the postmaterial political and social transformation occurring in the city and in the broader society.

Occurring in the context of the Club of Rome's *Limits to Growth*, which forecast humanity's imminent outstripping of the planet's carrying capacity, the Public Program revealed widespread anti-growth sentiment.[115] Lash's group responded with a proposal to distribute forecast population and employment growth across the region in such a way as to create areas of relative jobs-housing balance. The final vision statement contained growth targets for sectors of the region and proposals to decentralize employment to mixed-use "regional town centres" linked by a new light-rail rapid transit system.

The Livable Region Program (LRP) represented a far-reaching attempt to do planning differently – to "bring the people in" by developing a vision on the basis of shared values rather than narrow technical criteria. While the LRP eschewed static "blueprint" planning – a trap into which Lash believed the ORP had fallen – it articulated a generalized land-use concept that updated and nested within the

LMRPB's vision of "cities in a sea of green." The division of the Lower Mainland into metropolitan and rural valley regional districts, combined with the creation of the Agricultural Land Reserve, enabled the GVRD to shift the focus of regional planning from rural fringe development to the internal structure of the city. The result was a translation of the LMRPB's polycentric vision of a region of self-contained valley towns connected by highways to a metropolis of high-density mixed-use nodes connected by transit.

Yet transit was the one component of metropolitan infrastructure over which the GVRD had no control. The diesel and electric bus systems in the Vancouver and Victoria areas were operated by BC Hydro, the province-wide electric power utility nationalized by the Bennett government in 1961.[116] While the GVRD had voted in 1971 to assume jurisdiction over transit, the province ultimately retained control because it and the regional district could not agree on a cost-sharing formula. Although the GVRD's policy relationship to transportation infrastructure remained unresolved, the LRP vision would guide the expansion of the other systems under its control, principally water and sewer services.

Reconciling the LRP with the ORP

As the Livable Region Program concluded, it became clear that its implementation would require its translation into orthodox land-use regulation. Municipal politicians on the GVRD board pressured Lash and his staff to produce something more concrete – pressure that he resisted and that ultimately led to his departure. The natural instrument for moving forward was the 1966 ORP, which, if unloved by Lash and his crew, continued to be maintained and amended. With provincial encouragement, the Lower Mainland Review Panel created in 1969 to coordinate the four regional districts' administration of the ORP began discussing a formal update in September 1974. With provincial funding, the panel reviewed the ORP between 1978 and 1980. It concluded that the ORP's land-use designations, later reinforced by the ALR, had successfully slowed the urbanization of agricultural and floodplain land and the conversion of industrial land to residential uses.[117] More important was its role as an "inspiration and framework" for municipal planning, which had become considerably more sophisticated in the intervening years. The report also noted that, while rooted in the concerns of an earlier time, the LMRPB's land-use concept and policies were compatible with rising public interest in environmental quality, and so "establishing the relevance of the Official Regional Plan to contemporary circumstances is part of the challenge facing those responsible."[118]

The update was controversial among some municipal leaders. Although they were consulted, the review was a bureaucratically driven process. Perhaps forgetting that the 1966 plan remained in effect, municipal councillors in Delta, Surrey, and elsewhere groused that the revised plan undermined local autonomy.[119] Residents, councillors, and community groups in Surrey opposed not only the designation of large "urban reserve" areas that the municipality had designated as large-lot rural residential but also the regional plan's apparent resurrection of industrial zones that the city had earlier abandoned due to community opposition.[120] Surreyites were ultimately satisfied by terminological sleight of hand: the creation of a new "Urban 2" designation that permitted large-lot residential development yet was functionally equivalent to the "urban reserve" zone.

The revised ORP adopted by the regional district boards in October 1980 maintained and modernized the 1966 plan by bringing the agricultural zoning in line with the ALR, incorporated several of the LRP's features, and providing more detailed guidelines for different categories of urban and rural development.[121] The LRP's vision of mixed-use "regional town centres" was extended to the rest of the region, effectively fusing two ideas: nodal development within the contiguous urbanized area and the concentration of valley growth into existing towns. It also mapped existing and proposed transportation corridors. GVRD planner and review leader Ken Cameron publicly reconciled the LRP's policy statement with the ORP's regulatory framework using an appropriate metaphor: "The ORP provides the lot and the foundation of the house [while] the livable region program determines what the shape and the colour of the house is going to be and who is going to live in each room."[122]

Regional Planning Is Dead; Long Live Regional Planning

The ORP's revival was short-lived. In 1983, Bill Bennett's Social Credit government abolished statutory regional planning, and with it, the regional plan, in the name of efficiency and local autonomy.[123] Bennett's government responded to the deep recession of the early 1980s with a Thatcherite program of state retrenchment and marketization that was, in the words of journalist Allen Garr, "one of the most radical programs for social and economic change to hit the western world since the Second World War."[124] Debated for all of twenty-five minutes in the legislature, regional planning's elimination was but a small part of this agenda.[125] Nonetheless, the outcome devastated planning's advocates in Greater Vancouver, who saw the three-decade-long battle for a binding regional plan lost in an instant.

The plan's annulment did not lead to immediate changes in suburban development patterns, because the deep recession had slowed urban growth and the ALR remained in intact. While the Bennett Socreds had been no friends of the ALR in opposition and had called for its abolition in their victorious 1975 election campaign, they did not seek to dismantle it once in office. It had become popular with individual farmers, who were a crucial component of the Social Credit electoral base. A 1977 province-wide survey found that 80 per cent of farmers supported the ALR, with rates not much lower in the Lower Mainland.[126] The BC Federation of Agriculture, the farmers' lobby group, reversed its opposition and defended the system. Surveys of Vancouver-region residents found that agricultural land protection was a top-of-mind concern for urban, suburban, and rural residents alike.[127] The ALR's popularity, especially among the urban middle class, was in part the product of the ALC's reframing of agricultural protection as a livability issue rather than in relation to efficiency or the economic productivity of land.[128] This insulated it from political threat by linking it to the new urban postmaterial values that also animated the LRP. While the Social Credit government responded more permissively to applications for the exclusion of land from the ALR, it had no political interest in abolishing a popular program.[129] The long-term result has been the relative stability of the agricultural land base in the Lower Mainland and elsewhere in the province. Oberlander and Wilson's regional land-use concept remained intact.

Municipal leaders' appetite for coordinated regional planning re-emerged as economic growth returned in the late 1980s. Civic optimism bloomed following Vancouver's hosting of the Expo 86 world's fair.[130] After regional planning's abolition, the GVRD had maintained a "development services" department as a clearinghouse for land-use information and planning advice, but its limited resources and voluntary nature undermined its effectiveness. In 1988, the GVRD board formed a new development services committee to explore deeper regional collaboration. The ambitious and hard-driving Vancouver mayor (and future provincial Liberal premier) Gordon Campbell was persuaded to chair it. Elected to council in 1984 and as mayor in 1986, Campbell had served as executive assistant to progressive mayor Art Phillips between 1972 and 1976, during which time Phillips had served on the GVRD board and supported the LRP. The board also authorized the hiring of a new department head: New Westminster chief planner Ken Cameron, who had led the ORP review a decade earlier. The immediate goal was to put inter-municipal coordination on a more solid footing in order to respond to intensifying development pressures.

Campbell's role prior to his accession to provincial politics in 1993 was pivotal. He set the agenda and, perhaps more importantly, the tone. As long as regional planning and plans had no statutory basis, policymaking could occur only by inter-municipal consensus, which Campbell worked tirelessly to build. Despite representing the City of Vancouver, he perceived his GVRD role as distinct from his position as mayor and made a point of presenting himself a spokesperson for the regional interest.

In 1988–89, the GVRD took stock of the earlier Livable Region exercise, which retained great symbolic value among planners and area politicians. Planner Gerard Farry referred to the LRP period as the "Camelot days of regional planning," while Gordon Campbell characterized it as beyond criticism "because it was part of the mythos of what Greater Vancouver was."[131] A draft regional vision statement adopted the LRP's livability frame, equating it with environmental quality, a growing economy, and social equity. In 1989, Campbell launched a well-publicized consultation process, called Choosing Our Future, to identify goals and build community and municipal support for them. UBC's Walter Hardwick was asked to reprise the Urban Futures survey of residents, while the GVRD held public meetings and convened topic-based "challenge seminars" with international experts. Ultimately four thousand people participated between December 1989 and April 1990. The consultations revealed that people favoured a balance between environmental protection and economic growth.[132] This led to the articulation of fifty-four "regional actions" that reiterated the livability focus and rearticulated the LRP land-use concept of urban intensification coupled with rural land protection.[133] The GVRD board adopted the regional actions in September 1990. Campbell, Cameron, and GVRD communications and education manager Judy Kirk immediately embarked on a tour of every municipal council to introduce and promote them. While municipal councils were broadly supportive, some were concerned about the fiscal burdens their implementation might impose.[134]

By 1991–92, municipalities supported codifying the actions in a more specific regional plan, although its form and authority were not yet clear. Stakeholder conferences convened by the GVRD put flesh on the goal statements. The LRP's regional town centres policy was reaffirmed, and the notion of a "Green Zone" of protected rural areas supplemental to the ALR took shape. The process was designed to maintain local initiative and discretion within regional goals. The action statement called for the creation of a protected rural area but left its definition to municipalities. Municipalities ultimately came forward with proposals that would voluntarily foreclose urbanization on half the developable land in the GVRD. Importantly, the large developer-builders were supportive of a regional plan because of the investment certainty it provided. The provincial chapter of the Urban Development Institute, which represented larger developers, organized seminars on the need for more coordinated regional development.[135]

Deliberately referencing the earlier Livable Region Program, a draft *Livable Region Strategic Plan* (LRSP) was adopted by the GVRD board in late 1994. It mapped the Green Zone and designated and set growth targets for transit-connected "growth centres." To reduce congestion on river crossings, as well as development pressure on floodplain and unprotected agricultural land, it also sought to direct most growth to a "growth concentration area" that comprised the Burrard Peninsula, Anmore, Coquitlam, Port Coquitlam, and Port Moody, plus parts of Surrey and Delta across the Fraser River from New Westminster. (Richmond and Delta were excluded due to their earthquake- and flood-prone location, south of the Fraser River.)

While most councils quickly endorsed the plan, Surrey, Langley Township, Port Moody, and Richmond withheld approval. Surrey voted in 1994 to partially reject higher housing densities.[136] Both Surrey and Langley Township were concerned that the plan obliged them to reverse prior decisions. Both were mollified by agreements with the GVRD that explicitly grandfathered existing designations. The GVRD found Port Moody noncompliant with the plan when it refused to commit to a future population target in the absence of a funded capital investment plan for transit expansion. When a majority of Port Moody's pro-LRSP councillors were defeated in the 1996 elections, the new council unilaterally reduced the growth targets specified in its municipal plan.[137] Richmond was concerned that its exclusion from the growth concentration area would undermine its case for a rapid transit extension. Richmond councillors threatened to quit the GVRD, and Mayor Halsey-Brant removed councillor Bob Bose from his position as chair of the regional district's strategic planning committee.[138] The council approved a population target in excess of its agreed target in the LRSP. In a replay of the debate at the time of the LRSP's adoption, the GVRD and Richmond made a deal to increase the target.[139] Fearing for their electoral futures, local politicians in Coquitlam, Langley, Maple Ridge, and Surrey secured similar modifications.[140] While these changes were largely symbolic, they are symptomatic of the politics generated by fiscal pressure on land-use objectives.

Even when all municipalities endorsed the LRSP, it still lacked legal sanction. This would be provided by a new provincial government in 1995. After two decades in the political wilderness, the New Democratic Party had ended Social Credit's sixteen years in office in 1991. Led by former Vancouver mayor Mike Harcourt (who had sat on the GVRD board during the LRP period in the 1970s), the NDP was more urban in its policy focus and more sympathetic to planning than the Social Credit government it had replaced. Minister of Municipal Affairs Darlene Marzari, a former Vancouver councillor and community activist, worked with GVRD chief planner Ken Cameron to craft legislation. She feared that some of her cabinet colleagues (including future premier Glen Clark) would subvert the collaborative model developed by the GVRD by inserting the province directly into the process. In her view, provincial unilateralism would only generate conflict and prevent local governments from behaving as "consenting adults." Her overriding goal was to design a provincial framework that would "enhance the autonomy and underwrite the strengths of the municipal structures" by creating incentives to bottom-up collaborative action.[141]

The Growth Strategies Act (1995) passed in the legislature with only one dissenting vote. (LRSP champion Gordon Campbell was now leader of the main opposition party in the provincial legislature.) Under the legislation, a "regional growth strategy" – the word "plan" was still toxic in some parts of the province – would come into effect only with the consent of all affected local governments. Each municipality would have two years after the strategy's adoption to prepare a "regional context statement" detailing municipal implementation actions. In the event that a municipality disagreed with an adopted regional plan, or if the regional district rejected a regional context statement, a binding arbitration process would be invoked. Richmond's refusal to endorse the plan would have been the first test of this process, but a last-minute deal was worked out that designated a "strategic growth area" in exchange for the city's commitment to develop earthquake and flood mitigation plans.[142] Regional context statements for all member municipalities were agreed by 1999.

Institutional changes have further integrated regional planning. Internally, the GVRD restructured its administration to bring land-use planning into closer alignment with infrastructure provision.[143] The GVRD's membership expanded in two stages between 1988 and 1995, adding Pitt Meadows, Maple Ridge, and Langley City and Township. The remaining three Lower Mainland regional districts merged into a new Fraser Valley Regional District (FVRD) in 1995, which began to develop a regional growth strategy of its own that adopted many of the same principles as the GVRD plan.[144] The FVRD is no longer truly rural. Urban growth accelerated after Abbotsford and Matsqui Districts merged into a new City of Abbotsford in 1995. By 2011, three-quarters of the regional district's population lived in Abbotsford and Chilliwack's urban settlement areas.

Provincial Unilateralism and the Limits of the Regional Land-Use Consensus

Despite ongoing fights over municipal growth targets – including during the LRSP's *Metro Vancouver 2040* update in 2011 – the general consensus on the land-use concept first articulated in the early 1950s has held. The ALR remains in effect, foreclosing development on agricultural land across the region. Exclusive non-urban zoning – the successor to the Green Zone – is a foundation of the 2011 plan. The growth concentration area has been replaced by a tighter "urban containment area" that separates urban and rural zones, restricts infrastructure extension outside of contiguous urban areas, and seeks to channel population and housing growth to areas with frequent transit service.[145] An important signal of the acceptance of regional identity is the GVRD board's unanimous decision to rebrand itself as "Metro Vancouver" in 2007 – an extraordinary step, given other municipalities' history of suspicion of the city.

The Lower Mainland regional land-use consensus has been sustained for several reasons. The long tenures of municipal elected officials and planning staff at the regional district and local levels are an important factor, as is the long-term existence of inter-municipal institutions that routinize ongoing interaction between them. Moreover, dating back to the 1950s, the movement of personnel between UBC's planning school, the planning profession, public-sector planning authorities, and electoral politics has also reproduced planning ideas. (It is striking how many municipal and provincial politicians are UBC planning graduates.)

Achieving locally defined regional objectives has been frustrated, however, by provincial actions that directly undermine them. The Growth Strategies Act was designed to insulate regional goal setting and land-use planning from provincial intervention, yet local governments, the regional district, and TransLink (the regional transit operator) must rely on provincial funding for large capital projects. On the occasion of the Act's passage in 1995, then-GVRD chair and Richmond mayor Greg Halsey-Brandt acknowledged that the province had to do more than simply enable inter-municipal regional planning: "Unless the government comes up with the other half of the coin and puts in the transportation infrastructure for us, it will be very difficult for us to deliver on the promises of [reducing] air pollution and traffic congestion."[146] More recently, his successor as Richmond mayor and GVRD finance committee chair, Malcolm Brodie, stated in 2011 that, without provincial financial support, dramatic increases in user fees for water and sewer services would be needed to meet growth-related demand.[147]

Provincial unilateralism has been most evident in the transportation domain. The conventional light-rail system envisioned in the 1975 LRP was not built, due to the province's failure to commit capital funds. Instead, an elevated monorail – SkyTrain – using experimental technology was constructed for Expo 86, the theme of which was transportation and communication. Glen Clark, who became premier after Mike Harcourt's resignation in 1996, overrode the GVRD's preference for light rail for a Coquitlam line in 1998, imposing the more expensive SkyTrain technology instead. When the province failed to pay the difference, the new Millennium Line was truncated to serve only northern Burnaby and New Westminster.[148] It would be almost two decades before the opening of the Coquitlam extension, now known as the Evergreen Line, in 2016.

In principle, the provincial government's creation of a new regional transportation planning and operations body called TransLink in 1999

was supposed to bring transportation policy into alignment with the
GVRD's growth strategy.[149] Instead, its dependency on the province
for capital funds has created new avenues for provincial unilateralism.
The mode, route selection, and financing of a new SkyTrain line connecting downtown Vancouver to the airport and to Richmond's town
centre were driven as much by the intergovernmental politics of hosting
the 2010 Winter Olympics and Premier Campbell's desire for a legacy
project before leaving politics in 2011 as by forecast needs and technical requirements.[150] In their 2013 election platform, the governing
Liberals, led by Christy Clark following Gordon Campbell's departure,
promised a referendum on any new transportation taxes in Greater
Vancouver.[151] In 2015, voters defeated a ten-year transportation plan
developed by the region's mayors, its $7.7-billion price tag funded by
a 0.5 per cent sales tax increase. The Liberal government did little to
defend the plan, and taxpayers' rights groups successfully portrayed
it as a tax grab by an unaccountable agency. Lacking sufficient own-
source fiscal resources, TransLink had been unable to sustain incremental capital investment in new lines and service frequency
improvements.[152] The provincial insistence on a tax increase referendum – something unprecedented in the postwar Canadian context – fits
poorly with its unilateral decision-making on highway and bridge
infrastructure. The Liberal government's replacements of the Port
Mann Bridge, which opened in 2012, and the Massey Tunnel, which
broke ground in 2017, required no referendum. Both projects cost,
or are forecast to cost, about $6 billion dollars – almost as much as
the mayors' ten-year plan. Both were also opposed by Metro Vancouver
and Translink, which argued that they undermined the policy of concentrating growth north of the Fraser River. Provincial-municipal
relations have taken a different direction since the NDP's return to
power in 2017 with a minority government supported by the small
Green Party. Its electoral base concentrated in metropolitan Vancouver
and Victoria, the new government put the Massey Tunnel replacement
on hold pending review, and has committed to funding, along with
the federal government, the mayors' transit plan.

CONCLUSION

Much as in the Toronto case, Vancouver illustrates the benefits and
costs of the Westminster system's institutional foundations – the
potential for decisive and programmatic policymaking, especially in
the context of single-party dominance – but also its potential to be

disrupted by normative and political change. Metropolitan institutions have functioned best when politically supported by the provincial government. The Vancouver case also illustrates how the design of metropolitan institutions structures the incentives in which local actors operate. Indeed, the degree of inter-municipal collective action in Greater Vancouver has been unusually high compared to the other cases surveyed in this book as well as to other North American regions.

While British Columbia's provincial government was perhaps less visible and forceful in municipal affairs than Ontario's, its interventions were nonetheless essential to the establishment, maintenance, and effectiveness of regional institutions. As in Ontario, municipal insolvency during the Great Depression spurred the British Columbia government to institutionalize new capacities for the oversight of municipal affairs, and more robust land-use planning was a component of the postwar provincial "New Deal." While initially favouring two-tier metropolitan government reform for Greater Vancouver, the Social Credit government used carrots and sticks to encourage inter-municipal problem-solving. On the sewer issue, this took the form of more stringent water quality regulations, which compelled municipalities to the table. On the ORP, holdout municipalities were brought into line through quiet suasion on the part of the minister and his deputy. On the more thoroughgoing metropolitan integration of services, the regional district model was designed to infringe as little as possible on local initiative while incrementally pushing municipalities toward consolidating regional functions.

At the same time, institutionalized inter-municipal interaction through the water and sewer districts and the regional planning board during the 1950s and 1960s incubated a cadre of regionally minded local politicians. The consolidation of single-purpose bodies into the multi-purpose regional districts in 1967 reinforced inter-municipal collaboration while enabling more-integrated policymaking. While conflict never disappeared between the central city and its suburbs, and between both and the valley hinterland, the governing model managed it even as new challenges emerged.

New demands for public participation in planning and new concerns about the environment and quality of life threatened to delegitimize planning institutions and policies as the normative context changed in the late 1960s. Legitimacy was restored, however, by Harry Lash and the GVRD planners, who crafted a radical public engagement process that framed regional planning in terms of community values and the preservation of livability. The LMRPB's land-use concept was adapted to these new priorities through the Livable Region Program, the Agricultural Land Reserve, and subsequent planning processes. Uploading urban containment from the local to the provincial level redirected the GVRD's focus from the suburbanizing fringe to the internal structure of the city – where growth would go and how people would move. A new urban professional class sought to nurture the fragile complexity of the city, while protecting rural amenity spaces. Hitched to a livability discourse, urban containment attained totemic significance for planners and the general public alike. The refounding of regional planning and collaborative governance in the new normative context sustained commitment to the land-use concept even after the province abolished its statutory basis in 1983. The voluntary crafting of the LRSP during the late 1980s, with all of the attendant politicking and compromising, signalled the deep embeddedness of collaborative practices, public participation, and the land-use concept itself, as has the municipalities' continuing collaboration on updating and implementing the plan, as well as on prioritizing complementary transportation infrastructure projects.

Vancouver may be interpreted as an extreme case – an embodiment of collaborative "new regionalism" more thoroughgoing than found elsewhere in North America. As a model of sustained inter-municipal collaboration, it may serve as an example for bottom-up American regionalism.[153] In the Canadian context, elements of the regional district model have been copied in Alberta, New Brunswick, and Quebec. Still, the idiosyncratic historical evolution of British Columbia's inter-municipal regional governance model must be recognized. Greater Vancouver municipalities had been collaborating for decades through the sewer and water districts, and so were accustomed to multilateral policymaking and conflict management, along with the model's proportional allocation of representation, costs, and benefits. Even if identical institutions were created in a different context, this spirit of inter-municipal engagement and accommodation would not appear overnight. Casual observers of Vancouver's regional governance may overlook the essential historical and contemporary role of the provincial government, not just in creating institutions but in providing them with sustained political, fiscal, and legal support. In this regard, the Vancouver case also illustrates the limits of voluntary collaboration and strong land-use regulation in the context of scarce resources. As in Toronto, access to fiscal resources is controlled by the provincial government, which in recent decades has been an inconsistent enabler and supporter of regional policymaking. As a result, investment in capital infrastructure, and in particular for transportation, has not kept pace with population growth and physical urban development in the later postwar period.

7

Portland

Like Vancouver, Portland is celebrated as a "capital of good planning."[1] Since the late 1960s, a combination of downtown revitalization, innovative public-transportation planning, and state-level urban containment policies have enabled Portland to evade much of the core-area disinvestment and scattered fringe development experienced by many other American cities. Portland's multi-purpose metropolitan service district, or "Metro" – the only such directly elected body in the United States – is also a touchstone for urban governance reformers. There was, however, nothing inevitable about Portland's path of institutional and policy development. Each element was fiercely contested by contending advocates who strategically exploited Oregon's political institutions, which are arguably distinguished by unusually open access to external interests, even when compared to other American states.

Portland Metro is something of a "successful failure" because early postwar elite reformers failed to achieve their basic objective: regulating local government boundary change and consolidating the region's multiplicity of special-purpose infrastructure management and service-delivery bodies into a single operating authority. Through their efforts, several regional institutions were created between 1967 and 1970: an advisory regional planning body, a supervisory authority for local government boundary change (patterned, as in Minnesota, on the Ontario Municipal Board), and a flexible multi-purpose service district analogous to British Columbia's regional districts. Each was hobbled at birth by trade-offs made during legislative bargaining and by later erosion of its legitimacy and authority as opponents mobilized through the legislature, the courts, and electoral politics. Only through strategic

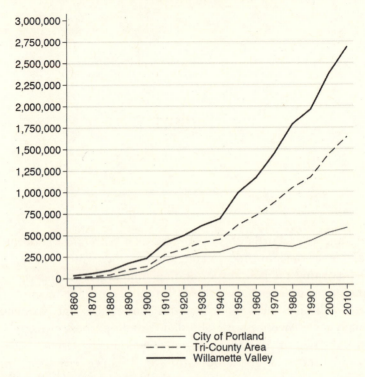

Figure 7.1 Portland population by zone, 1860–2010

Note: The City of Portland captured most growth in the tri-county area, and in the Willamette Valley as a whole, through the 1920s. Portland's population levelled off after the 1940s, as most growth flowed to other parts of Multnomah, Clackamas, and Washington Counties, and in other communities to the south.

use of Oregon's ballot initiative did reformers succeed, in 1978, in merging the regional planning body and the service district into the directly elected Metro. While Metro never became the infrastructure operator envisioned by its creators, it ultimately found purpose as the regional administrator of state land-use policies, including a regulatory urban containment device, the urban growth boundary. The result is the inverse of the metropolitan institutions established in the other three case cities: a directly elected regional policymaking body with few operating responsibilities. Its effectiveness is due to its adroit cultivation of advocacy groups and voters and the integration of local governments into its policymaking processes.

The Portland case illustrates both the pivotal role of state government in structuring policy responses to urbanization and the limits generated

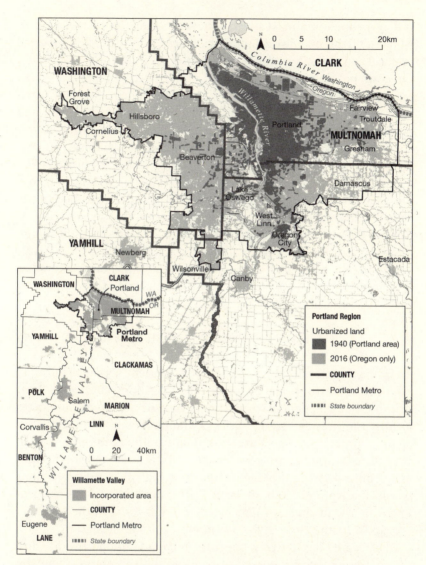

Figure 7.2 Administrative boundaries and urbanization in Portland and the Willamette Valley

Sources: 1940 urbanization redrawn from maps in *The Three Basic Services*; 2016 developed land redrawn from Portland Metro, Regional Land Information System.

by the institutional foundations of Oregon's version of the separated-powers system. For much of its history, Oregon has been both indecisive and irresolute – unable to rapidly and programmatically respond to policy problems and sustain policy programs over time. As in Minnesota, this inability delayed action until a distinct and short-lived political and normative conjuncture. In the late 1960s and early 1970s, Oregon's political parties converged on the need to protect resource extraction and agriculture from urban encroachment. At a time when trust in government and deference to elites was still high, committed policy entrepreneurs, working inside and outside the legislature, built coalitions in favour of metropolitan governance and land-use planning reforms. Legislators enacted these externally generated proposals in an atmosphere of urgency. The decline of bipartisan urban-rural consensus and rise of geographically and ideologically polarized politics signalled the end of this conjuncture. Similar to Vancouver's regional district, the evolution of Portland Metro also reveals how the design of institutions may facilitate collaboration and promote social learning. While the directly elected Portland Metro was not structured as a federation of local governments, institutionalized engagement with them has diffused conflicts and promoted collective action.

THE STATE AND THE PORTLAND REGION, 1848–1945

To frame the later discussion, we must first briefly survey the distinct political and institutional contexts of policymaking in Oregon. As in British Columbia, political conflict in Oregon has long pitted urbanites against rural residents, big business against labour, and metropolis against hinterland. The state's dominant political idiom has been populism. Indeed, Clucas and Henkels characterize Oregon politics as a conflict between progressive and conservative populists, factions of which are present in both parties.[2] This populism has been reproduced by the institutions that make up what is called the "Oregon system."[3] At the turn of the twentieth century, legislator William U'Ren secured legislative support for referenda to constitutionalize direct democracy in the form of ballot initiative, referral (whereby the legislature "refers" an adopted bill to the people for ratification), and citizen-initiated recall of public officials. The adoption of the open primary undermined party elites' control of candidate nomination, reducing state parties' organizational coherence and discipline. Well into the postwar period, Oregon legislators served on a part-time basis, were paid per diem, met in time-limited biennial sessions, and did their work without professional support. These factors undermined the cohesion and policymaking capacity of party caucuses in the legislature and privileged policy development by extra-governmental organized interests. Successful state politicians have won office by appealing to "common sense" rather than rigid ideology, developing personal followings, and mobilizing party factions and special interests.[4] Oregon also has a plural executive: the governor, state treasurer, attorney general, and secretary of state are separately elected statewide and may belong to different parties. The result: even by American standards, an unusually fragmented politics with many veto players.

This fragmentation is reflected in Oregon's local government organization and in the state-local relationship. Unlike in Minnesota and other midwestern states, where the survey grid became the basis of local government boundaries, and in contrast to British Columbia, where the province had encouraged "wall-to-wall" local government in settled areas, incorporated urban settlements floated like islands in largely unincorporated space. Although Oregon was divided into counties on accession to statehood in 1859, these functioned as administrative divisions of state government and provided few services. Residents of unincorporated areas were served by an expanding array of special taxing districts, which reduced the incentive to municipal incorporation. The state's legal authority over and capacity to assert an interest in the local government system was also constitutionally restricted at an early stage. Municipal home rule was constitutionalized in 1906.[5] As amended, the state constitution prohibited the legislature from unilaterally establishing, amending, or dissolving municipal corporations by special act, and, at the same time, citizens were granted broad authority to enact and amend home rule charters for new or existing cities. (Home rule would be extended to counties in 1958.) Municipal incorporation was virtually automatic, occurring without meaningful state oversight. Annexation was inhibited by the requirement for an affirmative vote in both the annexing municipality and the annexed territory. All of these factors promoted local government complexity as the Portland region and the state grew.

Portland Grapples with Growth

The territorial legislature incorporated Portland in 1851 at the request of local businessmen. Its population soon overtook that of rival Oregon City, and by the 1880s its dominance was assured by the arrival of the Northern Pacific Railway. Portland extended its boundaries several times over the next four decades, first by expanding the original town site's boundaries into surrounding unincorporated territory, then by annexing the separately incorporated cities of Albina and East Portland across the river in 1891, the city of Sellwood in 1893, additional unincorporated land to the east, and finally the towns of Linnton and St. Johns to the northwest in 1915.[6] While city boosters pursued annexation, the emerging suburbs desired annexation to gain access to Portland's water supply system. (Established in 1886, Portland's supply system transported water via aqueduct from Bull Run Lake, located at the northeast corner of Clackamas County near Mount Hood.) Propelled by a timber production boom, the combined population of the City of Portland and surrounding Multnomah County tripled between 1900 and 1930, while the statewide population merely doubled. By 1920, Portland accounted for all but 6 per cent of Multnomah County's population, and three-quarters of the tri-county population (see figure 7.1.)

Annexation largely ended in 1915, because fringe residents found ways to gain access to urban services without political union. In 1917, the state legislature authorized the formation of directly elected water districts, and the city adopted a policy of selling water to suburban districts and residents without requiring annexation. As discussed in detail later on, over thirty private water utilities and another thirty public water districts were active in the Portland region by the mid-1950s, each purchasing water from the City of Portland. Similarly, Portland's school district was detached from the control of the city commission, and its jurisdiction extended eastwards into unincorporated areas in Multnomah County. Private gas, electricity, and telephone providers also extended service to unincorporated areas. While Portland's population continued to increase in absolute terms, its share of tri-county population growth declined from 82 per cent during the second decade of the twentieth century to 10 per cent in the 1930s. By the Depression decade, tens of thousands of residents lived in unincorporated areas served by special-purpose bodies.

In was in this context that Portland's City Club in 1925 persuaded the legislature to appoint a Government Simplification Commission composed of politicians and citizens. Founded in 1916, the nonpartisan City Club was dominated by professionals – doctors, lawyers, engineers, architects, accountants, and teachers – who, like the later Twin Cities Citizens League, organized study committees on civic issues.[7] Private funding enabled the retainer of New York University professor Paul Studenski, a leading consolidationist and an affiliate of the New York Bureau of Municipal Research and the National Municipal League.[8] The commission's diagnosis was simple: although city dwellers and suburbanites possess common interests by virtue of their consumption of urban services, growing fragmentation of infrastructure and service provision, in particular water supply and fire protection, inhibited long-term planning and put safety at risk. While avoiding city taxes and regulations, fringe residents were found to pay more than Portlanders for the limited services they received. Consistent with the National Municipal League's reform program and anticipating postwar reform advocacy, the commission recommended reinvigorating annexation and consolidating the City of Portland with Multnomah County. While the legislature ignored the report, it was Portland's first attempt to grapple with metropolitan governance and the financing of services.

For their part, the City of Portland's council and local civic elites responded to rapid growth before the First World War and in the interwar period by hiring nationally recognized consultants, including John Olmsted, Edward Bennett, Charles Cheney, and Harland Bartholomew, to devise plans for parks and transportation systems, and a zoning bylaw.[9] These exercises were fuelled by a desire to emulate San Francisco, Chicago, and other growing American cities. Overlapping coalitions of business elites – the Committee of One Hundred and the Civic Improvement League – raised funds, promoted the plans, and pressed for their implementation. Yet the plans had little effect. By the start of the Great Depression, it was clear that, while urban civic elites and voters were enthusiastic about grand pictorial visions, they were less interested in the regulatory measures and projects required to carry them out. Growth within city limits was shaped by private interests rather than public priorities, and, more importantly, urban growth in the unincorporated hinterland remained unaddressed by any public body.

New Deal Planning Bypasses Oregon

The Great Depression devastated Oregon's forestry-based economy. Timber production dropped by almost two-thirds between 1926 and 1932. Statewide, the average per capita income fell by half, and the unemployment rate topped 25 per cent in early 1930.[10] High unemployment and relief demands quickly destabilized government finances.

In 1932–33 Oregon's property tax–delinquency rate and municipal debt levels were the fourth highest of all states.[11] Forty per cent of property taxes were uncollected or delinquent in the City of Portland in 1932–33 – the highest rate of any city of comparable size in the country.[12] Elsewhere, the crisis sparked debate over the need for regional economic and land-use planning, as well as metropolitan government reform. This debate largely bypassed Oregon. Unlike in Minnesota, the dominant state and local governing factions resisted the more far-reaching interventions of the New Deal. While urban and rural Oregonians, including many registered Republicans, supported Roosevelt's progressive Democrats federally, they rewarded anti–New Deal forces at home.

Elected mayor of Portland in 1932, conservative Democrat Joseph Carson, Jr. fulminated against relief, public works projects, and federal intervention, arguing instead for the restoration of individual and family self-reliance.[13] The conservative turn was mirrored at the state level. After the progressive independent governor Julius Meier declined to run again in 1934 due to ill health, he was succeeded by conservative Democrat congressman and retired military commander Charles "Iron Pants" Martin. He was Roosevelt's antithesis: nativist, pro-states' rights, anti-labour, and a champion of fiscal orthodoxy.[14] Likening social security to "national socialism," he proclaimed the Depression over in 1936, telling the federal government to keep its money.[15] Supported by business interests, private power utilities, and Mayor Carson, Martin opposed public hydroelectric power on the Tennessee Valley Authority model, a policy continued by his Republican successor, Charles A. Sprague.

It was in this inhospitable political context that Oregon joined other states in experimenting with "state planning" under the umbrella of the federal National Resources Planning Board (NRPB). In 1933 Governor Meier had appointed an Oregon State Planning Council to serve as the NRPB's interlocutor in Oregon. Following the 1935 election, the council was reconstituted as the Oregon State Planning Board (OSPB), with an economic focus.[16] There would be no analogue to Minnesota Governor Olson's support for a broad inquiry into the reform of local government structures and state-municipal relations in response to the fiscal crisis. Despite the gravity of the Portland's fiscal and social problems, the OSPB directed its attention toward inventorying economic and physical conditions and infrastructure needs to expand the exploitation and conservation of farmland and timber resources, and facilitate associated goods movement.[17] Its professional staff envisioned a hierarchy of land-use and infrastructure planning, with the county functioning as the "bridge" between city and state planning.[18] Ultimately these bodies accomplished little, partly because they lacked the necessary resources and expertise, and partly due to opposition from established interests. After 1935, the OSPB's sole operational focus was the development of the Willamette Valley Project, a scheme to construct dams to control floods and generate electricity, and also to divert water for irrigation.[19]

Little of this machinery survived into the postwar period. The legislature replaced the OSPB with the Oregon Economic Council in 1939, even before Congress abolished the NRPB, and, lacking institutional and fiscal support, the county planning commissions disbanded.[20] The last vestige of state planning was a Post War Readjustment and Development Commission created in 1943 to prepare for the expected postwar return to depression by prioritizing local public works projects.[21] As a result of Oregon's distinct patterns of political conflict, urban development never climbed the policy agenda in Oregon during the interwar and war years. As a result, state and local government would be ill prepared to mount a programmatic response to rapid urban growth after the war.

THE STATE AND LOCAL PLANNING, 1945–73

Industrial expansion was unleashed after 1937 with the arrival of cheap hydroelectric power from the Bonneville Dam on the Columbia River east of Portland. The United States' entry into the Second World War transformed Portland into a major shipbuilding centre, constructing over a thousand vessels.[22] The state population grew by almost 40 per cent during the 1940s. Overall, the tri-county area added about as many people between 1940 and 1950 as it had during the previous three decades combined. The majority of this growth occurred in unincorporated areas – the population of incorporated cities grew by about 90,000 people during the 1940s, while unincorporated areas added 100,000.[23] There was no meaningful coordination of urban development and infrastructure provision in the "no-man's land" beyond city limits.[24] (See figure 7.3.)

From County to Metropolitan Planning

Following a petition from the League of Oregon Cities in 1944, the legislature responded in 1947 by enabling counties, on affirmative

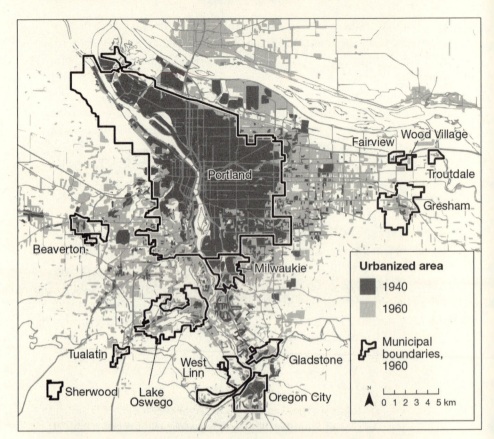

Figure 7.3 Municipal organization and urban growth in Portland, 1940–60

Note: While before 1940 most physical urban development had occurred within the corporate boundaries of Portland, Milwaukie, and Oregon City, extensive residential subdivision occurred in unincorporated portions of Multnomah, Clackamas, and Washington Counties between 1940 and 1960. Boundaries of incorporated municipalities circa 1961 are overlaid. Municipal boundaries are approximate – comparison of contemporaneous maps suggests that the smaller municipalities undertook a number of annexations in the early 1960s.

Source: Extent of urbanization in 1940 and 1960 redrawn from maps in *The Three Basic Services*.

vote of the people, to appoint advisory planning commissions that could zone and recommend long-term "development patterns" (later renamed "comprehensive plans") for unincorporated areas.[25] Counties were slow to embrace the new powers. By 1961, only the three Portland-area counties had formed planning commissions; of the other thirty-three, six had explicitly rejected planning, and many of the remainder locked in the status quo by zoning tracts in response to resident petitions.[26] Incorporated cities were expected to plan for themselves, yet few outside Portland did so, and city-county and inter-county coordination was not pursued. In fact, the law restricted a previous provision under which cities were required to approve all land subdivision within six miles of city limits. This authority disappeared when a county adopted its own land-use controls.[27]

Multnomah County's experience is illustrative.[28] During the 1940s and early 1950s, shacktowns sprang up as people moved self-built wartime houses by barge from Astoria at the mouth of the Columbia River to inexpensive sites in unincorporated areas east of Portland. Water came from wells and effluent was discharged into cesspools. The county sought zoning powers to stabilize property values and regulate unserviced development. Urban voters outnumbered rural opponents to create a county planning commission in 1952. At its inaugural meeting, however, the commission rejected joint planning with Portland and instead directed the young planning director Lloyd Anderson, recently recruited from Seattle, to prepare a comprehensive plan and zoning ordinance only for the unincorporated area. Anderson was rebuffed when he recommended that residential land subdivision be made conditional on connection to trunk sewer systems. Maintaining political support for even a minimal plan and zoning ordinance was difficult.

Linking land use to infrastructure extension paralleled another agenda during the 1950s: farmland protection. Much as in British Columbia's Lower Mainland, productive fertile land in the Willamette Valley was being subdivided, parcel by parcel, for non-agricultural residential use as farmers rationally capitalized on rising property values. What worked for the individual farmer, however, undermined the agricultural sector as a whole. Building on accepted practice in California and other states, the legislature enacted preferential property tax rates for agricultural land in 1961 as an incentive to keep land in production. As clarified in a further 1963 act, reduced taxes would apply in exclusive farm-use zones defined by counties, and, to avoid ad hoc spot rezoning, agricultural zoning had to be consistent with the county comprehensive plan.[29] These provisions provided new incentives for counties to engage in long-term planning and reinforced the notion that zoning should be subordinated to comprehensive plans. Yet initially, they were implemented only by Washington and Polk Counties, establishing a patchwork of regulation.

After Congress mandated the formation of advisory metropolitan planning commissions under the 1954 Housing Act, the Oregon legislature delegated its authority to administer grants to an obscure body: the State Board of Higher Education, which in turn authorized the Bureau of Municipal Research and Service (BMRS) on its behalf. Similar to Minnesota's Municipal Reference Bureau, the BMRS was an independent entity housed within a university. Through the University of Oregon's rural extension program, BMRS staff trained the first generation of local planners. Its director, Herman Kehrli, also led the League of Oregon Cities, a statewide municipal association.[30] Lloyd Anderson left Multnomah County to join the bureau in 1956, his express task being to leverage federal funds to promote city, county, and metropolitan planning.

One outcome was the formation of an advisory Metropolitan Planning Commission (MPC) covering the three metropolitan counties and the City of Portland in 1958.[31] Unlike its Twin Cities counterpart, the Portland MPC was not granted independent revenues. It existed at the whim of its members, which reauthorized its existence annually.[32] Two-thirds of its budget came from the federal government; half of the remainder came from the city, one-quarter from Multnomah County, and one-eighth each from Clackamas and Washington Counties. Over the next decade, the MPC undertook extensive mapping and survey work but enjoyed only lukewarm support from area local governments, not least because of its narrow representative structure.[33] The dozens of cities and freestanding special districts had no voice on the commission. Moreover, it was viewed primarily as a "talking shop" and technical information clearinghouse and was not empowered to produce a plan.

Also taking advantage of federal funds, the State Highway Commission convened the Portland-Vancouver Metropolitan Transportation Study (P-V MTS), a comprehensive transportation forecasting and needs-assessment study in collaboration with municipalities, counties, and the MPC in 1959. This mirrored other intergovernmental transportation studies of the era, including the Twin Cities' Joint Program and the Metro Toronto and Region Transportation Study. Unlike them, however, the Portland study was narrowly framed as an engineering exercise, disconnected from land-use objectives.[34]

The land-use question was at an impasse. Despite growing concern about farmland protection and haphazard unserviced urbanization on Portland's unincorporated fringe, these agendas were not yet linked, and, even if they had been, there was no public body (aside from state government) empowered to craft and implement a regional plan. The MPC was underpowered and disliked, proactive comprehensive planning (as opposed to reactive zoning) was only beginning to mature in counties that opted to pursue it, and the institutional foundations of state government established few incentives for part-time state legislators to engage in decisive and programmatic policymaking. Given these unpromising conditions, few would have predicted the state's imminent adoption of a far-reaching mandatory land-use planning framework.

Political Change

The politics of land use were rapidly transformed by partisan realignment and social and institutional change. Domestic migration was changing Oregon politics. Many of the new urban and rural residents who had arrived during and after the war brought liberal Democrat sympathies with them, bolstering the progressive impulse in Oregon politics and pulling both parties toward a progressive centre.[35] Republicans initially benefited more than Democrats, due to their party's superior cohesion. But the Democrats' electoral performance improved after 1956, due to high-quality candidates, the renewal of party machinery, and emerging disagreements between the state and federal Republican leaderships on energy and conservation policy. Democrat resurgence produced a competitive two-party system.[36] In addition, the growing Portland metropolitan area's representation increased after the state legislature was reapportioned on equal terms by a publicly initiated constitutional amendment in 1952. As in Minnesota fifteen years later, reapportionment brought forth a new generation of urban-based reformist legislators in both parties. The vigorous public debate over reapportionment, championed by the League of Women Voters, also mobilized and strengthened the civic elite networks that would later advocate for urban and regional planning and governance reform.[37]

Nonetheless, the government lacked the capacity to develop and decisively enact programmatic policy responses. Decisiveness was inhibited by the logrolling dynamic inherent in the separated-powers system. Part-time legislators had no resources to study issues.[38] Policy proposals typically entered the legislative agenda when advocacy groups recruited a sympathetic legislator to bring them forward.

Successive Oregon governors sought to modernize government to more programmatically respond to social and economic change.[39] In 1956, governor-elect Robert Holmes promised to reanimate state planning, and in 1957 the legislature authorized a Department of Planning and Development within the governor's executive office that would promote economic development, including local economic and land-use planning.[40] (The ubiquitous Lloyd Anderson served as deputy director of the department from 1961 to 1964, launching a statewide regional economic development program.) Holmes's successor, the young progressive Republican Mark Hatfield (in office 1959–67) also worked to strengthen the state's programmatic policymaking capacity, although he did not succeed in persuading the legislature to reorganize the executive branch.[41]

Normative Change

As elsewhere in North America, the 1960s and early 1970s brought a shift in the normative context. Environmentalism emerged on the political agenda in the 1960s, establishing new dimensions of land-use conflict. A new generation of (mostly urban) citizens and activists questioned the axiom that what was good for the timber and pulp-and-paper industries was good for Oregon and its citizens. At the same time, farmers sought to protect the viability of agricultural production from encroaching urbanization. Their activism dovetailed with the rise of a new quality-of-life discourse in the City of Portland.[42] As in other North American cities, concerns about urban livability generated a new mode of civic politics as inner-city residents organized to resist urban renewal and expressway megaprojects and demanded neighbourhood-focused planning. The new ethos was exemplified by charismatic public interest lawyer Neil Goldschmidt, who served as city councillor and mayor throughout the 1970s. He was joined on council by Lloyd Anderson, the earlier champion of county, metropolitan, and state planning. Supported by an activist planning staff, they initiated several projects that revived the declining downtown as a place of commerce and recreation: the development of Pioneer Courthouse Square, the conversion of a riverfront highway into a public park, and the creation of a car-free transit corridor. The latter, combined with the cancellation of the planned Mount Hood Freeway in favour of a new light-rail line, dramatically altered the calculus of downtown accessibility and induced downtown commercial and residential investment. This combination of normative, political, and institutional factors – charismatic governors interested in reinforcing programmatic policymaking coupled with an emerging consensus, that transcended the urban-rural divide, that Oregon would have to fight to maintain its quality of life – opened the door to non-incremental state and local policy change.

Creating the State Land-Use Program

Much like British Columbia's Lower Mainland, the combination of rapid urbanization, agriculture, and timber production and milling made the Willamette Valley fertile terrain for land-use conflict. The state's existing farmland preservation laws were proving ineffective. Residential subdivision and commercial and industrial development had reduced the Willamette Valley's agricultural land base by 20 per cent – 2,000 of 11,300 km^2 was lost between 1955 and 1965, much of it in the Portland area.[43] Farmers depended on the river for irrigation, yet fertilizer runoff, along with municipal sewer and industrial effluent, polluted the watershed. While the negative effects of river pollution had been known for decades, they remained unaddressed into the 1960s.[44] Working farmers also discovered that the proliferation of scattered exurban development undermined the viability of agricultural production. On the coast, expanding tourism-oriented development along Highway 101 fragmented beach access and threatened delicate coastal ecosystems.

Historian William Robbins describes public consciousness being gripped at this moment by a "siege mentality" – a fear that, without land-use restrictions, Oregon would become another California and the Willamette Valley another sprawling Los Angeles.[45] Environmentalism provided a powerful frame through which many Oregonians, and especially the growing urban middle class, would understand their relationship to the state's natural resources. This was crystalized by popular Portland television journalist Tom McCall, who made his public reputation with the broadcast of his documentary *Pollution in Paradise* in 1962.[46] Vividly dramatizing the discharge of industrial waste into the Willamette River, the documentary was a "tour de force" that "vaulted Tom McCall to the pinnacle of statewide politics."[47] In 1964 he was elected secretary of state on the Republican ticket; in 1967 he began the first of two terms as governor. While McCall was the not the first to identify water pollution as a problem

– the state chapter of the Izaak Walton League and others had been advocating for decades, with limited success – he put a face to it and elevated the natural environment to the highest level of state attention. A bipartisan consensus emerged. The state treasurer, Democrat Robert Straub, also advocated for environmental protection and the wise stewardship of the Willamette River and its valley. The centrist McCall worked easily with progressive legislators of both parties, often to the frustration of the parties' leadership groups. (From the late 1950s to the early 1970s, one or both chambers were controlled by a coalition of rural Republicans and conservative Democrats.) Straub would succeed the term-limited McCall as governor in 1974.[48]

In this political context, Oregon, like British Columbia, was an early adopter of environmental protection legislation. In 1968, two years before President Nixon signed the Environmental Protection Agency into law, the legislature transformed the Oregon State Sanitary Authority, a relatively toothless regulator of point-source pollution, into a powerful Department of Environmental Quality. Oregon also introduced the nation's first deposit-return program for bottles and cans in 1971, a year after British Columbia introduced the first such system in Canada.

While the political salience of pollution, farm viability, and ecosystem preservation in wilderness areas increased in the late 1950s and early 1960s, this did not in itself generate policy change. Propelled by inchoate public concern that the landscape was being changed by forces beyond their control, a bipartisan group of policy entrepreneurs fused these problems into a coherent policy package. Through their efforts, the legislature adopted landmark land-use and environmental protection legislation. Passed in 1969, Senate Bill (SB) 10 made city and county planning and zoning mandatory statewide. And in 1973, SB 100 subordinated the plans made under SB 10 to state-defined land-use goals.

The first step toward reform occurred in 1967. The absence of a programmatic land-use policy that protected agricultural land while preserving the natural environment was highlighted by a widely publicized conference – The Willamette Valley: What Is Our Future in Land Use? – which was organized by the chambers of commerce and assembled a wide range of stakeholders and opinion leaders.[49] That same year, Republican state representative L.B. Day introduced a bill that would permit local governments to create agricultural land preserves in "prime" areas based on their capability as assessed by federal soil surveys. Having served as secretary-treasurer of Oregon's largest food-processing workers' union since 1958, and as the regional director of the US Department of the Interior, he had a personal interest in, and direct knowledge of, farmland viability. The legislature shelved the bill, however, and instead appointed an interim committee to study the issue.[50]

The result of the committee's study was SB 10, which required (rather than merely enabled) all cities and counties to prepare comprehensive land-use plans and zoning ordinances. The major bone of contention was its requirement that county and city plans be completed by the beginning of 1972, or the state would impose plans at local expense. Local governments resisted state pre-emption of what they saw as their jurisdiction. Especially in the state's resource-dependent south, many residents remained opposed to land-use regulation in principle. Governor McCall proposed that comprehensive planning be undertaken by fourteen multi-county districts defined by his administration for the purposes of coordinating state and local government activity. Cities and counties would zone within the parameters of these regional comprehensive plans, ensuring cross-boundary coordination. (Reflecting the times, these regional bodies were analogous to the regional development councils Ontario created in 1966, the regional development commissions Minnesota created in 1967, and, somewhat less directly, the regional districts British Columbia established in 1965.) Legislators rejected McCall's regional approach, however, insisting on local control of planning.[51] At the same time, and for the same reason, the legislature also rejected a companion bill, SB 195, which would have defined uniform statewide zoning standards.

As ultimately passed, SB 10 contained two innovations. First, it required that zoning ordinances conform to comprehensive plans. The bill's major innovation, however, was the prescription of nine goals for "comprehensive physical planning," some of which are listed in this excerpt from section 3 of the bill:

Comprehensive physical planning should provide guidance ... responsive to economic development, human resource development, natural resource development and regional and metropolitan area development ... Goals for comprehensive physical planning are: (1) To preserve the quality of the air and water resources of the state. (2) To conserve open space and protect natural and scenic resources ... (4) To conserve prime farm lands for the production of crops and provide for an orderly and efficient transition from rural to urban land use ... (7) To develop a timely, orderly and efficient arrangement of public facilities and services to serve as a framework for urban and rural development ... (9) To ensure that the development of properties within the state is commensurate with the character and the physical limitations of the land.

These goals fused environmental and farmland protection objectives in relation to urbanization, all under the rubric of maintaining and improving quality of life. Governor McCall publicly endorsed the bill and promised to sign it and companion legislation into law. Parallel bills limited the construction of highways and infrastructure corridors on prime agricultural land, required new housing development to demonstrate adequate water source and sewer capacity, and supported additional soil classification surveys.

SB 10 would prove ineffective, however, because the political cost of imposing state plans on local governments was too high. Even eighteen months after the deadline, seventeen of thirty-six counties had not yet adopted plans and zoning ordinances, and many of the adopted plans were deemed of poor quality.[52] Still, the electorate favoured a bolder agenda. McCall won a second term in 1969 on a promise of strengthening SB 10, at the same time that voters rejected a ballot initiative to repeal the bill by a substantial margin. Pro-planning forces mobilized on two tracks, one initiated by the governor, the other by legislators.[53] In February 1970, McCall convened a committee of state staff and representatives from each of the four Willamette Valley councils of governments to discuss laying the groundwork for a valley-specific Environmental Protection and Development Plan. The governor's staff believed that securing public support for growth controls was essential.[54] Some 48,000 questionnaires were sent to area residents, and state staff held dozens of community-based public information meetings. Later, in 1971, the committee was converted into a "council" chaired by the secretary of state, with additional representation from state and federal agencies and departments. The council's first act was to launch Project Foresight – a participatory planning process in which citizens were asked to respond to six scenarios, the first representing current trends and the others premised on different controlled urban growth patterns. The scenarios were developed and pictorially represented by San Francisco landscape architect Lawrence Halprin, who was retained with federal funding.[55] Over 20,000 people attended 275 meetings, and 15,000 signed up to receive regular newsletters. McCall also launched a parallel process to develop a coastal plan. This mobilized the newly created Oregon State Public Interest Research Group (OSPIRG), America's first university-based policy advocacy group, which would go on to play a pivotal role in defending Oregon's land-use planning system. Through unprecedented and highly publicized mass participation and civic mobilization, McCall's ad hoc place-based policymaking initiatives set the stage for the legislature's reappraisal of SB 10.

This campaign was spearheaded by Linn County farmer and freshman Republican state senator Hector Macpherson, who had spoken at the 1967 land-use conference and become a convert to regulatory land-use planning.[56] Macpherson, as well as some environmentalists, interpreted the political problem primarily as one of local government capture by property development and industrial interests. Establishing a new balance between environmental, economic, and social interests in the land would require expanded state intervention in land-use decision making. The challenge would be to balance a muscular state role with home rule.

At the end of the 1971 session, the Senate leadership rebuffed Macpherson's request for an interim committee. Not taking no for an answer, he formed an unofficial Land Use Planning Committee. McCall supported his work by seconding to the group Bob Logan, his point man for local government relations. The group incorporated diverse interests: four city and county planning commissioners, representatives of Associated Oregon Industries and the Oregon Homebuilders Association, two environmentalists, two academics, a professional engineer, a member of the Governor's Commission for a Liveable Oregon, the president of the League of Oregon Cities, and the executive director of the Association of Oregon Counties.[57] The committee quickly concluded that achieving meaningful planning objectives and securing inter-jurisdictional coordination would require empowering a state-level agency not only to define goals and guidelines but also to supervise their implementation through local plans. Their final proposal provided for a governor-appointed Land Conservation and Development Commission (LCDC) supported by a professionally staffed Department of Land Conservation and Development (DLCD). Decisions of local planning bodies could be appealed to the LCDC.

The state would be authorized to declare critical areas of statewide concern for which it would define special rules. Logan revived the earlier idea of assigning coordinating authority to regional bodies, and the SB 195 minimum zoning standards were resurrected. Reflecting the atmosphere of crisis – 121 km² of farmland were reportedly urbanized in 1973 alone[58] – the draft bill contained an "emergency clause," meaning that it would take effect almost immediately rather than ninety days after the session's adjournment. Counties and cities were given one year to comply.

The Macpherson committee's proposal was not crafted in a vacuum. Beyond addressing the perceived failings of SB 10, it also drew on outside policy ideas and responded to a changing national policy context. Oregon's land-use debates occurred at the high-water mark of congressional debates on a proposed National Land Use Policy Act, which would have established federal mandates for state and local land-use planning in exchange for grants. The national debate was also buttressed by environmental scholars Fred Bosselman and David Callies's landmark report, *The Quiet Revolution in Land Use Control*, which critically evaluated nine case studies of state, metropolitan, and local land-use innovation (including the Twin Cities Metropolitan Council), recommending a robust state role in land-use planning. Macpherson would later refer to the *Quiet Revolution* as "our bible" in the drafting of SB 100.[59] Finally, the relationship between county comprehensive plans and zoning was clarified by the Oregon Supreme Court in the 1973 *Fasano* case, which required the latter to conform to the former.[60]

To a degree, McCall, Logan, and Macpherson and his colleagues were motivated by the expectation of future federal support. By establishing a state-level planning apparatus, Oregon could shape national debates and be ready when federal resources materialized. They also saw a federal-state-local policy hierarchy as essential to overcoming fragmented and parochial land-use decision making and to breaking the capture of local governments by economic interests. Congress never adopted national land-use legislation, however, and federal support for metropolitan and local land-use planning would disappear altogether with the Reagan revolution of the 1980s.

Despite McCall's express support in his opening address to the 1973 session – now regarded as one of Oregon's most famous political orations, in which he excoriated the "grasping wastrels of the land" – the bill did not receive an easy ride in the legislature. The Senate

Environment and Land Use Committee, which would deliberate on
the bill and on which Macpherson sat, was divided. A majority of
the committee's members would have to be persuaded if the bill was
to advance to the Senate floor. The chair, Democrat Ted Hallock, was
an enthusiastic supporter, as was Eugene Republican George Wingard.
The other four members, representing both parties and Portland-area
and rural locations of the state, were sceptical. (One sceptic was
future Republican governor Vic Atiyeh, a limited-government conservative who would nonetheless later defend the state land-use
system against repeal.)

Influential business lobbies opposed the bill – principally Associated
Oregon Industries and the Oregon Homebuilders Association, as well
as major timber-producing firms. (These groups' participation in
Macpherson's committee was apparently insufficient to sway their
leadership or membership.) Natural resource producers saw new
regulations as a brake on economic growth, and they especially
opposed the designation of critical areas as a *post hoc* impairment of
property rights without compensation. Cities and counties opposed
the bill's regionalizing of planning authority. They, along with the
Oregon Association of Realtors, argued that land-use decisions should
rest with electorally accountable local governments.

On the other side were environmentalist organizations, including OSPIRG and the Sierra Club. The state chapter of the American
Institute of Planners was also active, seeing Oregon as an important
test case in the development of state planning systems. Non-partisan
good-government groups, including the League of Women Voters and
Portland-focused Tri-County New Politics, were motivated by the
potential for greater citizen engagement in urban development. Not
all business leaders were opposed. Recreational land developer John
Gray, who was also president of Omark Industries, one of the largest
saw-chain manufacturers in the world, supported state planning and
the critical areas concept. The existing federally mandated councils of
governments, of which four were in the Willamette Valley, supported
the regionalizing planning authority because it would assign them a
new role in state law.

Faced with opposition from key stakeholders and legislators,
Hallock engineered the bill's redrafting by an ad hoc eight-member
committee chaired by Macpherson and with representation from the
bill's chief opponents: Associated Oregon Industries, the Association
of Oregon Counties, the Homebuilders Association, and the Oregon

Wheat Growers Association. A subordinate drafting committee, chaired by L.B. Day with McCall's endorsement, was created to work out legal details. The Association of Oregon Counties was brought on side by abandoning regionalization. Instead, counties were given responsibility for coordinating planning and zoning within their jurisdiction. Yet regionalism was preserved where it mattered most – in the state's largest metropolitan area. A companion bill, SB 769 (discussed below), assigned the coordinating role in the Portland region to its council of governments, the Columbia Region Association of Governments. A parallel bill was drafted that would appropriate $3 million to fund local planning work. A tug of war between environmentalists and industry groups over critical-area policies was resolved by removing their detailed description from the bill; instead the LCDC was authorized to designate and set rules for a narrow range of "critical activities." Finally, to meet the demands of good-government groups, the bill was amended to require extensive public hearings during the LCDC's development of statewide planning goals.

Hallock made two additional concessions to secure committee and Senate approval. The first was symbolic: the drafting of a statement of legislative intent stating that the bill's goal was to provide a framework for local action without compromising local discretion, and that institutionalized participation in goal drafting and later adjudication of disputes would ensure public control. Second, the emergency clause was dropped. This opened the bill to a ballot challenge. But opponents failed to gather the 26,600 required signatures, and so the bill was enacted without citizen ratification. The emergency clause's removal pushed the funding for local planning off the table – the legislature could not appropriate money in the current session for an agency that did not yet exist. Fearing that the reconciliation of different House and Senate bills would result in further watering down or even defeat, Hallock called in favours to secure the Senate Bill's passage by the House without amendment. The concessions made were minor; the core provisions remained intact.

Hallock was sanguine about the achievement, stating that SB 100 as passed was "a beginning" that "does not go far enough, having critical areas left out, and also relying on the archaic institution of the County rather than the COGs [councils of governments]."[61] McCall, Macpherson, and the various groups that desired stronger legislation agreed but were willing to accept a less directive bill rather than no bill at all.

A Temporary Conjuncture

The passage of SB 100 was the culmination of a quarter-century-long process of grappling with the impacts of rapid urban population growth and economic expansion. It reflected a temporary conjuncture. The legislature's initial responses in the 1940s and 1950s were modest – expanding enabling legislation for city and county planning without state-level oversight. Incrementalism reflected the constitutional and institutional limitations of Oregon's separated-powers system of government. A weak executive branch, a relatively unprofessionalized legislature, and opponents' access to the ballot initiative militated against the expansion of state administrative capacities by creating new departments or agencies. These limitations were temporarily overcome when a popular charismatic and activist governor and a group of able and committed legislators mobilized in concert with extra-governmental policy entrepreneurs to broker a solution among divergent interests. They did so in a temporary atmosphere of crisis, bipartisan consensus, and elevated national interest in state planning. Even in the context of Oregon's political populism and tradition of direct democracy, individual advocates could wield such extraordinary influence because of generalized trust in government and a deference to elites.

Crucially, urbanization – and Portland tri-county urbanization in particular – was only one of several drivers of the land-use policy agenda. Mobilization around farmland, coastal, and wilderness protection was statewide in scope and framed by a quality-of-life discourse that fused multiple policy objectives in relation to a diverse array of land-use conflicts. Had the state planning system been framed solely in relation to Portland-area urbanization, it would not have been politically salable at the state level. This is demonstrated by public and municipal resistance to successive Portland-area metropolitan agencies, both before and after the statewide system's creation – the subject of the next section.

CIVIC ELITES AND THE METROPOLITAN PROBLEM, 1955-78

As in the other three case studies that make up this book, the evolution of land-use controls is only half of the story. To understand their implementation in the Portland region, we must trace a separate set of developments: the push by good-government reformers to consolidate representative institutions, infrastructure provision, and service delivery at the metropolitan scale. This agenda was not motivated primarily by land-use concerns, although some reformers viewed inefficient land-use patterns as a byproduct of local government complexity. Rather, they sought to increase efficiency of service delivery and improve democratic expression and political accountability. These reformers perceived overlapping and multi-layered local governments as uncoordinated and opaque to voters. Although independently motivated and championed by different actors into the 1970s, metropolitan planning and local government reform would become linked during the 1990s.

Portland metropolitan governance had disappeared from the public agenda after the 1920s Government Simplification Commission. While agents of the Bureau of Municipal Research and Service in Eugene were well aware of the proliferation of special-purpose bodies in unincorporated areas, and especially in and around Portland, they did little more than collect and publish statistics and remark upon the desirability of governmental consolidation. Starting in the 1950s, Portland-area civic elites once again became interested in what they saw as a mismatch between governing arrangements and the scale of urbanization. These debates would culminate in the creation of four metropolitan institutions between 1967 and 1970: the Columbia Region Association of Governments (CRAG), a new planning body to replace the Metropolitan Planning Commission; a commission to regulate local government formation and boundary change; an area-wide public transportation authority; and a metropolitan multi-purpose service district (the Metropolitan Service District, or MSD). With the exception of the transit district, these bodies quickly foundered on opposition from the public, local governments, and legislators. In the late 1970s, the civic elites that had driven the agenda in the 1960s regrouped their forces and, through astute use of the ballot initiative, created Metro, the only directly elected regional government in the United States, by merging CRAG with the MSD.

The Problem of Special District Government in Unincorporated Areas

Single-purpose districts for various purposes proliferated after the First World War in Oregon, enabled by general legislation and created on petition from residents of unincorporated areas.[62] The first type to be authorized (aside from school districts) was the drainage district, in 1915. Four were established in Multnomah County along the Columbia River floodplain between 1917 and 1922. A more important intervention was the authorization of water supply districts in 1917. By the beginning of the Depression, there were twenty-two in the tri-county Portland area; by 1950, thirty-seven; and by 1956, forty-four. Most acquired water through contracts with Portland's municipal waterworks, although others relied on ground or surface water.[63] This system worked relatively well for those who received service, but many rural residents continued to draw water from wells. As unco-ordinated water services proliferated in the countryside, a new prob-lem emerged: the disposal of wastewater. Until the late 1940s, rural dwellers relied almost exclusively on septic tanks or cesspools. The State Board of Health cautioned that the hard clay soils surrounding Portland were ill suited to individual disposal systems, risking disease in areas dependent on groundwater. Only in 1949 did the legislature authorize sanitary sewer districts, spurring their formation. Fire pro-tection districts were authorized in 1929, in some cases supplanting self-organized volunteer fire departments. By 1950 there were twenty-three in the tri-county area. The real boom occurred in the 1940s, when the state responded to rapid growth by authorizing the forma-tion of districts for parks (1941) and for street lighting, water control, and zoning (all in 1947) (see figure 7.4).[64] Residents used zoning districts to lock in the status quo, and hence their property values, without reference to broader land-use goals.

The appeal of central-city annexation or suburban municipal incorporation decreased with each extension of the service district model. Statewide, the population of incorporated cities increased by 221,260 people during the 1940s, or 35 per cent, while the rural non-farm population grew by 237,886, a more than doubling.[65] Between 1921 and 1961, only one additional municipality was incor-porated in the tri-county area: Wood Village in eastern Multnomah County, a company town established by Reynolds Aluminum in 1951. During the same period, the proportion of the county's population living in incorporated areas declined from 94 to 72 per cent. By 1950 a patchwork of over 120 special districts of various kinds served many of the 200,000 tri-county residents living in unincorporated areas (see figure 7.5).[66]

The 1955 legislature established an Interim Committee on Local Government to study services in unincorporated areas.[67] Citing the B.C. Lower Mainland Regional Planning Board's *Urban Sprawl* report,

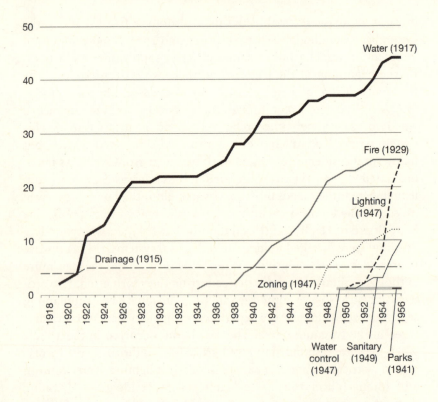

Figure 7.4 Cumulative number of special districts in the tri-county area, by type, 1917–56

Note: Years in parentheses indicate when legislative authorization of each type of district occurred. The general pattern is one of rapid adoption of special districts following their authorization.

Source: Compiled from Oregon, *Problems of the Urban Fringe*, 2: 51–5.

the commission highlighted the economic inefficiency of scattered and unserviced fringe development, which it believed to be the product of fragmented local government.[68] Easy creation of special districts removed any incentive residents might have had to separately incorporate or annex to cities. Counties were unwilling or unable to proactively fill the governance gap. In its final report, the committee concluded that the state must fully exercise its "responsibility for providing an adequate system of local government" in order to accommodate "the great growth in population of Oregon and particularly the growth in population and development in the unincorporated

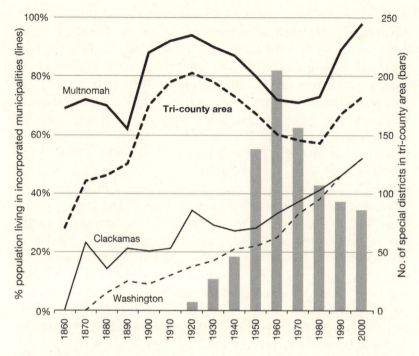

Figure 7.5 Incorporated area population and special districts, tri-county area, 1860–2000

Note: Until the 1920s, the proportion of the tri-county population living in incorporated areas generally increased as municipalities annexed suburbanizing areas. As annexation waned and more growth occurred in unincorporated areas, especially in Multnomah County, special districts proliferated. The proportion of the population living in municipalities has increased and reliance on special districts has decreased with new municipal incorporations and annexations since the 1970s.

Sources: Population from decennial census, various years; number of special districts for 1920–40 from Oregon, *Problems of the Urban Fringe*, 2: 51–5, and for later periods from Census of Governments, 1952–2002.

areas of the counties."[69] One option was to authorize differential tax treatment for annexed areas that were semi-rural and therefore did not yet benefit from the full range of city services. A more radical proposal was to require the compulsory annexation, without popular ratification, of areas deemed at risk of disease due to inadequate water and sewer systems. Others went further, calling for an end to the requirement of an affirmative vote in both the annexing municipality and the annexed territory. Either the vote would be tallied for the total area population (giving city residents an insuperable numerical advantage under most circumstances) or for the city alone. These proposals were rejected by the commission as incompatible with local self-government rights. The interim committee recommended that, absent annexation, existing service districts be encouraged to consolidate into countywide bodies. While stopping short of proposing specific legislation, it also recommended the formation of voluntary councils of governments to coordinate activities in urban areas, state-level "arbitration" of annexation disputes, and the creation of "metropolitan governments" in the state's large urban centres.[70] The committee's consultations were well attended and publicized. Its recommendations – approvingly characterized as "cautious" by the *Oregonian* newspaper – were endorsed by the Association of Oregon Counties and the League of Oregon Cities.[71] Yet few of the recommendations were ultimately enacted. While the legislature authorized differential tax treatment of annexed areas and consolidated countywide service districts, it chose not to enable new mechanisms of city-county coordination or regional governance. Nonetheless, the interim committee's thorough analysis would prove useful to later reform advocates.

In parallel, the three counties sought and received legislative authorization to establish a cooperative Tri-County Authority to collect and treat sewage in their suburban areas. Consulting engineers proposed a gravity system for a 388 km² area at a cost of $27.5 million. Almost immediately the limitations of the arrangement became clear. The cost of constructing a new treatment plant and trunk lines was to be offset by household connection fees, yet those already serviced by existing special districts had no desire to pay extra for equivalent service. Meanwhile, the City of Portland had no incentive to participate, because its wholesale water profits increased as the suburbs grew.[72] The scheme collapsed. Multnomah County was left in the curious position of owning a treatment plant in western Washington County, processing effluent on contract with several sanitary districts. Rich wryly concludes that "this experiment in intergovernmental cooperation to avoid 'any overriding authority' proved that an overriding authority is necessary to implement a Tri-County Plan."[73]

The proliferation of special districts and the 1960 census's revelation that the City of Portland had not grown over the previous decade led the city to initiate an aggressive annexation program. In almost all cases, suburban residents refused, instead maintaining their independence by incorporating new municipalities. In Washington County, Tigard incorporated in 1961, followed by North Plains in 1963, and Durham and King City in 1966. Part of northern Clackamas County organized as Happy Valley in 1965. Thus, the interim committee's recommendation of renewed central-city annexation as a means of addressing metropolitan malcoordination failed to bear fruit.

Civic Elites Forge a Consensus

It is in this context of increasing local government complexity that Portland's civic elites mobilized to advocate for regional governance. They framed the problem in two ways. First, they accepted the consolidationist argument that local government complexity generated higher aggregate service costs and inhibited the rational planning of physical urban growth. To produce a more efficient urban form would require subordinating infrastructure extension to a unified metropolitan plan. Second, they argued that the proliferation of special-purpose bodies, the small size of municipalities, and the remoteness of the Metropolitan Planning Commission undermined the meaningful exercise of local democracy. The MPC was deemed to have failed not only as a planner-coordinator, but also as an instrument of democratic decision making.

The agenda was initially defined by the League of Women Voters, which had emerged as an influential and respected voice after its role in securing electoral reapportionment in the early 1950s.[74] The Portland chapter launched a study of suburban growth in 1954. Its mostly urban middle-class members were concerned that suburbanization would undermine Portland's vitality, and they quickly grasped the disjuncture between governing structures and the physical pattern of development. The league's Metropolitan Planning Committee produced a memorandum, *The Mess We Are In*, in 1956, which recommended a two-tier metropolitan government to craft and implement a regional master plan. Counties and incorporated municipalities would remain intact, but the new area-wide body would assume all services currently provided by special districts and would be empowered to levy taxes and issue bonds. Its policymaking body "would be simple in structure, representative of the people in the area and responsible to them for its performance."[75]

The league's Portland, Beaverton, Oswego, and Milwaukie chapters then set the boundaries of future debate by jointly fleshing out a detailed proposal. In *A Tale of Three Counties: One Metropolitan Community*, published in 1960, the league emphasized the many interdependencies of the region's disparate parts while cataloguing the "crazy quilt map" of special districts that produced "Tri-County chaos."[76] After presenting a careful analysis of recently created metropolitan governments in Toronto, Seattle, and Miami, as well as of the older city-county of Honolulu, the league presented its own model of a "multi-purpose metropolitan district." The proposal contained four elements that presaged future debates. First, the district's boundaries would generally correspond to the built-up area, and would expand as urbanization spread outwards. Like the Metropolitan Toronto Planning Board, it would exercise extra-territorial jurisdiction over land use. Second, it would also have jurisdiction over pollution control and infrastructure planning and operations, including water and sewer services, transit, and major roads. Third, its governing board would be directly elected, in order to avoid capture by parochial municipal interests. Finally, to avoid veto by local interests, it would be given effect by affirmative vote of the entire area, rather than of each political subdivision. The report was widely publicized and praised in newspaper editorials.

The league concluded by calling for the creation of a permanent organization to study and educate the public on metropolitan questions, which it referred to as "Metropolis, Inc." Fulfilling this proposal, several league members joined with business and academic leaders to form a non-profit corporation called Metropolitan Area Perspectives (MAP) in 1960.[77] This well-connected group successfully lobbied the 1961 legislature for the creation of a new Interim Committee on Local Government and actively shaped its agenda. Proclaiming that "what is needed most for modernizing our sprawling urban settlements is not money, not cement, steel or labor … It is better governmental structure," the committee recommended that the 1963 session adopt legislation, drafted by MAP, for the creation of formal, state-funded study commissions to look into metropolitan problems and recommend changes to the legislature.[78] (While the law was general in its wording, its intended target was, of course, Portland.)

Taking this advice, the legislature appropriated $35,000 for the formation of a Portland Metropolitan Study Commission (PMSC), which was composed of thirty-eight members – one selected by each legislator representing a part of Multnomah, Clackamas, Washington, and Columbia Counties. It was authorized to consider a defined list of options: the creation of a multi-purpose service district as envisioned by the league; the creation of a regional "urban county"; transfers of service responsibilities between governments; the creation of joint bodies or contracts akin to Los Angeles's Lakewood Plan; the creation of a council of governments; and the establishment of a "metropolitan government" by charter.[79] The commission was intended to sunset after five years, but was renewed for another two, ultimately disbanding in 1971.

Its prime mover was its executive secretary, the intellectually acute and politically savvy A. McKay Rich. Having arrived in Oregon from Idaho only in 1960, after having briefly served as a schoolteacher, state representative, and city councillor, Rich had worked at the BMRS for two years before Frank Ivancie, Portland mayor Terry Schrunk's chief of staff, convinced him to apply for the job.[80] As the PMSC's top staff member, Rich carefully nurtured relationships with legislators, civic leaders, and organizations, including the City Club and the editorial board of the *Oregonian*. This generated support for the group's recommendations, virtually all of which were refinements of ideas initially championed by the League of Women Voters.

The PMSC leadership's motivations were exemplified by a 1968 brochure depicting the confusing life of everyman Marvin Metro, who tries and fails to navigate a welter of overlapping single-purpose governments, only to flip a coin at the ballot box. Marvin's "governmental burial" is framed in economic and political terms. Citing the federal Advisory Commission on Intergovernmental Relations (ACIR), the brochure sets out seven criteria for the proper organization of local government: that they should have "broad enough jurisdiction to cope with the problems," have the "ability to raise adequate revenues and do it equitably," have the "flexibility to adjust government boundaries," be "general purpose rather than single purpose form," have the "ability to take advantage of economies of scale," be "accessibility to the people and be controllable by them," and reflect "conditions which will allow active citizen participation."[81] These criteria represented an extension of the League of Women Voters' earlier framing, one that cast governmental rationalization as a precondition for efficient land-use and infrastructure planning, and as necessary for meaningful democratic self-government. As in Ontario in the same period, reformers proposed to save local government by reconstructing it.

Constructing Metropolitan Institutions

The PMSC was divided between radicals and pragmatists. Inspired by Metro Toronto, the radicals believed that a fundamental reconstruction of the local government system was necessary. The pragmatists, who came to dominate the group, believed that incremental change would be more likely not only to pass the legislature but also to survive any reform bill's likely referral to the people. The uneasy balance between the radicals and pragmatists was embodied in its 1966 Interim Report to the legislature.[82]

The PMSC's first recommendation, inspired by Metro Toronto, was the most radical – that a charter for a directly elected "metropolitan municipality" be referred to voters.[83] If approved, existing municipalities and special districts within the Portland-centred urban area, including the City of Portland, would be dissolved. Counties would remain intact. New "corporate communities" would be created – essentially incorporated boroughs governed by elected councils representing up to 75,000 residents. Major services would be delivered on an area-wide basis by a metropolitan tier of government, while essentially local services would be provided by the boroughs. (As cities and unincorporated areas would vote separately on inclusion, there was potential for a "swiss cheese" outcome.) The bill was vigorously opposed in the Senate by Donald Husband, an influential Eugene lawyer who specialized in representing special districts.[84] Outside Portland, editorialists attacked it as a form of forced annexation by the big city; within Portland it was viewed as the city's dismantling.[85] With no prospect of adoption, the proposal faded from view. The option's primary purpose may have been to render the other, more incremental proposals more palatable to cautious legislators and community interests.

The PMSC's first success occurred before the release of its interim report: the formation of a regional council of governments. In part, this formation was driven by federal mandates – as in the Twin Cities and other American metropolitan areas, Washington required that a permanently staffed and broadly representative body be charged with the task of reviewing federal funding applications. Independently of mandates, however, PMSC members believed that institutionalized inter-municipal coordination on land-use and infrastructure planning would produce better outcomes. They advanced the proposal as both a complement to, and, if necessary, a partial substitute for, more comprehensive local government reform.

During 1965 and 1966, the PMSC cultivated support among cities unhappy with the counties' control of the MPC, culminating in the formation of the Columbia Region Association of Governments (CRAG). (Direct reference to Portland in its title was politically unacceptable.) Representation on CRAG's general assembly reflected an uneasy compromise between Portland and its smaller neighbours. Each county received two seats, each municipality of over 300,000 residents three seats (only Portland qualified), and each smaller city one seat. Special districts were not represented. Fourteen cities joined, along with the three traditional Portland metropolitan counties and Clark County across the Columbia River in Washington State. Columbia County joined later. At its October 1966 inaugural meeting, Portland commissioner and MPC chair William Bowes recommended that CRAG assume the MPC's research and federal grant review functions.[86] This would occur in 1967, when CRAG was designated an A-95 clearinghouse and succeeded the MPC as Department of Housing and Urban Development's area-wide planning body. Beyond federal project grants, the membership agreed to contribute two cents per capita to support operating expenditures.

The PMSC's second major accomplishment was the legislature's establishment in 1969 of regional agencies to regulate local government formation and boundary change. In what turned out to be a pivotal move, Rich recruited Ron Cease, a young Portland State University public administration professor, to produce a study of state oversight of municipal incorporation and annexation. A native Portlander who had studied with municipal reform advocate Charles McKinley at Reed College, Cease had worked in Alaska on the design of the new state's municipal system and had been staff director of the Alaska Local Boundary Commission. Inspired by the reform proposals of the ACIR, the Council of State Governments, and the Committee for Economic Development, Cease was normatively committed to governmental rationalization. He examined institutions, legal frameworks, and practices in Alaska, Minnesota, Ontario, Alberta, New Mexico, California, Nevada, and Washington State.[87] Like Joe Robbie in Minnesota a decade earlier, Cease was impressed by the Ontario Municipal Board, which he correctly perceived as the strongest and most established entity. Cease's expert testimony, combined with adroit lobbying by the PMSC and the support of key legislators, including progressive Republican representative and future US senator Bob Packwood, led to the legislature's authorization of separate governor-appointed Local Government Boundary Commissions for the Portland, Salem, and Eugene-Springfield metropolitan areas.

Similar bills backed by the League of Women Voters had failed in the 1957, 1963, and 1967 legislative sessions.[88] These had foundered on three questions: whether review should be exercised at the county level or for broader areas, what provision there should be for voter ratification of annexations (concurrent majorities of residents of annexing and annexed territories, or a single majority of both), and the selection of members. The resistance of rural legislators was overcome by ruling out a statewide body akin to the Minnesota Municipal Commission or the Ontario Municipal Board. The scepticism of conservative legislative leaders in both parties was softened by the exhaustive airing of options and Cease's technical study, which had demonstrated the concept's practicability. The fact that two legislators, Frank Roberts and Hugh McGilvra, were also PMSC members provided an inbuilt source of support. By 1969, the legislative debate was no longer between supporters and opponents, but between supporters' contending proposals. Price emphasizes part-time legislators' deference to committee leadership: "At the time the bill was passed, not more than six of the ninety state legislators had significant knowledge of what the boundary commissions would do and how they would do it."[89] Had the rank and file fully understood the bill, they might not have supported it.

A further proposal – the creation of a multi-purpose metropolitan service district (MSD) to absorb the patchwork special-purpose bodies – first came before the legislature in 1967. As originally conceived, it would take on some or all of land-use planning, water and sewer services, parks and recreational facilities, air pollution control, and transportation. The bill failed in 1967, swamped by the negative attention given to the PMSC's higher-profile metropolitan municipality proposal. The PMSC tried again in 1969, this time having brought Senator Husband on board. The bill had formidable support from civic and business elites: the League of Women Voters, the City Club, the Portland Chamber of Commerce, and the Homebuilders' Association, but the City of Portland, which profited from sales to suburban water districts, remained opposed.[90]

In parallel to the introduction of the MSD bill, the City of Portland demanded that the legislature do something about the rapid deterioration of bus transit. Faced with declining ridership, and after years of conflict with the city, the private Rose City Transit Company demanded that Portland permit a hike to its already high fares or it would halt service. Instead, the city revoked its franchise and asked the state to authorize the creation of a regional public transit operator. Governor McCall quickly formed a task force that recommended the formation of the Tri-County Metropolitan Transportation District, or Tri-Met, that would assume the assets of Rose City and other small private suburban bus companies. In exchange, the city dropped its opposition to creating the MSD. To mollify advocates of a single multi-purpose agency, Senator Husband added a "marriage clause" that would enable the merger of the two entities at a later date.[91] To fund its operations, Tri-Met was granted a dedicated state-administered tax on for-profit business payrolls. The legislature referred the MSD bill to tri-county voters for ratification in the May 1970 primary election. Strong support in populous Multnomah County overwhelmed the measure's failure in Clackamas and Washington Counties.

The civic elite coalition at the core of the PMSC toasted its successes. In only a few short years it had replaced the failing MPC with a more powerful council of governments and created two institutions that promised to rationalize the region's local government complexity: the boundary commission and the MSD. The region also now had a unified regional public transit agency.

A Slow Unraveling

The establishment of new metropolitan institutions was one thing. Fulfilling their potential was another. While Tri-Met quickly mobilized its dedicated tax base, federal funds, and political support at all levels to consolidate existing private transit operators and lay the groundwork for the long-term development of a multi-modal transit system, the other regional institutions faltered.

Much like British Columbia's regional districts, the MSD had been sold to legislators and the public as an empty holding company – its lack of specific functions or authority made it politically palatable. Beginning life without any responsibilities, it was not granted an independent revenue source. Voters rejected a dedicated property tax in November 1970. Resisted by cities, counties, special districts, and residents alike, it never assumed control over water and sewer systems, nor did it merge with Tri-Met. The City of Portland chose to transfer two perennial money-losers to the new body: solid waste management and, in 1976, the Washington Park Zoo. After the legislature rejected its request for funding for new solid waste–processing stations, the MSD contemplated dissolution.[92] (Comparison to British Columbia's regional districts is apt. While the provincial government actively, if quietly, encouraged the assumption of local functions by regional districts during their first decade, the Oregon legislature did nothing to support the MSD.)

The Portland boundary commission also faced significant challenges, operating "under a political cloud since its inception."[93] Its first task was to differentiate itself from the other metropolitan bodies. Facing challenges of its own, CRAG had sought to legitimize itself and expand its influence by subsuming the boundary commission and supplying its staff. This was successfully resisted by the commission's inaugural chair, Ron Cease, who believed that control by the council of governments would compromise its neutrality as a state agency and undermine its technical expertise. The commission actively brokered special district consolidations, strengthened by a 1971 bill that eliminated referendum requirements. Between 1969 and 1977, 46 fire districts were reduced to 42; 116 street lighting districts to 6; 21 sanitary districts to 2; and 53 water districts to 45. All in all, the number of special districts was cut by almost 60 per cent, from 242 to 100, with many functions transferred to countywide service districts.[94] Perhaps more importantly, the wave of defensive municipal incorporations ended.

Despite these early successes, the boundary commissions came under fire when they were required to enforce the state's and (in Portland) CRAG's planning policies.[95] The enabling statute had charged them with preventing "illogical" boundary extensions and the "fragmentation of public services and local government," while assuring "adequate quantity and quality of public services" and the "financial integrity" of local government units.[96] These vague standards were negotiated with cities and counties on a case-by-case basis, relying on approved land-use plans where they existed. After 1973, they were legally required to enforce and implement the LCDC's land-use goals. Opposition inside and outside the legislature led the commissioners to adopt an increasingly cautious stance. Some legislators believed that SB 100 made the boundary commissions redundant, while other,

mostly rural, legislators viewed them as infringements on local autonomy. They were also opposed by homebuilder organizations, municipalities, and rural residents. This resistance reinforced the
commissions' restrained exercise of their legal authority.

CRAG also proved largely ineffective despite its substantial authority. Its chair, Richard Granger, argued that the organization would
have to actively gain public trust if it was to be effective, yet the public
remained largely ignorant of its existence and purpose.[97] More generally, the local governments represented in CRAG's general assembly
failed to transcend their narrow interests and adopt a regional perspective. The thirty-year *Interim Regional Land Use Plan* adopted in
October 1970 by CRAG's executive committee was perhaps unfairly
condemned by environmentalists and advocates of a more muscular
area-wide planning vision as a pasting together of existing local plans
rather than a fully articulated regional policy agenda. This criticism
was reinforced by municipalities' jockeying over industrial land designations and the future tax base they represented. On studying all
local plans, CRAG planners found that the amount of municipally
designated industrial land exceeded any reasonable forecast of future
need.[98] Local governments blocked CRAG staff's attempt to revise
the plan, each fearing that it would lose out on its "fair" share of
economic growth. The plan was also criticized for embodying status-
quo growth patterns as opposed to presenting an alternative future
vision. Critics referred to its schematic reference map as "the yellow
peril," because it displayed vast amounts of low-density residential
area, coloured yellow, at the region's edges.[99] With voluntary membership and its budget funded mostly by federal grants, local politicians had little incentive to invest in regional policymaking. Moreover,
local government dependence on the property tax militated against
cooperation – as competitors for residential growth and business
investment, they had little incentive to restrict urban development or
make trade-offs for the benefit of the whole.

Whatever its planners' aspirations, CRAG proved politically unable
to craft, negotiate, and implement regional objectives. It approved
virtually all federal grant applications that it reviewed. For critics,
CRAG's impotence was symbolized by its approval in 1971 of the
Charbonneau golf course community located across the Willamette
from Wilsonville in northwestern Clackamas County. The project
was located outside the extensive urban zone designated in the
Interim Regional Plan and would require extensive water and sewer

extensions onto agricultural land, yet CRAG's executive committee declined to reject the proposal.[100] The sole dissenting vote on the executive committee, Multnomah County commissioner Don Clark, later recalled that the decision was purely political. While CRAG's board generally supported more stringent urban growth controls, members feared that taking a stand on a particular project in the absence of a general policy risked igniting a "political firestorm" that would destroy the organization.[101]

Regional planning's advocates believed that institutional change was the only answer. The City Club, the League of Women Voters, and CRAG itself proposed that membership be made mandatory and that it be given stronger statutory planning authority.[102] The 1973 legislature took up this proposal. SB 769 made membership in CRAG mandatory and charged it with adopting regional goals and a "generalized, coordinated plan," to which local government plans would have to conform, to ensure the region's orderly development.[103] (It is important to note that SB 769 was passed before SB 100; CRAG's expanded planning powers would have existed even without the state land-use system.[104]) The basis of representation was also changed. Member governments would now vote in proportion to their population, thereby giving Portland a de facto veto. Don Clark, Lloyd Anderson, and other pro-planning board members engineered the resignation of CRAG executive director Homer Chandler, whom they saw as too passive, replacing him with former PMSC director A. McKay Rich.[105]

CRAG's reconstitution paralleled the development of a more proactive land-use policy framework. After the Charbonneau debacle, CRAG's staff began developing a more directive Interim Regional Development Policy, which encouraged infill and redevelopment as a steppingstone to a comprehensive regional plan.[106] This evolving scheme drew on experimentation by Washington County and the Salem-area Mid-Willamette Valley Council of Governments by designating urban service areas within which urban infrastructure would be provided and outside of which it would be prohibited.[107] This approach, which complemented earlier ideas about exclusive farm zoning, was carried into the LCDC's fourteenth statewide planning goal on urbanization, which came into effect at the beginning of 1975.[108] Represented as a line on a map, the urban service area came to be known as an "urban growth boundary" (UGB).

The designation of an urban service area to ensure orderly, contiguous urban expansion differed little from the contemporaneous metropolitan urban service area in the Twin Cities, or the Lower Mainland Regional Planning Board's and Metro Toronto's earlier insistence on contiguous, fully serviced urbanization. Planned infrastructure extension would be used to rationalize the location of market-led growth at the regional scale without necessarily altering its form at the neighbourhood, block, or parcel scale. Yet Oregon's framing of the urban service area as a *boundary* – a hard limit on urbanization – set it apart from the other jurisdictions' planning instruments, which were expressly designed to expand with urbanization. CRAG's deliberations on the interim regional land-use policy in 1973 reveal the bias toward slow- or no-growth policies – indeed, the word "moratorium" was replaced by "containment" only late in the process.[109] Ultimately, the infrastructure and servicing rationale for the UGB would fade from view as proponents and critics alike focused on it as a land-use designation and as a real and symbolic limit on the aspirations of property owners and local governments.

Despite extensive consultations with stakeholders and the public, and being backstopped by state mandate, rural local governments continued to resist CRAG's newly assertive planning agenda, which they saw, perhaps correctly, as a vehicle for Portland interests.[110] Hearings on the 1975 development framework drew an aggressive anti-planning public, including one man who was arrested for refusing to surrender his rifle.[111] Washington County resisted CRAG's incursion into its own planning efforts, symbolically voting to withdraw support from CRAG while continuing to "participate under protest."[112] The November 1976 election saw two publicly initiated questions on the statewide ballot – one to abolish all councils of governments, including CRAG, the other to repeal SB 100. While both failed, they revealed that the elite consensus in favour of regional and state planning masked substantial opposition.

Metropolitan Reform Elites Mobilize to Create Portland Metro

It was in this context that the 1960s-era civic elite network mobilized to consolidate its gains. A. McKay Rich had left CRAG to work for Multnomah County in 1973. When a National Academy of Public Administration (NAPA) call for applications to fund metropolitan governance research crossed his desk, he contacted Ron Cease. Using the boundary commission as a base, they won a $100,000 grant, which they used to reconstitute the core elements of the dissolved

PMSC, albeit without sanction by any government body. Cease, Rich, and journalist Jerry Tippens (who had also served on the boundary commission) formed the Ad Hoc Two-Tiered Planning Committee and raised an additional $50,000 from Portland State University, CRAG, the boundary commission, municipalities, and local corporations.

Ironically, Portland beat out Seattle for the NAPA grant largely on the basis of its strong neighbourhood organizations. Although the grant was intended to fund research on neighbourhood empowerment within metropolitan institutions, Cease and his colleagues focused almost entirely on democratic accountability and governmental efficiency at the metropolitan scale. They were cognizant of CRAG's legitimacy crisis and disappointed that the MSD had failed to consolidate the many special districts. They believed that merging the MSD and CRAG into a directly elected body would end disagreement over local government representation on metropolitan bodies, improve democratic accountability, and facilitate service consolidation on a metropolitan basis. Importantly, this agenda was detached from concurrent statewide and regional land-use debates. Neither Cease nor Rich viewed land-use planning as a primary rationale for metropolitan government.[113]

By the end of 1975 they had recruited a sixty-five-member steering group, the Tri-County Local Government Commission, deliberately composed of civic and business elites representing a diverse range of occupations who would use their influence to promote reform.[114] Cease was made chair, businessman and former Chamber of Commerce president Carl Halvorson vice-chair, and Rich the staff director. While Cease, Rich, and their fellow travellers were leaders in good-government reform circles, Halvorson's success in the construction and property development industries lent business prestige.[115]

Over eighteen months, the commission held two large conferences and dozens of public meetings, and informally engaged a broad range of stakeholders. Committees studied four potential governance models: Model I was the status quo; Model II a Metro Toronto–style two-tier general-purpose government that would replace existing counties; Model III a Twin Cities–style three-tier arrangement; and Model IV the consolidation of services into a series of single-purpose metropolitan service districts. The status quo and Model IV were rejected. The commission's leadership favoured Model II but saw Model III as more politically feasible. The commission adopted a final proposal for submission to the legislature at the end of 1976. As the M S D was less controversial than C R A G and, despite its travails, was grounded in a popularly ratified statute, its reconstitution as Metro would be the basis of the reform. Commission staff member Bill Cross recalls that the final proposal was orchestrated by Rich more than anyone else: "He had his preferences but deferred to the idea of broad political compromise. His goal was to pass *something*" rather than see a purer option fail.[116] Cease recalls his efforts at the final conference being focused on bringing the broader group into alignment with what "we knew ... what we wanted on the Metro side" without sacrificing the proposal's core elements.[117]

Testimony at the legislative hearings on H B 2070 aired predictable positions. Outer suburban business interests and rural politicians were opposed while their Portland counterparts were in favour.[118] Washington County municipalities Hillsboro and Cornelius, and the county itself, repeatedly asked to be removed from Metro's jurisdiction. The bill's legislative proponents came to believe that Metro's approval hinged on minimizing its actual and perceived impact on conservative rural voters. While the Tri-County Commission proposal called for the district to cover the entirety of the three counties, the legislative committee clipped off the rural fringes, leaving only urbanized and urbanizing areas. (There was precedent for this – the jurisdiction of the M S D and Tri-Met more or less corresponded with the extent of urbanization. C R A G, by contrast, had comprised whole counties. See figure 7.6.) While the question of what would happen when significant urbanization spilled beyond Metro's boundaries remained unanswered, the boundary commission could theoretically extend Metro's boundaries. The process of defining the boundary was political rather than technical. A legislative subcommittee chaired by Representative Mike Ragsdale requisitioned a National Guard helicopter and flew the entire committee and its staff around the region, sketching the boundary on US Geographical Survey maps.[119]

The bill provided for Metro to assume additional functions. Metro would maintain the M S D's "marriage clause" permitting the takeover of Tri-Met and was also empowered to absorb the authority of the Portland Boundary Commission, on the approval of voters. Metro was also authorized to become involved in regional aspects of water supply, social services, parks and recreation, libraries, and corrections, but only if it secured voter approval of a corresponding tax base – something that had eluded the M S D. It also maintained C R A G's roles

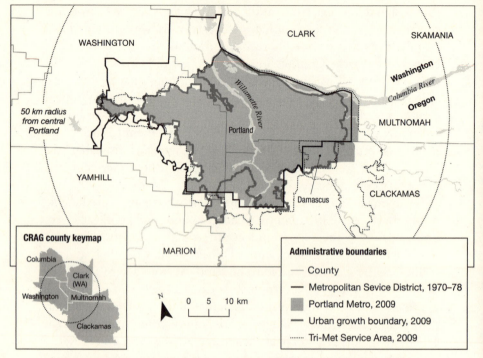

Figure 7.6 Administrative boundaries and the urban growth boundary in the
Portland Region

Note: The Columbia Region Association of Governments (CRAG) included local
governments within five counties spanning the Oregon–Washington state line. After
1973, Washington, Clackamas, and Multnomah Counties and their associated
cities were mandatory members of CRAG. Clark County and the cities of Columbia
County in Washington State were voluntary associate members, as were Tri-Met,
the Port of Portland, and the State of Oregon. The boundaries of the old
Metropolitan Service District (established in 1970), Tri-Met (1969), and Portland
Metro (1979) overlapped to a large extent but were not identical. The major difference between the current Urban Growth Boundary and the 1977 CRAG draft UGB
is the later addition of the Damascus area in Clackamas County. Each designation
reflected political compromises among urban and rural legislators. Also, the
Tri-Met boundary would certainly have been more restrictive at the time of its
creation, but I could locate no map of its historical boundaries.

Sources: Portland Metro, Tri-Met, and urban growth boundaries from Portland
Metro, Regional Land Information System CD-ROM (2009 edition); 1970 MSD
redrawn from *Metro: The Metropolitan Connection*.

as the coordinator of local land-use planning and zoning and as the
region's federal grants clearinghouse, as well as its authority to develop

land-use "goals and objectives," nested within the LCDC's policies, and "functional plans" for infrastructure and services, both binding on local comprehensive plans.[120] Metro would possess broad authority, yet it remained to be seen whether the legitimacy conferred by direct election would overcome the political barriers to its exercise.

Over the objection of the commission, which argued that the prior popular ratification of the original MSD "covered" the merger, the amended bill passed the legislature only with the proviso that it be referred to the voters. The commission leadership formed a "yes" campaign organization – the Citizen's Committee for Efficiency in Local Government – and adopted a "Trojan Horse" strategy that framed the ballot question as a "reorganization" of the MSD coupled with the "abolition" of the unpopular CRAG. The rhetoric remained squarely focused on accountability and efficiency:

> The case for Measure 6 [the ballot initiative to ratify the merger of CRAG and MSD] is a case for democracy, Measure 6 is needed to provide the people, through the ballot box, the same control over area-wide governmental matters that they now have at every other level. Measure 6 is also a classic case for efficiency in government ... Measure 6 is needed to help curb the costs of uncoordinated governmental growth.[121]

The proposal had considerable support from central-city opinion leaders – the editorial boards of the *Oregonian* and *Oregon Journal*, the Portland Chamber of Commerce, local Democratic Party organizations, and the League of Women Voters. Despite this, Ballot Measure 6 passed in the May 1978 election only because its vote surplus in urban Multnomah County was sufficiently large to compensate for its defeat in Clackamas County. Rich and others believe that the strategy was effective. Voters antagonistic to "big government" and planning may have voted yes in the belief that they were not only eliminating CRAG but also its activities and functions.

When Metro commenced operation on 1 January 1979, its territorial jurisdiction was smaller than the entities it replaced. The civic elite network's objective of consolidating local government and infrastructure systems into a single metropolitan authority was no closer to being achieved. What had changed was the basis of representation: Metro was directly elected. The impact of direct election on its legitimacy and effectiveness remained to be seen. While it had assumed

CRAG's planning role, its capacity to countervail municipal self-interest was untested.

As in the development and adoption of the state land-use system, policy entrepreneurs played an outsized role in developing legislative proposals. Taking advantage of their social position as professionals, academics, businesspeople, and legislators, normatively committed local government reformers constructed a coherent policy agenda and mustered majority support for it in the part-time legislature. But while a broadly perceived crisis spurred action on the land-use file, metropolitan reform was an elite-driven project. It may be that some of its elements (the creation of the boundary commissions and CRAG's expanded planning authority, for example) were enacted because they touched on land-use matters and were caught up in the crisis atmosphere. The rationalizing impulse that underlay the MSD, however, had no public constituency. Metro's creation in 1978 represented the end of the temporary conjuncture of factors – routine bipartisan cooperation, a broadly apprehended land-use crisis, and a normative context of trust in government and deference to elites – that had briefly countervailed the separated-powers system's tendency toward indecision and particularistic policymaking.

PORTLAND METRO AND THE OREGON LAND-USE SYSTEM SINCE 1979

Metro's creation coincided with the state land-use system's implementation. While Metro acquired a handful of operating responsibilities – principally for regional public facilities – it never assumed control over water and sewer systems or merged with Tri-Met. Over time, the boundary commission had incrementally reduced the number of special districts by negotiating mutually acceptable mergers and city annexations, yet many people continued to live in unincorporated areas, purchasing services from free-standing service districts. The objective of directly linking land-use and infrastructure planning and operations within a single metropolitan institution remained unachieved. In this sense, Metro was a failure. However, it found a new purpose as the administrator of the state land-use planning system, including, most visibly, the urban growth boundary. Backstopped by state mandates and an activist support coalition, Metro benefited from the popularity, especially in urban areas, of the state land-use system. Metro would become the primary institutional venue of conflict between the system's defenders and critics, whose stridency increased through the 1980s and 1990s. Over time, Metro maintained its legitimacy through a strategy of intensive stakeholder outreach, avoidance of public controversy, and the legal consolidation of its autonomy via a home-rule charter.

Metro's Context: Normative Change and the Contested State Land-Use System

The creation of the land-use system and metropolitan institutions had been separately driven by different constellations of elites. More so than the metropolitan reformers, the land-use advocates benefited from widespread and growing public concern about quality of life (to which they had successfully attached historically incompatible environmental protection and farmland preservation agendas) as well as the vigorous bipartisan support of governors McCall and Straub. Despite the mainstreaming of small-government conservatism and a newly radicalized property-rights lobby during the 1970s, the land-use system became firmly entrenched during its first two decades because it responded to inchoate public anxiety. As the administration of state land-use mandates became a central purpose of Metro and defined its public identity, its fortunes became increasingly intertwined with those of the statewide land-use system.

As in Minnesota, Ontario, British Columbia, and elsewhere, the 1970s featured a political reaction against state intervention and technocratic decision-making. While Democrats retained their advantage among registered voters, and would control the state legislature for much of the 1980s and 1990s, the political centre was shifting to the right. The Democrats' post-Watergate electoral gains were reversed by a newly radicalized Republican Party committed to limited government, deregulation, lower taxes, personal responsibility, and local autonomy. Bipartisanism dissolved as the Democrats ceded their rural labour electoral base to the Republicans, while many urban Republicans moved into the Democratic fold. This shift was complicated by a dramatic reversal in the state's resource-based economy. Statewide unemployment topped 12 per cent in 1975, almost half again the national rate.[122] Straub lost the 1978 election to Republican state senator Vic Atiyeh, who assumed the mantle of populist tax fighter and, anticipating the Reagan revolution two years later, painted the Democrats as tax-and-spend interventionists.[123] In 1974 Straub had defeated Atiyeh by the largest margin since 1950; in 1978 Atiyeh beat Straub by ten points. The same year saw the approval of California's Proposition 13, the landmark ballot initiative that constitutionalized local property tax limitation. Although a similar ballot measure – vigorously opposed by Straub – was defeated in November 1978, voters in nine states approved tax limits in that year.[124]

S B 100 had been passed in the twilight of McCall's second term. While they had twice run against each other for governor, McCall and Straub were united in their support for agricultural land and environmental protections. But as Straub's decisive 1974 victory over Atiyeh (with McCall's endorsement) was hailed as a de facto third McCall term, clouds massed on the horizon. McCall had presided over the legislative innovations of the late 1960s and early 1970s, but their implementation, and associated political costs, occurred under Straub.

Forestry and homebuilding groups mobilized to put an initiative on the 1976 ballot to repeal S B 100, arguing that it impeded economic growth. Straub dug in. In a 19 September 1975 speech to Associated Oregon Industries, he signalled that, if the timber industry launched a repeal initiative, he would "stand and fight" and "not give an inch and mobilize an army of good citizens who will stand behind us to protect what we have achieved."[125] The repeal measure was defeated by a fourteen-point margin after a bitterly fought campaign. A similar initiative failed by twenty-two points in November 1978. With the exception of the timber industry, anti-planning business interests eventually made their peace with land-use regulation. In particular, homebuilders came to see the LCDC as a source of market certainty through its ensuring that local governments zoned land in proportion to housing demand and that planning permissions occurred in a timely fashion.[126] Developer support contributed to the defeat of a third repeal initiative in 1982, as did the backing of Governor Atiyeh, who linked arms with past opponents Straub and McCall, as well as the influential industrialist and property developer John Gray.[127]

The state land-use system proved resilient during the politically polarizing and economically troubled 1980s and 1990s because it engendered a durable support coalition.[128] Two components have already been discussed: the Portland-area property development industry, which enjoyed the investment certainty provided by land-use planning, and central-city business and civic elites, who saw growth controls as essential to shoring up the downtown.[129] Farmers were ambivalent. While as landowners they resisted regulation, they also recognized, as had Macpherson, that without planning their livelihood was at risk. Most crucial was a new "watchdog" organization, 1000 Friends of Oregon.[130] Founded in 1975 with McCall's support, 1000 Friends represented a continuation of OSPIRG's earlier advocacy. (Henry Richmond, previously OSPIRG's staff lawyer, would serve as 1000 Friends' executive director for thirty years.) The organization engaged in lobbying and research, insisting on evidence-based planning. At the same time, it defended the system by mounting lawsuits (most of them successful) designed to reveal abuses of the land-use system and set legal precedents. This activism gave the LCDC and DLCD political cover by mounting an aggressive, third-party defense of the system, mobilizing fiscal resources and expertise beyond those available to the LCDC itself. As a non-partisan member-based organization, it was the hub through which a network of pro-planning advocates mobilized and connected.

Metro Acquires Unexpected Functions

Metro was hobbled by its ambiguous position in relation to the state and local governments, and by its minimal own-source resources: solid waste management and zoo user fees. Citizens voted down a dedicated property tax in 1980. Metro was forced to lay off forty-five employees when the federal government cancelled categorical grant funding for planning and other projects in early 1981.[131] (Only in 1990 was Metro granted an excise tax on its own operations, five years after Governor Atiyeh had vetoed a similar measure. Metro's user fees could be used only to recover costs for specific functions, while an excise tax on these fees could be pooled into a general fund.) Metro's early attempts at flood control planning and constructing new solid waste disposal facilities foundered on local political opposition.[132] Metro also had little public profile. It would be a half-decade before the *Oregonian* stopped referring to it as the "MSD" – its official name – and the telephone company agreed to list it as a "government," rather than as a "service district," in the blue pages of the directory.[133] At mid-decade it appeared that Metro was destined to accomplish little more than its predecessors.

The tide soon turned. Although federal support had diminished, it was not entirely gone. A deal to redirect federal funding from the cancelled Mount Hood Freeway to light-rail transit remained in effect. To meet the federal requirement that funds be managed by an intergovernmental body, Metro established a Joint Policy Advisory Committee on Transportation (JPACT). Composed of Metro councillors, municipal and county officials, and state agency representatives, JPACT "established the incentive for often competing interests to work together ... All parties recognized that the [light rail] system could not be built at once and that each part of the region had to wait for its 'turn.'"[134] JPACT institutionalized a role for Metro as an intergovernmental convener.

Metro also accrued legitimacy by assuming responsibility for the operation of new and existing regional "visitor facilities": the convention centre (1986); the Portland Center for the Performing Arts, Portland Civic Stadium, and Memorial Coliseum (1990); and Expo Centre (1994). These built on the MSD's earlier assumption of the Oregon Zoo. All but the convention centre were existing facilities taken over from the City of Portland or Multnomah County. Both the Port of Portland – a tri-county special-purpose body that operates airports and river terminals – and Metro were contenders to operate the convention centre. Ron Cease called on business leader Carl Halvorson, his associate from the earlier Tri-County Local Government Commission, to make the case for giving it to Metro, successfully arguing that "this is what we created Metro for."[135] Voters approved a $65 million general revenue bond for Metro to construct the centre, effectively locking in Metro's existence for the duration of the bond's twenty-five-year amortization period.[136] In the 1990s, Metro also became involved in parks and open space management, acquiring 1,450 hectares of parks, pioneer cemeteries, golf courses, and boat launches from Multnomah County.[137] After an initial failure at the ballot box in 1992, voters authorized a $135 million open-space acquisition program in 1995.

Metro acquired functions through improvisation rather than through programmatic action. The civic elite network that had championed its creation, and the MSD before it, intended it to absorb the profusion of water and sewer districts and ultimately Tri-Met. Instead, it acquired a hodgepodge of functions cast off from the city and Multnomah County. Even so, the facilities and parks and open space functions conferred legitimacy on Metro by increasing its public visibility and generating new support coalitions. The bond issues established long-term tasks and obligations, while giving Metro new discretionary resources.

Metro Gains Legitimacy through Administering the State Land-Use System

Metro's most visible and controversial task was the administration of state planning mandates inherited from CRAG. The draft urban service area boundary CRAG developed in 1975–76 was intended to fulfill the objectives of the LCDC's urbanization planning goal, which mandated the demarcation of a separation between a contiguous, fully serviced urban zone and productive rural land. As in the process that produced the 1970 "yellow peril" map, however, the politics of allocating population and employment growth proved difficult. CRAG's 1976 UGB enclosed 950 km², of which 36 per cent was "vacant," or non-urban.[138] The UGB was challenged by 1000 Friends of Oregon on the basis that CRAG had exceeded the LCDC's requirement that UGBs contain a twenty-year supply of developable land by adding on a 25 per cent "market factor." Metro had assumed CRAG's jurisdiction over the UGB in the meantime, and so it was Metro that the LCDC asked to justify the loose UGB. In the end, the LCDC acknowledged the boundary as originally submitted. This was a political move.[139] The LCDC recognized that an inhospitable political climate threatened both the land-use system and Metro. To survive, it needed to show progress toward acknowledging local plans, the statutory deadline for which was 1 July 1980, while also demonstrating its independence from 1000 Friends.

Metro's planning role amounted to little more than the passive coordination of local plans as they moved through the LCDC acknowledgment process.[140] Only in the second half of the 1980s did Metro assert a stronger regional planning role. This change had two catalysts. The first was the publicizing in 1988 of the Oregon Department of Transportation's nearly complete plans for a west-side highway bypass skirting Hillsboro, Beaverton, and Tigard – plans strongly opposed by 1000 Friends.[141] Initial studies by 1000 Friends found that the highway would undermine state land-use objectives by increasing urban development pressure on farmland inside and outside the UGB. The second catalyst was a DLCD-mandated review of the Portland UGB.[142] Metro realized that, in order to justify potential changes to the UGB, it would have to develop a land-use concept for the land within it. It also knew that exercising its legal authority to unilaterally produce "functional plans" binding on local governments would be political suicide.[143] Testimony before a 1987–88 legislative interim task force on metropolitan governance revealed strong opposition to Metro's using its existing powers, let alone expanding them. It had an "image problem" and was not yet seen to have proven itself.[144]

Metro established a Planning and Development Department in 1988 to review the UGB. Its work was supported by 1000 Friends' parallel development of a positive vision to counter the Department of Transportation's western bypass. With federal and foundation grants, 1000 Friends launched the Making the Land Use–Transportation–Air Quality Connection program (LUTRAQ). Better resourced than Metro itself, LUTRAQ involved a comprehensive analysis and multi-scenario forecast of transportation and housing demand. The definition of alternative land-use concepts was led by Berkeley-based architect–urban designer Peter Calthorpe, who would go on to national recognition as a founder of the New Urbanism movement and a pioneer of transit-oriented development. LUTRAQ was a national test bed for emerging professional planning ideas about concentrating residential, office, and commercial development into mixed-use, pedestrian-oriented nodes centred on higher-order transit corridors in suburban areas.[145] The notion of closely linking land-use and transportation infrastructure informed later expansion of the Tri-Met's Metropolitan Area Express light-rail system, the initial Portland–Gresham line of which had opened in 1986.

The policy development and advocacy work of 1000 Friends was complemented by Metro's stakeholder outreach, which built on JPACT. An Urban Growth Management Policy Advisory Committee (PAC), chaired by Metro councillor Jim Gardner, was composed of local and state officials, development industry representatives, and citizens. The PAC consulted widely, holding issue-focused workshops, two conferences, public hearings, and UGB tours, all while interacting directly with local government professional staff and distributing information materials to stakeholder groups and the public. Supported by Metro staff and a Technical Advisory Committee, the group developed a series of Regional Urban Growth Goals and Objectives (RUGGOs), which were adopted by Metro Council in 1991.[146] The first goal entrenched collaborative process by committing Metro to comprehensive engagement with citizens and local governments in plan development. The PAC was positioned as the lead actor, charged with making recommendations to Metro Council on any policy changes. In the event that a local government's plan was found to be not in conformity with regional goals, objectives, and plans, it was the PAC, not Metro itself, that would study the issue and recommend remedial actions. Through sustained formal and informal engagement, local governments previously antagonistic to Metro and regional planning found themselves designing its procedures and goals.[147]

Former Metro planning director John Fregonese credits the plan's successful implementation to the public engagement campaign, which presented stakeholders and residents with alternative scenarios and their implications.[148] Engagement built public credibility on which it could draw in future disputes. Metro also solidified its honest-broker role by assembling and disseminating regional land-use and other datasets. These became a trusted evidence base for policymaking, ending disputes between governments, and between governments and non-governmental interests over facts.[149]

The RUGGOs were amended in 1995 to include a Metro 2040 Growth Concept map and plan. This was followed in 1996–97 by implementing policy statements: the Urban Growth Management Functional Plan, to which local governments must conform, and the Regional Framework Plan, a guideline that adds policy detail to the RUGGOs. Periodically amended, these documents remain in effect today.

Home Rule for Metro Locks in Intergovernmental Relationships

This collaborative system was locked in when voters approved a home rule charter for Metro in 1992 – a proposal advanced by Metro's chief executive and endorsed by the interim legislative task force on metropolitan problems in 1988.[150] The charter, which was drafted by a committee chaired by Ron Cease, specified intergovernmental relationships and reoriented Metro's purpose.[151] The charter required Metro to prepare a "future vision" for the region and a "regional framework plan." It also defined the membership and role of the PAC. As Cotugno and Seltzer put it, "Through this charter, Metro and local governments develop binding expectations for the scope and authority for regional transportation and land-use planning, and the implementation of the regional vision through decision-making at the local level."[152] Much as in British Columbia's regional planning boards and regional districts, the institutionalization of collective interaction by local governments on regional issues built trust and norms of reciprocity. Through their routinized integration into Metro's policymaking, local officials came to accept that UGB expansion and other decisions were not winner-takes-all one-offs, but rather part of an ongoing process of problem-solving and mutual adjustment.

Becoming a home-rule entity also reoriented perceptions of Metro. Whereas previously it was viewed as a state agency responsible to the legislature, the charter reframed it as a novel form of local government, drawing its authority and legitimacy from the people. Unlike British Columbia's regional districts, Metro was not a federation of local governments, although it was formally linked to them through JPACT and the PAC. While Metro retained the authority to assume additional service functions, this was now secondary to its planning role, and could occur only through intergovernmental consensus.

Intergovernmental Relations in Perpetual Tension

From an unpromising beginning, Metro was transformed from an almost empty shell to an active policymaker. Created to consolidate infrastructure services, it found its purpose and legitimacy as a regional planner. This has put it at the centre of statewide debates that have pitted defenders of the land-use system against property rights advocates. No issue is ever permanently settled in Oregon land-use politics. Metro's role and authority in the region and within state land-use planning will remain open to challenge as antagonists pursue their goals through legislative lobbying, ballot initiatives, and lawsuits.

Ballot Measure 7, which passed by a six-point margin in 2000 but was overturned by the Oregon Supreme Court on technical grounds, required governments to financially compensate property owners for decreases in their property values caused by land-use regulation. Opponents were more successful in 2004 with a rephrased Measure 37. Recognizing that protecting agricultural and environmentally sensitive lands had majority support, opponents of the land-use system shifted from a negative message of repeal to a positive message of helping farmers.[153] As Measure 37 set no thresholds or procedural requirements, it led to a torrent of compensation requests to which cash-strapped local governments could respond only by lifting land-use controls. In the tri-county area alone, more than two thousand claims were lodged, pertaining to over 400 km² – an area one-third the size of Metro's jurisdiction. The legislature responded in 2007 with Measure 49, which maintained the possibility of compensation under specific conditions. Property rights advocacy remains a potent force in Oregon politics.

The UGB remains popular among urbanites yet controversial on the fringe. Local battles over UGB expansion have served as proxy campaigns for organized defenders and opponents of the land-use system. Metro resisted UGB expansion onto fertile farmland by the small Washington County city of Cornelius, which sought new employment areas. On the other side of the region, Metro undertook a large-scale UGB expansion in 2002 to include a part of Clackamas County called Damascus, largely on the basis that its clay soils are ill suited to agriculture. Its residents remain strongly opposed to urbanization, however, and little development has occurred.[154]

Metro and the counties have only recently ended a decade-long scuffle over further UGB expansion. At Metro's request in the context of the perceived failings of the Damascus UGB expansion, the state Senate passed a law in 2007 enabling Metro and the three counties to define "reserve" lands for long-term development through 2060. After hundreds of public meetings, extensive lobbying, and inter-municipal bargaining, an agreement was reached in 2010.[155] After opponents appealed the compromise, the courts overturned several of the reserve designations in 2014. Metro and stakeholders quickly hammered out a new compromise, which was enacted through state legislation to avoid further appeals of Metro's 2011 UGB adjustments, which depended on the earlier deal.

The integration of land-use planning and infrastructure provision remains incomplete. While Metro's plans are co-produced by counties and municipalities, and are binding on them, Metro does not finance and operate urban infrastructure and services, and so has little direct control over their extension. Without predictable and long-term capital funding aligned with metropolitan land-use objectives, Metro risks becoming a "paper planner." Alignment is strongest in transportation, where federal funds have incrementally expanded Tri-Met's rail network. Looking to the future, the state legislature's 2017 transportation "grand bargain," which raises taxes to fund projects across the state, will renew and expand road and transit systems in the region.[156] At the same time, Metro has taken over leadership from Tri-Met on a large bond issue that will go on the ballot in 2020 – a signal that local actors believe that Metro possesses sufficient influence and legitimacy to make the case to voters. The provision of other hard and soft infrastructure, from water and sewer mains to sidewalks and schools, depends on the availability of capital funding from senior governments. Indeed, high servicing costs, and the long-term decline of federal water and sewer grants, are credited with dooming development in Damascus.[157]

CONCLUSION

Oregon's version of the separated-powers system of government is virtually designed to be indecisive and irresolute. Together, the plural executive, the ballot initiative, legislative referral, and part-time legislative service have inhibited programmatic and durable policymaking except at extraordinary junctures.

Much as in Minnesota, the permeability of Oregon's legislative branch to outside actors enabled policy innovation, but only when external policymaking coalitions have been broad and unified in their objectives and the normative context was conducive. In the 1960s and 1970s, Portland metropolitan governance reform was driven by a bipartisan network of normatively committed civic elites – academics, public servants, and local and state politicians of both parties who were able to recruit influencers in the business world. The legislature was the transmission belt for policy ideas developed by the Bureau of Municipal Research and Service, the League of Women Voters, the City Club, OSPIRG, the Tri-County Local Government Commission, and 1000 Friends. The Portland Metropolitan Study Commission represented a version of the same mechanism – a state-sponsored analogue of the Twin Cities Citizens League. Policy entrepreneurs such as L.B. Day and Hector Macpherson also used elected office to advance their objectives.

Although Portland's civic elites persuaded the legislature to create new metropolitan bodies, they did not succeed in consolidating regional infrastructure systems and service delivery. (In the end, the panoply of special districts was partially rationalized not through regionalization, but through municipal annexation, at least in east Multnomah County.[158]) The MSD, CRAG, and the boundary commissions did not fulfill their framers' goals because they lacked the support of the general public and local governments. Metro claimed legitimacy not only the basis of direct election, but also by appealing to values, actively engaging the public, nurturing external support coalitions, and binding local governments to each other through collaborative process.

The state land-use system was devised and sustained by a separate coalition of working farmers, agricultural processing and tourism interests, activist environmental lawyers, and sympathetic politicians. If metropolitan governance reform was at its core a technocratic, elite-driven agenda, the drive to protect rural land through urban containment was the harbinger of a new politics based on appeals to values and quality of life. It is within the institutional framework of the state land-use system that Metro found its place in greater Portland's intergovernmental system. Should the foundations of the land-use system be undercut – as almost occurred with Measure 37 – Metro's legitimacy and authority would also be curtailed. Asked if anyone would be talking about Metro today if SB 100 had never been enacted, A. McKay Rich replied "probably not."[159]

This points to an important distinction between the Oregon and Minnesota cases, and indeed between Oregon and most American states: the land-use regime applies to the entire state, not only to the metropolitan area, and its support coalition crosscuts metropolitan and non-metropolitan space. Yet, as Seltzer notes, Oregon does not have a state plan. Rather, the state sets the rules and expectations for local governments, which make their own decisions subject to state acknowledgment.[160] In this sense, the Oregon system resembles Ontario's hierarchical planning regime, with its provincial policy statements and plans, more than it resembles the decentralized policy-making of Minnesota or British Columbia. Metro's independent authority in relation to the region's local governments is derived from state mandates, and, since these mandates operate statewide, Portland's metropolitan institutions are less vulnerable to legislative conflict divided on urban-rural lines. Still, as in Minnesota, polarization inside and outside the legislature between urban Democrats and suburban and rural Republicans is augmented by the growing social and economic distance between the metropolitan area and the state's rural hinterland.[161] While Oregon's permeable legislative process has enabled policy innovation, particularly in the early postwar normative context of greater trust in elites and bipartisan consensus, it remains a source of instability. Institutions and policies can never be durable when opponents can so easily mobilize through the legislature, the courts, and ballot initiative.

8

Urban Governance, Past and Future

A century and half ago, North American society, economy, and living environments were rural; today, the vast majority of Americans and Canadians reside in urban contexts and most live in expanding metropolitan areas. Throughout the industrial era, and especially in the years after the Second World War, rapid urbanization generated unprecedented policy demands, and governments mobilized resources and generated new capacities in response. The transition from an agrarian to an urban society may be nearly complete in North America and across the West. Sociologist Neil Brenner suggests that the world has reached a state of "planetary urbanization" in which the distinction between urban and rural is dissolved by the globalization of social and economic networks.[1] Yet the social and economic flows and the physical spaces of urban agglomeration remain, and are in constant flux.[2] The problems of urbanization do not end when agrarian societies are eclipsed by metropolitan ones; rather, urban flux generates new problems. At the beginning of this book, I suggested that most contemporary policy problems, and their solutions, are to be found in cities. The governance challenge is to mount an effective response.

In this final chapter, I summarize and draw lessons from my comparative historical interpretation of the development of urban governance in the United States and Canada. Comparing American and Canadian governance demonstrates that, since the beginning, governing institutions have structured the resources and capabilities of governments, imposing different incentives on those who work within them, and, through their cumulative effects, they have set each country's multi-level urban governance on different developmental paths. Westminster and separated-powers governments engage different

constellations of actors and interests in different venues, draw legitimacy from different sources, incentivize the construction of different
kinds of policy regimes and patterns of intergovernmental relations,
and perform more or less effectively in relation to a changing normative context. This framework shows why Canadian governments
responded more decisively, programmatically, and consistently from
the nineteenth century through the early postwar period than
American ones, and also why these characteristics have since declined
in both countries.

Importantly, my analysis highlights causal processes that many
American observers downplay. Focused on contemporary problems
in cities – racial conflict, insufficient inter-municipal collaboration in
metropolitan areas, the lack of accountability of special-purpose
bodies, and so on – Americans often presume a high degree of local
autonomy from state and federal government and look to bottom-up
mobilization for solutions. Taking a longer historical perspective
shows that American localism is not innate. Rather, it was constructed
through the accumulation of deliberate actions and unintended consequences, predominantly at the state level. To focus exclusively on
one level of government – and especially the local level – is to miss
the interactive evolution of the whole. Indeed, successive configurations of local, state, and federal influence over the urban sphere represent historical moments in the political development of multi-level
urban governance.

Decisive and programmatic urban governance is more necessary
now than ever. Large cities are where most Americans and Canadians
live out their lives and pursue their careers. They are the engines of
national wealth creation, the definers of mass culture, and magnets for
migrants seeking a better life. They are also at the epicentre of disruptive
societal transformations and the conflicts they produce: immigrant
integration, climate change, racialized poverty, the ageing society, the
opioid crisis, precarious work, and automation. Even ostensibly wealthy
and economically successful cities are sites of deepening economic
inequality, social segregation, and environmental injustice. This is what
Richard Florida calls the "urban contradiction."[3]

Urban governance is the combined effect on cities of actions by all
levels of government, not just the local. An important question for
our time is to work out how we can maximize the potential for a
multi-level urban governance that is inclusive and increases economic
opportunities and social sustainability, and that creates healthy and

efficient metropolitan environments. As urban societies confront a bewildering array of wicked problems, the programmatic mobilization of knowledge and resources across scales is vital. Yet, as the historical narratives in this book show, the very structure of our governing institutions inhibits programmatic multi-level urban governance.

INSTITUTIONAL FOUNDATIONS MATTER

The design of American and Canadian governing institutions – their institutional foundations – has structured the governance of cities and the character of urbanization itself. Centralized Westminster and decentralized separated-powers institutions generate different patterns of politics and different kinds of policies because they establish distinct sets of incentives for governmental and non-governmental actors in the policymaking process and incorporate external interests differently. These determine governments' capacity to rapidly enact policies in response to pressing problems, do so in ways that are coherent and general in application, and achieve durable settlements that sustain policies over extended periods of time. Using the terminology introduced in chapter 2, the performance of governing institutions can be understood as their ability to be *decisive* and *resolute*, and to generate *programmatic* rather than *particularistic* outputs.

The American Pattern

Policies in American states are made through legislative bargaining. Separated-powers systems are, and have always been, more open than Westminster systems to external interests and their ideas. Decentralized, legislature-centred policymaking has generated particularistic rather than programmatic outcomes as support for bills is assembled through appeals to individual legislators' self-interest, involving logrolling and the distribution of pork. In the nineteenth and early twentieth centuries, particularistic outputs included the proliferation of city charters, haphazard municipal incorporation, and the arbitrary and sometimes corrupt legislative intervention in local administration for partisan ends. The reformers' remedy to the latter problem was home rule – legal or constitutional restriction on the state's authority over local government. The erection of a legal firewall between state and local government, combined with the particularistic nature of state-level policymaking, limited the capacity of state governments to articulate a durable policy interest in urban and metropolitan affairs. No state established permanent administrative oversight of local government incorporation and boundary change. Although most states had adopted model enabling legislation for zoning during the 1920s, legislative frameworks for zoning, subdivision control, and comprehensive planning remain underdeveloped even today. The fiscal crisis of the Great Depression entrenched states' disengagement from urban affairs. Even the most successful of state-level radical parties, the Minnesota Farmer-Labor Party, could not overcome these barriers. Local governments would confront postwar urban development pressures with little assistance from state government, reproducing the emergent pattern of local government complexity and uncoordinated and unregulated local growth.

Only state governments had the jurisdiction to empower local government to respond to urbanization. The multiplicity of often small local governments had neither the administrative capacity nor the political incentive to craft and implement strategies that linked land-use regulation to infrastructure extensions. Few states – Oregon being the most far-reaching example – articulated an explicit policy framework to guide urban development and land-use change. As a result of municipal governments' low administrative capacity and weak coordination from above, the Twin Cities Metropolitan Council's urban service area and Portland's urban growth boundary, both conceived in the early 1970s, did not have demonstrable impacts until the late-1980s. By then, the majority of the regions' postwar urban development had already occurred, private-sector development practices were well entrenched, and the physical organization of urban settlement was set in place.

State inaction or incapacity paralleled a dramatic expansion of federal intervention, both fiscal and regulatory, in local communities. Building on New Deal precedent, Washington used conditional grants to induce coordination between local governments in metropolitan areas in the fields of housing and transportation. Federal "ownership" of the metropolitan file may have let the states off the hook, further undermining the potential for programmatic state action in its areas of exclusive jurisdiction: local government organization and land use. Few state governments gave federally mandated metropolitan planning commissions and councils of governments much in the way of political or fiscal support, Minnesota representing perhaps the most significant exception.[4] Although federal transportation, water, and sewer project grants renewed and extended the stock of metropolitan infrastructure, these interventions proved too indirect a mechanism to coordinate local land-use and infrastructure decision-making. Even these mechanisms were eliminated when federal review mandates were rolled back in the 1980s.

In Minnesota and Oregon, state governments' multiple veto points and tendency toward particularistic outputs were partially and temporarily overcome at critical junctures by bipartisan networks of civic elites. These grand coalitions of political, business, academic, professional, and media elites were glued together by interpersonal bonds and the social homogeneity of their membership. Their breadth and prestige gave the Citizens League in the Twin Cities, and the Metropolitan Study Commission and League of Women Voters in Portland, the capacity to perform roles performed by the professional bureaucracy in Westminster systems: studying problems; digesting and adapting imported policy ideas; and developing draft legislation, regulations, and policies. In a normative context of deference to elites and relative political consensus, bipartisan civic coalitions could drown out opposition and take advantage of intimate connections to both parties' leadership to insert their proposals directly into the legislative process. In Oregon and Minnesota, the civic elite networks advocated for the creation of what already existed in most Canadian provinces: provincial administrative oversight of local government formation and boundary change, not only in the negative sense of preventing undesirable outcomes, but also in the positive sense of initiating change.

Despite the civic elites' cohesion, influence, and discursive dominance, they could not fully countervail the incentives generated by the institutional foundations of the separated-powers system. It often took sustained lobbying over multiple biennial sessions before proposals were debated and approved by the legislature. The price of enactment was often the removal of the proposal's more coercive elements or fiscal resources. For example, the Minnesota Municipal Commission was established in 1959, twelve years after the League of Minnesota Municipalities first advocated for the reform of the state's laws on municipal incorporation and annexation, and without the power to impose municipal consolidation envisioned by its proponents. The Twin Cities Metropolitan Planning Commission was established in 1957, after a half-decade of concerted lobbying by C.C. Ludwig, and with only half the property tax base proposed. Similarly,

Portland's Metropolitan Service District was created in 1967 without access to the own-source revenues its supporters deemed essential to its success.

These institutional architectures and policy regimes faced existential challenges almost soon as they came into being. Local governments and counties actively resisted state mandates. Increasingly well-organized property developer groups viewed new standards and requirements as threats to their bottom line. As the new urban middle class demanded input into infrastructure project planning, rural residents opposed restrictions on their property rights. The civic elites that had created the new institutions and policies were ill equipped to defend them. The influence of the Twin Cities Citizens League and Leagues of Women Voters faded as public deference to elites waned. A crucial anchor of the civic elite networks, local business executives, came unmoored as home-grown firms consolidated into regional, national, and later international concerns. In Oregon, Minnesota, and other states, political support ebbed due to generational turnover among politicians and rising partisan polarization. Governors and legislators who had not been part of the earlier bipartisan elite consensus had little interest in expanding the authority of regional institutions or programmatically using them as instruments of state policy. And, as noted, federal retrenchment in the 1980s removed much of the external glue that induced state and local government collaboration through metropolitan institutions.

Lacking a support coalition, the Twin Cities Met Council lurched from one crisis to the next in the 1980s and 1990s. After a near-death experience in the 1990s, it was reconstituted as an infrastructure operator, its urban development policymaking role receding into the background. The creation of a virtually powerless Portland Metro in 1978 – approved only by playing to anti-government sentiment in a popular referendum – represented the last gasp of Portland's resurrected civic elite network. Its effectiveness since the late 1990s has stemmed from its assiduous cultivation of a broad societal support coalition, its embeddedness in the state land-use system, and the institutional bulwark afforded by the home-rule charter. Both the Met Council and Portland Metro – lauded as the most powerful and effective regional institutions in the nation – must always be mindful of political constraints imposed by fickle state politicians, antagonistic local governments jealous of their own prerogatives, and, in the Oregon case, single-interest groups mobilizing in the courts or on the ballot.

The Canadian Pattern

Policies in Canadian Westminster party government are crafted within the executive, which has the institutional means to decisively enact its preferences. Nineteenth- and early twentieth-century provincial governments in Ontario constructed a matrix of enduring urban governance institutions to facilitate local economic development and expand the fiscal viability and administrative capacity of local government so that it could provide an expanding array of infrastructure and services, including general municipal legislation, the Ontario Municipal Board, and the Ministry of Municipal Affairs. In the postwar period, the province applied this maturing legal and administrative toolkit to reconstruct local government in Toronto and across the province and expanded it to include a direct role in land-use planning. While tempered by electoral politics, the overall thrust was programmatic. Much the same pattern is visible in British Columbia. Regional planning was appended to existing municipal legislation in 1949 as a result of elite-level intra-party lobbying. Provincial political and bureaucratic elites consolidated and expanded the authority of the regional planning boards and, later, the regional districts during the 1950s, 1960s, and early 1970s. The decisiveness and resoluteness of provincial governments were reinforced by long periods of single-party dominance, which insulated governing parties from electoral challenge. Also important was a supportive normative context. The early postwar period was a time in which most people trusted government and professional, economic, and political elites to act in the societal interest. Governments in other provinces also intervened to integrate municipal authority over land-use planning and infrastructure and service delivery at the metropolitan scale. Without federally imposed consistency, individual provinces adopted different institutional formats. The common denominator was that regional governance, and therefore planning, was achieved through municipal institutions – either through their reorganization, as in Toronto, or through the institutionalization of inter-municipal collaboration, as in Vancouver.

In contrast to the American pattern, the concentration of decision-making power in the provincial executive and the close integration of provincial politicians and public servants brought much of the policymaking process inside the opaque walls of the provincial state. There was no equivalent to the Twin Cities Citizens League or the Portland League of Women Voters in Toronto or Vancouver. The historical record shows how business and labour groups and, as time went on, other organized interests including developers and environmentalists participated in formal consultation processes and lobbied provincial officials. Yet, however these interests were accommodated in the policymaking process, the accommodating was led by a relatively autonomous government that "held the pen" when laws and regulations were composed. The most visible exception was in wartime and early postwar Vancouver, when local enthusiasts mobilized through the Community Planning Association of Canada (CPAC) to advocate for regional planning legislation. But even this activity largely fits the pattern, as the provincial Post-War Reconstruction Council had already defined and studied economic development regions, and the CPAC group's point of access was the provincial executive.

Also in contrast to postwar America, the federal government has never attempted to articulate an urban or metropolitan policy, nor has it specifically used its spending power to programmatically influence provincial and local government urban development policies and decisions. The exceptions prove the rule. Federal involvement in urban housing and transportation finance and projects has been much smaller and less directive than that of the provinces. The two attempts to insert the federal government into provincial-municipal regulation of urban development – the Ministry of State for Urban Affairs (1971–78) and the Ministry of State for Infrastructure and Communities (2004–6) – were short-lived.

At least in principle, Westminster government's centralization and autonomy from societal interests permits it to act more decisively and programmatically than would the more decentralized and permeable separated-powers system. Centralized, executive-centred decision-making has been a double-edged sword, however. When electoral change occurs, incoming governments face few impediments if they wish to overturn up-and-running institutions and policies with their own agendas. Hence, long-term single-party dominance, disciplined by a centralized executive, exerted a stabilizing effect in early postwar Ontario, British Columbia, and other provinces.

While Westminster government's relative insulation from societal interests enables decisiveness and resoluteness, it may also undermine government's capacity to engage in policy innovation and adapt to changing norms and values. The shift in the normative context that occurred in the 1960s and 1970s generated new demands for public participation in policymaking, undermined deference to civic and political elites, sapped faith in state intervention as a progressive force, and elevated partisan conflict. On both sides of the border, these transformations delegitimized both the elite-driven process by which policies and institutions had been crafted and the technocratic rationalities they embodied. The very factors that had enabled decisive and programmatic provincial policymaking in the 1940s, 1950s, and 1960s – closed, executive-driven policy development – now worked against it. Restive voters increasingly opposed closed, technocratic policymaking. Policy ambition and continuity ebbed as the electoral security of long-serving governing parties eroded and fiscal deficits mounted. Up to this point, nominally conservative Canadian provincial governments had mobilized the fiscal and regulatory apparatus of the state to promote economic and social development. Thereafter, parties of the right adopted a populist, anti-statist agenda that viewed government, and policy elites within the bureaucracy, as part of the problem rather than part of the solution. The policy-making partnership between governing party elites and senior bureaucrats that had generated the previous era's institutional innovations weakened or disappeared.

This was especially visible in Ontario. Out of electoral self-preservation, Ontario's Conservative government abandoned its technocratic program of joined-up land-use, infrastructure, and economic planning by the late 1970s. The result was a half-built system: newly reformed upper-tier local governments in metropolitan areas were given new authority over urban development, yet the provincial policy framework that would coordinate their efforts was not implemented. Instead, regulatory authority and infrastructure system management was devolved to local governments. The cycling of one- or two-term governments of different parties from the mid-1980s through the early 2000s led to a series of policy reversals and the undermining of a coherent policy agenda. In British Columbia, Social Credit similarly withdrew its political support for coordinated local planning following the 1972–75 NDP interregnum, culminating with the abolition of regional planning as part of an austerity package in 1983.

Ontario, British Columbia, and other provinces have re-engaged with urban governance only inconsistently since the mid-1990s. Ontario enacted a set of regulatory policy directives binding on local governments for the greater Toronto region. British Columbia created a new statutory basis for planning by regional districts. Quebec established metropolitan agencies for economic development. All three provinces created coordinating agencies for metropolitan transit systems for their largest cities. Alberta re-established inter-municipal regional planning boards for Edmonton and Calgary. Yet all of these were primarily bureaucratically driven initiatives that have received inconsistent political support. They are also largely regulatory in nature and devolutionary in intent – features desirable to provincial governments averse to new open-ended fiscal commitments. While provincial (and federal) parties in power have avoided assuming responsibility for less visible expenditures, including for infrastructure maintenance and municipally administered human services, they have not shied away from funding megaprojects for which they can claim political credit, even if they undermine other local and provincial policy objectives.

In short, the conditions that made Ontario and other provincial governments decisive, programmatic, and resolute in the nineteenth and early twentieth centuries, and especially in the early postwar period, have diminished since the 1970s. The Westminster system's institutional foundations remain in place, but shifts in the political, normative, and societal context seem to militate against sustained and integrated multi-level urban governance.

Institutional "Genetics," Policymaking, and Democracy

The institutional foundations of the state are the genetic code of the body politic. They deeply structure governance inputs, processes, outputs, and outcomes. The case narratives showed how American state legislatures responded slowly and less coherently in part because the undisciplined legislature was highly permeable to external lobbies and societal interests. They also showed how Canadian provincial governments developed and implemented programmatic responses to urban growth in the early postwar period because political elites and the professional bureaucracy could act with relative autonomy from public opinion. This analysis raises difficult questions. Can governance be both programmatic and democratic at the same time? Is there a trade-off between the decisiveness of the legislative process and the inclusion of non-governmental actors in decision making?[5]

The indecisiveness of American state governments is not simply a matter of veto players setting a high bar for the adoption of programmatic policies. As seen in the Minnesota and Oregon cases, the very logic of legislative coalition-building generates particularistic rather than programmatic outputs. Overarching objectives and coherent means of implementation are often dissolved by the process of assembling sufficient support for enactment. Echoing Theodore Lowi's critique of the state's penetration by interest groups, Ira Katznelson suggests that America's postwar "permeable state lacked instruments of collective civic purpose" or "the idea of a common good based on shared goals."[6] Katznelson's argument is that contemporary American politics is defined by, and draws its legitimacy from, means rather than ends, from the processes and procedures through which groups battle to achieve their partial objectives rather than from the substantive social goals embodied in policy programs. Perhaps especially at the state level, where a weaker executive is less empowered to advocate for the whole in the face of a fractious legislature, the institutional foundations of American government inhibit the articulation of coherent societal projects and objectives. Moreover, Alan Ware argues that the institutional foundations of American government promote and prolong disagreements that in other countries would be submerged or defused by durable settlements.[7] In America, policy "losers" rarely accept the new status quo; rather, they exploit the permeability of the legislative and judicial process to seek another kick at the can. Nowhere is this more visible than in the Portland narrative, where the state land-use system and Portland Metro remain under permanent threat through lobbying, at the ballot box, and in the courts.

Bipartisan "consensus politics" has ebbed as parties have become more organizationally disciplined and ideologically polarized since the 1970s. In the 1950s, American political scientists believed that greater party coherence and policy differentiation would increase the capability of the American state to decisively develop and implement programmatic policies.[8] The Minnesota and Oregon cases suggest that the outcome has instead been a greater propensity to gridlock and policy whipsaw when party control of the legislature changes – in essence, to greater indecision and irresoluteness. In the early postwar period, the construction of legislative majorities generated particularistic outcomes on the basis of geography, as relatively autonomous representatives secured selective benefits for their constituents. Over time this has been overlaid and to some degree displaced by another dynamic. As legislative parties became more cohesive and organized interests consolidated, particularistic outputs have flowed from the allocation of selective benefits to interest groups that have become integral components of party coalitions: developers, environmentalists, farmers, property rights advocates, and so on. Growing social complexity, and the corresponding multiplication of demands for voice and collaboration in setting policy agendas, has generated new dimensions of conflict, rendering programmatic policy initiatives more elusive.

If American state-level separated-powers institutions are genetically prone to indecisiveness, particularism, and irresoluteness, Canadian provincial Westminster systems suffer from their own pathologies. Although provincial executives decisively enacted programmatic policies to manage metropolitan growth at an earlier stage, ultimately producing urban built environments with many enduring desirable characteristics, this was no golden age. Closed decision-making processes potentially restrict the scope of input from external voices and the airing of alternative ideas and proposals, sometimes resulting in mistakes, unintended consequences, and harmful outcomes with long-term effects. The technocratic planners of the 1950s and 1960s underestimated the social and economic costs of automobility and did not foresee how urban space and society would be transformed by the transition to a post-industrial economy. They also paid far too little attention to the perceptions, needs, and aspirations of those who would ostensibly benefit from their plans – ordinary people in their neighbourhoods. As the American founders recognized, there is always the risk that, while decisive, centralized majoritarian government may oppress the minority. In this regard, the erosion of deference to social, economic, political, media, and intellectual elites since the 1970s was a democratizing corrective. Still, the decline of trust in government and the emergence of more polarized and competitive provincial party systems has, as in the United States, reduced government's capacity to be decisive and resolute.

Especially in the United States, this analysis suggests that the bold interventions of the early postwar period were deviations from the policy styles generated by the national institutional foundations of governance. Again and again, people involved in the reforms of the 1960s told me there is no way they could be enacted today. An identical productive conjuncture of institutional foundations and social, political, and normative context will not be repeated. We cannot turn back the clock, nor would we want to. Urban societies in Canada and the United States are more diverse and tolerant than they were in the 1950s and 1960s. Urban economies are more integrated into broader ownership structures and circuits of labour, supply, and capital. No longer can a narrow stratum of political, business, or social elites legitimately speak for the whole. Given these transformations, can we democratically harness the positive characteristics of our governments' institutional foundations to confront emerging urgent challenges?

THE LIMITS OF LOCALISM

These days it is commonplace for urbanists to call for the enlargement of local autonomy. Influential American advocates now see federal and state government as part of the problem, not part of the solution, and direct their attention to locally driven leadership and bottom-up coalition building. From different angles, the Brookings Institution, journalist Neil Peirce, academic Manuel Pastor, and business consultant Doug Henton have championed the mobilization of regional civic and political coalitions composed of diverse interests to build consensus on social, economic, and environmental policy agendas.[9] Urban scholar David Imbroscio has argued for disadvantaged urban neighbourhoods to rebuild their economies from the bottom up through endogenous community economic development.[10]

In *If Mayors Ruled the World: Dysfunctional Nations, Rising Cities*, Benjamin Barber portrays local leadership as the antidote to the failures of the sclerotic nation-state. Given sufficient legal and fiscal autonomy, he argued, local leaders could experiment, learn from one another, and collaboratively construct collective responses to global policy challenges such as climate change. In his view, sovereign national and state or provincial governments should simply get out of the way: "Cities can govern globally where states can't, but only insofar as national states let them or look the other way."[11] And city leaders are increasingly occupying "the spaces being vacated by a sovereignty that is disappearing or minimally is being displaced by economic power."[12] The legal theorist Gerald Frug similarly focuses on how states' local government laws block the progressive and integrative tendencies of local governments.[13] Canadian philanthropist Alan Broadbent has called for the political "liberation" of Canada's metropolitan areas by converting them into their own provinces.[14] Political theorist Warren Magnusson makes a compelling case for viewing the urban as an alternative to state sovereignty as the organizing principle of political life, highlighting the emancipatory possibilities of the self-organizing, multipolar, and networked politics of the city over the authoritative, monopolistic, and hierarchical state.[15]

This localist discourse is seductive. Nonetheless, it raises questions for which there are no easy answers. Those who suggest that local autonomy can flourish only by lifting the heavy hand of the state – "home rule" in its purest form – do not have a good answer to the question of how much variation the broader society is willing to tolerate between local places, or, more bluntly, how much we are willing to allow local jurisdictions to make mistakes. Local jurisdictions are, as Paul Peterson wrote in *City Limits*, highly permeable to external forces and flows, and can easily be escaped if others possess more desirable characteristics. Of what benefit is a broad scope of local autonomy if its unilateral exercise has undesirable effects – for example, the repression of minority groups; the imposition of negative externalities on non-residents, such as pollution; or economic or urban development policies that reduce residents' quality of life? What happens if localities become undesirable places, entering a downward spiral of depopulation and economic decline? Unlike bankrupt firms, failed places do not simply disappear; their disinvested built environments and least advantaged populations remain. Is letting places "fail" the price of local autonomy?

Devolution's advocates tend to focus on economically successful cities and, in particular, on their innovative and entrepreneurial central-city mayors. Barber, for example, celebrates New York City's Michael Bloomberg as an exemplar of local agency, a harbinger of a new kind of bottom-up global governance. This focus brackets out the fact that "New York" is not simply the five boroughs, but a metropolis spanning over a thousand municipalities, school boards, and other special-purpose bodies. The problem of goal setting to distribute costs and benefits across governmentally complex metropolitan areas is ignored. Consider the City of St. Louis, Missouri, in which resides barely 10 per cent of the metropolitan population. St. Louis's mayor is just that – he or she has no more material interest in or authority over the economic, environmental, and social health of its troubled neighbour Ferguson than the president of France has in the economic, environmental, and social health of Italy or Greece. And for all the celebration of local political and civic leadership in smaller metropolitan areas and non-metropolitan "strong towns," these places' structural position is weak compared to global cities like New York or even nationally important cities like Minneapolis–St. Paul and Portland.[16] Neither Ferguson nor even St. Louis shall see its Bloomberg take his seat in Barber's imagined "global parliament of mayors."

We should also be careful not to expect too much of local business leaders and civic entrepreneurs. To be sure, these groups have built coalitions around specific projects and agendas. The Twin Cities and

Portland cases showed the early postwar civic elite networks to be decisive actors in policy development. But civic associations are not legislatures. They can develop policy programs, advocate for projects, and build support for them, but they cannot enact them. Nor should we be naive about the self-interest and blind spots of these groups. While the Citizens League, Leagues of Women Voters, and 1000 Friends of Oregon are positively portrayed in the historical narratives – indeed, the institutional and policy changes would not have occurred without them – scholars of urban political economy correctly view state and market actors as in tension.[17]

Perhaps the most fundamental deficiency of the localist perspective is its zero-sum portrayal of the authority and capacity of the multi-level state. Localist advocates explicitly or implicitly argue that, for local autonomy to increase, the scope of autonomous action at other levels must correspondingly diminish. The historical narratives in this book belie this analysis. They illustrate how, over the past two centuries, urbanization has spurred the creation of new instruments of state authority, new capacities to govern, and new venues of cooperation and conflict – what Michael Mann calls the "infrastructural power" of the state.[18] This process has generated an ever more complex field of institutions and actors that span multiple scales, from the local to the global. We need not choose between centralization and devolution; we can have powerful, effective, and accountable local and provincial or state governments at the same time.

STATES AND PROVINCES AS ENABLERS AND PROTECTORS OF LOCAL AUTONOMY

As we contemplate the potential of local autonomy, we must recognize the centrality – even the indispensability – of state and provincial governments in each country's field of multi-level urban governance. Only states and provinces have the legal authority to create rules and incentives, and distribute resources, that can minimize destructive competition and encourage the meaningful exercise of local authority while enhancing efficiency and equity across the greater polity. By building up the capacity of local governments, states and provinces can enable them to become more effective, democratically accountable, and innovative. As Hank Savitch and Paul Kantor put it, intergovernmental support is a resource on which localities can draw to chart their course in the global economy.[19] The performance of local governments, individually and as a system, is determined as much from above, by the choices of provincial and state governments, as it is from below, by the engagement of the local civil society.

Acknowledging this does not require us to accept that state and provincial governments are intrinsically virtuous or have consistently made good policy in the past. Indeed, historical narratives reveal that they have been inconsistent in their attention to cities and urban policy problems and have often been arbitrary in their actions. Rather, it is to recognize both the structural limits on local action *and* the unique position of states and provinces in the national constitutional order to mitigate or reverse those limits. State and provincial "ownership" of local governance does not mean that municipalities and other local governments must be passive administrators of provincial policies or colonies of state capitals.

When wielded constructively, states' and provinces' constitutional jurisdiction over local government has underwritten democratic accountability and problem-solving capacities. It does so in two ways. Provinces and states *enable* insofar as they can deploy their constitutional and legal authority, political support, and fiscal resources to maximize the productive exercise of local autonomy. They *protect* insofar as they establish ground rules and incentives that shield localities, individually and as a system, not only from external threats but also from making choices that harm their own residents or others. These are tests against which we can measure the performance of multi-level urban governance.

The historical narratives in the preceding chapters contain numerous examples of states and provinces playing enabling and protecting roles. In Minnesota, the state's intention to increase policy alignment among the Twin Cities region's more than three hundred local governments was signalled by the legislature's replacement of the 1930s Sanitary District with the Waste Control Commission; its generation of the Metropolitan Transit Commission out of the ashes of the bankrupt private Twin City Lines; and its creation of the Metropolitan Council, the metropolitan fiscal equalization scheme, and the mandates in the Land Planning Act. The legislature also sought to promote a more capable system of local governments with the earlier establishment of the Minnesota Municipal Commission. Similar legislative actions occurred in Oregon during the same period: the creation of the metropolitan agencies for transit, infrastructure and facilities management, and local government boundary review, as

well as the state land-use system. Oregon's land-use system remains
a positive American example of what Richard Whitman calls "vertical integration":

> If the system establishes spatially appropriate state-level goals
> and desired outcomes; monitors performance toward those out-
> comes; adapts its tools for achieving those outcomes over time;
> and updates those outcomes as needed over time; it can be suc-
> cessful over the long term ... The key in such a system is the deli-
> cate political art of vertical integration and the degree of tension
> and control among state, regional, and local governing entities.[20]

The legislators and advocates who supported initiatives in both states
had no desire to usurp local autonomy. Rather, their goal was to
improve the capability and democratic accountability of local governments in each state's growing metropolitan areas.

In Canada, from the passage of the 1849 Baldwin Act through the
1960s, Ontario pursued a policy of expanding local capability within
general frameworks of rules. Over time, provincial oversight and
regulation extended to the formation of local governments, changes
to their boundaries, local taxation and borrowing, and land-use planning. Provincial grants redistribute resources to municipalities with
weak tax bases. Provincial mandates and grants make access to services
and facilities more equitable by requiring, incentivizing, or supporting
their provision. Prohibitions or limitations on tax holidays and subsidies to attract business investment reduce destructive competition
between municipalities. Crucially, the provincial government's goal in
creating Metro Toronto in 1954 and appointing the Local Government
Review commissions in the 1960s was not to replace local autonomy
with provincial control. Rather, it was to create more capable and
democratically accountable local governments that could assume
greater responsibility. British Columbia's support for inter-municipal
infrastructure governing bodies for Greater Vancouver in the early
twentieth century, and the later creation of regional planning boards,
regional districts, and the binding arbitration approach for adopting
regional growth strategies, represents a similar impulse. So too does
the Agricultural Land Reserve, which reduces political pressures at
the local level to develop high-quality farmland. In each case, the
provincial government established a mechanism that lowered the cost

of, and encouraged, inter-municipal collaboration on goal setting or service delivery, with the effect of empowering local communities.

CAN PROVINCES AND STATES ARTICULATE
AN ENDURING INTEREST IN CITIES TODAY?

The case studies show that states and provinces have enabled and protected local governments by providing supportive rules and fiscal frameworks in the past. But are they capable of doing so today and the future? The historical narratives point to a pessimistic conclusion: that, even given the tendencies generated by their institutional foundations, state and provincial governments are less capable of decisive, programmatic, and enduring responses to urban problems than they were in earlier decades.

In the American context, the Brookings Institution's Bruce Katz and Jeremy Nowak put the blame on "the exceptional level of partisanship and the consequent withdrawal of the federal and state governments as reliable partners" to cities.[21] History suggests that programmatic policymaking was more likely when a durable majority electoral coalition was anchored in cities but also crosscut urban cores and suburban and non-metropolitan constituencies. Today's partisan polarization plays out geographically, with electoral support in urban cores increasingly tilted to the left and non-metropolitan areas to the right, with postwar suburbs often holding the balance of power.[22] Reinforced in the United States by gerrymandering, this electoral geography aligns with deep social cleavages, principally around race and socioeconomic status. In the United States, a sustained majority legislative coalition in favour of programmatic policymaking for metropolitan areas is unlikely except in the few states that have developed single-party (Democrat) dominance rooted in urban constituencies, California being perhaps the clearest example. Many more state legislatures remain dominated by a rural-suburban partisan formation that, as Tom Ogorzalek writes, is not grounded in the historically evolved organizational complexity of the inner city and finds no electoral benefit in resolving urban and metropolitan problems.[23]

Given the hyperpolarization of politics in the American states, many now look to the federal government to discipline the states using mandates and conditional grants. In *Place Matters*, for example, Peter Dreier, John Mollenkopf, and Todd Swanstrom argue that "only the nation as a whole can limit, and ultimately reverse, the factors that created the current situation."[24] Yet the election of Donald Trump shows that Washington should not be viewed as a consistent counterweight to the states. Moreover, the historical narratives suggest that the impact of federal mandates will be limited without states' commitment to programmatically exercise the most powerful levers available to shape the metropolis: local government law and regulation of the use of land. By virtue of their constitution, state government remains the essential venue and actor in American multi-level urban governance.

The situation in Canada is less extreme. Cities and suburbs are not divided by race. Gerrymandering is virtually eliminated by the delineation of electoral district boundaries by independent non-partisan commissions. Political parties in Ontario, British Columbia, and other provinces have in recent years continued to assemble electoral coalitions that crosscut urban, suburban, and rural lines. Nonetheless, the trend in federal and provincial politics has been toward the geographic polarization of parties. Ontario's recently elected populist Conservative government is the least urban in the composition of the government caucus and cabinet in a generation. Its early actions indicate that the reversal of many of the previous urban-centred policies of the previous Liberal government is in the offing.

Still, Canadian provinces are better placed than American states to productively engage in multi-level urban governance, because the Westminster system's institutional foundations remain more conducive to decisive and programmatic governance. Today's provincial policymakers inherit an institutional architecture with many positive characteristics: sophisticated general enabling legislation for local government and local land-use planning; an up-and-running provincial administrative apparatus to monitor and incentivize their use; rules that inhibit destructive inter-municipal competition and the emergence of fiscal problems; and, perhaps most importantly, a system of capable local governments.

An important question for both countries is this: Will the increasing urbanization and metropolitan concentration of the electorate, both nationally and within states and provinces, lock in durable electoral coalitions supportive of programmatic urban governance? Or will parties differentiate on cleavages that divide metropolitan residents from one another – ethnicity, language, and class? Given the incentives embedded in their institutional foundations, the former path seems more likely for Canada than for the United States.

WHAT SHOULD URBAN GOVERNANCE LOOK LIKE?

What *should* twenty-first-century urban governance look like? First, it should leverage the authority, resources, and capacities of governments and societal actors at all levels. No single level of government can go it alone. While national governments have superior technical knowledge and expertise, and can redistribute resources across the entire territory of the nation, their remoteness from local contexts inhibits the tailoring of policies to specific needs and conditions. Moreover, in the North American context, national governments lack constitutional jurisdiction over land use and local government institutions. While provincial and state governments possess this jurisdiction, they also may be too distant to be sensitive to variations in local conditions. Local governments and groups possess superior "tacit knowledge" – they know local needs and conditions best – yet they may lack the legal authority, technical expertise, and fiscal and administrative capacity to mount effective responses to problems. Effective multi-level urban governance consists of each level of government compensating for the limitations of the other as they collectively govern urban spaces. This book has chronicled numerous examples in both countries of national and provincial or state governments crafting new institutional and fiscal arrangements and legal and policy frameworks that have increased the capacity of local governments to respond to urbanization and urban problems.

Second, and more specifically, state and provincial governments should create general frameworks of incentives and prohibitions that enable and protect local democratic initiative while compelling local actors to consider how their choices affect their neighbours. In doing so, they can productively recognize and assert the distinct interests of states and provinces in the economic, social, and environmental health of their metropolitan areas while sustaining local autonomy and democratic accountability. Of the four cases examined, Vancouver comes closest to meeting this ideal. The province created powerful incentives to inter-municipal collaboration when it established the regional districts and their precursors, and also the Growth Strategies Act. These institutions have contained conflict, built trust, facilitated the exchange of ideas, and generated and sustained shared policy programs. While their idiosyncratic historical evolution militates against their ready adoption by other North American jurisdictions, their real-world operation over time deserves careful study. The Vancouver model has successfully reconciled municipal interests and integrated land-use planning with infrastructure operations at the regional scale while maintaining democratic input and accountability, but it remains vulnerable to resource constraints and arbitrary provincial action – vulnerabilities it shares with the other three regions studied. Institutional enabling must be accompanied by the fiscal means necessary for local governments to carry out their responsibilities.

Third, multi-level urban governance should be directed toward the definition and achievement of broad policy programs rather than specific projects. To be sure, ad hoc task- or project-based collaborations among governments and other actors are essential to accomplish narrow goals such as waterfront regeneration, constructing a major public facility, or addressing a localized public health crisis. Indeed, the multiplicity of regional intergovernmental organizations identified by Miller and Nelles and public authorities described by Savitch and Adhikari are focused primarily on specific tasks or the execution of projects.[25] However, the allocation of localized benefits and costs across metropolitan space in the interest of collective objectives – equitable access to services, economic growth, or environmental quality – requires either external coercion or some other means of securing broad voluntary agreement. Individual general- and special-purpose local governments have no incentive to make such trade-offs. Ontario took the path of coercion when it established Metro Toronto, its planning board, and the regional conservation authority in the 1950s, and when it enacted the regional policy framework for the Toronto region in the middle of the first decade of the twenty-first century. The latter approach is exemplified by British Columbia's quiet efforts over many decades to construct and support collaborative metropolitan institutions. While less elaborate, much the same outcome has been secured by Portland Metro's engagement of local governments and other stakeholders as institutionalized in its home-rule charter and state land-use rules. The Twin Cities Met Council's lack of institutionalized engagement with the local governments that implement its plans has made them antagonists rather than partners, undermining the potential for the bottom-up development of regional objectives within the state's enabling framework.

Finally, the designers of policy programs and decision-making processes must be mindful of changing public norms and values. In each of the four cases, up-and-running institutions and policies were delegitimized by normative change. The abstract technical logics of Ontario's Toronto-Centred Region scheme and the Twin Cities Metropolitan Council's development framework, both crafted in the late 1960s and early 1970s, were premised on a depoliticized understanding of urban development. Absent an attachment to the changing spirit of the times and lacking a support coalition inside and outside of government, their influence faded. Again, we can perhaps learn the most from Vancouver. Harry Lash and his staff at the Greater Vancouver Regional District responded to public sentiment by reframing the economic and infrastructural logic of the Lower Mainland Planning Board's "cities in a sea of green" in quality-of-life terms.

This book is premised on the notion that history, and particularly cross-national comparative history, can help us understand why our cities are governed the way they are and how we can govern them better. Institutions and norms are powerful factors because they are relatively inflexible; in any given historical moment, they are parameters rather than variables. Taking a long historical view reveals their evolution through the collision of social forces amid profound economic and technological change. As in the past, it is in this potential for change that the seeds of future forms of urban governance lie, and it is with these seeds that we may find ways to grow more successful cities.

Notes

CHAPTER ONE

1 Rusk, *Inside Game/Outside Game*; Calthorpe and Fulton, *The Regional City*; Weitz, "Growth Management in the United States."

2 Henry and Sherraden, *Costs of the Infrastructure Deficit*; Stiff and Smetanin, *Public Infrastructure Underinvestment*.

3 Scott and Storper, "Regions, Globalization, Development"; Jonas and Ward, "Introduction to a Debate on City-Regions"; Cooke and Morgan, *The Associational Economy*; Rosabeth Moss Kantor, "Business Coalitions as a Force for Regionalism"; Clarke and Gaile, *The Work of Cities*; Florida, *Cities and the Creative Class*.

4 Swanstrom, *Regional Resilience*; Pendall, Foster, and Cowell, "Resilience and Regions"; Christopherson, Michie, and Tyler, "Regional Resilience."

5 World Bank, *Cities and Climate Change*; Satterthwaite et al., *Adapting to Climate Change in Urban Areas*; Jabareen, *The Risk City*; Hunt and Watkiss, "Climate Change Impacts and Adaptation."

6 Bishop and Cushing, *The Big Sort*; Glaeser, Resseger, and Tobio, "Urban Inequality"; *Dynamics of Urban Poverty in the 1990s*; Altshuler et al., *Governance and Opportunity in Metropolitan America*; Orfield, *Metropolitics*; Walks, "New Divisions"; Dreier, Mollenkopf, and Swanstrom, *Place Matters*.

7 Hunter, *Community Power Structure*; Dahl, *Who Governs?*; Banfield, *Political Influence*. While Canadian scholars have been less theoretically motivated, their empirical attention has also been trained on local government institutions and policies, especially in central cities. For an overview, see Taylor and Eidelman, "Canadian Political Science and the City."

8 Logan and Molotch, *Urban Fortunes*; Harvey, "The Urban Process under Capitalism"; Kantor, *The Dependent City Revisited*.

9 C. Stone, *Regime Politics* and "Reflections on Regime Politics."

10 DiGaetano and Strøm, "Comparative Urban Governance"; Savitch and Kantor, *Cities in the International Marketplace*.

11 Pierre, *The Politics of Urban Governance*.

12 Studenski, *The Government of Metropolitan Areas*; Victor Jones, *Metropolitan Government*.

13 See Ostrom, Tiebout, and Warren, "The Organization of Government in Metropolitan Areas"; Bish, "Vincent Ostrom on Local Government"; Tiebout, "A Pure Theory of Local Expenditures."

14 Dreier, Mollenkopf, and Swanstrom, *Place Matters*.

15 Savitch and Vogel, "Introduction"; Pastor, Benner, and Matsuoka, *This Could Be the Start of Something Big*.

16 Feiock, *Metropolitan Governance*.

17 Visser, "Understanding Local Government Cooperation."

18 Foster, "Regional Capital."

19 A. Wallis, "Governance and the Civic Infrastructure of Metropolitan Regions"; Hamilton, "Organizing Government Structure."

20 Nelles, *Comparative Metropolitan Policy*, 44. See also Wolfe, *21st Century Cities in Canada*, chap. 4.

21 D. Miller and Nelles, *Discovering American Regionalism*; Savitch and Adhikari, "Fragmented Regionalism"; Spicer, *The Boundary Bargain*.

22 Steinacker, "Game-Theoretic Models of Metropolitan Cooperation."

23 Rosan, *Governing the Fragmented Metropolis*, 163.

24 Legal scholars are a notable exception. See Briffault, "Our Localism: Part I"; Frug and Barron, *City Bound*. David Y. Miller and collaborators distinguish between the "vertical" and "horizontal" dimensions of metropolitan governance, while Myron A. Levine uses the phrase "intergovernmental city" to frame discussion of federal-state-local relations in metropolitan areas. See D. Miller and Lee, "Making Sense of Metropolitan Regions"; Levine, *Urban Politics*; Hamilton, Miller, and Paytas, "Exploring the Horizontal and Vertical Dimensions."

25 Brenner, "Is There a Politics of 'Urban' Development?" 121; see also Wood, "Comparative Urban Politics and the Question of Scale."

26 Horak and Young, *Sites of Governance*; Sellers, "The Nation-State and Urban Governance."

27 Tomalty and Mallach, *America's Urban Future*; Wolman, "Looking at Regional Governance Institutions"; Birkhead, *A Look to the North*.

28 D. Miller and Cox, *Governing the Metropolitan Region*, 101–12.

29 Foster, *The Political Economy of Special-Purpose Government*; Burns, *The Formation of American Local Governments*; Bollens, *Special District Governments in the United States*, chap. 3.

30 See Stephens and Wikstrom, *Metropolitan Government and Governance*, 19; Burns, *The Formation of American Local Governments*, 9–11.

31 Sancton, *Canadian Local Government*, chap. 4; Richmond and Siegel, *Agencies, Boards, and Commissions*.

32 L. Stone, *Urban Development in Canada*, 207–8.

33 My findings are consistent with those of others. Comparing density gradients in three Canadian and twelve US metropolitan areas, Filion and his colleagues found that the Canadian cities are most similar to older northeastern American cities and that the greatest difference in density is found in areas developed in the early postwar period – those developed predominantly between 1945 and 1970. See Filion et al., "Canada-US Metropolitan Density Patterns"; see also Edmonston, Goldberg, and Mercer, "Urban Form in Canada and the United States." Similarly, Miron found that a larger proportion of Americans than Canadians tend to live in lower-density neighbourhoods. See Miron, "Urban Sprawl in Canada and America."

34 Lopez and Hynes, "Sprawl in the 1990s." The neighbourhood population density threshold used is 3,500 per square mile, or 13.5 per hectare. Rural areas are excluded by dropping all census tracts with less than 200 people per square mile, or 0.8 per hectare. Index scores for the US metropolitan statistical areas are drawn from Lopez, "Urban Sprawl in the United States." Scores for Canada were calculated from the 1971, 1981, 1991, 2001, and 2011 Census of Population. Lopez and Hynes note that, while density-based measurements of "sprawl" capture only a single aspect of land-use performance, they are simple to calculate and correlate with more elaborate multivariate sprawl indicators. See also Laidley, "Measuring Sprawl."

35 See, for example, Hamidi and Ewing, "A Longitudinal Study of Changes in Urban Sprawl"; Paulsen, "Geography, Policy or Market?"

36 See Burchell et al., *Sprawl Costs*. For similar American and Canadian findings, see Carruthers and Úlfarsson, "Does 'Smart Growth' Matter to Public Finance?"; Carruthers and Úlfarsson, "Urban Sprawl and the Cost of Public Services"; Blais, *The Economics of Urban Form*; IBI Group, *The Implications of Alternative Growth Patterns*.

37 Berke et al., "Greening Development to Protect Watersheds"; Daniels and Lapping, "Land Preservation"; Pendall, Martin, and Fulton, *Holding the Line*.

38 Newman and Kenworthy, *Sustainability and Cities*, 100–9; Ewing and Rong, "The Impact of Urban Form on US Residential Energy Use"; Ewing and Hamidi, "Compactness versus Sprawl."

39 Carruthers and Úlfarsson, "Fragmentation and Sprawl," 334–5; P. Lewis, *Shaping Suburbia*, chap. 2.

40 Fulton et al., *Who Sprawls Most?*, 13.

41 P. Lewis, *Shaping Suburbia*, chap. 3; Fulton et al., *Who Sprawls Most?*; Glaeser, Kahn, and Chu, *Job Sprawl*.

42 Carruthers and Úlfarsson, "Fragmentation and Sprawl"; Carruthers, "Growth at the Fringe."

43 Regressing DBI against the number of general-purpose local governments per 100,000 residents and logged metropolitan population yields statistically significant positive coefficients for both, and an R^2 of 0.47. That is, 47 per cent of the variation in DBI is explained by variation in per capita governments and metropolitan population. DBI is also strongly associated with vehicle-distance travelled, a common measure of travel behaviour. The less compact the urban form, the longer the distance people commute, accounting for metropolitan area population size. Regressing daily vehicle kilometres travelled against DBI and logged metropolitan population yields a R^2 of 0.38, meaning that 38 per cent of the variation in vehicle kilometres travelled (VKT) is explained by variation in the other terms. Canadian VKT values are from Kriger et al., *Urban Transportation Indicators*; Hollingworth et al., *Urban Transportation Indicators*. United States VKT values are calculated from Federal Highway Administration, "Highway Statistics 2015." All data are for 2015 except for Edmonton and Montreal, which are for 2010. The analysis includes the 367 metropolitan areas for which comparable data are available.

44 Kim and Jurey, "Local and Regional Governance Structures."

45 Ahrend et al., "What Makes Cities More Productive?"; Boulant, Brezzi, and Veneri, "Income Levels and Inequality in Metropolitan Areas"; Bartolini, "Municipal Fragmentation and Economic Performance."

46 Razin and Rosentraub, "Are Fragmentation and Sprawl Interlinked?"

47 Stephens and Wikstrom, *Metropolitan Government and Governance*, chap. 7. See also Hendrick and Shi, "Macro-Level Determinants of Local Government Interaction." These difficulties are exemplified in Smith and Spicer's comparison of local autonomy in ten large Canadian municipalities. See A. Smith and Spicer, "The Local Autonomy of Canada's Largest Cities."

48 Gyourko, Saiz, and Summers, "A New Measure of the Local Regulatory Environment for Housing Markets," 699.

49 See R. Lewis and Knaap, "Institutional Structures for State Growth Management"; Paulsen, "Geography, Policy or Market?" They collectively identify California, Connecticut, Delaware, Florida, Maryland, New Jersey, Oregon, Rhode Island, and Washington as states that have state-level development plans or mandate local planning objectives.

50 The Community Environmental Legal Defense Fund reports that, as of 2015, forty-three states have some form of home rule. See Community Environmental Legal Defense Fund, "Home Rule." On state pre-emption trends, see DuPuis et al., *City Rights in an Era of Preemption.*

51 Hall and Soskice, *Varieties of Capitalism*; Pontusson, *Inequality and Prosperity*; Arts and Gelissen, "Three Worlds of Welfare Capitalism or More?"; Esping-Andersen, *The Three Worlds of Welfare Capitalism.*

52 Filion, "Balancing Concentration and Dispersion"; Relph, *The Modern Urban Landscape.*

53 Anisef and Lanphier, *The World in a City*; Ornstein, *Ethno-Racial Groups in Toronto*; Ornstein, *Ethno-Racial Groups in Montreal and Vancouver.*

54 Hitchings, "A Typology of Regional Growth Management Systems"; D. Miller and Cox, *Governing the Metropolitan Region*, 189–91.

55 Abbott, "The Capital of Good Planning"; Berelowitz, *Dream City*, 1.

56 The rich literature on American political development has recently taken comparative and urban turns. See Dilworth, *The City in American Political Development*; Orren and Skowronek, *The Search for American Political Development*; Lucas and Vipond, "Back to the Future."

CHAPTER TWO

1 See Sellers and Kwak, "State and Society in Local Governance"; Shah and Shah, "The New Vision of Local Governance"; Norton, *International Handbook of Local and Regional Government*; Ivanyna and Shah, "How Close Is Your Government to Its People?"

2 Lipset, *Continental Divide*, 212; Banting, Hoberg, and Simeon, "Introduction," 13.

3 Norris, "Prospects for Regional Governance"; Norris, Phares, and Zimmerman, "Metropolitan Government in the United States?"; Goldberg and Mercer, *The Myth of the North American City*; Rothblatt, "Summary and Conclusions," 449–50.

4 On the origins and nature of national political cultures, see Hartz, *The Liberal Tradition in America*; Jackson, *Crabgrass Frontier*, 68–72; Wiseman, *In Search of Canadian Political Culture*. On contemporary national differences in Canadian and American values and value change, see Nevitte, *The Decline of Deference*; M. Adams, *Fire and Ice*.

5 Romney, "From the Rule of Law to Responsible Government," 90; Taylor, *The Civil War of 1812*.

6 Grabb and Curtis, *Regions Apart*.

7 Ware, *Political Conflict in America*, chap. 3, esp. 59. See also Hartz, *The Founding of New Societies*.

8 See Noel, "Oliver Mowat, Patronage, and Party Building," 98–100; E. Jones, "Localism and Federalism in Upper Canada to 1865"; Vipond, *Liberty and Community*, 26–7; Wickett, "City Government in Canada," 150; Jacek, "Regional Government and Development."

9 Crawford, "The Independence of Municipal Councils in Ontario," 553.

10 Brittain, *Local Government in Canada*, v.

11 Boudreau, "Strategic Territorialization"; Horak, *The Power of Local Identity*; McDougall, *John P. Robarts*, chap. 16.

12 Sancton, *Governing the Island of Montreal*.

13 Spicer, "The Rise and Fall of the Ministry of State for Urban Affairs."

14 Iton, "The Backlash and the Quiet Revolution."

15 Boychuk, *National Health Insurance in the United States and Canada*.

16 Katznelson, *Fear Itself*.

17 McKinnon, *The Black Population in the United States*, 2.

18 On this discursive shift, see Pritchett, "Which Urban Crisis?"

19 King and Smith, "Racial Orders in American Political Development."

20 See Ogorzalek, *The Cities on the Hill*, 15–21.

21 See also Rasch, "Institutional Foundations of Legislative Agenda-Setting." While not directly focused on governing institutions, Hall and Soskice, in *Varieties of Capitalism*, also place "institutional foundations" at the base of their framework for explaining how differences in the organization of national political economies translate into comparative advantage.

22 Moe and Caldwell, "The Institutional Foundations of Democratic Government," 172.

23 See Bagehot, *The English Constitution*; W. Wilson, *Congressional Government*.

24 Comparisons of national institutional performance typically focus on national-scale outcomes. Lijphart, for example, defines national

institutional performance in terms of measurable outcomes, including female legislative representation, political violence, voter turnout, economic growth, the inflation rate, income inequality, and the unemployment rate. See Lijphart, *Patterns of Democracy*. A "macro" outcomes focus is less tenable when considering the performance of subnational political institutions because spillover effects make it impossible to assign credit for any given outcome to any one unit. Instead, assessment of performance should focus on decision-making processes and their policy outputs. See Z. Taylor, *Good Governance at the Local Level*. On different institutions generating different policy outputs, see, for example, King, "The Establishment of Work-Welfare Programs" and Weir, "Ideas and the Politics of Bounded Innovation." Perhaps the most detailed comparison between the American separated-powers system and the British parliamentary system is Weaver and Rockman, *Do Institutions Matter?*

25　Tsebelis, *Veto Players*.

26　Squire, *The Evolution of American Legislatures*, chap. 7.

27　Malloy, "Prime Ministers and Their Parties in Canada," 156, 60–2.

28　Weaver and Rockman, "Assessing the Effects of Institutions," 27.

29　Tsebelis and Money, *Bicameralism*; Congleton, "On the Merits of Bicameral Legislatures"; Buchanan and Tullock, *The Calculus of Consent*.

30　Cox and McCubbins, "The Institutional Determinants of Economic Policy Outcomes," 26–7. For a similar argument, see Moe and Caldwell, "The Institutional Foundations of Democratic Government."

31　Much of the literature on political regime type is concerned with governability or the performance of different institutional designs, both generically and in light of transitions from dictatorship to democracy. See Lijphart, *Parliamentary versus Presidential Government*; Gerring, Thacker, and Moreno, "Are Parliamentary Systems Better?"; Lijphart, *Patterns of Democracy*; Linz, "Democracy, Presidential or Parliamentary"; Cheibub, *Presidentialism, Parliamentarism, and Democracy*; Haggard and McCubbins, *Presidents, Parliaments, and Policy*, chaps. 4–9.

32　On sunset clauses, see Kearney, "Sunset." In twenty-four states, citizens can put questions, or measures, on the election ballot if they meet specific criteria, including a minimum number of petition signatures. These are called initiatives. Among these states, eighteen permit constitutional amendment by ballot measure, and twenty-one permit proposals for legislation. Twenty-four states also permit referenda to repeal adopted legislation. In all fifty states, the legislature may place a question on the referendum ballot. This is sometimes called a "referral." Initiative and referendum are also common at the local level. According to a survey by the International City Managers Association, over 90 per cent of American local governments have a mechanism for initiative or referendum. See Initiative and Referendum Institute, "Initiative and Referendum Institute at the University of Southern California."

33 Dicey, *Introduction to the Study of the Law of the Constitution*, 3–4, 24–5.

34 Weaver and Rockman, "Assessing the Effects of Institutions," 20.

35 Averages do not include tenures of parties elected before 1940 or that were still in power as of the end of 2016.

36 Cox and McCubbins, "The Institutional Determinants of Economic Policy Outcomes," 47–52. For a similar distinction and argument, see Moe and Caldwell, "The Institutional Foundations of Democratic Government," 178.

37 Dahl, *Who Governs*; Lowi, *The End of Liberalism*.

38 Weaver and Rockman, "Assessing the Effects of Institutions," 28.

39 Hall, "Policy Paradigms, Social Learning, and the State."

40 Triadafilopoulos, *Becoming Multicultural*, 7.

41 J. Campbell, "Institutional Analysis and the Role of Ideas in Political Economy," 385. See also Skogstad and Schmidt, "Introduction," 6–10.

42 Weir, "Innovation and Boundaries in American Employment Policy," 264. See also Hall, "Conclusion," 370–5.

43 Weaver and Rockman, "Assessing the Effects of Institutions," 40.

44 Bell, *The Coming of Post-Industrial Society*; Inglehart, "The Silent Revolution in Europe"; Huntington, "Postindustrial Politics." See also Dalton, "The Social Transformation of Trust in Government."

45 See Leo, *The Politics of Urban Development*; Ley, "Gentrification and the Politics of the New Middle Class."

46 Swanstrom, "Beyond Economism"; T. Weaver, *Blazing the Neoliberal Trail*.

47 Simeon, Hoberg, and Banting, "Globalization, Fragmentation, and the Social Contract," 407–15.

48 Hays, "From Conservation to Environment."

49 Ware, *Political Conflict in America*, 70.

50 Cochrane, *Left and Right*.

51 Hinchliffe and Less, "Party Competition and Conflict in State Legislatures"; Shor, "Polarization in American State Legislatures."

52 Ware, *Political Conflict in America*, 83.
53 See Mahoney and Thelen, "A Theory of Gradual Institutional Change."
54 Simeon and Willis, "Democracy and Performance."

CHAPTER THREE

1 For example, see Skowronek, *Building a New American State*;
Stevenson, *Ex Uno Plures*. Important American exceptions include
Weir, "States, Race, and the Decline of New Deal Liberalism; Mettler,
Dividing Citizens; and Kantor, *The Dependent City Revisited*.
2 Isin, *Cities without Citizens*, chaps. 3–5; W.P.M. Kennedy, *The
Constitution of Canada*, chap. 12.
3 J. Taylor, "Urban Autonomy in Canada," 271; Whebell, "Robert
Baldwin and Decentralization"; Isin, *Cities without Citizens*, 131–42;
Aitchison, "The Municipal Corporations Act of 1849"; Romney,
"From the Rule of Law to Responsible Government"; Buckner, *The
Transition to Responsible Government*.
4 Between 1832 and 1840, elected boards of police able to levy taxes
were authorized in nine village settlements in Upper Canada. This
meaning of "police" was broader than in contemporary usage; it
referred to the general power to regulate, among other activities, nui-
sances, building materials to prevent fire, the fire service, and wharves.
5 Isin, *Cities without Citizens*, chap. 4; Aitchison, "The Municipal
Corporations Act of 1849"; Whebell, "Robert Baldwin and
Decentralization."
6 Bloomfield, Bloomfield, and McCaskell, *Urban Growth and Local
Services*, 12–13.
7 Wickett, "City Government in Canada," 244; James Anderson, "The
Municipal Government Reform Movement in Western Canada," 76,
86; Crawford, *Canadian Municipal Government*, 32.
8 Drawing on Magnusson, Johnson suggests that the Baldwin Act was
directly inspired by earlier American general municipal acts. Yet, as
Munro describes, these were viewed as ineffective even in their own
time. A more plausible inspiration is the British Municipal Corporations
Act of 1835, which replaced many of the medieval "rotten boroughs"
with elected councils that drew their authority from the general act
rather than special-act charters. Still, the 1835 act applied only to a
particular category of urban municipality. The remaining unreformed
boroughs were brought into the system by 1886, and the 1888 and
1894 Local Government Acts instituted a uniform system of elected

county and urban and rural district councils. See Magnusson, "Introduction," 6; K. Johnson, "'The Glorified Municipality,'" 404; W. Munro, *The Government of American Cities*, 55–6.

9 J. Taylor, "Urban Autonomy in Canada," 272.

10 Wickett, "City Government in Canada," 250.

11 J. Weaver, *Shaping the Canadian City*, 50.

12 Hodos, "Against Exceptionalism," 49.

13 W. Anderson, *Local Government and Finance in Minnesota*, 15.

14 Piva, *The Borrowing Process*, chap. 4; Piva, "Government Finance and the Development of the Canadian State," 260–8; Whebell, "The Upper Canada District Councils Act," 204.

15 Weingast and Wallis, "Dysfunctional or Optimal Institutions?" 344, 351–5; J. Wallis, "Constitutions, Corporations, and Corruption," 245.

16 Teaford, *The Unheralded Triumph*, chap. 10; Weingast and Wallis, "Dysfunctional or Optimal Institutions?" 355–7; Griffith, *A History of American City Government: The Conspicuous Failure*, chap. 3; Sbragia, *Debt Wish*, chap. 5.

17 Goodnow, *Municipal Home Rule*, 53; Goodnow, *Municipal Problems*, 37–8; W. Anderson, *American City Government*, 43–4.

18 Stewart, *A Half Century of Municipal Reform*, 8–9; Steffens, *The Shame of the Cities*; Patton, *The Battle for Municipal Reform*, chap. 2; Griffith, *A History of American City Government: The Conspicuous Failure*, chap. 8.

19 Bryce, *The American Commonwealth*, 432; for similar sentiment, see also Goodnow, *Municipal Home Rule*.

20 Stivers, *Bureau Men*, 25.

21 Ibid., 25; J. Weaver, *Shaping the Canadian City*, 64–5; J. Weaver, "'Tomorrow's Metropolis' Revisited," 403–9.

22 Griffith, *A History of American City Government: The Conspicuous Failure*, chap. 7.

23 J. Weaver, "Order and Efficiency," 224; Careless, *Toronto to 1918*, 143; Rutherford, "Introduction," xiv–xv.

24 W. Munro, *American Influences on Canadian Government*, 99.

25 J. Weaver, "Order and Efficiency," 225.

26 J. Weaver, *Shaping the Canadian City*, 46.

27 Wickett, "City Government in Canada," 245.

28 J.D. Anderson, "The Municipal Government Reform Movement in Western Canada," 74–5, 101; J. Weaver, "'Tomorrow's Metropolis' Revisited," 409–10.

29 J. Weaver, *Shaping the Canadian City*, 40.

30 Gelfand, *A Nation of Cities*, 6–7.
31 Goodnow, *Municipal Home Rule*, 22–3.
32 Bryce, *The American Commonwealth*, 435.
33 Schlesinger, *The Rise of the City*, 395.
34 Teaford, *The Unheralded Triumph*, ch. 4; Teaford, "Special Legislation and the Cities."
35 See also Griffith and Adrian, *A History of American City Government: The Formation of Traditions*, chap. 3.
36 W. Anderson, *City Charter Making in Minnesota*, 13.
37 Goodnow, *Municipal Home Rule*, 28–9; W. Anderson, *Local Government and Finance in Minnesota*, 61.
38 Teaford, *The Unheralded Triumph*, 84.
39 Ibid., chap. 5.
40 Goodnow, *Municipal Home Rule*, 8–9.
41 Ibid., 57–61; Binney, "Restrictions upon Local and Special Legislation."
42 Patton, *The Battle for Municipal Reform*, 71; W. Anderson, *American City Government*, 47, 59–60.
43 Goodnow, *Municipal Problems*, 46.
44 W. Anderson, *Local Government and Finance in Minnesota*, 59.
45 Ibid., 61–9, 319; W. Munro, *The Government of American Cities*, 55.
46 Goodnow, *Municipal Problems*, 40–6.
47 Laskin, "The Ontario Municipal Board," 5n9, 20n74.
48 Rutherford, "Tomorrow's Metropolis," 214–15.
49 Ontario, *First Report of the Commission on Municipal Institutions*, 75.
50 Noel, *Patrons, Clients, Brokers*, chap. 15.
51 Chipman, "Policy-Making by Administrative Tribunals," 68.
52 Humphries, *"Honest Enough to Be Bold,"* 138–9.
53 Ibid., 77.
54 Armstrong and Nelles, *Monopoly's Moment*, 188, 93.
55 The first and second purposes are evident in the actions of the ORMB's architect, former Conservative leader William Meredith, who had earlier resisted the conversion of the Education Office to a full-fledged government department on the basis that it would expose education to political influence and legislative logrolling. With similar motivations, Meredith also played important roles in the creation of the Hydro-Electric Power Commission and the Workmen's Compensation Board. See Hodgetts, *From Arm's-Length to Hands-On*, 141–3.
56 Teaford, *The Rise of the States*, 21–5.
57 Humphries, *"Honest Enough to Be Bold,"* 141; Chipman, "Policy-Making by Administrative Tribunals," 69–70.

58 While in Ontario, Nova Scotia, New Brunswick, Alberta, and, later, Quebec the regulation of utilities and municipal affairs were commingled, other provinces set up separate municipal commissions, boards, or inspectorates, as in British Columbia and Saskatchewan in 1913. Quebec set up agencies to oversee local bond issues first for greater Montreal (1921) and then separately for the rest of the province (1932). See Fischler and Wolfe, "Regional Restructuring in Montreal," 97. Similarly, Manitoba set up an oversight board for Winnipeg's suburbs in 1921. See Brittain, *Local Government in Canada*, 33–4.

59 National Bureau of Economic Research, Series A08166, "US Gross National Product in 1929 Prices, 1919–1955" (table), at http://www.nber.org/databases/macrohistory/contents/chapter08.html.

60 Horn, *The Great Depression*, 3; Canada, Royal Commission on Dominion-Provincial Relations, *Report*, 1: 148.

61 Zagorsky, "Was Depression Era Unemployment Really Less in Canada," 130.

62 Canada, Royal Commission on Dominion-Provincial Relations, *Report* 1: 148, 50.

63 Hillhouse, *Municipal Bonds*, 248–56.

64 Canadian gross municipal debt data for 1913 are from Canada, Royal Commission on Dominion-Provincial Relations, *Report*, 3: tables 57–8, and for 1920 and 1932 from Hillhouse, *Municipal Bonds*, 215. American nationwide and state local debt per capita are from Hillhouse, *Municipal Bonds*, 485 and 488–9 and United States, *Financial Statistics of State and Local Governments*, table 5.

65 Teaford, *The Twentieth-Century American City*, 80.

66 United States, *Realty Tax Delinquency*, vol. 1; Dearborn, *City Financial Emergencies*, table 2.6.

67 Teaford, *The Twentieth-Century American City*, 80.

68 Brittain, *Local Government in Canada*, 101.

69 Tassonyi, *Municipal Debt Limits and Supervision*, 6.

70 United States, *Realty Tax Delinquency*, 1: 6.

71 Teaford, *The Rise of the States*, 122.

72 Abbott, *Portland in Three Centuries*, 110–11; Mullins, "'I'll Wreck the Town If It Will Give Employment,'" 111.

73 Riendeau, "A Clash of Interests," 54.

74 Gathercole, "The City of Toronto in Depression and Recovery," 34, 75.

75 Lemon, *Toronto since 1918*, 59.

76 Riendeau, "A Clash of Interests," 52.

77 Bradbury, "The Road to Receivership."

78 Hillhouse, *Municipal Bonds*, 215.

79 Ibid., 217.

80 Hodgetts, *From Arm's-Length to Hands-On*, 124–5; Bird and
    Tassonyi, "Constraints on Provincial and Municipal Borrowing," 93;
    Hillhouse, *Municipal Bonds*, 218.

81 Bradbury, "The Road to Receivership"; Hillhouse, *Municipal Bonds*,
    22, 220.

82 Edsforth, *The New Deal*, 93.

83 Valelly, *Radicalism in the States*, 83–5.

84 Teaford, *The Rise of the States*, 124.

85 Lutz, "State Supervision of Local Finance," 292.

86 The US Constitution, Article I, s. 10, cl. 1 prohibits state legislatures
    from retroactively modifying the provisions of private contracts. This
    was a remedy to a problem that had been endemic in the Revolutio-
    nary period prior to the constitution's adoption in 1789: state legisla-
    tures used special legislation to arbitrarily absolve influential people
    of their debts – in essence the abrogation of legally binding private
    contracts. To halt this abuse, a clause was added to the constitution
    granting the national Congress exclusive authority over contract law.

87 M. McConnell and Picker, "When Cities Go Broke," 425–7.

88 Gelfand, *A Nation of Cities*, 51.

89 Teaford, *The Twentieth-Century American City*, 80–1; Bird, *The
    Present Financial Status of 135 Cities*; Edsforth, *The New Deal*,
    91–2.

90 Teaford, *The Rise of the States*, 125.

91 Hart, *Debts and Recovery*, 227–28.

92 Hillhouse, *Municipal Bonds*, 295–320.

93 J. Smith, *Building New Deal Liberalism*, 2.

94 Edsforth, *The New Deal*, 226.

95 Fishback, Horrace, and Kantor, "Did New Deal Grant Programs
    Stimulate Local Economies?"

96 Hart, *Debts and Recovery*, 114, 229.

97 See Clawson, *New Deal Planning*; M. Scott, *American City Planning
    since 1890*, chaps. 5–6; Hancock, "The New Deal and American
    Planning."

98 Gray and Johnson, *The TVA Regional Planning and Development
    Program*.

99 Friedmann and Weaver, *Territory and Function*, 77.

100 Ethington and Levitus, "Placing American Political Development,"
    166.

101 Canada, Royal Commission on Dominion-Provincial Relations, *Report*, 1: 151–60.
102 Struthers, "Prelude to Depression."
103 Canada, Royal Commission on Dominion-Provincial Relations, *Report*, 1: 163; Canada, *Report of the Dominion Director of Unemployment Relief*, appendix F.
104 Quoted in Gathercole, "The City of Toronto in Depression and Recovery," 64; see also Spanner, "The Straight Furrow," chaps. 6–7.
105 Kulisek and Price, ""Ontario Municipal Policy Affecting Local Autonomy."
106 Ontario, *Report of the Royal Commission on Border Cities Amalgamation*, 4–6.
107 Crawford, *Canadian Municipal Government*, 349.
108 Laskin, "The Ontario Municipal Board," 75–7.
109 G. Bell and Pascoe, *The Ontario Government*, 129.
110 Metropolitan Area Committee of the Council of the County of York, *Interim Report*, January 1934, in Archives of Ontario, RG 19-145, Records of the Metropolitan Area Committee of the County of York, box 1.
111 Ontario, *Report of the Royal Commission on Border Cities Amalgamation*.
112 Brittain, *Local Government in Canada*, 34–6; Feldman, "Legislative Control of Municipalities in Ontario," 294; Crawford, *Canadian Municipal Government*, 344–55.
113 Quoted in Kulisek and Price, "Ontario Municipal Policy Affecting Local Autonomy," 262.
114 Hillhouse, *Municipal Bonds*, 260.
115 J. Allen, "How a Different America Responded to the Great Depression."
116 Patterson, *Congressional Conservatism and the New Deal*.
117 Clawson, *New Deal Planning*, chap. 13; Conant and Myers, *Toward a More Perfect Union*, chap. 7; M. Scott, *American City Planning since 1890*, chap. 5.
118 W. Young, *The Anatomy of a Party*.
119 Horn, *The League for Social Reconstruction*; Owram, *The Government Generation*.
120 Canada, Royal Commission on Dominion-Provincial Relations, *Report*, vol. 2; Bradford, *Commissioning Ideas*.
121 Bright, "Planning to Plan"; Gotlieb, "George Drew and the Dominion-Provincial Conference on Reconstruction"; Thorpe, "Historical Perspective on the 'Resources for Tomorrow' Conference."

122 Stephens and Wikstrom, *Metropolitan Government and Governance*; Cassella, "Evolution of National Civic League Policies."

123 Bollens, *Special District Governments in the United States*, 103–4, chap. 8.

124 In central and eastern Canada, counties follow the traditional English model of indirect representation. Organized as federations, their councils are composed of delegates of elected township and village councils rather than being directly elected. This contrasts with the traditional American practice of directly electing the county commission. Indirect representation remains the norm in the regional county municipalities and urban agglomeration councils established in post-1979 local government reorganizations in Quebec. The conversion of some Ontario urban counties to "regional municipalities" in the late 1960s and early 1970s led in some cases to direct election of regional councillors.

125 Weiner, *Urban Transportation Planning in the United States*, chaps. 3–5; Solof, *History of Metropolitan Planning Organizations*.

126 Flanagan, "The Housing Act of 1954."

127 Feiss, "The Foundations of Federal Planning Assistance," 183.

128 Scott, *American City Planning since 1890*, 504.

129 See Wikstrom, *Councils of Governments*.

130 Solof, *History of Metropolitan Planning Organizations*, 21; Weiner, *Urban Transportation Planning in the United States*, chaps. 6–7.

131 Weir, "Planning, Environmentalism, and Urban Poverty"; Connolly, "Institutional Change in Urban Environmentalism," chap. 4.

132 American Law Institute, *A Model Land Development Code.*

133 Weir, "Planning, Environmentalism, and Urban Poverty"; Connolly, "Institutional Change in Urban Environmentalism," chap. 4.

134 On state planning, see Bosselman and Callies, *The Quiet Revolution in Land Use Control*; American Law Institute, *A Model Land Development Code*. The US Department of Commerce published a standard state zoning enabling act in 1924. All states had adopted some variation of it by the end of the decade. See Meck, "Model Planning and Zoning Enabling Legislation." By the end of the 1960s, 68 per cent of municipalities in metropolitan areas had adopted zoning ordinances, and 59 per cent had adopted subdivision regulations. Their effectiveness was undermined, however, by inconsistent or inappropriate use and by lack of coordination at the metropolitan scale. See United States, *Building the American City*, 209–17.

135 Canadian planning legislation bore much closer resemblance to American than British policy ideas. See, for example, the planning

legislation and procedures manual of the International City
Managers' Association and the community planning guide jointly
produced by the ICMA, the American Municipal Association, and the
American Society of Planning Officials: Segoe, *Local Planning
Administration*; *Action for Cities*. Both lay out schemes for the formation of city planning commissions authorized to conduct studies,
approve an official map of land uses and infrastructure systems, and
exercise zoning and subdivision control. Canadian provinces did not
copy the key features of Britain's 1947 Town and Country Planning
Act, which allowed for the nationalization of development rights and
the use of discretionary development control instead of zoning. On
the adoption of planning legislation in other provinces, see G. Hodge
and Gordon, *Planning Canadian Communities*, 227–33. Quebec was
the laggard, adopting a general planning act only in 1979. This may
perhaps be explained by the separate evolution of local and metropolitan planning mechanisms in Montreal, the province's largest city.

136 Brownstone and Plunkett, *Metropolitan Winnipeg*.
137 Z. Taylor, Burchfield, and Kramer, "Alberta Cities at the Crossroads."
138 Fischler and Wolfe, "Regional Restructuring in Montreal";
      Cullingworth, *Urban and Regional Planning in Canada*, 347–58.
139 Bollens and Schmandt, *The Metropolis*, 169, 370–1.
140 Kerner, *Report of the National Advisory Commission on Civil
      Disorders*.
141 Douglas, *Building the American City*, 1.
142 Powell, "Addressing Regional Dilemmas for Minority Communities."
143 Douglas, *Building the American City*, 26.
144 On the transformation of the parties' racial bases and policy agendas
      from the 1930s through the 1960s and its emergent geography, see
      Schickler, *Racial Realignment*; Ogorzalek, *The Cities on the Hill*.
145 Solof, *History of Metropolitan Planning Organizations*, 26; Weiner,
      Urban Transportation Planning in the United States, chaps. 10–11.
146 D. Miller and Cox, *Governing the Metropolitan Region*, 181.
147 Knaap and Lewis, "Regional Planning for Sustainability and
      Hegemony"; Seltzer and Carbonell, "Regional Practice, Regional
      Prospect."
148 D. Johnson et al., *Planning for Smart Growth*; Weitz, "From Quiet
      Revolution to Smart Growth"; Cobb, "Toward Modern Statutes."
149 Garcea and LeSage, *Municipal Reform in Canada*.
150 Climenhaga, "The Death and Life of Regional Planning in the
      Calgary Area."

151 Fischler and Wolfe, "Regional Restructuring in Montreal."
152 Z. Taylor, Burchfield, and Kramer, "Alberta Cities at the Crossroads."
153 Stoney and Graham, "Federal-Municipal Relations in Canada."
154 Z. Taylor and Bradford, "Governing Canadian Cities."

CHAPTER FOUR

1 S.M. Wickett, Memorandum re: Metropolitan Area, n.d. (but catalogued as 1909), microform, Toronto Reference Library. See also J.
Weaver, "Order and Efficiency," 226–7.
2 Stott, "Enhancing Status through Incorporation."
3 Harris, *Unplanned Suburbs*, 40; Careless, *Toronto to 1918*, 124;
Moore, "Public Services and Residential Development," 455. See also
unsigned letter to Minister David Croll from the York County
Metropolitan Area Committee, 19 Nov. 1934, Archives of Ontario
(hereafter A O), R G 19–145, Records of the Metropolitan Area
Committee of the County of York, box 1, file Ont. (misc.).
4 Only forty-two American municipalities are independent of county
structures. Of these, thirty-nine are in Virginia; the others are
Baltimore, Maryland; Carson City, Nevada; and St. Louis, Missouri.
These so-called independent cities are distinct from city-county
consolidations, in which the administration of the municipality and
county are merged yet remain legally distinct. See Pinchbeck, "City-
County Separation in Virginia"; V. Jones, 130–5.
5 Colton, *Big Daddy*, 53.
6 For a detailed summary of early suburban municipal organization
and its motivations, see "Discontent in the Suburbs," 11.
7 See letter from the Metropolitan Area Committee to Minister David
Croll, 20 Nov. 1934, A O, R G 19-145, Records of the Metropolitan
Area Committee of the County of York, box 1.
8 This event has received virtually no attention in secondary accounts.
Colton mentions it only in passing, and Frisken bases her brief description on Colton. See Colton, *Big Daddy*, 55; Frisken, *The Public
Metropolis*, 55–6. It is also not mentioned in Henry's only biography.
See Spanner, "The Straight Furrow."
9 See "The Toronto Metropolitan District Act, 1924," undated draft
typescript, A O, R G 37-6-2, Record of Hearings into Toronto Amalgamation, Records of the Ontario Municipal Board, box 968, exhibit 28.
10 Colton, *Big Daddy*, 55; "Metropolitan Area Advocated by Henry Is
Carefully Studied"; "Metropolitan Area Plan Means Mill and a Half

Tax"; "A Metropolitan Area"; "Mr. Henry's Project"; "Metropolitan Area Seems Unpopular with School Board"; "Metropolitan Area Meets Opposition of Urban Boards."

11 "Metropolitan Area Plan Means Mill and a Half Tax"; "Metropolitan Area Advocated by Henry Is Carefully Studied."

12 Colton, *Big Daddy*, 56.

13 Meeting minutes, 22 Dec. 1933, AO, RG 19-145, Records of the Metropolitan Area Committee of the County of York, box 1, file Metropolitan Area Committee.

14 Letter to Minister Finlayson from A.J.B. Gray, 15 March 1934, and Metropolitan Area Committee of the Council of the County of York, *Interim Report*, Jan. 1934, both in AO, RG 19-145, Records of the Metropolitan Area Committee of the County of York, box 1, unlabelled file.

15 Letter to Minister Finlayson signed by Hollis Beckett on behalf of the Committee, 24 Jan. 1934, AO, RG 19-145, Records of the Metropolitan Area Committee of the County of York, box 1, file Ontario (Misc.).

16 See AO, RG 19-145, Records of the Metropolitan Area Committee of the County of York, box 1, file Questionnaires.

17 Wrong, "Ontario Provincial Elections."

18 Plumptre, *Report on the Government of the Metropolitan Area of Toronto*. On the controversy, see Lemon, *Toronto since 1918*, 74.

19 Colton, *Big Daddy*, 56.

20 McKenty, *Mitch Hepburn*, chap. 8.

21 See McConnell, "Toronto May Be Forced to 'Adopt' Suburbs."

22 "Suburban Municipalities Divided on Annexation"; "House to Rule on Annexation Says Hepburn"; "Changing Tone in Legislature."

23 AO, RG 19–145, Records of the Metropolitan Area Committee of the County of York, box 6, Briefs 1938 and 1939.

24 See letter from Reeve Warren to Metropolitan Area Committee A.J.B. Gray, 13 Dec. 1938, AO, RG 19–145, Records of the Metropolitan Area Committee of the County of York, box 1, unlabelled file.

25 McConnell, "Toronto May Be Forced to 'Adopt' Suburbs." See also "Cross Assails Mayor for Stand on Annexation."

26 "Toronto Annexation Parlay Is Proposed"; "Cross Assails City Plebiscite on Annexation."

27 Colton, *Big Daddy*, 56. Letter from Minister Eric Cross to Committee Chair A.J.B. Gray, 12 Oct. 1939, AO, RG 19-145, Records of the Metropolitan Area Committee of the County of York, box 1. The

report was expected to be tabled in late summer or early autumn. See "Toronto Annexation Parlay Is Proposed."

28 Manthorpe, *The Power and the Tories*, 31–2.

29 See Lemon, *Toronto since 1918*, 81; R. White, *Planning Toronto*, 42–6.

30 Gotlieb, "George Drew and the Dominion-Provincial Conference on Reconstruction," 31.

31 G. White, *Change in the Ontario State*, 13.

32 On the history of Ontario planning legislation, see Gomme, "Municipal Planning in Ontario," 28–60.

33 Under the 1912 City and Suburbs Plans Act and the 1917 Planning and Development Act, city and town planning commissions could review requests for land subdivision within a specified distance from their borders (five miles for cities and three miles for towns).

34 White notes Bunnell's close connection to Walter Blucher, who served as president of ASPO in the 1940s and played an important advisory role in the preparation of model planning legislation and procedures in the United States, to which the 1946 Ontario act bears considerable resemblance. See R. White, *Planning Toronto*, 45. For American ideas, see *Action for Cities*; Segoe, *Local Planning Administration*.

35 A. Richardson, *Conservation by the People*, chap. 1.

36 Shrubsole, "The Evolution of Public Water Management Agencies in Ontario," 51–3.

37 A. Richardson, *Conservation by the People*, 20–1.

38 Ibid., 28; see also McLean, *Pathways to the Living City*.

39 Ontario, *Report of Conference on Planning and Development*, 6; A. Richardson, *Conservation by the People*, 19.

40 See "Far More Cruel Than Nazi"; R. White, *Planning Toronto*, 46.

41 Gomme, "Municipal Planning in Ontario," 66.

42 Toronto and York Planning Board, *Report*, 9, 44.

43 "Sees 5,000,000 Living in Toronto in 50 Years."

44 An inventory presented in evidence to the OMB listed 163 agreements between Toronto and its neighbours dating back to 1915. AO, RG 37-6-2, Records of Hearings into Toronto Amalgamation, box 968, exhibit 65.

45 "Hints York May Offer Alternative to Merger."

46 "Tax Bills of Suburbanites Soar"; "City Homeowners Face Greater Share of Taxes."

47 R. White, *Urban Infrastructure and Urban Growth*, 12–13.

48 Gore and Storrie, *Report on Water Supply and Sewage Disposal*, 13.

49 "Want Legislature to Give City Seven Suburbs."

50 "Two-Gun Buck'"; "A Metropolitan Problem."

51 Lemon, *Toronto since 1918*, 82; Colton, *Big Daddy*, 57; "The Single Community," n.p.

52 "Planning Is Basis," n.p.

53 "Strength in Union," n.p.

54 "No Magician's Wand." See also "Annexation by Negotiation"; "Amalgamation, Unification, Annexation?" In late 1951, the *Star* endorsed mayoral candidate Nathan Phillips on the basis of his opposition to amalgamation. See "What Amalgamation Would Mean."

55 The potency of anti-communist rhetoric should not be underestimated. During the OMB's hearings on Toronto's application for amalgamation, the counsel for Forest Hill repeatedly accused fiscal unification's advocates of communist sympathies. See "Gray Says He's No Red in Amalgamation Views"; "Research Bureau Views Held Akin to Marxism by Forest Hill's Counsel."

56 Gore and Storrie, *Report on Water Supply and Sewage Disposal*; N. Wilson, *A Transportation Plan for Metropolitan Toronto*.

57 Colton, *Big Daddy*, 61.

58 Civic Advisory Council, *First Report*, 77–81.

59 Toronto and York Planning Board, *Report*.

60 Resolutions of County Council, 1 and 3 Feb. 1950, AO, RG-147, Toronto Area Committee files, box 2, file T.A.C. 2.

61 "Distorting the Facts."

62 "Annexation by Negotiation."

63 Memorandum on "Greater Toronto" by A.E.K. Bunnell, 15 Nov. 1949, AO, RG 19-147, Toronto Area Committee files, box 4, file Planning.

64 Proceedings of the first special meeting of a committee of the mayors and reeves of the thirteen municipalities in the Toronto area, 26 Jan. 1950, AO, RG 19-147, Toronto Area Committee files, box 1, file Proceedings – Metropolitan Scheme.

65 Colton, *Big Daddy*, 65.

66 R. Graham, *Old Man Ontario*, 201.

67 Instead of seeking a new seat in the legislature, Drew resigned the premiership and set his sights on becoming leader of the federal Progressive Conservative Party. This triggered the leadership contest won by Frost.

68 R. Graham, *Old Man Ontario*, 146–50.

69 "Report of the Toronto Area Committee," 30 March 1950, AO, RG 19-147, Toronto Area Committee files, box 2, file Toronto Area Committee 1.

70 On 3 February 1950, York County council voted to request that the
province give it authority over intermunicipal services and that the
City of Toronto be permitted to join the county for these purposes.
See memorandum in AO, RG 19-147, Toronto Area Committee files,
box 1, file Metropolitan Area File – Department. See also an information bulletin released by the Advisory Information Council of York
County on April 11, which outlines the proposed duties of the empowered county. See AO, RG 37-6-2, Record of Hearings into Toronto
Amalgamation, box 966, file 1a, General Correspondence –
Amalgamation Report.
71 It is not clear why Mimico switched its preference from a joint-services
board to amalgamation. In September 1950, Mimico informed the
OMB of its support for Toronto's amalgamation proposal but asked
that consideration of a special-purpose body continue should amalgamation prove impracticable. See "Mimico Supports City in Area
Amalgamation."
72 "Interim Joint Control of Sewage and Water Likely Merger Move."
73 "Mayor Invites Suburbs to Discuss Unification."
74 "Hearing on Merger Deferred 2 Weeks"; "Proposes Area Board to
Handle Services without a Merger"; "Amicable Solution Sought";
"County Approaches City to Start Merger Talks."
75 "Sees 5,000,000 Living in Toronto in 50 Years"; "All 23 Municipalities
Should Merge: Council."
76 "Bylaws Block Housing."
77 See the report by Horace Brittain of the Citizens Research Institute,
"The Government of the Toronto Metropolitan Area," AO, RG 37-6-2,
Record of Hearings into Toronto Amalgamation, box 966, folder 1a,
General Correspondence – Amalgamation Report; letter from the
Greater Toronto chapter of CPAC, 9 June 1950, ibid., folder 4a, Misc.
Reports Not Filed as Exhibits; Bureau of Municipal Research, issue of
Civic Affairs, 16 Jan. 1950.
78 "All Suburbs Better Off under Amalgamation."
79 "Toronto, Scarboro Benefitting by Merger"; "Sound Financial State
Reason York Opposes Merger."
80 "Rapid Expansion Hits Municipalities."
81 "12 Reassessments in Toronto Area near Completion"; "Three Assessors
to Draft System."
82 Colton, *Big Daddy*, 69–70.
83 *Decision of the Board Dated January 20, 1953*, 27, 9–32.
84 Ibid., 25, 39–41.

85   AO, RG 37-6-2, Record of Hearings into Toronto Amalgamation, box 968, file 28.

86   The creation of a Metropolitan Toronto School Board was provided for by the act. This was a modification of Cumming's original proposal, which assigned authority over education directly to Metro Council.

87   *Decision of the Board Dated January 20, 1953*, 72–4.

88   Ibid., 87–9. Gardiner also wanted future reviews to consider boundary expansion. Interview with Stevenson.

89   "Decide to Fight Unification."

90   "Federation to Cut Toronto Taxes."

91   "Basically Undemocratic."

92   "Elected Representation."

93   "Gradual Merger Plan Favored by Oliver."

94   "Rap Federation."

95   White, *Planning Toronto*, 79.

96   Colton, *Big Daddy*, 69–71.

97   Byrnes, "29 Amendments in Bill Clear Path."

98   McLean, *Pathways to the Living City*, chap. 1; A. Richardson, *Conservation by the People*, chap. 3; White, *Planning Toronto*, 124–7.

99   These built on the Toronto and York Planning Board's earlier water and sewer and transportation studies. See Gore and Storrie, *Report on Water Supply and Sewage Disposal*; N. Wilson, *A Transportation Plan for Metropolitan Toronto and the Suburban Area Adjacent*.

100   R. White, *Planning Toronto*, 118–22.

101   Colton, *Big Daddy*, 160.

102   Goldenberg, *Report of the Royal Commission on Metropolitan Toronto*, 11, 79.

103   Rose, *Governing Metropolitan Toronto*, 31. In his comprehensive review of house-building industry concentration, Buzzelli reports that, in Ontario, large firms (those producing more than 100 units per year) accounted for 21 per cent of all units in 1960 and 57 per cent in 1973 – the highest percentage among all provinces in both years. See Buzzelli, "Firm Size Structure in North American Housebuilding," 541. Colton reports that, in 1962, 34 per cent of all units in Metro financed with federally backed mortgages were constructed by large firms. He credits this in part to Metro's policy of imposing cash exactions to pay for infrastructure (what today would be called development charges or impact fees) and also to its use of subdivision control to manage a long-term land supply. These

conditions favoured larger firms with access to capital. See Colton, *Big Daddy*, 163. See also Sorensen and Hess, "Building Suburbs, Toronto-Style."

104 Rose, *Governing Metropolitan Toronto*, chap. 4.
105 Goldenberg, *Governing Metropolitan Toronto*, 70–1.
106 R. White, *Planning Toronto*, 86–95, 113–22.
107 Rose, *Governing Metropolitan Toronto*, 39.
108 Ibid., 157.
109 Colton, *Big Daddy*, chap. 5, esp. 98–9.
110 Ibid., 74, 97, 123–32.
111 G. White, *Change in the Ontario State*.
112 Macdonald interview.
113 McDougall, *John P. Robarts*, 86, 96.
114 Ibid., 135–9.
115 N. Richardson, "Guest Editor's Foreword," 89.
116 United States, *Statistical Abstract of the United States*, 396, 420.
117 Rose, *Governing Metropolitan Toronto*, 102–3.
118 AO, RG 18-147, Royal Commission on Metropolitan Toronto (1963–65), box 10 General Files, file University of Toronto – Speech by Goldenberg at Centre for Urban Studies Seminar, 1 Oct 1965, Reorganization of Metropolitan Toronto: Problems and Proposals, Second Seminar on Problems of Metropolitan Reorganization.
119 Ibid., boxes 4 and 5, Briefs; boxes 11 and 12, Comments Regarding Report.
120 The OWRC was a provincial agency established in 1956 to regulate and finance municipal water and sewer systems. See Bordessa and Cameron, "Servicing Growth in the Metropolitan Toronto Region."
121 R. White, *Planning Toronto*, 133–4.
122 "Metro Fringe Faces Crisis Too." See also "Planning Chief Metro 'Black Sheep.'"
123 Goldenberg, *Governing Metropolitan Toronto*, 169–71.
124 Baker, "Metro to Be Enlarged to 8 Boroughs."
125 See letter from Forest Hill MPP Edward Dunlop to Spooner, 23 Aug. 1965, AO, RG 18-147, Royal Commission on Metropolitan Toronto (1963–65), box 11, Comments Regarding Report, file Goldenberg Report – M.L.A. Opinions. For Gardiner's opinion, see Best, "Fred Gardiner Says Goldenberg Plan Won't Work." Gardiner was appointed by Robarts to advise on the report's implementation.
126 Letter from Cumming to Robarts, 20 Dec. 1965, in AO, RG 18-147, Royal Commission on Metropolitan Toronto (1963–65), box 11,

Comments Regarding Report, file Amendments to the Municipality of Metropolitan Toronto Act.

127 McKeough interview.

128 A.M. Campbell, "The Boundaries of Metropolitan Toronto." The Toronto Board of Trade and the Bureau of Municipal Research continued to advocate for Metro's expansion, the former to include the land within the MTPB area, the latter to include only the urbanizing areas of York County. Metro itself recommended annexing portions of Vaughan and Markham to North York and Scarborough. In November 1968, Pickering Township council petitioned to join Metro as a new borough, a proposal endorsed both by Metro Council and Pickering residents in a referendum.

129 L. Smith, *Report*, 2: 545.

130 McDougall, *John P. Robarts*, 210.

131 Address by Lorne Cumming to the Association of Ontario Counties conference, 5 April 1967, AO, RG 19-8, Records of the Special Advisor on Local Government Studies, box 14, file Association of Ontario Counties conference.

132 "The Rebirth of Counties in the United States," address by Bernard F. Hillenbrand, executive director of the National Association of Counties, n.d. (but stamped received 22 May 1964), in AO, RG 19-8, Records of the Special Advisor on Local Government Studies, box 6, file Association of Ontario Counties.

133 Beckett, *Fourth and Final Report*.

134 AO, RG 49-146, Select Committee on the Municipal and Related Acts, boxes C112–C113.

135 Extracts from Public Speeches by Hon. J.P. Robarts and Hon. J.W. Spooner, re: Regional Government, in AO, RG 19-8, Records of the Special Advisor on Local Government Studies, box 1, file Regional Government.

136 McDougall, *John P. Robarts*, 210–11.

137 Macdonald interview. McKeough recalls that while compromise on the boundary question was dictated by political resistance, county reform "was a good place to start" and that the larger game was to reduce the number of lower-tier municipalities in order to make them more capable (interview).

138 Stevenson interview.

139 Extracts from Public Speeches by Hon. J.P. Robarts and Hon. J.W. Spooner, re: Regional Government.

140 In both cases, the commissions recommended the division of the area into two single-tier urban and rural municipalities. On Murray Jones's Ottawa-Carleton report, see Milner, "Statutes," 81. See also letter from Spooner to Robarts, 20 Nov. 1966, AO, RG 19-8, Records of the Special Advisor on Local Government Studies, box 3, file Memoranda to the Prime Minister. On the Peel-Halton inquiry, see Plunkett, *Report of the Peel-Halton Local Government Review.*

141 Feldman, *Ontario, 1945–1973,* 14.

142 In a speech to the Ontario Municipal Association on 25 August 1965, Robarts emphasized Metro Toronto as the dominant precedent for the regional government program, noting that "regional government has always been based on the county." See Extracts from Public Speeches by Hon. J.P. Robarts and Hon. J.W. Spooner, re: Regional Government. In interviews, Lionel Feldman and Darcy McKeough both suggest that Cumming favoured Metro-style two-tier empowered county arrangements and was instrumental in rejecting Jones's scheme for Ottawa. Cumming retired after the completion of the Ottawa process, and McKeough, who favoured single-tier units, was then able to pursue a single-tier amalgamation for Thunder Bay.

143 While the new Durham Region contained most of the territory of the former Ontario and Durham Counties, it should be noted that the northern tip of Ontario County was transferred to Simcoe County, and the northeast corner of Durham County was transferred to Victoria County (now the City of Kawartha Lakes).

144 L. Smith, *Report,* 2: 550.

145 Ontario, *Government Reform in Ontario,* 41–4; Ontario, *Municipal Reform.*

146 G. White, *Change in the Ontario State,* 16; McDougall, *John P. Robarts,* 211.

147 For an overview of these programs, see R. White, *Planning Toronto,* chap. 4.

148 Ontario, *Growth and Travel,* 80.

149 Ontario, *Choices for a Growing Region,* 7.

150 Ontario, *Transportation for the Regional City.*

151 Ibid.

152 Ontario, *Choices for a Growing Region,* chaps. 12–13.

153 L. Gertler, *Regional Development.*

154 Macdonald, "A Retrospective View from the Top," 93; Macdonald interview.

155 Robarts, *Design for Development: Statement*, 2.
156 Ibid., 6.
157 N. Richardson, "Insubstantial Pageant," 565.
158 Robarts, *Design for Development: Statement*, 7; Robarts, *Design for Development: Phase Two.*
159 Ontario, *Design for Development: The Toronto-Centred Region.*
160 Cullingworth, "The Provincial Role in Planning and Development," 145–8.
161 Established in June 1968 with Charles Macnaughton as minister, the Department of Treasury and Economics was an amalgam of the traditional fiscal management functions previously located in the Treasury Department, and the economic research and forecasting functions of the former Department of Economics and Development. The latter had been created in 1960 with the breakup of the Department of Planning and Development (established in 1944), at which time land-use planning had been transferred to the Department of Municipal Affairs.
162 McKeough interview.
163 McDougall, *John P. Robarts*, 214.
164 See a May 1970 speech by McKeough quoted in Saunderson, *Submission to the Government of Ontario on Design for Development*, 11–12.
165 R. White, *Planning Toronto*, 244–6.
166 W. Davis, *Design for Development.*
167 Feldman, *Ontario 1945–1973*, 24–5.
168 See Ontario, *Report to the Advisory Committee on Urban and Regional Planning*; McKeough, *Toronto-Centred Region Program Statement.*
169 McDougall, *John P. Robarts*, 232–3.
170 Manthorpe, *The Power and the Tories*, 9. For example, Hoy quotes McKeough as believing that, while Robarts was committed to the regional government agenda, Davis was not. See Hoy, *Bill Davis*, 125.
171 See Ontario, *Report* (Planning Act Review Committee), 57–8; Robarts, *Report of the Royal Commission on Metropolitan Toronto*, 131–3, 225–6; Ontario, *White Paper on the Planning Act*, 45–6.
172 Frisken, *The Public Metropolis*, 160–1.
173 Ibid., 186–8.
174 Bordessa and Cameron, "Servicing Growth in the Metropolitan Toronto Region"; R. White, *Planning Toronto*, 250.

175 N. Richardson, "Guest Editor's Foreword," 90.

176 Brochure, "What Is the OGTA?" n.d., AO, RG 19-162, Correspondence of the Office for the Greater Toronto Area, 1986–94, file B336366, PER-01-2 GTA Organization/Role and Mandate of OGTA. See also slide presentation dated 31 October 1989 in same location.

177 Ontario Legislative Assembly, Hansard, 34th Parl, 2nd Sess., 3 Nov. 1987, 15: 10.

178 Metro Toronto and the surrounding regional municipalities of Halton, Peel, York, and Durham started to be referred to as the Greater Toronto Area, or GTA, in the late 1980s. A search of the ProQuest Canadian Newsstand database reveals no use of the acronym "GTA" before 1989 and no use of "Greater Toronto Area" in the contemporary territorial meaning before 1987. Since the government began using the term in policy in 1987, it may be responsible for its popularization.

179 Its head, Deputy Minister (DM) Gardner Church, favoured the title "Greater Toronto Office of Urban Development," but this was nixed by the minister. See Memorandum from Church to Mary Mogford, DM of Treasury and Economics, 20 Oct. 1988, AO, RG 19-162, Correspondence of the Office for the Greater Toronto Area, 1986–94, file B336366, PER-01-2 GTA Organization/Role and Mandate of OGTA.

180 Memoranda, "Mandate" and "Challenges," n.d., AO, ibid.

181 On lack of resources and buy-in, see author interview with Elizabeth McLaren, also memorandum from Church to Elaine Todres, DM of the Human Resources Secretariat, 29 Nov. 1989, AO, ibid.

182 Clayton Research, *Projections of Population and Households in the Greater Toronto Area*; Hemson Consulting, *Employment Forecasts for the Greater Toronto Area*.

183 IBI Group, *Greater Toronto Region Urban Concepts Study*.

184 Interview with McLaren and correspondence with Grier.

185 Ontario, *Growing Together*; Ontario, *GTA 2021*.

186 Ontario, *Shaping Growth in the GTA*.

187 AO, RG 19-162, Correspondence of the Office for the Greater Toronto Area, 1986–94, file B336366, CON48 GTA Policy Statement – Background Reports.

188 In an interview, the then chief of staff to Minister of Municipal Affairs Ian Fawcett recalls that, while the premier strongly supported Planning Act reform, there was no political direction on the creation of a GTA policy.

189 Donald, "Economic Change and City Region Governance," 141–53.
190 M. Gertler, *A Region in Transition*.
191 See Stein, "What We Must Do to Prosper"; Stein, "What's Wrong with the Greater Toronto Area"; Stein, "Nobody Is Running the Show."
192 On Rae's motivations, see Donald, "Economic Change and City Region Governance," 158–9.
193 Boston Consulting, *The Fourth Era*.
194 Ontario, *Report of the GTA Task Force*, s. 6.
195 See Donald, "Economic Change and City Region Governance," 165–74; Sancton, "Differing Approaches to Municipal Restructuring."
196 Crombie, "Recommendations of the 'Who Does What' Panel"; K. Graham and Phillips, "Who Does What in Ontario."
197 McLaren interview.
198 Cobban, "Bigger Is Better."
199 Eidelman, "Managing Urban Sprawl in Ontario"; Sandberg, Wekerle, and Gilbert, *The Oak Ridges Moraine Battles*, chap. 5.
200 Interviews with MacKenzie and Faught.
201 Ontario, *Oak Ridges Moraine Conservation Plan*. The Oak Ridges Moraine has been recognized as geological feature since the 1940s. It had long been recognized as a scenic landscape and the location of the headwaters of numerous rivers, but by the late 1980s it was increasingly the subject of urban development, especially in York Region. The Liberal and NDP governments took steps toward developing a policy to regulate land use on the moraine, although they stopped short of imposing a provincial plan, as had been done for the Niagara Escarpment some years earlier. See Kanter, *Space for All*. Work on a provincial moraine policy was halted by the incoming Conservative government in 1995.
202 Winfield, *Blue-Green Province*, 149.
203 Ontario, *Greenbelt Plan 2005*.
204 Ontario, *Places to Grow*.
205 Allen and Campsie, *Implementing the Growth Plan for the Greater Golden Horseshoe*, 33–4.
206 Howlett, "Subway Plan Could Benefit Sorbara Family."
207 Pagliero, "How Kathleen Wynne's Liberals Secretly Helped Kill the Scarborough LRT."
208 Pagliero and Spurr, "Cost of Scarborough Subway Extension Rises."

CHAPTER FIVE

1 "Twin City Metropolitan Area Planning Commission Proposed."

2 "Meeting to Launch Twin City Planning Commission Move"; "Twin City Engineers Will Organize Association"; "Twin City Planning Commission Forms"; "Communities Near Cities Included in Planning Program."

3 "Metropolitan Plan Group Is Organized for 25 Mile Radius."

4 Scott, *American City Planning since 1890*, 215.

5 "Metropolitan Unit Financing Starts"; "Metropolitan Planning Board Maps 1,000 Mile Program"; "Minneapolis Foes Renew Attack on Metropolitan Zone"; "800 Leaders Called to Help Map Metropolitan Plan"; "New Metropolitan Area Group Formed "; "Regional Board Starts Plan for 3,000-Mile Area"; "Planning Unit Head Asks Aid"; "Planning Group Begins Work Here."

6 Mick, "The Minneapolis-Saint Paul Sanitary District"; *50 Years*.

7 "Joint Twin Cities Proposed."

8 Citizens League, *Twin Cities Metropolitan Area Sewage Needs*, 29.

9 See Valelly, *Radicalism in the States*. This mode of politics was not limited to the United States. Similarly motivated agrarian socialist or progressive party movements operated in the Canadian provinces, winning power in Alberta, Manitoba, and Ontario in the first two decades of the twentieth century, fragments of which later coalesced as the Co-operative Commonwealth Federation (CCF) in 1932. Although the CCF never gained power in British Columbia or Ontario during this period, it influenced politics and policy in both provinces through what Maurice Duverger called "contagion from the left."

10 Mitau, *Politics in Minnesota*, chap. 3.

11 Mayer, *The Political Career of Floyd B. Olson*, chap. 4.

12 Valelly, *Radicalism in the States*, 135.

13 See Minnesota Historical Society and State Archives (hereafter MNHS), Minnesota State Planning Board Fonds, loc. 101.G.15.2(F), box 13, Reports 1934–1937 and loc. 109.B.15.4(F), box 11, Meeting Minutes.

14 *Report of the Committee on Taxation*, 6–9.

15 *Report of the Committee on Administrative Units*, 3.

16 *Report of the Metropolitan Committee*, 10.

17 A general enabling act for zoning by cities and villages existed, but only Minneapolis's charter provided for the preparation of a comprehensive plan as distinct from a zoning ordinance. This did not stop St. Paul from appointing a planning commission in 1919 and adopting a comprehensive plan and zoning ordinance in 1922. There was no legal means, however, for jurisdictions to exercise these powers jointly. See Planning in Minnesota Prior to 1933, MSPB memorandum no. 162,

in MnHS, Minnesota State Planning Board fonds, loc. 109.B.15.4(F), box 11, Meeting Minutes.

18 *Report of the Metropolitan Committee*, 8.

19 Herrold, "State Planning Boards and Their Relation to Other Planning Agencies."

20 See, for example, "Policies Affecting Urban Land Planning and Utilization" adopted by the American City Planning Institute at its annual meeting, Cincinnati, 19 May 1935, reprinted in MSPB memorandum no. 189, in MnHS, Minnesota State Planning Board Fonds, loc. 109.B.15.4(F), box 11, Meeting Minutes.

21 *Report of the Minnesota State Planning Board, Part 1: Digest and Interpretations* (1934), 30.

22 Olson had won the 1934 election, but the conservative caucus retook the legislature. Olson's rural base was weakened by his conciliatory resolution of a violent multi-month truckers' strike in Minneapolis in 1934, in which Trotskyite unionists openly skirmished with the Citizens Alliance, a business-backed group that refused to recognize the union and fought for the retention of the open shop. See Valelly, *Radicalism in the States*, chap. 7; Mayer, *The Political Career of Floyd B. Olson*, chap. 10. The contrast with the Ontario Liberal government's repression of the 1937 Oshawa General Motors strike is intriguing. In Ontario, anti-labourism contributed to the rise of the socialist CCF, leading to the Progressive Conservative Party's "left turn" in the 1940s and the Liberals' reduction to a rural rump until the 1980s.

23 *Report of the Minnesota State Planning Board, Part I: Digest and Interpretations* (1936), 86.

24 MnHS, Gov. Elmer Benson Fonds, file Planning Board – Olson/Peterson/Benson Admin 1938, loc. 110.E.7.6(F), box 46.

25 Valelly, *Radicalism in the States*, chaps. 8–9; Haynes, *Dubious Alliance*, chaps. 1 and 2.

26 Blegen, *Minnesota*, 536–8; Hinderaker, "Harold Stassen"; Kirby, Rothmann, and Dalin, *Harold E. Stassen*, chaps. 1–2.

27 Harold Stassen, "Keynote Address before the Republican National Convention," 24 June 1940, MnHS, JK 2357 1940s.

28 MnHS, Records of the Minnesota Postwar Council, loc. 109.F.9.1(B).

29 *Selected Determinants of Residential Development*.

30 Cavanaugh, *Politics and Freeways*, s. 2.

31 Diers and Isaacs, *Twin Cities by Trolley*, appendix A.

32 Qtd. in Nathanson, *Minneapolis in the Twentieth Century*, 163.

33 Grosenick, *Boundary Change by Administrative Commission*, Part 1, tables III-4 and III-5.

34 Interview with Ed Maranda.

35 In American government, interim commissions are committees of legislators struck to study issues between biennial legislative sessions. The closest Canadian analogue is the select committee of the legislature or the royal commission.

36 Grosenick, *Boundary Change by Administrative Commission*, Part 1, 7.

37 Vance, *Inside the Minnesota Experiment*, 18–19.

38 Grosenick, *Boundary Change by Administrative Commission*, Part 1, I-9.

39 Minnesota, *Report* (Commission on Municipal Annexation and Consolidation).

40 Ibid., 10.

41 Ibid., 11.

42 *A Report on the Minnesota Municipal Commission*, 1; Hady and Hein, "Administrative Control of Municipal Incorporation."

43 *A Report on the Minnesota Municipal Commission*, 2; Citizens League, *The Minnesota Municipal Commission: Where Now?*; Citizens League, *Minnesota Municipal Commission*; Grosenick, *Boundary Change by Administrative Commission*, Part 1, 18; *Governmental Structure, Organization, and Planning in Metropolitan Areas*.

44 Grosenick, *Boundary Change by Administrative Commission*, Part 2, V-1.

45 For a detailed account of the MPC's creation, see Sharifi, "The Twin Cities Metropolitan Planning Commission," chap. 2.

46 Interviews with James Solem, 16 June 2009 and 4 May 2010.

47 Andersen, *A Man's Reach*, 151–3.

48 C.C. Ludwig, "Metropolitan Planning Commission 'Observations,'" 3 June 1959, MnHS, MPC Fonds, loc. 102.E.14.4F, box 1. This sentiment is echoed in the March 1962 resignation speech of Ludwig's successor as chair, Robert Edman, MnHS, MPC Fonds, loc. 102.E.14.5B, box 2.

49 In 1963 the levy was increased to 0.13 mills from 0.10 mills, adding about $39,000 to its budget. In 1965, the legislature upped the levy to 0.2 mills. See *1963 Annual Report*, 9–10; *1965–1966 Biennial Report*, 11.

50 *Meeting the Challenge of Metropolitan Growth*, 24.

51 *1965 Annual Report*, 3–4.

52 Rhees, *Minnesota's Planning and Zoning Enabling Laws*.

53 *Local Planning Bulletin* 1.

54 *Local Planning Bulletin* 4.

55 *4,000,000 by 2000*, 14.

56 *50 Years*, 6.

57 *Metropolitan Sewerage Study*.

58 R. Miller, "Minneapolis–St. Paul," 60.

59 Baldinger, *Planning and Governing the Metropolis*, 77–9; Minnesota, *Report* (Commission on Municipal Laws).

60 MNHS, Gov. Elmer L. Andersen Fonds, Committee Files, loc. 115.K.17.1B, box 4, folder Metropolitan Coordinating Committee.

61 *50 Years*, 7, 26.

62 MNHS, Metropolitan Waste Control Commission Fonds, Southwest Sanitary Sewer District files, loc. 118.H.15.4F.

63 Citizens League, *Twin Cities Metropolitan Area Sewage Needs*.

64 T. Berg, *Minnesota's Miracle*, 9–10; Mitau, *Politics in Minnesota*, 98–100.

65 R. Miller, "Minneapolis–St. Paul," 103.

66 Elazar, Gray, and Spano, *Minnesota Politics and Government*, 116.

67 See *1968 State Legislative Program*, part C; *State Planning and Federal Grants*; *State Planning*.

68 Harrigan and Johnson suggest that legislature would have created the Metropolitan Council in 1967 in the absence of federal mandates, but it would likely have had considerably less authority. See Harrigan and Johnson, *Governing the Twin Cities Region*, 51.

69 "Speech Given at CMAL General Meeting, April 6, 1965 by Ted Kolderie," mimeo, MNHS, Citizens League Fonds, loc. 149.I.G.6F.

70 "Editorial: Metropolitan Council."

71 Berg, *Minnesota's Miracle*, 14–15.

72 For detailed descriptions of actors' motivations, see R. Miller, "Minneapolis–St. Paul," chap. 3; Davis, "An Analysis of the Factors and Forces Leading to the Creation of the Twin Cities Metropolitan Council," chaps. 3–4; Baldinger, *Planning and Governing the Metropolis*, chaps. 4–5.

73 *Governmental Structure, Organization, and Planning in Metropolitan Areas*; *Alternative Approaches*; *Metropolitan America*; Hansen, *Metropolitan Councils of Government*; Gulick, *The Metropolitan Problem and American Ideas*.

74 Harrigan and Johnson, *Governing the Twin Cities Region*, 27.

75 "The Metro Government Trend."

76 Matlin, "The Citizens League of Minnesota," chap. 2; Citizens League, "History of the Citizens League"; Kolderie and Gilje, "The Citizens League."

77 Hetland interview; Matlin, "The Citizens League of Minnesota," 26–7.

78 *Governmental Procedures in Metropolitan Areas*; *Metropolitan Maze*.

79 Interview with Kolderie.

80 Gulick, *The Metropolitan Problem and American Ideas*, 128–30.

81 Kolderie, "Our Metropolitan Future"; Kolderie, "Metropolitan Unity."

82 Kolderie, "Our Metropolitan Future," 2.

83 Minnesota's electoral boundaries are drawn such that each Senate district contains two House districts. The legislative delegation from each senatorial district therefore contains two House representatives and one senator. Boundaries crosscut county and municipal borders and therefore break down the historic city-suburb division.

84 Kolderie, "Our Metropolitan Future," 3.

85 The CED had separately made far-reaching recommendations: a nationwide reduction in the number of local governments by at least 80 per cent, the encouragement of strong-mayor systems, and the direct election of metropolitan policymaking bodies. See *Modernizing Local Government to Secure a Balanced Federalism*.

86 R. Miller, "Minneapolis–St. Paul," 80–1. Dayton, who would later serve on the first Metropolitan Council, is a pivotal figure in the development of a regionalist sensibility among elites. The Dayton Company had opened Southdale Mall, the first enclosed shopping centre in the world, in suburban Edina in 1956, and the first Target discount retail outlet was opened in suburban Roseville in 1962. Through his business dealings, Dayton saw, perhaps more clearly than policymakers, how suburbanization was reshaping the regional economy and infrastructure demand. Dayton's central role was stressed in interviews with Einsweiler, Maranda, and Solem (16 June 2009).

87 Kolderie, *Governing the Twin Cities Area*.

88 Shoop, "New Government Unit Needed."

89 Ackerberg, "Businessmen Urge Metro Rule Unit." Business leadership was fragmented. Only in 1963 did nineteen area chambers of commerce collaborate to form a joint council for the seven-county area. See "Area Chambers of Commerce Unit Elects Chief."

90 Shoop, "St. Paul's Byrne to Push Metro Council Plan."

91 Honsey and Bergstrom, *Report on Study of the Municipality of Metropolitan Toronto*.

92 Speech by Gov. Rolvaag to the Metropolitan Affairs Conference of the DFL, Minneapolis, 5 Feb. 1966, MnHS, Gov. Rolvaag – General Files, loc. 110.F.18.1B, folder Metropolitan Affairs 1966. In a 10 August 1966 letter to Robbie, Rolvaag acknowledged Robbie's influence on the DFL platform.

93 Quoted in Davis, "An Analysis of the Factors and Forces Leading to the Creation of the Twin Cities Metropolitan Council," 68–9.

94 Wilensky, "The Twin Cities Metropolitan Council," 82.

95 Ibid., 82.

96 Interview with Laukka.

97 See Davis, "An Analysis of the Factors and Forces Leading to the Creation of the Twin Cities Metropolitan Council," 47–51. Later polls showed metropolitan-area residents to be more supportive of election than appointment, regardless of party affiliation. See "Elected Met Council Favored"; "Elective Metro Council Preferred"; "2 out of 3 in Twin Cities Say Met Council Should Be Elected."

98 *A Metropolitan Council.*

99 For detailed accounts of the legislative debate, see R. Miller, "Minneapolis–St. Paul," chap. 4; Wilensky, "The Twin Cities Metropolitan Council," chap. 5; Baldinger, *Planning and Governing the Metropolis*, chap. 7.

100 Both quotes are from Vanderpoel, "Metro Unit Compromise Seen."

101 See *Local Consent Requirements to State Law.*

102 Interview with James Hetland.

103 Citizens League, *Breaking the Tyranny of the Local Property Tax.*

104 Orfield and Wallace, "The Minnesota Fiscal Disparities Act of 1971," s. II.

105 Hinze, *The Fiscal Disparities Program.*

106 For detailed accounts of the changes discussed see Vanderpoel, "The Twin Cities Metro Council"; Harrigan and Johnson, *Governing the Twin Cities Region*, 32–8; Baldinger, *Planning and Governing the Metropolis*, chap. 9.

107 *50 Years*, 36–7.

108 *1967–1968 Biennial Report.*

109 Baldinger, *Planning and Governing the Metropolis*, 193.

110 Vance, *Inside the Minnesota Experiment*, 16.

111 Bosselman and Callies, *The Quiet Revolution in Land Use Control*, 144.

112 Minnesota Laws, ch. 892, HF 359, "Twin Cities Area Metropolitan Transit Commission Act," enacted 25 May 1967. A voluntary MTC

had been established under joint-powers legislation by twenty-three municipalities the previous year, after the failure of the 1965 bill. The entity's impotence intensified calls for a statutory commission.

113 Citizens League, *The Transit Problem in the Twin Cities Area.*

114 *Regional Fixed Guideway Study.*

115 Citizens League, *Statement by the Citizens League.*

116 Harrigan and Johnson, *Governing the Twin Cities Region*, 34–5; US Congress, *Assessment of Community Planning for Mass Transit.*

117 PRT had been championed by aerospace engineering firms for a decade with federal Urban Mass Transportation Administration funding. It was designed to avoid the negative aspects of conventional mass transit – long wait times, time-consuming mode changes between origin and destination, and sharing vehicles with strangers – while decongesting roads. See Cole and Merritt, *Tomorrow's Transportation.* Locally, University of Minnesota engineering professor Edward Anderson lobbied strongly for PRT during the 1960s and 1970s, organized major conferences at the university in 1971 and 1973, and produced a complete design for a system for the Twin Cities in 1974. See Anderson, *Progress, Problems, and Potential.* PRT turned out to be a technocratic illusion, and interest faded by the end of the 1970s. Only one system was constructed, a Boeing-built demonstration project in Morgantown, West Virginia between 1970 and 1975. The long-term effect of the Twin Cities' dalliance with PRT was to halt development of rapid transit. Until the first decade of the twenty-first century, when a light rail line from downtown Minneapolis to the international airport and the Mall of America opened, the Twin Cities had the largest all-bus system in the United States.

118 T. Berg, *Minnesota's Miracle*, 146–51.

119 See *Regional Park System.*

120 *Twin Cities Area Metropolitan Development Guide.*

121 Interviews with Robert Einsweiler and Ed Maranda. For Einsweiler's ideas, see Einsweiler, "Metropolitan Planning and Implementation" and Einsweiler, "Planning for the Minnesota Twins."

122 Einsweiler, "Metropolitan Planning and Implementation," 117.

123 Typescript of interview with Hetland by Suburban Newspapers editors, as recorded in the *Minnetonka Herald*, 25 Jan. 1968, MnHS, Citizen League Files, loc. 149.1.6.7(B), box 24, file Citizens League: Metropolitan Development Guide Committee files 1967–68.

124 Reichert, *Growth Management in the Twin Cities Area*, 8, 11.

125 Vance, *Inside the Minnesota Experiment*, 20–1; Baldinger *Planning and Governing the Metropolis*, 60–3; Rhees, *Minnesota's Planning and Zoning Enabling Laws*.

126 Minnesota, *Protecting the Environment through Regulation of Land Use*.

127 Knudson, *Regional Politics in the Twin Cities*, 5–6.

128 The Minnesota Housing Institute (MHI) was established by residential tract housing and apartment builders opposed to the Land Planning Act. Its first president was west-side developer-builder Larry Laukka, who played a key role in lobbying against the bill. The MHI was a precursor to the later merger of the separate Minneapolis and St. Paul associations of residential builders. Laukka correspondence.

129 Reichert, *Growth Management in the Twin Cities Area*, 16–19.

130 Ibid., 36.

131 The 1975 urbanized area and staged expansions to the MUSA in 1980 and 1990 are mapped in Reichert, *Growth Management in the Twin Cities Area*, 39.

132 Knudson, *Regional Politics in the Twin Cities*, 32–4.

133 Heying describes this process as the "delocalization of capital." See Heying, "Civic Elites and Corporate Delocalization." On the Twin Cities, see Galaskiewicz, "An Urban Grants Economy Revisited"; Harrigan, "Minneapolis–St. Paul," 220–1.

134 Interview with Solem (4 May 2010).

135 The DFL was not helped by Governor Anderson's decision to appoint himself to the federal Senate seat vacated by Walter Mondale after he became vice-president in 1976. The electorate saw this as self-serving, and Republicans took both Senate seats in the 1978 federal election. (Both Senate seats were up simultaneously due to the death of senator and former vice-president Hubert Humphrey.) Lieutenant Governor Rudy Perpich assumed the governorship on Anderson's departure for Washington, only to be defeated by Quie in 1978. See Berg *Minnesota's Miracle*, 158–62, chap. 9.

136 Crosby and Bryson, "The Twin Cities Metropolitan Council," 99; Barton and Starr, "The Regional-Local Planning Process."

137 The Land Planning Act's mandating of municipal planning had the desired effect. A 1978 survey to which 140 of 189 municipalities responded found that while 29 had adopted a zoning ordinance prior to 1968, 109 had done so since that time, and 88 per cent reported regulating subdivision. Virtually all municipalities reported having hired, or an intention to hire, professional planning staff or

consultants. Although aggregate statistics do not indicate the quality or sophistication of local planning activities, they show a dramatic increase since the mandate came into effect. See *Survey of Local Planning in the Twin Cities Metropolitan Area*; *Local Planning in the Twin Cities Metropolitan Area*; Bryson and Boal, "Strategic Management in a Metropolitan Area."

138 Daniel, "Land Use Planning," 1959; Pinel, "Regional Planning as Mediation," 402–9; Poradek, "Putting the Use Back in Metropolitan Land-Use Planning," 1357.

139 Orfield, *Metropolitics*, 105.

140 Israel, "Images of an Organization," 70.

141 Kaszuba, "Met Council Ends Review of Subdivision Proposals."

142 Ohm also faults the vague wording of the original law, which is unclear on which planning instruments fall under the consistency requirement, and also grandfathers existing zoning bylaws. See Ohm, "Growth Management in Minnesota"; "Reviving Comprehensive Planning in the Twin Cities Metropolitan Area."

143 Citizens League, *The Metropolitan Council*, 18; Haigh, "The Metropolitan Council," 172.

144 Harrigan, "Minneapolis–St. Paul," 217–19; J. Martin, "In Fits and Starts," 233; Orfield, "Politics and Regionalism," 244–5.

145 Harrigan, "Minneapolis–St. Paul," 218.

146 Orfield, "Politics and Regionalism," 246.

147 *Coordination of Light Rail Transit Planning for the Twin Cities Area*

148 Harrigan, "Minneapolis–St. Paul," 222; Israel, "Images of an Organization," 27–8.

149 Klauda, "Latimer Talks of Metro Council's 'Receding Leadership.'" On Perpich's negative influence, see also Kaszuba and Blake, "A Vision Clouded."

150 Blake, "Carlson Puts 2-Year Limit on 'Laid Back' Met Council."

151 See Orfield, *Metropolitics*, chap. 7.

152 On the implementation of "fair share" housing policy in the Twin Cities, see Goetz, "Fair Share or Status Quo"; Goetz, Chapple, and Lukermann, "The Minnesota Land Use Planning Act." The council's influence receded as federal housing funding diminished in the 1980s and 1990s.

153 Israel, "Images of an Organization," 114, 20–1.

154 Ibid., 115.

155 "The Met Council Takes Housing Dive."

156 Harrigan, "Minneapolis–St. Paul," 224.

157 D. Smith, "Bill to Make Met Council Elected Is Narrowly Defeated in House"; D. Smith, "House Votes to Group Metropolitan Agencies"; D. Smith, "Legislators Push to Wrap up Key Bills."
158 Interview with James Solem (16 June 2009).
159 Ohm, "Reviving Comprehensive Planning in the Twin Cities Metropolitan Area."
160 Haigh, "The Metropolitan Council," 172–4.
161 Goetz, "Fair Share or Status Quo"; Goetz, Chapple, and Lukermann, "The Minnesota Land Use Planning Act."
162 S. Berg, "Peter Bell Looks Back on the Metro Landscape."
163 Interview with Ohrn.
164 Orfield and Luce, Region, 61, 228.
165 Orfield, Metropolitics, 125.
166 Dornfeld, "Minnesota's Planning Laws Lag Behind Leaders."
167 Mondale and Fulton, Managing Metropolitan Growth.
168 S. Berg, "Peter Bell Looks Back on the Metro Landscape."
169 Ballou, "A Future for the Met Council," 143. The 2012 bill was endorsed by the Association of Metropolitan Municipalities. See Findings and Recommendations.
170 J. Johnson, "Jeff Johnson for Governor."
171 See Roper, "Senate OKs Bill to Overhaul the Met Council."
172 "Metro Transit Finds Firmer Financial Footing."
173 Carver and Scott counties never joined the arrangement. See Haigh, "The Metropolitan Council," 188; Ferraro, "Tentative Deal Pays Off Dakota County."
174 Roper, "Budget Bill Could Invite More Challenges of Met Council's Regional Plans"; Roper, "Insert in Bonding Bill Erodes Met Council Planning Power."

CHAPTER SIX

1 Berelowitz, Dream City, 1.
2 See Birkhead, A Look to the North; Hamilton, Measuring the Effectiveness of Regional Governing Systems, chap. 6; Tomalty and Mallach, America's Urban Future, 117–18; Wolman, "Looking at Regional Governance Institutions in Other Countries."
3 Z. Taylor and Burchfield, Growing Cities; Filion et al., "Intensification and Sprawl."
4 Grant, "Experiential Planning," 362.
5 Crawford, Canadian Municipal Government, 73–6.

6 Bish and Clemens, *Local Government in British Columbia*, 21–2.

7 Bottomley, "Ideology, Planning and the Landscape," 106–7.

8 Cain, "Water and Sanitation in Vancouver"; Keeling, "Sink or Swim."

9 For deliberations between 1911 and 1913, see City of Vancouver Archives (hereafter CVA), Town Planning Commission Fonds, Add. MSS. 1257 loc. 63-A-1, Burrard Peninsula Joint Sewerage Board (1911–23), vol. 1, Minute Book, Joint Sewerage Committee, City of Vancouver.

10 Letter from E.A. Cleveland, Chief Commissioner, Greater Vancouver Water District to J. Clark Keith, Chief Engineer, Essex Border Utilities Commission, Windsor, Ontario, 25 March 1931, CVA, Add MSS 1257 loc. 64-C-5.

11 CVA, Town Planning Commission Fonds, Add. MSS. 1257 loc. 64-C-1, Greater Vancouver Water District, file 2, Administration – General, 1927–35; and loc. 64-C-5, Greater Vancouver Water District – General, letter from Delta, 28 Nov. 1927, and reply, 1 Dec. 1927, and letter to Major A.C. Taylor, 6 Dec. 1935.

12 See Dilworth, *The Urban Origins of Suburban Autonomy*; Teaford, *City and Suburb*, chaps. 2, 5.

13 Ward, "The International Diffusion of Planning," 60–3; Bartholomew, *A Plan for the City of Vancouver*.

14 Letter to area municipalities from H.V. Jackson, 29 Nov. 1937, CVA, Town Planning Commission Fonds, s. 397 loc. 61-D-6, file 9, Regional Planning 1937–52. The cities of Vancouver, North Vancouver, New Westminster, Port Coquitlam, Port Moody, and West Vancouver, and the districts of Burnaby, Coquitlam, Delta, Richmond, and Surrey participated. On the association's dissolution see Report of H.V. Jackson, chairman, Lower Mainland Regional Planning Association, 27 June 1939, in CVA, Town Planning Commission Fonds, s. 397 loc. 61-D-6, file 9, Regional Planning 1937–52.

15 Robin, *Pillars of Profit*, chap. 1.

16 Ormsby, "T. Dufferin Pattullo and the Little New Deal"; Fisher, "The Decline of Reform."

17 The legislation was passed at the behest of the B.C. Bond Dealers' Association in the 1932 session. See Bradbury, "The Road to Receivership," 157–8. A commissioner responsible to the provincial inspector of municipalities, the senior public servant in the Ministry of the Attorney General (later converted to being the deputy minister of municipal affairs on the department's creation), was deemed preferable to a court-appointed receiver. An elected council was not restored to

Burnaby until 1942 and to the City and District of North Vancouver until 1944 and 1951, respectively. The interior cities of Merritt and Prince Rupert also defaulted and were placed under commissioner control.

18 Robin, *Pillars of Profit*, 69–70.

19 In some Canadian provinces, village and township heads of council are called reeves. On Paton's membership on the Water Board, see CVA, Greater Vancouver Water District fonds, Add MSS. 1257 loc. 64-C-1, file 2, Administration – General, 1927–35.

20 Sherman, *Bennett*, 45–7.

21 Perry, *Reports of the Post-War Rehabilitation Council*, 143.

22 "Proposed Provincial Planning Act with Supporting Brief," prepared by the Vancouver Town Planning Commission, presented to the Executive Council, Provincial Government, 23 Nov. 1943, CVA, Town Planning Commission Fonds, s. 588 RD 1363; see also Minutes of the TPC – General (1936–42), minutes for 11 June and 2 July 1942, ibid., s. 397 loc. 77-A-1.

23 Mitchell, *W.A.C. Bennett and the Rise of British Columbia*, 74–5.

24 British Columbia, *Preliminary Report*.

25 Mitchell, *W.A.C. Bennett and the Rise of British Columbia*, 86–94; Robin, *Pillars of Profit*, 66–7.

26 Mitchell, *W.A.C. Bennett and the Rise of British Columbia*, 85.

27 Carver, *Compassionate Landscape*, 88–90, 104–5.

28 Correspondence in CVA, TPC Fonds, loc. 61-D-6, file 9.

29 Elkins, "Politics Makes Strange Bedfellows."

30 "Progress Report on the Work of the Lower Mainland Regional Planning Board," 14 April 1950, CVA, box 61-D-6, file 9.

31 Oberlander and Newbrun, *Houser*, esp. chap. 7. Oberlander's deep assimilation of New Deal regionalism is apparent in his master's thesis on the Ottawa Valley as a natural region. See Oberlander, "Ottawa and the Ottawa Valley."

32 Carver, *Compassionate Landscape*, 104, 16–20. See also Donaldson, "Alumni Interviews: Peter Oberlander." See also Chadwick interview with Oberlander.

33 Memorandum, "Regional Planning in British Columbia," n.d. (labelled "about 1953"), University of British Columbia Archives (hereafter UBCA), GVRD Fonds, box 12, file 2, History, LMRPB.

34 Chadwick interview with Wilson. Wilson's professional biography can be found in CVA, CPAC Fonds, Add. MSS. 683, loc. 580-B-5, file 5-8, Biographies. The TVA's planning-assistance program is described in

Gray and Johnson, *The TVA Regional Planning and Development Program*, chap. 2, postscript.

35 J. Wilson, "A Land Use Plan for Chapel Hill."

36 UBCA, Thomas McDonald Fonds, box 3, LMRPB, various LMRPB staff memoranda from 1951.

37 "Review of Objectives," 5 July 1951, UBCA, GVRD Planning Dept. Fonds, box 12, file 2.

38 *The Lower Mainland Looks Ahead.*

39 See Whyte, "Urban Sprawl."

40 *Economic Aspects of Urban Sprawl*; Real Estate Research Corporation, *Costs of Sprawl.*

41 *Land for Living*, 10.

42 *Chance and Challenge*, 14.

43 *Land for Farming.*

44 Chadwick interview with O'Gorman. Planner and senior Ministry of Municipal Affairs staff member Don South also emphasizes the reinforcing linkages between the UBC planning school, the LMRPB, and the PIBC as it matured. See South, "The Choices We Had in the Fifties."

45 Remarks by Wilson, Joint conference of CPAC and the Pacific Northwest Chapter of the AIP, Oct. 1953, CVA. Add. MSS 683, CPAC, loc. 580-B-3, file 10, Conferences – CPAC Division conference programs (1953–56).

46 See *Reference Book – Lower Mainland Regional Planning Board* (1969), Section F, "Members of the Board, 1949–69," Simon Fraser University Archives (hereafter SFUA), James Wood Wilson Fonds, loc. F-132-1-0-2.

47 James Wood Wilson, "The Lower Mainland's Regional Plan: A Retrospective Introduction" (1988), SFUA, James Wood Wilson Fonds, loc. F-132-1-0-1.

48 Calculated from annual lists in *Reference Book – Lower Mainland Regional Planning Board* (1969).

49 "LMRPB Reaches First Decade."

50 *Chance and Challenge.*

51 Commissioner K.E. Patrick's Report to the Greater Vancouver Water District Administration Board, 10 April 1964, UBCA, GVRD Fonds, box 1, file 13, Council Reactions.

52 For a summary of the consultations on *Chance and Challenge*, see *The People and the Plan*. See also consultation records in CVA, Add. MSS. 683, CPAC-BC, loc. 580-B-6 box 3, files 2–4, Lower Mainland Regional Planning Board – minutes (1962–69); UBCA, GVRD Fonds,

box 1, file 13, Council Reactions, and box 1, file 15, Consultation with
Municipal Councils, Dec. 1965–May 1966. Major business and pro-
fessional groups that publicly supported *Chance and Challenge* and
the idea of a regional plan were the Westminster County Real Estate
Board, the Vancouver District Labour Council, the Vancouver Board of
Trade, the BC Telephone Company, the BC Institute of Agrologists, the
Associated Chambers of Commerce, the Architectural Institute of BC,
and CPAC-BC.

53 Royal British Columbia Archives (hereafter RBCA), GR-0239, Minister
of Municipal Affairs Records, 1964–67, box 5, file 2, Regional
Planning Area – Lower Mainland 1964, and box 19, file 4, Regional
Planning – Lower Mainland. See also "'Last Word' Should Be with
Council"; "Councillors Fear Planning Board Might Usurp Municipal
Authority."

54 "District Still Holds Region Plan Doubts."

55 "Economic Survey of Regional Plan."

56 UBCA, GVRD Fonds, box 1, file 13, Council Reactions.

57 *Official Regional Plan of the Lower Mainland Planning Area.*

58 "Councillors Weigh Bd ... Surrey Plans."

59 See "Concepts in Planning"; "Regional Plan Effect Will Be Studied."

60 RBCA, GR-0239, Minister of Municipal Affairs Records, 1964–67, box
19, file 4, Regional Planning – Lower Mainland.

61 Ibid., box 5, file 2, Regional Planning Area – Lower Mainland 1964.

62 Parker complained to Campbell that the Highways and Lands, Forests,
and Water Resources Ministries refused to cooperate with the LMRPB,
undermining the coordination of activities. See ibid., box 17, file 2,
LMRPB 1966, letter dated 24 March 1966.

63 Petter, "Sausage Making in British Columbia's NDP Government,"
6fn17. See also ""LMRPB Plan Gets District Heave"; "Split Vote in
Kent Council Defeats Final Regional Plan."

64 RBCA, GR-0239, Minister of Municipal Affairs Records, 1964–67, box
17, file 2, LMRPB 1966.

65 The ALC estimates that between 4,000 and 6,000 hectares were lost
annually to non-agricultural uses in this period. See *Ten Years of
Agricultural Land Preservation.* However, a report of the Lower
Mainland Review Panel suggests a smaller impact: "In the seven years
between 1966 and 1973, when the Agricultural Land Reserve was
introduced, 1755 hectares were redesignated from Rural 2 and Rural 3
[zoning] to other designations (primarily Urban). This amounts to only
1.4 percent of the Lower Mainland's agricultural land." See *The Way*

Ahead, 14. In the three valley regional districts between 1970 and 1977 the ORP was amended 138 times, of which 85 were considered "major." Between 1966 and 1977 in the GVRD 84 amendments were proposed, 35 of them in rapidly urbanizing Surrey. For analyses of amendments, see Furuseth, "Planning for Agricultural Lands," 301; *Amendments, August 29, 1966–March 31, 1969*; M. Jones and Connelly, *Review of the Official Regional Plan,* appendix IIB.

66 The internal political battles over the implementation of the ALR, and the more general travails of the chaotic and short-lived Barrett government, are chronicled in Garrish, "Unscrambling the Omelette"; Kavic and Nixon, *The 1200 Days*; Meggs and Mickleburgh, *The Art of the Impossible,* chap. 3; Petter, "Sausage Making in British Columbia's NDP Government"; Resnick, "Social Democracy in Power"; Tennant, "The NDP Government of British Columbia."

67 *The Way Ahead,* 13.

68 The legislature had been reapportioned only twice in the three decades prior to 1966 despite a more than doubling of the provincial population. Urban areas remained profoundly underrepresented. Robin summarizes: "There were as many voters registered in the three largest provincial ridings – Point Grey, Vancouver-East and Delta – as there were in the twenty-six non-urban ridings ... Thirty per cent of the voters in Vancouver received only nine members or 17.3% of the legislative representation." See Robin, *Pillars of Profit,* 259. Social Credit's fortunes in the Lower Mainland steadily increased. They won 6 of 15 (40%) seats in the region in 1952, 10 of 15 (67%) in 1953, and 14 of 18 (78%) in 1956. The Lower Mainland's representation in the Socred caucus also increased over the three elections, from 32 to 42 per cent.

69 Keeling, "The Effluent Society," 48–9.

70 Rawn, Hyde, and Oliver, *Sewerage and Drainage Survey.*

71 Churchill, *Local Government and Administration,* 2, 38–9.

72 Keeling, "Sink or Swim," 88–90.

73 Keeling, "The Effluent Society," 59–64.

74 Keeling, "Sink or Swim," 92.

75 *The Lower Mainland Looks Ahead.*

76 *Greater Vancouver Metropolitan Community,* 31.

77 "Some Notes on the Organization for Planning in the Greater Vancouver Metropolitan Area as Presented Orally to the Minister of Municipal Affairs on April 18th, 1956," UBCA, GVRD Planning Department Fonds, box 9, file 6, Metropolitan Planning Organizations.

78 See minutes of 18 March and 10 June 1954, CVA, Vancouver Board of Trade Fonds, loc. 527-E-5, Civic Bureau Minutes 1940–55.

79 Churchill, *Local Government and Administration*, 2, 47.

80 See "Minister to Call Parley on Metro." The eleven municipalities were Burnaby, Coquitlam, Fraser Mills, New Westminster, Port Coquitlam, Port Moody, Richmond, Vancouver, the City and District of North Vancouver, and West Vancouver. Surrey and Delta were later invited but declined.

81 Citation from an article in the *Vancouver Province*, 15 May 1956, in paper by J.T. Pennington, CVA, [Halford] Wilson Family Fonds, Add. MSS. 362, loc. 551-D-2, file 3, Metropolitan Government Proposals.

82 Untitled address by Black, 10 Jan. 1958, RBCA, MS-1926, Hugo Ray Fonds, box 1, file 8, Correspondence & Papers 1957.

83 Ray had been interested in the issue for some time. At CPAC's fifth annual conference in 1953, he, as reeve of West Vancouver, had moved that CPAC sponsor the creation of a committee to study how to make metropolitan planning more effective. The motion passed unanimously. See CVA, CPAC (BC Division) Fonds, Add. MSS. 683, loc. 580-B-3, file 9, Conferences – CPAC Division conference programs.

84 See "Resume of Field Investigation," Sept. 1959, RBCA, GR-0575, Minister of Municipal Affairs Records, Metro Joint Commission, box 7, file 7.

85 Ray, *Final Report*. The terms of reference restricted the study to water, sewer, public health and air pollution, public hospitals, land-use planning, and parks.

86 "Address – Hugo Ray," n.d., p. 7, RBCA, MS-1926, Hugo Ray Fonds, box 1, file 8, Correspondence and Papers 1957.

87 "Single Metro Board Oked by Probers." On parks, see also "Municipal Officials Favor Board for Development of Recreational Areas."

88 See RBCA, GR-0238 Minister of Municipal Affairs Records, 1953–64, box 2, file 5, LM Metrop. Area – Briefs. See also "Richmond Says Metro Won't Solve Problems." Robert McMath was the only member of Richmond's seven-member council to vote in favour of the report's recommendations.

89 "Burnaby Board Opposed to Metro."

90 "Five-Year Trial Urged for Metro"; "Ray Concedes Metro Would Lose in Vote."

91 "Mayors, Reeves Want Metro Vote"; "Step-by-Step Metro Plan Approved."

92 "Seven New Faces on Metro Board."

93 See memorandum Re: Metropolitan Vancouver, 1 March 1962, RBCA, GR-0238 Minister of Municipal Affairs Records, 1953–64, box 2, file 2.

94 "Step-by-Step Metro Plan Approved."

95 In a memo from Deputy Minister Brown to Minister Black dated 29 July 1962, Brown suggests that the minister could combine the existing water, sewer, public health, and regional boards without municipal approval or plebiscite if their functions remained unmodified and if the principle of voluntary participation remained intact. Black evidently chose not to pursue the scheme, although it may have been the germ of the regional district structures imposed by his successor, Dan Campbell. RBCA, GR-0238, Minister of Municipal Affairs Records, 1953–64, box 2, file 2.

96 Meligrana, "Developing a Planning Strategy," 132.

97 Letters patent are roughly equivalent to executive orders in the United States.

98 Confidential memorandum, n.d., "Legislation – Joint Services Board," RBCA, GR-0239, box 10, file 3, Legislation 1965.

99 Quoted in Rashleigh, "A Progress Report on B.C.'s Regional Districts."

100 Tennant and Zirnhelt, "Emergence of Metropolitan Government," 12–13.

101 Ibid., 16.

102 South, "The Rise? And Fall? Of Regional Planning in B.C."

103 *Report No. 1, February 20, 1969.*

104 Tennant and Zirnhelt, "Emergence of Metropolitan Government," 28.

105 Ibid., 8–11. This interpretation is supported by participants in the process. See Chadwick interview with Farry.

106 Minutes, 20 Dec. 1967, CVA, CPAC (BC Division) Fonds, Add. MSS. 683, loc. 580–B-6, box 3, Lower Mainland Regional Planning Board – minutes.

107 UBCA, GVRD Fonds, box 34, file 56, Review Panel.

108 For this perspective, see South, "The Rise? And Fall? Of Regional Planning in B.C."; Harcourt, Cameron, and Rossiter, *City Making in Paradise*, 78–9. On the LMRPB's opposition to Robert's Bank, see *Our Southwestern Shores.*

109 Young, "Three Accused of Hatchet Job."

110 "Planning's Death Sentence "; "Chambers Deplore Planning Dispersal"; "Councillor Hits Assassination"; "Campbell Plan Okayed"; "City Defends Planners."

111 "Campbell Denies 'Hatchet Job' Tag."

112 Ramsay, "Restrain Planners, Minister Urges."

113 Gutstein, *Vancouver, Ltd.*

114 On the transformation of Vancouver-region planning in this period, see Gerecke, "Toward a New Model of Urban Planning"; Harcourt, Cameron, and Rossiter, *City Making in Paradise*, chap. 4; Lash, *Planning in a Human Way*; Rashleigh, *Documentary Review*. Author interviews with Cameron, Rashleigh, and Spaxman, and Chadwick interview with Farry provide additional context.

115 Meadows et al., *The Limits to Growth.*

116 Roy, "Direct Management from Abroad"; Meligrana, "Toward Regional Transportation Governance."

117 *The Way Ahead*, 13–14.

118 Ibid., 5.

119 Maitland, "Powerful Land-Use Plan in Wings"; L. Smith, "New Development Strategy Will Give Surrey Problems"; "Delta Attacks Updated GVRD Regional Plan"; "Regional Plan Gets Opposition."

120 "Clayton Residents Oppose Industry"; "Surrey Residents Oppose GVRD Plan."

121 *Plan for the Lower Mainland.*

122 Maitland, "Powerful Land-Use Plan in Wings."

123 Harcourt, Cameron, and Rossiter, *City Making in Paradise*, 70–2.

124 Garr, *Tough Guy*, 1, see also chap. 7. See also Magnusson and Carroll, *The New Reality*; Resnick, "Neo-Conservatism on the Periphery."

125 Harcourt, Cameron, and Rossiter, *City Making in Paradise*, 70–3.

126 Manning and Eddy, *The Agricultural Land Reserves of British Columbia*, table 6.3.

127 Wilson and Pierce, "The Agricultural Land Commission of British Columbia," 288.

128 Garrish, "Unscrambling the Omelette," 38.

129 On post-adoption political support and land use change, see Cocking, "A Comparison of the NDP and Social Credit Agricultural and Land Commission Policy"; Furuseth, "Planning for Agricultural Lands in British Columbia"; B. Smith, "A Work in Progress."

130 On this period, see Harcourt, Cameron, and Rossiter, *City Making in Paradise*, chaps. 6–7; *Establishing a Regional Strategic Plan.*

131 See Chadwick interview with Farry and author interview with Campbell.

132 "Environment a Concern, Survey Shows."

133 *Creating Our Future.*

134 Harcourt, Cameron, and Rossiter, *City Making in Paradise,* 120–1; *Establishing a Regional Strategic Plan.*

135 *Back to the Future.* Also author interview with Enser.

136 Tomalty, *Compact Metropolis,* 54–6.

137 H. Munro, "GVRD, Port Moody at Odds over Population Growth."

138 See Strachan, "Coquitlam Transit Link Defended"; "Regional Plan a Good Beginning Despite Its Flaws"; "Richmond Considers Separation from GVRD"; Bellett, "Reprisal by Richmond Suspected in Bose Losing Post."

139 Pynn, "Richmond, GVRD Reach Compromise."

140 H. Munro, "Councils Resist GVRD Population Targets."

141 Chadwick interview with Marzari.

142 Harcourt, Cameron, and Rossiter, *City Making in Paradise,* 144–8. See also Bocking, "Richmond, GVRD Take Step to Resolving Growth Issue"; "Floodplain Follies."

143 *1999 Annual Report: Livable Region Strategic Plan.*

144 *Choices for Our Future.*

145 *Metro Vancouver 2040.*

146 Bohn, "Proposed Planning Law Welcomes."

147 Sinoski, "Cost of Metro Services Could Rise 44 Per Cent."

148 Puil, "Regional District Must Renegotiate Skytrain Costs"; Simpson, "Skytrain Uncertainty Angers Coquitlam."

149 Harcourt, Cameron, and Rossiter, *City Making in Paradise,* chap. 8.

150 Siemiatycki, "Mega-Projects in the Making."

151 *Strong Economy, Secure Tomorrow,* 17–18.

152 Bula, "Cash-Strapped Translink Can't Keep Up with Growth."

153 See, for example, Wolman, "Looking at Regional Governance Institutions in Other Countries."

CHAPTER SEVEN

1 Abbott, "The Capital of Good Planning."

2 Clucas and Henkels, "A State Divided."

3 McClintock, "Seth Lewelling, William S. U'ren and the Birth of the Oregon Progressive Movement."

4 Burton, *Democrats of Oregon,* 10–16.

5 Montague, "Law of Municipal Home Rule in Oregon."

6 Voorsanger, "Problems of Annexation," chap. 4.

7 Lucia, *The Conscience of a City,* 18, 33.

8 Montague, "Government in the Portland Metropolitan Area." One of the commission's members was C.C. Ludwig, who would go on to play a crucial role in the development of metropolitan governance in the Twin Cities.

9 See Abbott, *Portland*.

10 Mullins, "'I'll Wreck the Town If It Will Give Employment,'" 109, 17.

11 United States, *Realty Tax Delinquency*, 1: 6–7; United States, *Financial Statistics of State and Local Governments*, 63.

12 United States, *Realty Tax Delinquency*, 2: 21.

13 Abbott, *Portland*, 111; Barker, "Portland's Works Progress Administration," 430–3.

14 Murrell, *Iron Pants*; Burton, *Democrats of Oregon*, 77–87.

15 Murrell, *Iron Pants*, 158–9.

16 Van Beuren Stanbery, "The Planning Program for Oregon: First Preliminary Report of the State Planning Consultant to National Resources Board," 25 July 1934, Oregon State Archives (hereafter OSA), loc. 4/10/4/4, National Resources Committee Records, folder 7/7, Correspondence 1934–37; Philip A. Parsons, "County and Community Planning in Oregon," National Planning Conference, Detroit, MI, 1–3 June 1937, Multnomah County Library (hereafter MCL), O-353.901 P26.

17 Van Beuren Stanbery, "The Field of State Planning," paper presented to the Third Pacific Northwest Regional Planning Conference, Spokane, WA, 13 Feb. 1936, MCL, O-353.901 S78f.

18 "Report of Committee on Community, City, and County Planning," 19 Nov. 1934, OSA, loc. 4/10/4/4, Oregon State Planning Council Records, folder 8/1, Committee Reports.

19 Dewing, *Regions in Transition*, 109; *Oregon Looks Ahead*, 63–4.

20 Bessey, *Pacific Northwest Regional Planning*, 48.

21 Oregon, *Oregon Blue Book*, 217–18; Robbins, *Landscapes of Conflict*, 27–30.

22 Abbott, *Portland*, chap. 6.

23 *Interim Report of the Portland Metropolitan Study Commission*, 3.

24 Robbins, *Landscapes of Conflict*, 284–5.

25 Richard L. Barron, "Staff Report Concerning Planning within the Tri-County Area," n.d. (marked received 12 June 1967), City of Portland Archives (hereafter CPA), loc. 15-06-43/1, box 1, file 6, PMSC – Collected Reports and Studies, 1962–1970". See also Sullivan, "The Quiet Revolution Goes West," 361.

26 Adler, *Oregon Plans*, 25. In the Portland area, Washington County formed a planning commission in 1950, Multnomah in 1953, and Clackamas in 1955.

27 *Planning by Local Government in Oregon.*
28 Interview with Lloyd Anderson.
29 Sullivan and Eber, "The Long and Winding Road," 4–6; Adler, *Oregon Plans*, 25.
30 Rich interview.
31 Rich, "The Politics of Governmental Reorganization in the Portland Metropolitan Area," chap. 9. On the MPC's formation, see CPA, Administrative – Metropolitan Planning Subject File – Metropolitan Planning Project – 1955, box 5, folder 28.
32 Richard L. Barron, "Staff Report Concerning Planning within the Tri-County Area," n.d. (marked received 12 June 1967), p. 10, CPA, loc. 15-06-43/1, box 1, file 6, PMSC – Collected Reports and Studies, 1962–1970; MPC, *A Review of the Status of the Metropolitan Planning Commission*, prepared for the Executive Committee of CRAG, 15 Dec. 1966, CPA, loc. 09-09-19/3, box 50, file 13, Metropolitan Planning Commission Status Review – 1966.
33 *How Should Our Community Grow*; *Urban Area: Basic Data Maps*; *The Three Basic Services*; *Interim Report of the Portland Metropolitan Study Commission*, 18.
34 City Club, "Report on Planning for Transportation in the Portland Metropolitan Area," 278.
35 Burton, *Democrats of Oregon*, 3; McKay, *An Editor for Oregon*, 100.
36 Burton, *Democrats of Oregon*, chap. 7.
37 G. Baker, "Reapportionment by Initiative in Oregon," see esp. 519.
38 Squire, *The Evolution of American Legislatures.*
39 Teaford, *The Rise of the States*, 187–91.
40 Bessey, *Pacific Northwest Regional Planning*, 122.
41 Hatfield, *Not Quite So Simple*, 42–9.
42 Abbott, *Portland*, chaps. 8–10; Thompson, "Taming the Neighborhood Revolution."
43 Walth, *Fire at Eden's Gate*, 244.
44 Robbins, *Landscapes of Promise*, 306; Robbins, *Landscapes of Conflict*, 248–65; Walth, *Fire at Eden's Gate*, 134–41; Carter, "Pioneering Water Pollution Control in Oregon," 260–1.
45 Robbins, *Landscapes of Conflict*, 287.
46 Tom McCall and Oregon's Environmental Legacy, *Pollution in Paradise.*
47 Robbins, *Landscapes of Conflict*, 266.
48 At that time, the state treasurer and attorney general were elected in presidential election years, while the governor was elected at midterm. This enabled Straub to challenge McCall for the governorship in 1966

and 1970 while retaining his position as treasurer. McCall could not run in 1974 due to term limits. On the two men's cooperation and competition, and shared interest in the natural environment, see Walth, *Fire at Eden's Gate*, chap. 8.

49 Abbott and Howe, "The Politics of Land Use Law in Oregon," 11.

50 On the work of the Interim Committee and the drafting of SB 10, see Sullivan and Eber, "The Long and Winding Road," 8–9; Adler, *Oregon Plans*, chap. 1.

51 Cogan interview. As McCall's state planning coordinator in McCall's office, Cogan designed the fourteen-district system to insert the state's interest into the functioning of the federally mandated councils of government in urban areas while creating a policy coordination capacity in rural areas. The districts, eleven of which corresponded to existing federally mandated councils of government, were established by executive order in 1970 and so had no statutory base. Counties resisted regionalization, which was abandoned by the time McCall left office in 1974.

52 Adler, *Oregon Plans*, 81.

53 See ibid., chap. 2.

54 Cogan interview.

55 Halprin, *The Willamette Valley*.

56 The ensuing discussion is synthesized from several sources. Senate Bill 100's complex history and its influences are exhaustively chronicled in Zachary, "Politics of Land Use." The recollections of Macpherson and others are collected in Abbott and Howe, "The Politics of Land Use Law in Oregon." Adler summarizes the work of the Macpherson committee and the legislative process in *Oregon Plans*, chaps. 2–3. External influences are discussed in Sullivan, "The Quiet Revolution Goes West," 366–7; Walker and Hurley, *Planning Paradise*, 24–6, chap. 3.

57 Zachary, "Politics of Land Use," 14–15.

58 Knaap and Nelson, *The Regulated Landscape*, 21.

59 Abbott and Howe, "The Politics of Land Use Law in Oregon," 20.

60 Sullivan, "The Quiet Revolution Goes West," 369.

61 Adler, *Oregon Plans*, 75.

62 See Oregon, *Problems of the Urban Fringe*; Oregon, *Findings and Recommendations*.

63 Oregon, *Problems of the Urban Fringe*, 35.

64 Tollenaar, *Organization for Water Distribution in the Portland Area*, 53.

65 Oregon, *Findings and Recommendations*, 10.

66 Tollenaar, *Organization for Water Distribution in the Portland Area*, 19.

67 Rich, "The Politics of Governmental Reorganization," chap. 6.

68 Oregon, *Findings and Recommendations*, 12; *Urban Sprawl*.

69 Oregon, *Findings and Recommendations*, 1.

70 The latter idea was fleshed out in a draft metropolitan charter prepared by BMRS assistant director Ken Tollenaar, who may have been influenced by emergent ideas in metropolitan government and planning reform, and the contemporaneous Seattle–King County and Metro Toronto reforms. See "Metropolitan Government Act," n.d., OSA, Acc. No. 58–20, 1955–57 Interim Committee on Local Government, box 12.

71 Rich, "The Politics of Governmental Reorganization," 113–14. See also "Oregon Legislative Interim Committee Reviews Local Government Structure," n.d., OSA, Acc. No. 58-20, 1955–57 Interim Committee on Local Government, box 12.

72 By 1954, 15 per cent of the city's water revenue came from external sales, up one-third from a decade earlier. See Tollenaar, *Organization for Water Distribution in the Portland Area*, 16; Abbott, *Portland*, 254. In the absence of annexation, Portland's profits from external sales increased as unincorporated suburbs expanded.

73 Rich, "The Politics of Governmental Reorganization," 142.

74 On the Portland League's advocacy of metropolitan reform, see Stevens, "Feminizing the Urban West," chap. 2. Stevens suggests that "sprawl" and inefficient service delivery were especially visible and troubling to the educated middle-class women of the league by virtue of their lived experience as homemakers. The women's influence was certainly aided by the status of many of their husbands, some of whom were legislators, academics, and business leaders.

75 Quoted in ibid., 71.

76 *A Tale of Three Counties*, 5.

77 The bridge between the league, MAP, and business elites may have been the husband-and-wife team of Reed College professor Charles McKinley and his wife, Nellie. Charles was a nationally recognized urban reformer and former president of both the American Political Science Association and the Portland City Club, while Nellie had served on the Metropolitan Planning Committee of the Portland League of Women Voters. See Stevens, "Feminizing the Urban West," 72; Rich, "The Politics of Governmental Reorganization," 238–9. See also Rich interview, 24 Aug. 2009.

78 Oregon, *Metropolitan and Urban Area Problems*, 15; Rich, "The Politics of Governmental Reorganization," 238–9.

79 Oregon, *Metropolitan and Urban Area Problems*. The committee did not clarify the distinction between a "metropolitan government" and an "urban county." A background report treats the two separately, dismissing the creation of a "federation" as overly complex. See R. Kennedy, "Subject: Summary of Approaches to Metropolitan Government."

80 Rich, "The Politics of Governmental Reorganization."

81 Portland Metropolitan Study Commission, "Anticipating the Challenges of Tomorrow or Continuing the Governmental Burial of Marvin Metro?"

82 *Interim Report of the Portland Metropolitan Study Commission.*

83 *Discussion Leaders' Material*, 8–11; *Interim Report of the Portland Metropolitan Study Commission*, 9–10.

84 Rich interview, 24 Aug. 2009.

85 Rich, "The Politics of Governmental Reorganization," 253.

86 CRAG, Minutes of the First Meeting, October 13, 1967, PCA, loc. 15-06-39/3, box 1, file 9, CRAG Misc. 1966–67.

87 Cease, *A Report on State and Provincial Boundary Review Boards.*

88 Price, "The Portland Boundary Commission," chap. 2.

89 Ibid., 37.

90 Abbott, *Portland*, 254.

91 Rich interview, 24 Aug. 2009.

92 Seymour, "Board Lacks Public Trust"; Ruble, "Service District to Weigh Future."

93 Price, "The Portland Boundary Commission," 203.

94 Ibid., 137.

95 Ibid., chap. 8.

96 Ibid., 128–9.

97 "Panel to Evaluate Direction of CRAG."

98 Barron, *Columbia Region Association of Governments (CRAG)*, 6.

99 "Interim Regional Land Use Plan" (map). Rich recalls that Portland and Multnomah County planners who favoured a more aggressive approach used this term (interview). The yellow zone was designated for residential development at a density of between 0.5 and 20 housing units per acre (1.25 to 50 units per hectare) – a fairly high density at the upper end. However the map gave the impression of unchecked low-density development in the region's agricultural fringe.

100 Barron, *Columbia Region Association of Governments (CRAG)*, 12–13.

101 Clark interview. In an interview with the author (24 August 2009), Rich notes that, while CRAG had not yet produced policies against which to measure development proposals and therefore would have faced criticism of arbitrary behaviour had it opposed specific proposals, it had conducted careful studies of the land's carrying capacity and had begun developing what later became the urban growth boundary – a defined urban service area.

102 City Club, "Interim Report on Columbia Region Association of Governments (CRAG)."

103 See Huston, *The Columbia Region Association of Governments*, 25-31.

104 "Blueprint for Planning."

105 Clark interview. See also interviews with Rich, 24 Aug. 2009, and Anderson.

106 *Planning in the CRAG Region: An Appraisal; Planning in the CRAG Region: The Second Step; Columbia-Willamette Region Comprehensive Plan*; see also Huston, *The Columbia Region Association of Governments*, 29-30; CRAG *Goals and Objectives; Proposed CRAG Land Use Framework Element.*

107 Washington County, *Comprehensive Framework Plan; Papers and Discussion Outlines.*

108 Adler, *Oregon Plans*, 143-4.

109 "CRAG Approves Containment Policy of Interim Land-Use Planning"; "'Containment' Plan Endorsed."

110 Abbott and Abbott, *Historical Development of the Metropolitan Service District*, 17-18; Abbott, *Portland*, 252-3.

111 Mancuso, "Rifle-Toting Meeting-Goer Rides Elevator to Jail"; "CRAG Sets Hillsboro Hearing on Comprehensive Plan Ideas"; "CRAG's Urban-Limits Plan Faces Double-Barreled Attack"; "Suspicion, Hostility Handicap."

112 Mancuso, "Withdrawal from CRAG 'Political.'"

113 Interviews with Cease, 17 Aug. 2009, and Rich, 24 Aug. 2009.

114 Cease interview, 17 Aug. 2009.

115 Interviews with Cease, 17 Aug. 2009, and Cross.

116 Cross interview.

117 Cease interview, 17 Aug. 2009.

118 OSA, Hearings on HB 2070, House Committee on Intergovernmental Affairs, 14-16 Feb. 1977.

119 Ragsdale interview. According to Ragsdale, the House committee's goal was to define a contiguous area that included all urban and

urbanizing land, plus sufficient room for twenty years of urban development. This is identical to the UGB definition criteria in the LCDC's urbanization goal, yet Ragsdale does not recall using the CRAG's draft UGB as a guide to establishing Metro's boundaries. This may explain why Metro's borders and the UGB differ.

120 *Urban Growth Boundary*, 13–14.

121 *Ballot Measure 6.*

122 C. Johnson, *Standing at the Water's Edge*, 195.

123 Atiyeh's candidacy was strengthened by McCall's decision to enter the Republican primary. (He was limited to two consecutive terms but was eligible to run in subsequent non-consecutive elections.) While still popular, he was organizationally outgunned by Atiyeh, who won the primary. This weakened Straub, due to his strong identification with McCall and his legacy. See C. Johnson, *Standing at the Water's Edge*, 243–4.

124 Martin, *The Permanent Tax Revolt*; Johnson, *Standing at the Water's Edge*, 246–51.

125 Johnson, *Standing at the Water's Edge*, 219.

126 Ibid., 231; Seltzer, "Land Use Planning in Oregon," 66.

127 Johnson, *Standing at the Water's Edge*, 255–6; Zusman, "John Gray, the Quiet Lion, Dies at 93."

128 Walker and Hurley, *Planning Paradise*, 67–75.

129 Indeed, state planning Goal 10, which bans exclusionary zoning by requiring every municipality and unincorporated county area within the UGB to provide a mix of housing types suitable for all income levels, is credited with levelling the playing field for small local developers in the face of national single-family tract housing developers. See Abbott, "The Portland Region," 29.

130 Adler, *Oregon Plans*, chaps. 7 and 9.

131 Gustafson interview.

132 Abbott and Abbott, *Historical Development of the Metropolitan Service District*, 26–8.

133 Gustafson interview.

134 Cotugno and Seltzer, "Towards a Metropolitan Consciousness in the Portland Oregon Metropolitan Area," 293.

135 Cease interview, 17 Aug. 2009.

136 Abbott and Abbott, *Historical Development of the Metropolitan Service District*, 28–9.

137 *Metro's Portfolio of Natural Areas*, chaps. 2–3.

138 *Proposed CRAG Land Use Framework Element.*

139 Leonard, *Managing Oregon's Growth*, 97–104.
140 On the development of Metro's planning program, see Seltzer, "Regional Planning and Local Governance."
141 1000 Friends, *Making the Connections*, 1, 6.
142 The 1981 legislature amended the state land-use planning law to require all governments with planning authority, including Metro, to conduct periodic reviews of their UGBs in order to ensure they remained compliant with state policy and reflected changing conditions. Despite having been approved by LCDC in December 1979, the Portland UGB was not given full effect until 1986 due to a further legal appeal by 1000 Friends. The DLCD requested the review in August 1987 with a due date of February 1989. See *Urban Growth Boundary*, 21.
143 Seltzer, "Regional Planning and Local Governance," 284.
144 Oregon, *Final Report*, 15.
145 Metro planning director John Fregonese, the principal author of the Metro 2040 Growth Concept, would later go into business with Calthorpe. See Carlton, *Histories of Transit-Oriented Development*, esp. 12–17; Calthorpe, *The Next American Metropolis*.
146 *Regional Urban Growth Goals and Objectives*.
147 Abbott, "The Portland Region," 31.
148 Fregonese and Gabbe, "Engaging the Public and Communicating Successfully in Regional Planning," 235–6.
149 Seltzer, "Regional Planning and Local Governance," 284–5.
150 See Oregon, *Final Report*. The legislature referred a state constitutional amendment to the statewide electorate in 1990 permitting home rule for metropolitan service districts, of which Portland Metro was the only one. This was approved, and Metro successfully put its charter proposal on the ballot in 1992.
151 *1992 Metro Charter*, s. 5.
152 Cotugno and Seltzer, "Towards a Metropolitan Consciousness," 289.
153 Bassett, "Framing the Oregon Land Use Debate."
154 Walker and Hurley, *Planning Paradise*, 162–79.
155 Christensen, "A 50 Year Map"; Christensen, "Metro, Clackamas County and Cities Celebrate Adoption of Urban and Rural Reserves Plan"; "Urban and Rural Reserves."
156 "Regional Leaders on Transportation Bill."
157 Christensen, "A 50 Year Map"; Copeland, *Water Infrastructure Financing*.

158 Martin interview. In the mid-1980s, the unincorporated area of
    Multnomah County between Portland and Gresham applied to the
    Boundary Commission to incorporate as a city. The commission
    denied the application, instead encouraging Portland and Gresham to
    pursue annexation. By the end of the 1990s, the area was completely
    annexed, and the corresponding special-purpose bodies were rolled
    into municipal utilities.
159 Rich interview, 27 July 2010.
160 Seltzer, "Land Use Planning in Oregon," 70.
161 Hibbard et al., *Toward One Oregon*.

CHAPTER EIGHT

1 Brenner, *Implosions/Explosions*.
2 See Shaw, "Planetary Urbanisation."
3 Florida, *The New Urban Crisis*.
4 Wikstrom, *Councils of Governments*, chaps. 2 and 5.
5 See, for example, Dahl, "A Democratic Dilemma."
6 Katznelson, *Fear Itself*, 19, 478.
7 Ware, *Political Conflict in America*, 67–71.
8 See *Toward a More Resonsible Two-Party System*.
9 Peirce, *Citistates*; Pastor, Benner, and Matsuoka, *This Could Be the
   Start of Something Big*; Henton, Melville, and Walsh, *Grassroots
   Leaders for a New Economy*; Katz and Nowak, *The New Localism*.
10 Imbroscio, *Urban America Reconsidered*.
11 Barber, *If Mayors Ruled the World*, 166.
12 Ibid., 170.
13 Frug, *City Making*.
14 Broadbent, *Urban Nation*.
15 Magnusson, *Politics of Urbanism*.
16 Charles Marohn, for example, celebrates local leadership and creativity in his widely read Strong Towns blog. See Marohn, "Three
   Lessons from Muskegon." Bliss's analysis of small-town economic
   governance in Minnesota and Illinois is an important bookend to
   Savitch and Kantor's work on global cities. He finds substantial local
   agency despite external constraints but also acknowledges the importance of state-level frameworks in enabling local leadership. See Bliss,
   Economic Development and Governance in Small Town America.
17 C. Stone, *Regime Politics*.
18 Mann, *The Sources of Social Power*, 59–60.

19 Savitch and Kantor, *Cities in the International Marketplace.*
20 Whitman, "Commentary," 91.
21 Katz and Nowak, *The New Localism,* 12.
22 Gainsborough, *Fenced Off.*
23 Ogorzalek, *The Cities on the Hill.*
24 Dreier, Mollenkopf, and Swanstrom, *Place Matters,* 253.
25 D. Miller and Nelles, *Discovering American Regionalism*; Savitch and Adhikari, "Fragmented Regionalism."

Bibliography

LIST OF INTERVIEW SUBJECTS

Portland

Lloyd Anderson (17 August 2009): director, Multnomah County Planning Commission, 1953–56; associate director, Bureau of Municipal Research and Service, 1956–61; deputy director, Oregon State Department of Planning and Development, 1961–64; consulting planner, 1964–69; Portland City commissioner, 1969–74; member, board of CRAG, 1974

Ronald Cease (17 August 2009 and 2 August 2010): professor, political science and public administration, Portland State University, 1966–00; member, Portland Metropolitan Area Local Government Boundary Commission, 1969–78 (chair, 1969–72); director, Tri-County Local Government Commission, 1975–78; Oregon state representative and senator, 1985–97; member, Metro Home Rule Charter Committee, 1992–93

Arnold Cogan (26 August 2009): planner, City of Portland, 1959–62; planning director, Port of Portland, 1962–67; state planning coordinator, 1967–73; director, LCDC, 1973–75; principal, Cogan Owens Cogan LLC

Bill Cross (27 July 2010): public information coordinator, Tri-County Local Government Commission, 1975–77; professional lobbyist

Rick Gustafson (19 August 2009): Oregon state representative, 1974–78; executive officer, Portland Metro, 1978–87

Ken Martin (5 July 2010): analyst and executive officer, Portland Local Boundary Commission, 1972–98

Mike Ragsdale (18 July 2010): Oregon state representative and senator,
   1973–80; Portland Metro councillor, 1986–90
A. McKay Rich (24 August 2009 and 27 July 2010): research associate,
   Bureau of Municipal Research and Service, 1962–64; executive director,
   PMSC, 1964–71; assistant director, 1971–73; staff director, Tri-County
   Local Government Commission, 1975–78

Toronto

Jim Faught (15 March 2012): executive director, Federation of Ontario
   Naturalists, 1999–2005
Ian Fawcett (30 July 2014), chief of staff to the Ontario minister of muni-
   cipal affairs, 1993–95.
Lionel Feldman (17 February 2010): staff member, Goldenberg
   Commission, 1965; independent consultant on local government issues
Ruth Grier (correspondence 4 June 2014): Ontario minister of the
   environment, 1990–93
H. Ian Macdonald (20 June 2012), chief economist, Province of Ontario,
   1965–67; deputy treasurer, Province of Ontario, 1967–74
John MacKenzie (25 May 2010): special assistant to the Ontario minister
   of municipal affairs and housing, 2003–5
Darcy McKeough (21 June 2012): Ontario MPP, 1963–78; minister of
   municipal affairs, 1967–71; minister of treasury and economics, 1971–
   72; minister of treasury, economics, and intergovernmental affairs,
   1975–78
Elizabeth McLaren (29 November 2010): assistant deputy minister, OGTA,
   1990–95; executive director, GTA Task Force, 1995–96; executive director, GTSB, 2002
Don Stevenson (12 June 2013): senior public servant, province of Ontario,
   1950s–80s

Twin Cities

Robert Einsweiler (12 August 2010): Transportation Division head,
   TCMPC, 1959; Metropolitan Studies Division head, TCMPC, 1961–62;
   supervisor of the Joint Program's technical studies, TCMPC, 1962–67;
   planning director, Metropolitan Council, 1967–71
James Hetland (26 June 2009): member, Citizens League, late 1960s, early
   1970s; chair, Metropolitan Council, 1967–71

Ted Kolderie (24 June 2009): reporter and editorial writer, *Minneapolis Star*, 1956–67; executive director, Citizens League, 1967–80

Larry Laukka (5 May 2010; also correspondence 13 Nov. 2013): suburban property developer, 1962–present; founder, Minnesota Housing Institute, c. 1972

Ed Maranda (4 May 2010), demographer and planner, MPC and Metropolitan Council, 1960s–80s

Carl Ohrn (23 June 2009): land-use and transportation planner, Metropolitan Council 1980–present

James Solem (16 June 2009 and 4 May 2010): research director, Ramsey County League of Cities, 1964–66; staff member, State Planning Agency, 1970–78; regional administrator, Metropolitan Council, 1994–2000

Vancouver

Ken Cameron (6 October 2009): planner, GVRD 1978–85, 1988–2004

Gordon Campbell (26 January 2011): mayor of Vancouver, 1986–93; premier of British Columbia, 2001–11

Maureen Enser (29 April 2016): president and CEO, Urban Development Institute–Pacific Region, 1982–2012

Ted Rashleigh (20 April 2009): planner, LMRPB, 1962–66; planner, GVRD, 1970–75; executive director of CPAC–BC

Ray Spaxman (8 April 2009): chief planner, City of Vancouver, 1973–88

UBC Regional Planning Project interviews by Narissa Chadwick (1999–2000)

Gerard Farry (25 February 2000): UBC planning graduate; planner, City of Vancouver, 1952–69; director planning, GVRD, late 1970s

Darlene Marzari (28 February 2000): Vancouver councillor, 1970s; BC minister of municipal affairs, 1993–96

Denis O'Gorman (3 March 2000): UBC planning graduate; staff at LMRPB

Peter Oberlander (17 February 2000): professor of planning, UBC, 1950s–2000s

Jim Wilson (15 March 2000): director, LMPRB, 1952–64

SOURCES

Abbott, Carl. "The Capital of Good Planning: Metropolitan Portland since 1970." Chap. 9 in *The American Planning Tradition: Culture and Policy*, edited by Robert Fishman, 241–62. Washington, DC: Woodrow Wilson Center Press, 2000.

– *Portland: Planning, Politics, and Growth in a Twentieth Century City*. Lincoln: University of Nebraska Press, 1983.

– *Portland in Three Centuries: The Place and the People*. Corvallis: Oregon State University Press, 2011.

– "The Portland Region: Where Cities and Suburbs Talk to Each Other – and Often Agree." *Housing Policy Debate* 8, no. 1 (1997): 11–51.

Abbott, Carl, and Margery Post Abbott. *Historical Development of the Metropolitan Service District*. Portland, OR: Metropolitan Service District, 1991.

Abbott, Carl, and Deborah A. Howe. "The Politics of Land Use Law in Oregon: Senate Bill 100 Twenty Years After." *Oregon Historical Quarterly* 94, no. 1 (1993): 5–39.

Ackerberg, Peter. "Businessmen Urge Metro Rule Unit." *Minneapolis Star*, 19 Sept. 1966.

Action for Cities: A Guide for Community Planning. Chicago: Public Administration Service, 1943.

Adams, John S., and Barbara J. VanDrasek. *Minneapolis–St. Paul: People, Place, and Public Life*. Minneapolis: University of Minnesota Press, 1993.

Adams, Michael. *Fire and Ice: The United States, Canada and the Myth of Converging Values*. Toronto: Penguin, 2003.

Adler, Sy. *Oregon Plans: The Making of an Unquiet Land Use Revolution*. Corvallis: Oregon State University Press, 2012.

Advisory Commission on Intergovernmental Relations. *Alternative Approaches to Governmental Reorganization in Metropolitan Areas*. Washington, DC: Author, 1962.

Ahrend, Rudiger, Emily Farchy, Ioannis Kaplanis, and Alexander C. Lembcke. "What Makes Cities More Productive? Evidence on the Role of Urban Governance from OECD Countries." *OECD Regional Development Working Papers* 2014/05. Paris: OECD, 2014.

Aitchison, J.H. "The Municipal Corporations Act of 1849." *Canadian Historical Review* 30, no. 2 (1949): 107–22.

"All 23 Municipalities Should Merge: Council," *Toronto Globe and Mail*, 9 April 1951.

"All Suburbs Better Off under Amalgamation, Municipal Board Told." *Toronto Globe and Mail*, 28 Sept. 1950.

Allen, Jodie T. "How a Different America Responded to the Great Depression." Pew Research Center, 14 Dec. 2010. http://www.pewresearch.org/2010/12/14/how-a-different-america-responded-to-the-great-depression/.

Allen, Rian, and Philippa Campsie. *Implementing the Growth Plan for the Greater Golden Horseshoe: Has the Strategic Vision Been Compromised?* Toronto: Neptis Foundation, 2013.

Altshuler, Alan, William Morrill, Harold Wolman, and Faith Mitchel, eds. *Governance and Opportunity in Metropolitan America*. Washington, DC: Committee on Improving the Future of US Cities through Improved Metropolitan Area Governance, National Research Council, 1999.

Alternative Approaches to Governmental Reorganization in Metropolitan Areas. Washington, DC: Advisory Commission on Intergovernmental Relations, 1962.

"Amalgamation, Unification, Annexation?" *Toronto Daily Star*, 1 March 1952.

Amendments, August 29, 1966–March 31, 1969. Amendments to the 1966 Official Regional Plan. New Westminster, BC: Lower Mainland Regional Planning Board, 1969.

American Law Institute. *A Model Land Development Code*. Washington, DC, 1976.

"Amicable Solution Sought: Toronto, York County Resume Merger Talks." *Toronto Globe and Mail*, 16 Jan. 1951.

Andersen, Elmer L. *A Man's Reach*. Minneapolis: University of Minnesota Press, 2000.

Anderson, J. Edward, ed. *Progress, Problems, and Potential: 1973 International Conference on Personal Rapid Transit*. Minneapolis: Center for Urban and Regional Affairs, University of Minnesota, 1973.

Anderson, James D. "The Municipal Government Reform Movement in Western Canada, 1880–1920." Chap. 3 in *The Usable Urban Past: Planning and Politics in the Modern Canadian City*, edited by Alan F.J. Artibise and Gilbert A. Stelter, 73–111. Toronto: Macmillan, 1979.

Anderson, William. *American City Government*. New York: Henry Holt and Company, 1925.

– *City Charter Making in Minnesota*. Minneapolis: Bureau for Research in Government, University of Minnesota, 1922.

– *Local Government and Finance in Minnesota*. Minneapolis: University of Minnesota Press, 1935.

Anisef, Paul, and Michael Lanphier, eds. *The World in a City*. Toronto: University of Toronto Press, 2003.

"Annexation by Negotiation." *Toronto Daily Star*, 18 May 1950.

"Area Chambers of Commerce Unit Elects Chief." *Minneapolis Tribune*, 4 Jan. 1966.

Armstrong, Christopher, and H.V. Nelles. *Monopoly's Moment: The Organization and Regulation of Canadian Utilities, 1830–1930*. Philadelphia: Temple University Press, 1986.

Arts, Wil, and John Gelissen. "Three Worlds of Welfare Capitalism or More? A State-of-the-Art Report." *Journal of European Social Policy* 12, no. 2 (2002): 137–58.

Back to the Future: Re-Designing Our Landscapes with Form, Place and Density. Burnaby, BC: Urban Development Institute, Pacific Region, 1993.

Bagehot, Walter. *The English Constitution*. Boston: Little Brown, 1873.

Baker, Alden. "Metro to Be Enlarged to 8 Boroughs by 1977." *Toronto Globe and Mail*, 2 April 1966.

Baker, Gordon E. "Reapportionment by Initiative in Oregon." *Western Political Quarterly* 13, no. 2 (1960): 508–19.

Baldinger, Stanley. *Planning and Governing the Metropolis: The Twin Cities Experience*. New York: Praeger, 1971.

Ballot Measure 6: Reorganizes Metropolitan Service District, Abolishes CRAG. Portland, OR: Citizen's Committee for Efficiency in Local Government, 1978.

Ballou, Brendan. "A Future for the Met Council." *University of St. Thomas Law Journal* 12, no. 1 (2015): 131–45.

Banfield, Edward. *Political Influence: A New Theory of Urban Politics*. New York: Macmillan, 1961.

Banting, Keith, George Hoberg, and Richard Simeon. "Introduction." In *Degrees of Freedom: Canada and the United States in a Changing World*, edited by Keith Banting, George Hoberg, and Richard Simeon, 3–19. Montreal and Kingston: McGill-Queen's University Press, 1997.

Barber, Benjamin R. *If Mayors Ruled the World: Dysfunctional Nations, Rising Cities*. New Haven, CT: Yale University Press, 2013.

Barker, Neil. "Portland's Works Progress Administration." *Oregon Historical Quarterly* 101, no. 4 (2000): 414–41.

Barron, Jillian. *Columbia Region Association of Governments (CRAG): A Critical Look at Regional Planning*. Corvallis, OR: Oregon State Public Interest Research Group, 1973.

Bartholomew, Harland. *A Plan for the City of Vancouver, British Columbia, Including Point Grey and South Vancouver and a General Plan of the Region*. Vancouver: Vancouver Town Planning Commission, 1929.

– *A Preliminary Report upon Decentralization and Regional Planning.* Vancouver: Vancouver Town Planning Commission, 1946.

Bartolini, David. "Municipal Fragmentation and Economic Performance of OECD Tl2 Regions." *OECD Regional Development Working Papers* 2015/02. Paris: OECD, 2015.

Barton, James, and Lee Starr. "The Regional-Local Planning Process: Making It Work in the 1980s." In *Challenge and Choice in the New Decade: A Collection of Staff Essays about the 1980s. Prepared for the Council's 1980 State of the Region Conference, February 12, 1980,* 61–73. St. Paul: Twin Cities Metropolitan Council, 1980.

"Basically Undemocratic." *Toronto Globe and Mail,* 26 Jan. 1953.

Bassett, Ellen M. "Framing the Oregon Land Use Debate: An Exploration of Oregon Voters' Pamphlets, 1970–2007." *Journal of Planning Education and Research* 29 (2009): 157–72.

Beckett, Hollis. *Fourth and Final Report, Select Committee on the Municipal Act and Related Acts.* Toronto: Government of Ontario, 1965.

Bell, Daniel. *The Coming of Post-Industrial Society: A Venture in Social Forecasting.* New York: Basic Books, 1973.

Bell, G.G., and A.D. Pascoe. *The Ontario Government.* Toronto: Wall and Thompson, 1988.

Bellett, Gerry. "Reprisal by Richmond Suspected in Bose Losing Post." *Vancouver Sun,* 9 Jan. 1996, A1.

Berelowitz, Lance. *Dream City: Vancouver and the Global Imagination.* Vancouver: Douglas and McIntyre, 2005.

Berg, Steve. "Peter Bell Looks Back on the Metro Landscape." *MinnPost (Minneapolis),* 1 Dec. 2010.

Berg, Tom. *Minnesota's Miracle: Learning from the Government That Worked.* Minneapolis: University of Minnesota Press, 2012.

Berke, Philip R., Joe MacDonald, Nancy White, Michael Holmes, Dan Line, Kat Oury, and Rhonda Ryznar. "Greening Development to Protect Watersheds: Does New Urbanism Make a Difference?" *Journal of the American Planning Association* 69, no. 4 (2003): 397–413.

Bessey, Roy T. *Pacific Northwest Regional Planning: A Review.* Bulletin No. 6. Olympia, WA: Division of Power Resources, State of Washington, 1963.

Best, Michael. "Fred Gardiner Says Goldenberg Plan Won't Work." *Toronto Star,* 15 July 1965.

Binney, Charles Chauncey. "Restrictions upon Local and Special Legislation in the United States." *American Law Register and Review* 41, no. 12 (1893): 1109–61.

Bird, Frederick L. *The Present Financial Status of 135 Cities in the United States and Canada.* New York: Municipal Administration Office, 1931.

Bird, Richard M., and Almos T. Tassonyi. "Constraints on Provincial and Municipal Borrowing in Canada: Markets, Rules, and Norms." *Canadian Public Administration* 44, no. 1 (2001): 84–109.

Birkhead, Guthrie. *A Look to the North: Canadian Regional Experience.* Vol. 5 of Substate Regionalism and the Federal System. Washington, DC: Advisory Commission on Intergovernmental Relations, 1974.

Bish, Robert L. "Vincent Ostrom on Local Government: The Evolution of an Inquiry." Typescript. Prepared for the Public Choice Society Meeting, Charleston, SC, 2014.

Bish, Robert L., and Eric G. Clemens. *Local Government in British Columbia.* 4th ed. Richmond, BC: Union of British Columbia Municipalities, 2008.

Bishop, Bill, and Robert G. Cushing. *The Big Sort: Why the Clustering of Like-Minded America Is Tearing Us Apart.* Boston: Houghton Mifflin, 2008.

Blais, Pamela. *The Economics of Urban Form.* Toronto: Berridge Lewinberg Greenberg Dark Gabor, 1995.

Blake, Laurie. "Carlson Puts 2-Year Limit on 'Laid Back' Met Council." *Minneapolis Star-Tribune*, 20 March 1991.

Blegen, Theodore Christian. *Minnesota: A History of the State.* 2nd ed. Minneapolis: University of Minnesota Press, 1975.

Bliss, Daniel. *Economic Development and Governance in Small Town America: Paths to Growth.* New York: Routledge, 2018.

Bloomfield, Elizabeth, Gerald Bloomfield, and Peter McCaskell. *Urban Growth and Local Services: The Development of Ontario Municipalities to 1981.* Guelph, ON: Department of Geography, University of Guelph, 1983.

"Blueprint for Planning," *Oregonian* (Portland, OR), 16 May 1973.

Bocking, Mike. "Richmond, GVRD Take Step to Resolving Growth Issue." *Vancouver Sun*, 27 Jan. 1996, A9.

Bohn, Glenn. "Proposed Planning Law Welcomes: Cash Needed to Improve Rapid Transit, Region Says." *Vancouver Sun*, 20 April 1995.

Bollens, John Constantinus. *Special District Governments in the United States.* Berkeley: University of California Press, 1957.

Bollens, John Constantinus, and Henry J. Schmandt. *The Metropolis: Its People, Politics, and Economic Life.* 4th ed. New York: Harper and Row, 1982.

Bordessa, Ronald, and James M. Cameron. "Servicing Growth in the
  Metropolitan Toronto Region during the Early Years of the Ontario
  Water Resources Commission, 1956–1968." *Canadian Water Resources
  Journal* 5, no. 1 (1980): 1–29.
Bosselman, Fred P., and David L. Callies. *The Quiet Revolution in Land
  Use Control.* Washington, DC: Council on Environmental Quality, 1972.
Boston Consulting. *The Fourth Era: The Economic Challenges Facing the
  GTA. Summary of a Study Prepared by the Toronto Office of the Boston
  Consulting Group for the GTA Task Force.* Toronto: Boston Consulting
  Group, 1995.
Bottomley, John. "Ideology, Planning and the Landscape: The Business
  Community, Urban Reform and the Establishment of Town Planning in
  Vancouver, British Columbia, 1900–1940." PhD diss., University of
  British Columbia, 1977.
Boudreau, Julie-Anne. "Strategic Territorialization: The Politics of Anglo-
  Montrealers." *Tijdscrift voor Economische en Sociale Geografie* 92,
  no. 4 (2001): 405–19.
Boulant, Justine, Monica Brezzi, and Paolo Veneri. "Income Levels and
  Inequality in Metropolitan Areas: A Comparative Approach in OECD
  Countries." *OECD Regional Development Working Papers* 2016/06.
  Paris: OECD, 2016.
Boychuk, Gerard William. *National Health Insurance in the United States
  and Canada: Race, Territory, and the Roots of Difference.* Washington,
  DC: Georgetown University Press, 2008.
Bradbury, Bettina. "The Road to Receivership: Unemployment and Relief
  in Burnaby, North Vancouver City and District and West Vancouver,
  1929–1933." Master's thesis, Simon Fraser University, 1975.
Bradford, Neil. *Commissioning Ideas: Canadian National Policy
  Innovation in Comparative Perspective.* Toronto: Oxford University
  Press, 1998.
Brenner, Neil, ed. *Implosions/Explosions: Towards a Study of Planetary
  Urbanization.* Berlin, DE: Jovis, 2014.
– "Is There a Politics of 'Urban' Development? Reflections on the US
  Case." Chap. 6 in *The City in American Political Development*, edited
  by Richardson Dilworth, 121–40. New York: Routledge, 2009.
Briffault, Richard. "Our Localism: Part I – The Structure of Local
  Government Law." *Columbia Law Review* 90, no. 1 (1990): 1–115.
Bright, Steven J. "Planning to Plan: Cyril James, the Ottawa Mandarins
  and the Committee on Reconstruction, 1941–1943." Master's thesis,
  Royal Military College, 2005.

British Columbia. *Preliminary Report on "Proposed Lower Mainland Regional Plan."* Victoria, BC: Regional Planning Division, Bureau of Post-War Rehabilitation and Reconstruction, 1945.

Brittain, Horace L. *Local Government in Canada.* Toronto: Ryerson, 1951.

Broadbent, Alan. *Urban Nation: Why We Need to Give Power Back to the Cities to Make Canada Strong.* Toronto: HarperCollins, 2008.

Brownstone, Meyer, and Thomas J. Plunkett. *Metropolitan Winnipeg: Politics and Reform of Local Government.* Berkeley: University of California Press, 1983.

Bryce, James. *The American Commonwealth.* 3rd ed. Vol. 1. 1888; Indianapolis: Liberty Fund, 1995.

Bryson, John M., and Kimberly B. Boal. "Strategic Management in a Metropolitan Area: The Implementation of Minnesota's Metropolitan Land Planning Act of 1976." In *Academy of Management Proceedings, 1983,* edited by K. Cheung, 332–6. Briarcliff Manor, NY: Academy of Management, 1983.

Buchanan, James M., and Gordon Tullock. *The Calculus of Consent: The Logical Foundations of Constitutional Democracy.* Ann Arbor: University of Michigan Press, 1962.

Buckner, Phillip A. *The Transition to Responsible Government: British Policy in British North America, 1815–1850.* Westport, CT: Greenwood Press, 1985.

Bula, Frances. "Cash-Strapped Translink Can't Keep Up with Growth." *Toronto Globe and Mail,* 28 May 2014.

Burchell, Robert W., Anthony Downs, Barbara McCann, and Sahan Mukherji. *Sprawl Costs: Economic Impacts of Unchecked Development.* Washington, DC: Island Press, 2005.

"Burnaby Board Opposed to Metro." *Vancouver Sun,* 19 Jan. 1960.

Burns, Nancy. *The Formation of American Local Governments: Private Values in Public Institutions.* New York: Oxford University Press, 1994.

Burton, Robert E. *Democrats of Oregon: The Pattern of Minority Politics, 1900–1956.* Eugene: University of Oregon, 1970.

Buzzelli, Michael. "Firm Size Structure in North American Housebuilding: Persistent Deconcentration, 1945–98." *Environment and Planning A* 33 (2001): 533–50.

"Bylaws Block Housing, Builders Favor Merger." *Toronto Globe and Mail,* 13 April 1951.

Byrnes, Bruce. "29 Amendments in Bill Clear Path for Metropolitan Area." *Toronto Evening Telegram,* 26 March 1953.

Cain, Louis P. "Water and Sanitation in Vancouver: An Historical Perspective." *BC Studies* 30, no. 1 (1976): 27–43.

Calthorpe, Peter. *The Next American Metropolis: Ecology, Community, and the American Dream.* Princeton, NJ: Princeton Architectural Press, 1993.

Calthorpe, Peter, and William Fulton. *The Regional City: Planning for the End of Sprawl.* Washington, DC: Island Press, 2001.

Campbell, A.M. "The Boundaries of Metropolitan Toronto: Submission to the Metropolitan Executive Committee, Sept. 16, 1971." In *Regional Planning and Government: A Policy to Implement the Toronto-Centred Region Development Concept.* Toronto: Municipality of Metropolitan Toronto, 1971.

Campbell, John L. "Institutional Analysis and the Role of Ideas in Political Economy." *Theory and Society* 27 (1998): 377–409.

"Campbell Denies 'Hatchet Job' Tag." *Vancouver Sun*, 31 Jan. 1969.

"Campbell Plan Okayed." *Vancouver Sun*, 28 Nov. 1968.

Canada. *Report of the Dominion Director of Unemployment Relief.* Ottawa: Department of Labour, 1941.

– Royal Commission on Dominion-Provincial Relations. *Report.* Vol. 1. *Canada, 1867–1939.* Ottawa: Author, 1940.

– Royal Commission on Dominion-Provincial Relations. *Report.* Vol. 2. *Recommendations.* Ottawa: Author, 1940.

– Royal Commission on Dominion-Provincial Relations. *Report.* Vol. 3. Appendix. Ottawa: Author, 1940.

Careless, J.M.S. *Toronto to 1918: An Illustrated History.* Toronto: James Lorimer and National Museum of Man, National Museums of Canada, 1984.

Carlton, Ian. *Histories of Transit-Oriented Development: Perspectives on the Development of the TOD Concept.* Working Paper 2009–02. Berkeley: University of California – Berkeley, Institute of Urban and Regional Development, 2007.

Carruthers, John I. "Growth at the Fringe: The Influence of Political Fragmentation in United States Metropolitan Areas." *Papers in Regional Science* 82 (2003): 475–99.

Carruthers, John I., and Gudmundur F. Úlfarsson. "Does 'Smart Growth' Matter to Public Finance?" *Urban Studies* 45, no. 9 (2008): 1791–823.

– "Fragmentation and Sprawl: Evidence from Interregional Analysis." *Growth and Change* 33, no. 3 (2002): 312–40.

– "Urban Sprawl and the Cost of Public Services." *Environment and Planning B* 30, no. 4 (2003): 503–22.

Carter, Glen D. "Pioneering Water Pollution Control in Oregon." *Oregon Historical Quarterly* 107, no. 2 (2006): 254–72.

Carver, Humphrey. *Compassionate Landscape*. Toronto: University of Toronto Press, 1975.

Cassella, William N. "Evolution of National Civic League Policies: A Retrospective." *National Civic Review* 83, no. 3 (1994): 311–17.

Cavanaugh, Patricia. *Politics and Freeways: Building the Twin Cities Interstate System*. Minneapolis: Center for Transportation Studies and Center for Urban and Regional Affairs, University of Minnesota, 2006.

Cease, Ronald C. *A Report on State and Provincial Boundary Review Boards*. Portland, OR: Portland Metropolitan Study Commission, 1968.

The Challenge of Metropolitan Growth. St. Paul, MN: Twin Cities Metropolitan Planning Commission, 1958.

Cheibub, José Antônio. *Presidentialism, Parliamentarism, and Democracy*. New York: Cambridge University Press, 2007.

"Chambers Deplore Planning Dispersal." *Vancouver Sun*, 14 Jan. 1969.

Chance and Challenge: A Concept and Plan for the Development of the Lower Mainland Region. New Westminster, BC: Lower Mainland Regional Planning Board, 1963.

"Changing Tone in Legislature." *Toronto Globe and Mail*, 29 April 1939, 7.

Chipman, John George. "Policy-Making by Administrative Tribunals: A Study of the Manner in which the Ontario Municipal Board Has Applied Provincial Land Use Planning Policies and Has Developed and Applied Its Own Planning Policies." JSD thesis, University of Toronto, 1999.

Choices for Our Future: Regional Growth Strategy. Chilliwack, BC: Fraser Valley Regional District, 2004.

Christensen, Nick. "A 50 Year Map: Years of Research, Public Input Led to Agreement on Reserves Plan." Portland Metro, 30 Nov. 2015. http://www.oregonmetro.gov/news/50-year-map-years-research-public-input-led-agreement-reserves-plan.

– "Metro, Clackamas County and Cities Celebrate Adoption of Urban and Rural Reserves Plan." Portland Metro, 29 June 2017. http://www.oregonmetro.gov/news/metro-clackamas-county-and-cities-celebrate-adoption-urban-and-rural-reserves-plan.

Christopherson, Susan, Jonathan Michie, and Peter Tyler. "Regional Resilience: Theoretical and Empirical Perspectives." *Cambridge Journal of Regions, Economy and Society* 3, no. 1 (2010): 3–10.

Churchill, Dennis Michael. *Local Government and Administration in the Lower Mainland Metropolitan Community*. Vol. 2. Vancouver: Metropolitan Joint Committee, 1959.

Citizens League. *Breaking the Tyranny of the Local Property Tax.* Minneapolis: Citizens League, 1969.

– "History of the Citizens League." N.d. http://www.citizensleague.org/who/history/.

– *The Metropolitan Council: Recalibration for the Future.* St. Paul, MN: Citizens League, 2016.

– *Minnesota Municipal Commission.* Report. St. Paul, MN: Citizens League, 1963.

– *The Minnesota Municipal Commission: Where Now?* St. Paul, MN: Citizens League, 1965.

– *Statement by the Citizens League to the Public Hearing on the Transportation Chapter of the Metropolitan Development Guide, Nov. 9, 1972.* Minneapolis: Citizens League, 1972.

– *The Transit Problem in the Twin Cities Area.* 1965.

– *Twin Cities Metropolitan Area Sewage Needs.* Report. St. Paul, MN: Citizens League, 1965.

City Club. "Interim Report on Columbia Region Association of Governments (CRAG)." *City Club Bulletin* 53, no. 42 (1973): 193–8.

– "Report on Planning for Transportation in the Portland Metropolitan Area." *Portland City Club Bulletin* 49, no. 27 (1968): 261–88.

"City Defends Planners." *Vancouver Sun,* 21 Nov. 1968.

"City Homeowners Face Greater Share of Taxes If Merger Is Approved." *Toronto Globe and Mail,* 8 Oct. 1952.

Civic Advisory Council. *First Report.* Section One. *The Committee on Metropolitan Problems.* Toronto: Civic Advisory Council of Toronto, 1949.

Clark, Don. Interview by Ernie Bonner. Transcript. PlanPDX Oral History Project, 8 March 2002.

Clarke, Susan E., and Gary L. Gaile. *The Work of Cities.* Minneapolis: University of Minnesota Press, 1998.

Clawson, Marion. *New Deal Planning: The National Resources Planning Board.* Baltimore: Johns Hopkins University Press, 1981.

Clayton Research. *Projections of Population and Households in the Greater Toronto Area.* Toronto: Greater Toronto Coordinating Committee, 1989.

"Clayton Residents Oppose Industry." *Surrey (BC) Delta Messenger,* 12 March 1980.

Climenhaga, David J. "The Death and Life of Regional Planning in the Calgary Area." Master's thesis, Carleton University, 1997.

Clucas, Richard A., and Mark Henkels. "A State Divided." Chap. 1 in *Oregon Politics and Government: Progressive versus Conservative*

Populists, edited by Richard A. Clucas, Mark Henkels, and Brent S. Steel, 1–16. Lincoln: University of Nebraska Press, 2005.

Cobb, Rodney L. "Toward Modern Statutes." Chap. 2 in *Planning Communities for the 21st Century*, edited by Stuart Meck, 7–24. Washington, DC: American Planning Association, 1999.

Cobban, Timothy W. "Bigger Is Better: Reducing the Cost of Local Administration by Increasing Jurisdiction Size in Ontario, Canada, 1995–2010." *Urban Affairs Review* Online (2017).

Cochrane, Christopher. *Left and Right: The Small World of Political Ideas.* Montreal and Kingston: McGill-Queen's University Press, 2015.

Cocking, Florence Irene. "A Comparison of the NDP and Social Credit Agricultural and Land Commission Policy." Masters's. thesis, University of British Columbia, 1982.

Cole, Leone M., and Harold W. Merritt. *Tomorrow's Transportation: New Systems for the Urban Future.* Washington, DC: US Department of Housing and Urban Development, Office of Metropolitan Development, 1968.

Colton, Timothy. *Big Daddy: Frederick G. Gardiner and the Building of Metropolitan Toronto.* Toronto: University of Toronto Press, 1980.

Columbia-Willamette Region Comprehensive Plan: Discussion Draft. Portland, OR: Columbia Region Association of Governments, 1974.

"Communities near Cities Included in Planning Program." *Minneapolis Journal*, 20 Jan. 1924.

Community Environmental Legal Defense Fund. "Home Rule." 25 Aug. 2015. https://celdf.org/law-library/local-law-center/home-rule/.

Conant, Ralph Wendell, and Daniel J. Myers. *Toward a More Perfect Union: The Governance of Metropolitan America.* Novato, CA: Chandler and Sharp, 2002.

"Concepts in Planning." *Surrey (BC) Leader*, 23 Sept. 1965.

Congleton, Roger D. "On the Merits of Bicameral Legislatures: Intergovernmental Bargaining and Policy Stability." Chap. 6 in *Democratic Constitutional Design and Public Policy: Analysis and Evidence*, edited by Roger D. Congleton and Birgitta Swedenborg, 174–88. Cambridge, MA: MIT Press, 2006.

Connolly, James. "Institutional Change in Urban Environmentalism: A Case Study Analysis of State-Level Land Use Legislation in California and New York." PhD diss., Columbia University, 2012.

"'Containment' Plan Endorsed." *Oregonian* (Portland, OR), 13 Sept. 1973.

Cooke, Phillip, and Kevin Morgan. *The Associational Economy: Firms, Regions, and Innovation.* Oxford: Oxford University Press, 1998.

Coordination of Light Rail Transit Planning for the Twin Cities Area: A Report to the Minnesota Legislature. St. Paul, MN: Twin Cities Metropolitan Council, 1988.

Copeland, Claudia. *Water Infrastructure Financing: History of EPA Appropriations (96-647).* Washington, DC: Congressional Research Service, 2012.

Cotugno, Andrew, and Ethan Seltzer. "Towards a Metropolitan Consciousness in the Portland Oregon Metropolitan Area." *International Planning Studies* 16, no. 3 (2011): 289–304.

"Councillor Hits Assassination." *Vancouver Sun,* 16 Dec. 1968.

"Councillors Fear Planning Board Might Usurp Municipal Authority." *Delta (BC) Optimist,* 13 April 1966.

"Councillors Weigh Bd ... Surrey Plans." *Surrey (BC) Leader,* 22 Dec. 1965.

"County Approaches City to Start Merger Talks." *Toronto Daily Star,* 10 Jan. 1951.

Cox, Gary W., and Matthew D. McCubbins. "The Institutional Determinants of Economic Policy Outcomes." Chap. 2 in *Presidents, Parliaments, and Policy,* edited by Stephan Haggard and Matthew D. McCubbins, 21–63. Cambridge: Cambridge University Press, 2001.

"CRAG Approves Containment Policy of Interim Land-Use Planning." *Oregonian* (Portland, OR), 17 March 1973, 26.

CRAG Goals and Objectives. Portland, OR: Columbia Region Association of Governments, 1976.

"CRAG Sets Hillsboro Hearing on Comprehensive Plan Ideas." *Oregonian* (Portland, OR), 18 Feb. 1976.

"CRAG's Urban-Limits Plan Faces Double-Barreled Attack." *Oregonian* (Portland, OR), 14 March 1976.

Crawford, Kenneth Grant. *Canadian Municipal Government.* Toronto: University of Toronto Press, 1954.

– "The Independence of Municipal Councils in Ontario." *Canadian Journal of Economics and Political Science* 6, no. 4 (1940): 543–54.

Creating Our Future: Steps to a More Livable Region. Burnaby, BC: Greater Vancouver Regional District, 1990.

Crombie, David. "Recommendations of the 'Who Does What' Panel on Local Governance." Toronto: Government of Ontario, 1996.

Crosby, Barbara C., and John M. Bryson. "The Twin Cities Metropolitan Council." Chap. 6 in *The Government of World Cities: The Future of the Metro Model,* edited by L.J. Sharpe, 91–109. New York: John Wiley and Sons, 1995.

"Cross Assails City Plebiscite on Annexation." *Toronto Globe and Mail*, 2 June 1939.

"Cross Assails Mayor for Stand on Annexation." *Toronto Globe and Mail*, 30 March 1939, 15.

Cullingworth, J. Barry. "The Provincial Role in Planning and Development." *Plan Canada* 24, nos. 3/4 (1984): 142–55.

– *Urban and Regional Planning in Canada*. Oxford: Transaction Press, 1987.

Dahl, Robert. "A Democratic Dilemma: System Effectiveness Versus Citizen Participation." *Political Science Quarterly* 109, no. 1 (1994): 23–34.

– *Who Governs? Democracy and Power in an American City*. New Haven, CT: Yale University Press, 1961.

Dalton, Russell J. "The Social Transformation of Trust in Government." *International Review of Sociology* 15, no. 1 (2005): 133–54.

Daniel, Carrie. "Land Use Planning – The Twin Cities Metropolitan Council: Novel Initiative, Futile Effort." *William Mitchell Law Review* 27, no. 3 (2001): 1941–69.

Daniels, Tom, and Mark Lapping. "Land Preservation: An Essential Ingredient in Smart Growth." *Journal of Planning Literature* 19, no. 3 (2005): 316–29.

Davis, Roger A. "An Analysis of the Factors and Forces Leading to the Creation of the Twin Cities Metropolitan Council." Master's thesis, Mankato State College, 1968.

Davis, William G. *Design for Development: Phase Three*. Toronto: Government of Ontario, 1972.

Dearborn, Philip. *City Financial Emergencies: The Intergovernmental Dimension*. Washington, DC: Advisory Commission on Intergovernmental Relations, 1973.

"Decide to Fight Unification after Eight Hours of Debate." *Toronto Globe and Mail*, 3 Feb. 1953.

Decision of the Board Dated January 20, 1953. Toronto: Ontario Municipal Board, 1953.

"Delta Attacks Updated GVRD Regional Plan." *Columbian* [n.p.], 1980.

Dewing, Rolland. *Regions in Transition: The Northern Great Plains and the Pacific Northwest in the Great Depression*. Lanham, MD: University Press of America, 2006.

Dicey, A.V. *Introduction to the Study of the Law of the Constitution*. 8th ed. London: Macmillan, 1915.

Diers, John W., and Aaron Isaacs. *Twin Cities by Trolley: The Streetcar Era in Minneapolis and St. Paul.* Minneapolis: University of Minnesota Press, 2007.

DiGaetano, Alan, and Elizabeth Strøm. "Comparative Urban Governance: An Integrated Approach." *Urban Affairs Review* 38, no. 3 (2003): 356–95.

Dilworth, Richardson, ed. *The City in American Political Development.* New York: Routledge, 2009.

– *The Urban Origins of Suburban Autonomy.* Cambridge, MA: Harvard University Press, 2005.

"Discontent in the Suburbs: Splintering Followed the Rail Lines." *Toronto Globe and Mail*, 18 June 1965, 11.

Discussion Leaders' Material: Study and Evaluation of the Comprehensive Plan to Be Proposed by the Metropolitan Study Commission. Portland, OR: League of Women Voters of Beaverton, Milwaukie, Oswego, and Portland, Tri-County Metro Committee, 1967.

"Distorting the Facts." *Toronto Evening Telegram*, 12 Nov. 1951.

"District Still Holds Region Plan Doubts." *Langley (BC) Advance*, 30 Dec. 1965.

Donald, Betsy. "Economic Change and City Region Governance: The Case of Toronto." PhD diss., University of Toronto, 1999.

Donaldson, Jim. "Alumni Interviews: Peter Oberlander." School of Architecture, McGill University, 1998. http://www.mcgill.ca/architecture/aluminterviews/oberlander/.

Dornfeld, Steven. "Minnesota's Planning Laws Lag Behind Leaders." *MinnPost (Minneapolis)*, 26 June 2012.

Douglas, Paul H. *Building the American City: Report of the National Commission on Urban Problems to the Congress and to the President of the United States.* Washington, DC: US Government Printing Office, 1968.

Dreier, Peter, John Mollenkopf, and Todd Swanstrom. *Place Matters: Metropolitics for the Twenty-First Century.* 2nd ed. Kansas City: University Press of Kansas, 2004.

– *Place Matters: Metropolitics for the Twenty-First Century.* 3rd ed. Kansas City: University Press of Kansas, 2014.

DuPuis, Nicole, Trevor Langan, Christiana McFarland, Angelina Panettieri, and Brooks Rainwater. *City Rights in an Era of Preemption: A State-by-State Analysis.* Washington, DC: Center for City Solutions, National League of Cities, 2017.

The Dynamics of Urban Poverty in the 1990s: A Canadian Profile.
Ottawa: Canadian Council on Social Development, 2008.

Economic Aspects of Urban Sprawl: A Technical Report. New
Westminster, BC: Lower Mainland Regional Planning Board, 1956.

"Economic Survey of Regional Plan." *Surrey (BC) Leader,* 3 Sept. 1965.

"Editorial: Metropolitan Council." MPC *Newsletter* (Twin Cities
Metropolitan Planning Commission) 4, no. 10 (1964): 2.

Edmonston, Barry, Michael A. Goldberg, and John Mercer. "Urban Form
in Canada and the United States: An Examination of Urban Density
Gradients." *Urban Studies* 22, no. 3 (1985): 209–17.

Edsforth, Ronald. *The New Deal: America's Response to the Great
Depression.* Malden, MA: Blackwell Publishers, 2000.

Eidelman, Gabriel. "Managing Urban Sprawl in Ontario: Good Policy or
Good Politics?" *Politics and Policy* 38, no. 6 (2010): 1211–36.

"800 Leaders Called to Help Map Metropolitan Plan." *Minneapolis
Journal,* 9 Jan. 1927.

Einsweiler, Robert C. "Metropolitan Planning and Implementation."
*Journal of the Urban Planning and Development Division, Proceedings
of the American Society of Civil Engineers* 96, no. UP2 (1970): 113–21.

– "Planning for the Minnesota Twins." Paper presented at the AASHO
54th Annual Meeting, Minneapolis, 6 Dec. 1968.

Elazar, Daniel J., Virginia Gray, and Wyman Spano. *Minnesota Politics and
Government.* Lincoln: University of Nebraska Press, 1999.

"Elected Met Council Favored – Metro-Poll." *Minneapolis Star,* 28 Jan.
1969.

"Elected Representation." *Toronto Evening Telegram,* 6 Feb. 1953.

"Elective Metro Council Preferred – Metro-Poll." *Minneapolis Star,*
19 Jan. 1971.

Elkins, David J. "Politics Makes Strange Bedfellows: The B.C. Party
System in the 1952 and 1953 Provincial Elections." *BC Studies*
30 (1976): 3–26.

"Environment a Concern, Survey Shows." *Vancouver Sun,* 10 March
1990, A2.

Esping-Andersen, Gøsta. *The Three Worlds of Welfare Capitalism.*
Cambridge, MA: Polity Press, 1990.

Establishing a Regional Strategic Plan: A Review of the Process. Burnaby,
BC: Strategic Planning Department, Greater Vancouver Regional
District, 1996.

Ethington, Philip J., and David P. Levitus. "Placing American Political
Development: Cities, Regions, and Regimes, 1789–2008." Chap. 8 in

The City in American Political Development, edited by Richardson Dilworth, 154–76. New York: Routledge, 2009.

Ewing, Reid, and Shima Hamidi. "Compactness versus Sprawl: A Review of Recent Evidence from the United States." *Journal of Planning Literature* 30, no. 4 (2015): 413–32.

Ewing, Reid, and Fang Rong. "The Impact of Urban Form on US Residential Energy Use." *Housing Policy Debate* 19, no. 1 (2008): 1–30.

"Far More Cruel than Nazi Drew Says of Inside Russia." *Toronto Daily Star*, 20 June 1946, 10.

Federal Highway Administration. "Highway Statistics 2015, Urbanized Area Summaries, Tables HM-71 and HM-72." https://www.fhwa.dot.gov/policyinformation/statistics/2015/.

"Federation to Cut Toronto Taxes: Lamport." *Toronto Evening Telegram*, 10 March 1953.

Feiock, Richard C., ed. *Metropolitan Governance: Conflict, Competition, and Cooperation*. Washington, DC: Georgetown University Press, 2004.

Feiss, Carl. "The Foundations of Federal Planning Assistance: A Personal Acount of the 701 Program." *Journal of the American Planning Association* 51, no. 2 (1985): 175–84.

Feldman, Lionel D. "Legislative Control of Municipalities in Ontario." *Canadian Public Administration* 4, no. 3 (1961): 294–301.

– *Ontario, 1945–1973: The Municipal Dynamic*. Toronto: Ontario Economic Council, 1974.

Ferraro, Nick. "Tentative Deal Pays Off Dakota County, Allows Breakup of Transit Board." *St. Paul Pioneer Press*, 9 May 2017.

50 Years: Treating the Mississippi Right. St. Paul, MN: Metropolitan Waste Control Commission, 1988.

Filion, Pierre. "Balancing Concentration and Dispersion? Public Policy and Urban Structure in Toronto." *Environment and Planning C: Government and Policy* 18 (2000): 163–89.

Filion, Pierre, Trudi Bunting, Kathleen McSpurren, and Alan Tse. "Canada-US Metropolitan Density Patterns: Zonal Convergence and Divergence." *Urban Geography* 25, no. 1 (2004): 42–65.

Filion, Pierre, Trudi Bunting, Dejan Pavlic, and Paul Langlois. "Intensification and Sprawl: Residential Density Trajectories in Canada's Largest Metropolitan Areas." *Urban Geography* 31, no. 4 (2010): 541–69.

Findings and Recommendations, Task Force on Metropolitan Governance. St. Paul, MN: Metro Cities, 2012.

Fischler, Raphaël, and Jeanne M. Wolfe. "Regional Restructuring in Montreal: An Historical Analysis." *Canadian Journal of Regional Science* 23, no. 1 (2000): 89–114.

Fishback, Price V., William C. Horrace, and Shawn Kantor. "Did New Deal Grant Programs Stimulate Local Economies? A Study of Federal Grants and Retail Sales during the Great Depression." *Journal of Economic History* 65, no. 1 (2005): 36–71.

Fisher, Robin. "The Decline of Reform: British Columbia Politics in the 1930s." *Journal of Canadian Studies* 25, no. 3 (1990): 74–89.

"Five-Year Trial Urged for Metro." *Vancouver Sun*, 24 Mar. 1960.

Flanagan, Richard M. "The Housing Act of 1954: The Sea Change in National Urban Policy." *Urban Affairs Review* 33, no. 2 (1997): 265–86.

"Floodplain Follies." *Vancouver Sun*, 29 Jan. 1996, A8.

Florida, Richard. *Cities and the Creative Class*. New York: Routledge, 2005.

– *The New Urban Crisis*. New York, NY: Basic Books, 2017.

Foster, Kathryn Ann. *The Political Economy of Special-Purpose Government*. Washington, DC: Georgetown University Press, 1997.

– "Regional Capital." Chap. 5 in *Urban-Suburban Dependencies*, edited by Rosalind Greenstein and Wim Wiewel, 83–118. Cambridge, MA: Lincoln Institute of Land Policy, 2000. *4,000,000 by 2000! Preliminary Options for Guiding Change*. St. Paul, MN: Twin Cities Metropolitan Planning Commission, 1964.

Fregonese, John, and C.J. Gabbe. "Engaging the Public and Communicating Successfully in Regional Planning." Chap. 8 in *Regional Planning in America: Practice and Prospect*, edited by Ethan Seltzer and Armando Carbonell, 222–42. Cambridge, MA: Lincoln Institute of Land Policy, 2011.

Friedmann, John, and Clyde Weaver. *Territory and Function: The Evolution of Regional Planning*. London: Edward Arnold, 1979.

Frisken, Frances. "Canadian Cities and the American Example: A Prologue to Urban Policy Analysis," *Canadian Public Administration* 29 (1986): 345–76.

– *The Public Metropolis: The Political Dynamics of Urban Expansion in the Toronto Region, 1924–2003*. Toronto: Canadian Scholars Press, 2008.

Frug, Gerald E. *City Making: Building Communities without Building Walls*. Princeton, NJ: Princeton University Press, 1999.

Frug, Gerald E., and David J. Barron. *City Bound: How States Stifle Urban Innovation*. Ithaca, NY: Cornell University Press, 2008.

Fulton, William, Rolf Pendall, Mai Nguyen, and Alicia Harrison. *Who Sprawls Most? How Growth Patterns Differ across the US* Washington, DC: Brookings Institution, 2001.

Furuseth, Owen J. "Planning for Agricultural Lands in British Columbia: Progress and Problems." *Environmentalist* 1 (1981): 299–309.

Gainsborough, Juliet. *Fenced Off: The Suburbanization of American Politics.* Washington, DC: Georgetown University Press, 2001.

Galaskiewicz, Joseph. "An Urban Grants Economy Revisited: Corporate Charitable Donations in the Twin Cities, 1979–81, 1987–89." *Administrative Science Quarterly* 42, no. 3 (1997): 445–71.

Garcea, Joseph, and Edward C. LeSage, eds. *Municipal Reform in Canada: Reconfiguration, Re-Empowerment, and Rebalancing.* Toronto: Oxford University Press, 2005.

Garr, Allen. *Tough Guy: Bill Bennett and the Taking of British Columbia.* Toronto: Key Porter, 1985.

Garrish, Christopher. "Unscrambling the Omelette: Understanding British Columbia's Agricultural Land Reserve." *BC Studies*, no. 136 (2002/3): 25–55.

Gathercole, George E. "The City of Toronto in Depression and Recovery, 1929–1939." Master's thesis, University of Toronto, 1945.

Gelfand, Mark I. *A Nation of Cities: The Federal Government and Urban America, 1933–1965.* New York: Oxford University Press, 1975.

Gerecke, John Kent. "Toward a New Model of Urban Planning." PhD diss., University of British Columbia, 1974.

Gerring, John, Strom C. Thacker, and Carola Moreno. "Are Parliamentary Systems Better?" *Comparative Political Studies* 42, no. 3 (2009): 327–59.

Gertler, Leonard O., ed. *Regional Development: Selected Background Papers.* Toronto: Department of Economics and Development, Government of Ontario, 1965.

Gertler, Meric S. *A Region in Transition: The Changing Structure of Toronto's Regional Economy.* Toronto: University of Toronto and Neptis Foundation, 2000.

Gilhousen, Marlin. *A Brief History of Municipal Incorporations in the Twin Cities Metropolitan Area.* St. Paul, MN: Twin Cities Metropolitan Council, 1983.

Glaeser, Edward L., Matthew Kahn, and Chenghuan Chu. *Job Sprawl: Employment Location in US Metropolitan Areas.* Washington, DC: Brookings Institution, Center on Urban and Metropolitan Policy, 2001.

Glaeser, Edward L., Matthew G. Resseger, and Kristina Tobio. "Urban Inequality." *National Bureau of Economic Research Working Paper Series,* no. 14419 (2008).

Goetz, Edward G. "Fair Share or Status Quo: The Twin Cities Livable Communities Act." *Journal of Planning Education and Research* 20 (2000): 37–51.

Goetz, Edward G., Karen Chapple, and Barbara Lukermann. "The Minnesota Land Use Planning Act and the Promotion of Low- and Moderate-Income Housing in Suburbia." *Law and Inequality* 22 (2004): 31–72.

Goldberg, Michael, and John Mercer. *The Myth of the North American City: Continentalism Challenged.* Vancouver: U B C Press, 1986.

Goldenberg, H. Carl. *Report of the Royal Commission on Metropolitan Toronto.* Toronto: Government of Ontario, 1965.

Gomme, Ted. "Municipal Planning in Ontario." Unpublished typescript, 1983.

Goodnow, Frank J. *Municipal Home Rule: A Study in Administration.* New York: Macmillan, 1895.

– *Municipal Problems.* New York: Macmillan, 1897.

Gore and Storrie. *Report on Water Supply and Sewage Disposal for the City of Toronto and Related Areas.* Toronto: Toronto and York Planning Board, 1949.

Gotlieb, Marc J. "George Drew and the Dominion-Provincial Conference on Reconstruction of 1945–6." *Canadian Historical Review* 66, no. 1 (1985): 27–47.

Governmental Procedures in Metropolitan Areas. Minneapolis, M N: Council of Metropolitan Area Leagues, League of Women Voters of Minnesota, 1963.

Governmental Structure, Organization, and Planning in Metropolitan Areas: Suggested Action by Local, State, and National Governments. Washington, D C: Advisory Commission on Intergovernmental Relations, 1961.

Grabb, Edward, and James Curtis. *Regions Apart: The Four Societies of Canada and the United States.* Toronto: Oxford University Press, 2005.

"Gradual Merger Plan Favored by Oliver." *Toronto Evening Telegram,* 10 March 1953.

Graham, Katherine A., and Susan D. Phillips. "Who Does What in Ontario: Disentangling Provincial-Municipal Relations." *Canadian Public Administration* 41, no. 2 (1998): 175–209.

Graham, Roger. *Old Man Ontario: Leslie M. Frost.* Toronto: University of Toronto Press, 1990.

Grant, Jill L. "Experiential Planning: A Practitioner's Account of Vancouver's Success." *Journal of the American Planning Association* 75, no. 3 (2009): 358–70.

Gray, Aelred J., and David A. Johnson. *The TVA Regional Planning and Development Program: The Transformation of an Institution and Its Mission.* Aldershot, UK: Ashgate, 2004.

"Gray Says He's No Red in Amalgamation Views." *Toronto Globe and Mail,* 18 Oct. 1950.

The Greater Vancouver Metropolitan Community: A Preliminary Factual Study. New Westminster, BC: Lower Mainland Regional Planning Board, 1954.

Griffith, Ernest. *A History of American City Government: The Conspicuous Failure, 1870–1900.* New York: Praeger, 1974.

Griffith, Ernest, and Charles R. Adrian. *A History of American City Government.* Vol. 2. *The Formation of Traditions, 1775–1870.* Washington, DC: Published for the National Municipal League by University Press of America, 1983.

Grosenick, Leigh E. *Boundary Change by Administrative Commission: The Minnesota Experience.* Part 1. *The Minnesota Municipal Commission.* Minneapolis: Municipal Reference Bureau, General Extension Division, University of Minnesota, 1968.

– *Boundary Change by Administrative Commission: The Minnesota Experience.* Part 2. *Standards for Incorporation and Municipal Boundary Change: Recommendations Based on a Study of Statutory and Case Law in the United States.* Minneapolis: Municipal Reference Bureau, General Extension Division, University of Minnesota, 1968.

Gulick, Luther Halsey. *The Metropolitan Problem and American Ideas: Five Lectures Delivered on the William W. Cook Foundation at the University of Michigan, March 6–10, 1961.* New York: Alfred A. Knopf, 1962.

Gutstein, Donald. *Vancouver, Ltd.* Toronto: Lorimer, 1975.

Gyourko, Joseph, Albert Saiz, and Anita Summers. "A New Measure of the Local Regulatory Environment for Housing Markets: The Wharton Residential Land Use Regulatory Index." *Urban Studies* 45, no. 3 (2008): 693–729.

Hady, Thomas F., and Clarence J. Hein. "Administrative Control of Municipal Incorporation: The Search for Criteria." *Western Political Quarterly* 19, no. 4 (1966): 697–704.

Haggard, Stephan, and Matthew D. McCubbins, eds. *Presidents, Parliaments, and Policy.* Cambridge: Cambridge University Press, 2001.

Haigh, Susan. "The Metropolitan Council." *William Mitchell Law Review* 40, no. 1 (2013): 160–223.

Hall, Peter A. "Conclusion." Chap. 14 in *The Political Power of Economic Ideas: Keynesianism across Nations,* edited by Peter A. Hall, 361–91. Princeton, NJ: Princeton University Press, 1989.

– "Policy Paradigms, Social Learning, and the State: The Case of Economic Policymaking in Britain." *Comparative Politics* 25, no. 3 (1993): 275–96.

Hall, Peter A., and David Soskice. *Varieties of Capitalism: The Institutional Foundations of Comparative Advantage.* Oxford: Oxford University Press, 2001.

Halprin, Lawrence. *The Willamette Valley: Choices for the Future. Illustrated Scenarios Showing Consequences of Alternative Approaches to Development in the Valley for the Next Thirty Years.* Salem, OR: Executive Department, State of Oregon, 1972.

Hamidi, Shima, and Reid Ewing. "A Longitudinal Study of Changes in Urban Sprawl between 2000 and 2010 in the United States." *Landscape and Urban Planning* 128 (2014): 72–82.

Hamilton, David K. *Governing Metropolitan Areas: Growth and Change in a Networked Age.* 2nd ed. New York: Routledge, 2014.

– *Measuring the Effectiveness of Regional Governing Systems: A Comparative Study of City Regions in North America.* New York: Springer, 2013.

– "Organizing Government Structure and Governance Functions in Metropolitan Areas in Response to Growth and Change: A Critical Overview." *Journal of Urban Affairs* 22, no. 1 (2000): 65–84.

Hamilton, David K., David Y. Miller, and Jerry Paytas. "Exploring the Horizontal and Vertical Dimensions of the Governing of Metropolitan Regions." *Urban Affairs Review* 40, no. 2 (2004): 147–82.

Hancock, John. "The New Deal and American Planning: The 1930s." Chap. 8 in *Two Centuries of American Planning,* edited by Daniel Schaffer, 197–230. Baltimore, MD: Johns Hopkins University Press, 1988.

Hansen, Royce. *Metropolitan Councils of Government.* Washington, DC: Advisory Commission on Intergovernmental Relations, 1966.

Harcourt, Mike, Ken Cameron, and Sean Rossiter. *City Making in Paradise: Nine Decisions that Saved Vancouver.* Vancouver: Douglas and McIntyre, 2007.

Harrigan, John J. "Minneapolis–St. Paul: Structuring Metropolitan Government." Chap. 9 in *Regional Politics: America in a Post-City Age,* edited by Hank V. Savitch and Ronald K. Vogel, 206–28. Thousand Oaks, CA: Sage, 1996.

Harrigan, John J., and William C. Johnson. *Governing the Twin Cities Region: The Metropolitan Council in Comparative Perspective.* Minneapolis: University of Minnesota Press, 1978.

Harris, Richard. *Unplanned Suburbs: Toronto's American Tragedy, 1900 to 1950.* Baltimore, MD: Johns Hopkins University Press, 1996.

Harris, Richard, and Martin Luymes. "The Growth of Toronto, 1861–1941: A Cartographic Essay." *Urban History Review* 18, no. 3 (1990): 244–55.

Hart, Albert Gailord. *Debts and Recovery: A Study of Changes in the Internal Debt Structure from 1929 to 1937 and a Program for the Future.* New York: Twentieth Century Fund, 1938.

Hartz, Louis. *The Founding of New Societies: Studies in the History of the United States, Latin America, South Africa, Canada, and Australia.* New York: Harcourt, Brace and World, 1964.

– *The Liberal Tradition in America: An Interpretation of Americal Political Thought since the Revolution.* New York: Harcourt, Brace, Jovanovich, 1955.

Harvey, David. "The Urban Process under Capitalism: A Framework for Analysis." *International Journal of Urban and Regional Research* 2, nos. 1–3 (1978): 101–31.

Hatfield, Mark O. *Not Quite So Simple.* New York: Harper and Row, 1968.

Haynes, John Earl. *Dubious Alliance: The Making of Minnesota's DFL Party.* Minneapolis: University of Minnesota Press, 1984.

Hays, Samuel P. "From Conservation to Environment: Environmental Politics in the United States since World War Two." *Environmental Review* 6, no. 2 (1982): 14–41.

"Hearing on Merger Deferred 2 Weeks." *Toronto Evening Telegram,* 22 Jan. 1951.

Hemson Consulting. *Employment Forecasts for the Greater Toronto Area to 2031.* Toronto: Greater Toronto Coordinating Committee, 1989.

Hendrick, Renecca, and Yu Shi. "Macro-Level Determinants of Local Government Interaction: How Metropolitan Regions in the United States Compare." *Urban Affairs Review* 51, no. 3 (2015): 414–38.

Henry, Shayne, and Samuel Sherraden. *Costs of the Infrastructure Deficit.* Washington, DC: New America Foundation, 2011.

Henton, Douglas, John Melville, and Kimberly Walsh. *Grassroots Leaders for a New Economy: How Civic Entrepreneurs Are Building Prosperous Communities.* San Francisco: Jossey-Bass, 1997.

Herrold, G.H. "State Planning Boards and Their Relation to Other Planning Agencies." *Civil Engineering* 5, no. 4 (1935): 234.

Heying, Charles. "Civic Elites and Corporate Delocalization." *American Behavioral Scientist* 40, no. 5 (1997): 657–68.

Hibbard, Michael, Ethan Seltzer, Bruce Weber, and Beth Emshoff, eds. *Toward One Oregon: Rural-Urban Interdependence and the Evolution of a State*. Corvallis: Oregon State University Press, 2011.

Hillhouse, Albert Miller. *Municipal Bonds: A Century of Experience*. New York: Prentice-Hall, 1936.

Hinchliffe, Kelsey L., and Frances E. Less. "Party Competition and Conflict in State Legislatures." *State Politics and Policy Quarterly* 16, no. 2 (June 2016): 172–97.

Hinderaker, Ivan. "Harold Stassen and Developments in the Republican Party in Minnesota, 1937–1943." PhD diss., University of Minnesota, 1949.

"Hints York May Offer Alternative to Merger but Hearing Goes On." *Toronto Globe and Mail*, 1 July 1950.

Hinze, Steve. *The Fiscal Disparities Program: Commercial-Industrial Tax-Base Sharing*. St. Paul, MN: Research Department of the Minnesota House of Representatives, 2012.

Hitchings, Benjamin G. "A Typology of Regional Growth Management Systems." *Regionalist* 3, nos. 1–2 (1998): 1–14.

Hodge, Gerald, and David L.A. Gordon. *Planning Canadian Communities: An Introduction to the Principles, Practice, and Participants*. 6th ed. Toronto: Nelson Education, 2014.

Hodgetts, J. E. *From Arm's-Length to Hands-On: The Formative Years of Ontario's Public Service, 1867–1940*. Toronto: University of Toronto Press, 1995.

Hodos, Jerome. "Against Exceptionalism: Intercurrence and Intergovernmental Relations in Britain and the United States." In *The City in American Political Development*, edited by Richardson Dilworth, 44–63. New York: Routledge, 2009.

Hollingworth, Brian, Mori Anna, Dylan Cham, and Neal Irwin. *Urban Transportation Indicators, Fourth Survey*. Ottawa: Transportation Association of Canada, 2010.

Honsey, Milton C., and Vernon E. Bergstrom. *Report on Study of the Municipality of Metropolitan Toronto*. Minneapolis: Hennepin County League of Municipalities, 1965.

Horak, Martin. *The Power of Local Identity: C4LD and the Anti-Amalgamation Mobilization in Toronto*. Toronto: Centre for Urban and Community Studies, University of Toronto, 1998.

Horak, Martin, and Robert Young, eds. *Sites of Governance: Multilevel Governance and Policy Making in Canada's Big Cities*. Montreal and Kingston: McGill-Queen's University Press, 2012.

Horn, Michiel. *The Great Depression of the 1930s in Canada*. Ottawa: Canadian Historical Association, 1984.

– *The League for Social Reconstruction: Intellectual Origins of the Democratic Left in Canada, 1930–1942*. Toronto: University of Toronto Press, 1980.

"House to Rule on Annexation Says Hepburn." *Toronto Globe and Mail*, 7 April 1939, 19.

Howlett, Karen. "Subway Plan Could Benefit Sorbara Family." *Toronto Globe and Mail*, 23 March 2006.

How Should Our Community Grow? Portland, OR: Portland Metropolitan Planning Commission, 1966.

Hoy, Claire. *Bill Davis: A Biography*. Toronto: Methuen, 1985.

Huber, John D., and Charles R. Shipan. *Deliberate Discretion: The Institutional Foundations of Bureaucratic Autonomy*. Cambridge: Cambridge University Press, 2002.

Humphries, Charles W. *"Honest Enough to Be Bold": The Life and Times of Sir James Pliny Whitney*. Toronto: University of Toronto Press, 1985.

Hunt, A., and P. Watkiss. "Climate Change Impacts and Adaptation in Cities: A Review of the Literature." *Climatic Change* 104, no. 1 (2011): 13–49.

Hunter, Floyd. *Community Power Structure*. New York: Anchor, 1953.

Huntington, Samuel P. "Postindustrial Politics: How Benign Will It Be?" *Comparative Politics* 6, no. 2 (1974): 163–91.

Huston, Michael. *The Columbia Region Association of Governments: The Agency and Its Accomplishments, National Perspective, History, Legal Status*. Portland, OR: Columbia Region Association of Governments, 1977.

IBI Group. *Greater Toronto Region Urban Concepts Study*. Toronto: Office for the Greater Ontario Area, 1990.

– *The Implications of Alternative Growth Patterns on Infrastructure Costs*. Calgary, AB: Author, 2009.

Imbroscio, David. *Urban America Reconsidered: Alternatives for Policy and Governance*. Ithaca, NY: Cornell University Press, 2010.

Inglehart, Ronald. "The Silent Revolution in Europe: Intergenerational Change in Post-Industrial Societies." *American Political Science Review* 65, no. 4 (1971): 991–1017.

Initiative and Referendum Institute. "Initiative and Referendum Institute at the University of Southern California." University of Southern California, 2013. http://www.iandrinstitute.org/.

"Interim Joint Control of Sewage and Water Likely Merger Move." *Toronto Globe and Mail*, 7 July 1950.

"Interim Regional Land Use Plan." [Map]. Portland, OR: Columbia Region Association of Governments, 1970.

Interim Report of the Portland Metropolitan Study Commission. Salem, OR: Portland Metropolitan Study Commission, 1966.

Isin, Engin. *Cities without Citizens: Modernity of the City as a Corporation*. Montreal: Black Rose, 1992.

Israel, Roger R. "Images of an Organization: A New Historical and Theoretical Perspective on the Twin Cities Metropolitan Council." PhD diss., University of Southern California, 1996.

Iton, Richard. "The Backlash and the Quiet Revolution: The Contemporary Implications of Race and Language in the United States and Canada." In *Canada and the United States: Differences that Count*, edited by David M. Thomas, 141–64. Peterborough, ON: Broadview Press, 2000.

Ivanyna, Maksym, and Anwar Shah. "How Close Is Your Government to Its People? Worldwide Indicators on Localization and Decentralization." *Economics Discussion Papers: Kiel Institute for the World Economy*, no. 38 (2013).

Jabareen, Yosef. *The Risk City: Cities Countering Climate Change*. Dordrecht, NL: Springer, 2015.

Jacek, Henry J. "Regional Government and Development: Administrative Efficiency versus Local Democracy." Chap. 9 in *The Government and Politics of Ontario*, edited by Donald C. MacDonald, 145–64. Toronto: Van Nostrand Reinhold, 1980.

Jackson, Kenneth T. *Crabgrass Frontier: The Suburbanization of the United States*. New York: Oxford University Press, 1985.

Johnson, Charles K. *Standing at the Water's Edge: Bob Straub's Battle for the Soul of Oregon*. Corvallis: Oregon State University Press, 2012.

Johnson, Denny, Patricia E. Salkin, Jason Jordan, and Karen Finucan. *Planning for Smart Growth: 2002 State of the States*. Washington, DC: American Planning Association, 2002.

Johnson, Jeff. "Jeff Johnson for Governor: Issues." http://www.johnson forgovernor.org/issues. Accessed 12 June 2017.

Johnson, Katherine N. "'The Glorified Municipality': State Formation and the Urban Process in North America." *Political Geography* 27 (2008): 400–17.

"Joint Twin Cities Proposed but Only for Drainage Tax." *Minneapolis Journal*, 26 Aug. 1928.

Jonas, Andrew E.G., and Kevin Ward. "Introduction to a Debate on City-Regions: New Geographies of Governance, Democracy, and Social Reproduction." *International Journal of Urban and Regional Research* 31, no. 1 (2007): 169–78.

Jones, Elwood H. "Localism and Federalism in Upper Canada to 1865." Chap. 2 in *Federalism in Canada and Australia: The Early Years*, edited by Bruce W. Hodgins, Don Wright, and W.H. Heick, 19–41. Waterloo, ON: Wilfrid Laurier University Press, 1978.

Jones, Murray V., and T. John Connelly. *Review of the Official Regional Plan, Lower Mainland B.C.* Vancouver, 1977.

Jones, Victor. *Metropolitan Government*. Chicago: University of Chicago Press, 1942.

Kanter, Ron. *Space for All: Options for a Greater Toronto Area Greenlands Strategy*. Toronto: Government of Ontario, 1990.

Kanter, Rosabeth Moss. "Business Coalitions as a Force for Regionalism." Chap. 6 in *Reflections on Regionalism*, edited by Bruce Katz, 154–81. Washington, DC: Brookings Institution, 2000.

Kantor, Paul. *The Dependent City Revisited: The Political Economy of Urban Development and Social Policy*. Boulder, CO: Westview Press, 1995.

Kaszuba, Mike. "Met Council Ends Review of Subdivision Proposals." *Minneapolis Star-Tribune*, 9 April 1992.

Kaszuba, Mike, and Laurie Blake. "A Vision Clouded: Met Council's Future Uncertain as Its Influence Drops Sharply." *Minneapolis Star-Tribune*, 14 April 1991.

Katz, Bruce, and Jeremy Nowak. *The New Localism: How Cities Can Thrive in the Age of Populism*. Washington, DC: Brookings Institution Press, 2017.

Katznelson, Ira. *Fear Itself: The New Deal and the Origins of Our Time*. New York: Liveright Publishing, 2013.

Kavic, Lorne J., and Garry Brian Nixon. *The 1200 Days: A Shattered Dream – Dave Barrett and the NDP in BC, 1972–75*. Coquitlam, BC: Kaen Publishers, 1978.

Kearney, Richard C. "Sunset: A Survey and Analysis of the State Experience." *Public Administration Review* 50, no. 1 (1990): 49–57.

Keeling, Arn. "The Effluent Society: Water Pollution and Environmental Politics in British Columbia, 1889–1980." PhD diss., University of British Columbia, 2004.

– "Sink or Swim: Water Pollution and Environmental Politics in
  Vancouver, 1889–1975." *BC Studies* 142/143 (2004): 69–101.
Kennedy, Richard L. "Subject: Summary of Approaches to Metropollitan
  Government in the United States and Canada. Informational Report
  No. 5." Salem, OR: Legislative Interim Committee on Local
  Government, 1961.
Kennedy, W.P.M. *The Constitution of Canada, 1534–1937: An
  Introduction to Its Development, Law, and Custom.* 2nd ed. London:
  Oxford University Press, 1938.
Kerner, Otto. *Report of the National Advisory Commission on Civil
  Disorders.* New York: Bantam Books, 1968.
Kim, Jae Hong, and Nathan Jurey. "Local and Regional Governance
  Structures: Fiscal, Equity, and Environmental Outcomes." *Journal of
  Planning Literature* 28, no. 2 (2013): 111–23.
King, Desmond S. "The Establishment of Work-Welfare Programs in the
  United States and Britain: Politics, Ideas, and Institutions." Chap. 8 in
  Structuring Politics: Historical Institutionalism in Comparative Analysis,
  edited by Sven Steinmo, Kathleen Thelen, and Frank Longstreth, 217–
  50. New York: Cambridge University Press, 1992.
King, Desmond S., and Rogers M. Smith. "Racial Orders in American
  Political Development." *American Political Science Review* 99, no. 1
  (2005): 75–92.
Kirby, Alec, John F. Rothmann, and David G. Dalin. *Harold E. Stassen:
  The Life and Perennial Candidacy of the Progressive Republican.*
  Jefferson, NC: McFarland, 2013.
Klauda, Paul. "Latimer Talks of Metro Council's 'Receding Leadership.'"
  Minneapolis Star-Tribune, 14 Oct. 1989.
Knaap, Gerrit-Jan, and Rebecca Lewis. "Regional Planning for
  Sustainability and Hegemony of Metropolitan Regionalism." Chap. 7
  in *Regional Planning in America: Practice and Prospect*, edited by Ethan
  Seltzer and Armando Carbonell, 176–221. Cambridge, MA: Lincoln
  Institute of Land Policy, 2011.
Knaap, Gerrit-Jan, and Arthur C. Nelson. *The Regulated Landscape:
  Lessons on State Land Use Planning from Oregon.* Cambridge, MA:
  Lincoln Institute of Land Policy, 1992.
Knudson, Ed. *Regional Politics in the Twin Cities*. St. Paul, MN: Twin
  Cities Metropolitan Council, 1976.
Kolderie, Ted. *Governing the Twin Cities Area. Background Paper for the
  Conference on Governmental Structure, St. Thomas College, November*

10, 1966. Minneapolis: Upper Midwest Research and Development Council, 1966.

– "Metropolitan Unity: Time for Action." *Minneapolis Star*, 9–13 Jan. 1967.

– "Our Metropolitan Future." *Minneapolis Star*, 25–29 Oct. 1965.

Kolderie, Ted, and Paul Gilje. "The Citizens League: Report on Its Achievement of a Record of Cumulative Effectiveness in the Twin Cities Area." *National Civic Review* 65, no. 7 (July 1976): 322–42.

Kriger, David, Andreas Rose, Erhan Baydar, Jeff Moore, Lawrence Frank, Jim Chapman, and Alan E. Pisarski. *Urban Transportation Indicators, Fifth Survey*. Ottawa: Transportation Association of Canada, 2016.

Kulisek, Larry, and Trevor Price. "Ontario Municipal Policy Affecting Local Autonomy: A Case Study Involving Windsor and Toronto." *Urban History Review* 16, no. 3 (1988): 255–70.

Laidley, Thomas. "Measuring Sprawl: A New Index, Recent Trends, and Future Research." *Urban Affairs Review* 52, no. 1 (2016): 66–97.

Land for Farming. New Westminster, BC: Lower Mainland Regional Planning Board, 1962.

Land for Living: Outlook for Residential Development in the Lower Mainland. New Westminster, BC: Lower Mainland Regional Planning Board, 1963.

Lash, Harry. *Planning in a Human Way: Personal Reflections on the Regional Planning Experience in Greater Vancouver*. Ottawa: Ministry of State for Urban Affairs, Government of Canada, 1976.

Laskin, Bora. "The Ontario Municipal Board." Master's thesis, Harvard Law School, 1937.

"'Last Word' Should Be with Council." *Chilliwack (BC) Progress*, 9 March 1966.

Lemon, James. *Toronto since 1918*. Toronto: Lorimer, 1985.

Leo, Christopher. *The Politics of Urban Development: Canadian Urban Expressway Disputes*. Toronto: Institute of Public Administration of Canada, 1977.

Leonard, H. Jeffrey. *Managing Oregon's Growth: The Politics of Development Planning*. Washington, DC: Conservation Foundation, 1983.

Levine, Myron A. *Urban Politics: Cities and Suburbs in a Global Age*. 9th ed. New York: Routledge, 2015.

Lewis, Paul G. *Shaping Suburbia: How Political Institutions Organize Urban Development*. Pittsburgh: University of Pittsburgh Press, 1996.

Lewis, Rebecca, and Gerrit-Jan Knaap. "Institutional Structures for State Growth Management: An Examination of State Development Plans." *State and Local Government Review* 44, no. 1 (2012): 33–44.

Ley, David. "Gentrification and the Politics of the New Middle Class." *Environment and Planning D: Society and Space* 12, no. 1 (1994): 53–74.

Lijphart, Arend, ed. *Parliamentary versus Presidential Government.* Oxford: Oxford University Press, 1992.

– *Patterns of Democracy: Government Forms and Performance in Thirty-Six Countries.* 2nd ed. New Haven, CT: Yale University Press, 2012.

Linz, Juan J. "Democracy, Presidential or Parliamentary: Does It Make a Difference?" Chap. 1 in *The Failure of Presidential Democracy: The Case of Latin America*, edited by Juan J. Linz and Arturo Valenzuela, 3–89. Baltimore, MD: Johns Hopkins University Press, 1994.

Lipset, Seymour Martin. *Continental Divide: The Values and Institutions of the United States and Canada.* New York: Routledge, 1990.

The Livable Region 1976/1986: Proposals to Manage the Growth of Greater Vancouver. Burnaby, BC: Greater Vancouver Regional District, 1975.

The Livable Region Strategic Plan. Burnaby, BC: Greater Vancouver Regional District, 1996.

"LMRPB Plan Gets District Heave." *Langley (BC) Advance*, 14 July 1966.

"LMRPB Reaches First Decade." *Community Planning BC* [Newsletter of the BC Division of Community Planning Association of Canada] 11, no. 1 (1960).

Local Consent Requirements to State Law. St. Paul, MN: Citizens League, 1965.

Local Planning Bulletin 1: Development Districts. St. Paul, MN: Twin Cities Metropolitan Planning Commission, 1959.

Local Planning Bulletin 4: County Planning Guide. St. Paul, MN: Twin Cities Metropolitan Planning Commission, 1965.

Local Planning in the Twin Cities Metropolitan Area: A 1975 Inventory and Analysis. St. Paul, MN: Twin Cities Metropolitan Council, 1975.

Logan, John R., and Harvey L. Molotch. *Urban Fortunes: The Political Economy of Place.* 20th anniversary ed. Berkeley: University of California Press, 2007.

Lopez, Russell. "Urban Sprawl in the United States: 1970–2010." *Cities and the Environment* 7, no. 1 (2014), n.p.

Lopez, Russell, and H. Patricia Hynes. "Sprawl in the 1990s: Measurement, Distribution, and Trends." *Urban Affairs Review* 38, no. 3 (2003): 325–55.

The Lower Mainland Looks Ahead: A Report and Outline Plan for the Development of the Lower Mainland Region of British Columbia. New Westminster, BC: Lower Mainland Regional Planning Board, 1952.

Lowi, Theodore J. *The End of Liberalism: The Second Republic of the United States.* 2d ed. New York: W.W. Norton, 1979.

Lucas, Jack, and Robert Vipond. "Back to the Future: Historical Political Science and the Promise of Canadian Political Development." *Canadian Journal of Political Science* 50, no. 1 (2017): 219–41.

Lucia, Ellis. *The Conscience of a City: Fifty Years of City Club Service in Portland.* Portland, OR: City Club of Portland, 1966.

Lutz, Harley L. "State Supervision of Local Finance." *Journal of Political Economy* 43, no. 3 (June 1935): 289–305.

Macdonald, H. Ian. "A Retrospective View from the Top." *Plan Canada* 24, nos. 3/4 (1984): 92–9.

Magnusson, Warren. "Introduction: The Development of Canadian Urban Government." In *City Politics in Canada*, edited by Andrew Sancton and Warren Magnusson, 3–57. Toronto: University of Toronto Press, 1983.

– *Politics of Urbanism: Seeing Like a City.* New York: Routledge, 2011.

Magnusson, Warren, and William K. Carroll, eds. *The New Reality: The Politics of Restraint in British Columbia.* Vancouver: New Star Books, 1984.

Mahoney, James, and Kathleen Thelen. "A Theory of Gradual Institutional Change." Chap. 1 in *Explaining Institutional Change: Ambiguity, Agency, and Power*, edited by James Mahoney and Kathleen Thelen, 1–37. New York: Cambridge University Press, 2010.

Maitland, Andrea. "Powerful Land-Use Plan in Wings." *Vancouver Sun*, 26 Nov. 1979.

Malloy, Jonathan. "Prime Ministers and Their Parties in Canada." Chap. 7 in *Understanding Prime-Ministerial Performance: Comparative Perspectives*, edited by Paul Strangio, Paul 'T Hart, and James Walter, 151–71. Oxford: Oxford University Press, 2013.

Mancuso, Jo. "Rifle-Toting Meeting-Goer Rides Elevator to Jail." *Oregonian* (Portland, OR), 10 Feb. 1976.

– "Withdrawal from CRAG 'Political.'" *Oregonian* (Portland, OR), 16 Sept. 1976.

Mann, Michael. *The Sources of Social Power: The Rise of Classes and Nation-States, 1960–1914.* New York: Cambridge University Press, 1993.

Manning, Edward S., and Sandra S. Eddy. *The Agricultural Land Reserves of British Columbia: An Impact Analysis.* Ottawa: Lands Directorate, Environment Canada, 1978.

Manthorpe, Jonathan. *The Power and the Tories: Ontario Politics, 1943 to the Present.* Toronto: Macmillan, 1974.

Marohn, Charles. "Three Lessons from Muskegon, America's Strongest Town." 7 Sept. 2018. https://www.strongtowns.org/journal/2018/9/7/muskegon-americas-strongest-town.

Martin, Isaac William. *The Permanent Tax Revolt: How the Property Tax Transformed American Politics.* Stanford, CA: Stanford University Press, 2008.

Martin, Judith A. "In Fits and Starts: The Twin Cities Metropolitan Framework." Chap. 5 in *Metropolitan Governance: American/Canadian Intergovernmental Perspectives*, edited by Donald N. Rothblatt and Andrew Sancton, 205–41. Berkeley: Institute of Governmental Studies Press, University of California, 1993.

Matlin, John S. "The Citizens League of Minnesota." Master's thesis, Brunel University London, 2004.

Mayer, George H. *The Political Career of Floyd B. Olson.* Minneapolis: University of Minnesota Press, 1951.

"Mayor Invites Suburbs to Discuss Unification," *Toronto Globe and Mail*, 29 Feb. 1952.

"Mayors, Reeves Want Metro Vote." *Vancouver Sun*, 22 July 1960, 3.

McClintock, Thomas C. "Seth Lewelling, William S. U'ren and the Birth of the Oregon Progressive Movement." *Oregon Historical Quarterly* 68, no. 3 (1967): 196–220.

McConnell, Michael W., and Randal C. Picker. "When Cities Go Broke: A Conceptual Introduction to Municipal Bankruptcy." *University of Chicago Law Review* 60 (1993): 425–95.

McConnell, R.W. "Toronto May Be Forced to 'Adopt' Suburbs." *Toronto Evening Telegram*, 1 April 1939, 18.

McDougall, Allan Kerr. *John P. Robarts: His Life and Government.* Toronto: University of Toronto Press, 1986.

McKay, Floyd J. *An Editor for Oregon: Charles A. Sprague and the Politics of Change.* Corvallis: Oregon State University Press, 1998.

McKenty, Daniel Neil. *Mitch Hepburn.* Toronto: McClelland and Stewart, 1967.

McKeough, W. Darcy. *Toronto-Centred Region Program Statement.* Toronto: Government of Ontario, 1976.

McKinnon, Jesse. *The Black Population in the United States, March 2002.* Washington, DC: United States Census Bureau, 2003.

McLean, Bill. *Pathways to the Living City: The Story of the Toronto and Region Conservation Authority.* Toronto: Toronto and Region Conservation Authority, 2004.

Meadows, Donella, H., Dennis L. Meadows, Jørgen Randers, and William W. Behrens III. *The Limits to Growth: A Report for the Club of Rome's Project on the Predicaments of Mankind.* New York: Universe Books, 1972.

Meck, Stuart. "Model Planning and Zoning Enabling Legislation: A Short History." In *Modernizing State Plannng Statutes*, edited by Stuart Meck, 1–19. Washington, DC: American Planning Association, 1996.

Meeting the Challenge of Metropolitan Growth: A Prospectus for the Joint Program. St. Paul, MN: Joint Program/Twin Cities Metropolitan Planning Commission, 1963.

"Meeting to Launch Twin City Planning Commission Move." *Minneapolis Journal,* 14 Sept. 1923.

Meggs, Geoff, and Rod Mickleburgh. *The Art of the Impossible: Dave Barrett and the NDP in Power, 1972–1975.* Madeira Park, BC: Harbour Publishing, 2012.

Meligrana, John F. "Developing a Planning Strategy and Vision for Rural-Urban Fringe Areas: A Case Study of British Columbia." *Canadian Journal of Urban Research* 12, no. 1 (2003): 119–41.

– "Toward Regional Transportation Governance: A Case Study of Greater Vancouver." *Transportation* 26 (1999): 359–80.

"The Met Council Takes Housing Dive." *Minneapolis Star-Tribune,* 27 March 1993.

Metro: The Metropolitan Connection. Portland, OR: League of Women Voters of Portland, 1978.

"Metro Fringe Faces Crisis Too: Comay." *Toronto Star,* 14 May 1964, 3.

"The Metro Government Trend." *Minneapolis Star,* 14 April 1966.

"Metro Transit Finds Firmer Financial Footing – for Now." *Minneapolis Star-Tribune,* 15 June 2017.

Metro Vancouver 2040: Shaping Our Future. Burnaby, BC: Greater Vancouver Regional District Board, 2011.

Metro's Portfolio of Natural Areas, Parks and Trails: Opportunities and Challenges. Portland, OR: Portland Metro, 2011.

Metropolitan America: Challenge to Federalism. Washington, DC: Advisory Commission on Intergovernmental Relations, 1966.

"A Metropolitan Area." *Toronto Daily Star*, 1 Feb. 1924, 8.

"Metropolitan Area Advocated by Henry Is Carefully Studied." *Toronto Globe*, 2 Feb. 1924, 1, 14.

"Metropolitan Area Meets Opposition of Urban Boards." *Toronto Globe*, 3 March 1924, 2.

"Metropolitan Area Plan Means Mill and a Half Tax." *Toronto Daily Star*, 30 Jan. 1924, 5.

"Metropolitan Area Seems Unpopular with School Board." *Toronto Globe*, 21 Feb. 1924, 1.

A Metropolitan Council for the Twin Cities Area. Minneapolis: Citizens League, 1967.

Metropolitan Maze ... the Council-Watcher's Guide. St. Paul, MN: Council of Metropolitan Area Leagues of Women Voters, 1967.

"Metropolitan Plan Group Is Organized for 25 Mile Radius." *Minneapolis Journal*, 10 Jan. 1924.

"Metropolitan Planning Board Maps 1,000 Mile Program, Engineers Club Votes Funds." *Minneapolis Journal*, 17 Jan. 1925.

"A Metropolitan Problem." *Toronto Evening Telegram*, 14 Aug. 1951.

Metropolitan Sewerage Study. Metropolitan Planning Reports. St. Paul, MN: Twin Cities Metropolitan Planning Commission, 1960.

"Metropolitan Unit Financing Starts." *Minneapolis Journal*, 7 Dec. 1924.

Mettler, Suzanne. *Dividing Citizens: Gender and Federalism in New Deal Public Policy*. Ithaca, NY: Cornell University Press, 1998.

Mick, Kerwin L. "The Minneapolis-Saint Paul Sanitary District: Operation and Expansion." *Journal* (Water Pollution Control Federation) 39, no. 10 (1967): 1684–700.

Miller, David Y., and Raymond W. Cox. *Governing the Metropolitan Region: America's Next Frontier*. Armonk, NY: M.E. Sharpe, 2014.

Miller, David Y., and Joo Hun Lee. "Making Sense of Metropolitan Regions: A Dimensional Approach to Regional Governance." *Publius* 41, no. 1 (2009): 126–45.

Miller, David Y., and Jen Nelles. *Discovering American Regionalism: An Introduction to Regional Intergovernmental Organizations*. New York: Routledge, 2018.

Miller, Richard James. "Minneapolis–St. Paul: An Analysis of Metropolitan Cooperation." Master's thesis, University of Wisconsin, 1968.

Milner, J.B. "Statutes: The Regional Municipality of Ottawa-Carleton Act, 1968." *University of Toronto Law Journal* 19 (1969): 80–5.

"Mimico Supports City in Area Amalgamation," *Toronto Globe and Mail*, 8 Sept. 1950.

"Minister to Call Parley on Metro." *Vancouver Province*, 20 July 1957.

"Minneapolis Foes Renew Attack on Metropolitan Zone." *Minneapolis Journal*, 19 March 1925.

Minnesota. *Protecting the Environment through Regulation of Land Use.* St. Paul, MN: State Planning Agency, 1972.

– *Report.* St. Paul, MN: Commission on Municipal Annexation and Consolidation, 1959.

– *Report.* St. Paul, MN: Commission on Municipal Laws, 1961.

Miron, John R. "Urban Sprawl in Canada and America: Just How Similar?" Paper presented at the Annual Meeting of the Association of American Geographers. New Orleans, 2003.

Mitau, G. Theodore. *Politics in Minnesota.* 2nd ed. Minneapolis: University of Minnesota Press, 1970.

Mitchell, David Joseph. *W.A.C. Bennett and the Rise of British Columbia.* Vancouver: Douglas and McIntyre, 1983.

Modernizing Local Government to Secure a Balanced Federalism: A Statement on National Policy. New York: Committee for Economic Development, 1966.

Moe, Terry M., and Michael Caldwell. "The Institutional Foundations of Democratic Government: A Comparison of Presidential and Parliamentary Systems." *Journal of Institutional and Theoretical Economics* 150, no. 1 (1994): 171–95.

Mondale, Ted, and William Fulton. *Managing Metropolitan Growth: Reflections on the Twin Cities Experience.* Washington, DC: Brookings Institution, 2003.

Montague, Richard W. "Government in the Portland Metropolitan Area: A Report by the Government Simplification Commission to the Governor of Oregon." *Portland City Club Bulletin* 7, no. 14 (1926): 1–12.

– "Law of Municipal Home Rule in Oregon." *California Law Review* 8 (1919): 151–68.

Moore, Peter W. "Public Services and Residential Development in a Toronto Neighbourhood, 1880–1915." *Journal of Urban History* 9, no. 4 (1983): 445–71.

"Mr. Henry's Project." *Toronto Globe*, 12 Feb. 1924, 4.

Mullins, William H. "'I'll Wreck the Town If It Will Give Employment':
Portland in the Hoover Years of the Depression." *Pacific Northwest
Quarterly* 79, no. 3 (1988): 109–18.

"Municipal Officials Favor Board for Development of Recreational
Areas." *Vancouver Province*, 12 Aug. 1961.

Munro, Harold. "Councils Resist GVRD Population Targets as Voters
Oppose Growth." *Vancouver Sun*, 14 May 1998, B4.

– "GVRD, Port Moody at Odds over Population Growth." *Vancouver
Sun*, 30 May 1998, B1.

Munro, William Bennett. *American Influences on Canadian Government*.
Toronto: Macmillan, 1929.

– *The Government of American Cities*. New York: Macmillan, 1919.

Murrell, Gary. *Iron Pants: Oregon's Anti-New Deal Governor, Charles
Henry Martin*. Pullman: Washington State University Press, 2000.

Nathanson, Iric. *Minneapolis in the Twentieth Century: The Growth of
an American City*. St. Paul: Minnesota Historical Society Press, 2010.

Nelles, Jen. *Comparative Metropolitan Policy: Governing beyond Local
Boundaries in the Imagined Metropolis*. New York: Routledge, 2012.

Nevitte, Neil. *The Decline of Deference: Canadian Value Change in Cross-
National Perspective*. Peterborough, ON: Broadview Press, 1996.

"New Metropolitan Area Group Formed to Draft Master Development
Plan." *Minneapolis Journal*, 11 Jan. 1927.

Newman, Peter, and Jeffrey R. Kenworthy. *Sustainability and Cities:
Overcoming Automobile Dependence*. Washington, DC: Island Press,
1999.

1999 Annual Report: Livable Region Strategic Plan. Burnaby, BC: Greater
Vancouver Regional District, 1999.

1992 Metro Charter. Portland, OR: Metro Charter Committee, 1992.

*1968 State Legislative Program of the Advisory Commission on
Intergovernmental Relations (M-35)*. Washington, DC: Advisory
Commission on Intergovernmental Relations, 1967.

1965 Annual Report. St. Paul, MN: Twin Cities Metropolitan Planning
Commission, 1966.

1967–1968 Biennial Report to the Minnesota Legislature. St. Paul, MN:
Twin Cities Metropolitan Council, 1969.

1965–1966 Biennial Report to the Minnesota Legislature. St. Paul, MN:
Twin Cities Metropolitan Planning Commission, 1967.

1963 Annual Report: A Year of Intergovernmental Action. St. Paul, MN:
Twin Cities Metropolitan Planning Commission, 1964.

"No Magician's Wand." *Toronto Daily Star*, 18 April 1950.

Noel, S.J.R. "Oliver Mowat, Patronage, and Party Building." In *Ontario since Confederation: A Reader*, edited by Edgar-André Montigny and Lori Chambers, 94–104. Toronto: University of Toronto Press, 2000.

– *Patrons, Clients, Brokers: Ontario Society and Politics, 1791–1896*. Toronto: University of Toronto Press, 1990.

Norris, Donald F. "Prospects for Regional Governance under the New Regionalism: Economic Imperatives Versus Political Impediments." *Journal of Urban Affairs* 25, no. 3 (2001): 557–71.

Norris, Donald F., Don Phares, and Tonya Zimmerman. "Metropolitan Government in the United States? Not Now ... Not Likely." In *Governing Metropolitan Regions in the 21st Century*, edited by Don Phares, 11–38. Armonk, NY: M.E. Sharpe, 2009.

Norton, Alan. *International Handbook of Local and Regional Government*. Cheltenham, UK: Edward Elgar, 1994.

Oberlander, H. Peter. "Ottawa and the Ottawa Valley: A Critical Analysis of a Regional Concept." Master's thesis, School of City Planning, Harvard University, 1946.

Oberlander, H. Peter, and Eva Newbrun. *Houser: The Life and Work of Catherine Bauer*. Vancouver: UBC Press, 1999.

Official Regional Plan of the Lower Mainland Planning Area. New Westminster, BC: Lower Mainland Regional Planning Board, 1966.

Ogorzalek, Thomas K. *The Cities on the Hill: How Urban Institutions Transform National Politics*. New York: Oxford University Press, 2018.

Ohm, Brian W. "Growth Management in Minnesota: The Metropolitan Land Planning Act." *Hamline Law Review* 16 (1992–93): 359–87.

– "Reviving Comprehensive Planning in the Twin Cities Metropolitan Area: The 1995 Amendments to the MLPA." *Minnesota Real Estate Law Journal* 8, no. 6 (1995): 81–6.

1000 Friends. *Making the Connections. A Summary of the LUTRAQ Project: Integrating Land-Use and Transportation Planning for Livable Communities*. Portland, OR: 1000 Friends of Oregon, 1997.

Ontario. *Built Boundary for the Growth Plan for the Greater Golden Horseshoe, 2006*. Toronto: Ministry of Public Infrastructure Renewal, 2008.

– *Choices for a Growing Region*. Vol. 2. Toronto: Metropolitan Toronto and Region Transportation Study, 1967.

– *Design for Development: The Toronto-Centred Region*. Toronto: Department of Treasury and Economics, Regional Development Branch, 1970.

– *First Report of the Commission on Municipal Institutions*. Vol. 1. Toronto: Warwick and Sons, 1888.

- *Government Reform in Ontario.* Toronto: Ontario Economic Council, 1969.
- *Greenbelt Plan, 2005.* Toronto: Ministry of Municipal Affairs and Housing, 2005.
- *Growing Together: Towards an Urban Consensus in the Greater Toronto Area.* Toronto: Office for the Greater Toronto Area, 1991.
- *Growth and Travel, Past and Present.* Vol. 1. Toronto: Metropolitan Toronto and Region Transportation Study, 1966.
- *GTA 2021. The Challenge of Our Future: A Working Document.* Toronto: Office for the Greater Toronto Area, 1992.
- *Municipal Reform: A Proposal for the Future.* Toronto: Ontario Economic Council, 1971.
- *Oak Ridges Moraine Conservation Plan.* Toronto: Ministry of Municipal Affairs and Housing, 2002.
- *Places to Grow: Growth Plan for the Greater Golden Horseshoe.* Toronto: Ministry of Public Infrastructure Renewal, 2006.
- *Report.* Toronto: Planning Act Review Committee, 1977.
- *Report of Conference on Planning and Development Held at Toronto, Ontario, May 8th and 9th, 1944.* Toronto: Department of Planning and Development, 1944.
- *Report of the GTA Task Force.* Toronto: GTA Task Force, 1996.
- *Report of the Royal Commission on Border Cities Amalgamation.* Toronto: Department of Municipal Affairs, 1935.
- *Report to the Advisory Committee on Urban and Regional Planning.* Toronto: Central Ontario Lakeshore Urban Complex Task Force, 1974.
- *Shaping Growth in the GTA: A Commentary Report.* Toronto: Office for the Greater Toronto Area, 1992.
- *Transportation for the Regional City: Statement of Principles and Recommendations.* Vol. 3. Toronto: Metropolitan Toronto and Region Transportation Study, 1967.
- *White Paper on the Planning Act.* Toronto: Ministry of Housing, 1979.
Oregon. *Final Report.* 1987–88 Interim Task Force on Metropolitan Regional Government, Oregon State Legislature, 1988.
- *Findings and Recommendations of the Joint Legislative Interim Committee on Local Government: Prepared in Accordance with Senate Joint Resolution 31, Oregon Laws, 1955.* Salem, OR: Joint Legislative Interim Committee on Local Government, 1956.
- *Metropolitan and Urban Area Problems in Oregon: Findings of the Legislative Interim Committee on Local Government. Prepared in*

Accordance with House Joint Resolution 23, Fifty-First Legislative Assembly. Salem, OR: Legislative Interim Committee on Local Government, Oregon, 1963.

– *Oregon Blue Book*. Salem, OR: Secretary of State, Oregon, 1947.

– *Problems of the Urban Fringe*. Vol. 2. *Portland Area*. Salem, OR: Legislative Interim Commitee on Local Government, Oregon, 1956.

Oregon Looks Ahead. Salem, OR: Oregon State Planning Board, 1938.

Orfield, Myron. *Metropolitics: A Regional Agenda for Community and Stability*. Washington, DC: Brookings Institution and the Lincoln Institute of Land Policy, 1997.

– "Politics and Regionalism." Chap. 9 in *Urban Sprawl: Causes, Consequences, and Policy Responses*, edited by Gregory D. Squires, 237–54. Washington, DC: Urban Institute Press, 2002.

Orfield, Myron, and Thomas F. Luce Jr. *Region: Planning the Future of the Twin Cities*. Minneapolis: University of Minnesota Press, 2009.

Orfield, Myron, and Nicholas Wallace. "The Minnesota Fiscal Disparities Act of 1971: The Twin Cities' Struggle and Blueprint for Regional Cooperation." *William Mitchell Law Review* 33 (2006–7): 591–612.

Ormsby, Margaret A. "T. Dufferin Pattullo and the Little New Deal." *Canadian Historical Review* 43, no. 4 (1962): 277–97.

Ornstein, Michael. *Ethno-Racial Groups in Montreal and Vancouver, 1971–2001: A Demographic and Socio-Economic Profile*. Toronto: Institute for Social Research, York University, 2007.

– *Ethno-Racial Groups in Toronto, 1971–2001: A Demographic and Socio-Economic Profile*. Toronto: Institute for Social Research, York University, 2006.

Orren, Karen, and Stephen Skowronek. *The Search for American Political Development*. Cambridge: Cambridge University Press, 2004.

Ostrom, Vincent, Charles M. Tiebout, and Robert Warren. "The Organization of Government in Metropolitan Areas: A Theoretical Inquiry." *American Political Science Review* 55, no. 4 (1961): 831–42.

Our Southwestern Shores. New Westminster, BC: Lower Mainland Regional Planning Board, 1968.

Owram, Doug. *The Government Generation: Canadian Intellectuals and the State, 1900–1945*. Toronto: University of Toronto Press, 1986.

Pagliero, Jennifer. "How Kathleen Wynne's Liberals Secretly Helped Kill the Scarborough LRT." *Toronto Star*, 5 June 2018.

Pagliero, Jennifer, and Ben Spurr. "Cost of Scarborough Subway Extension Rises to $3.35 Billion as Number of New Riders Fall." *Toronto Star*, 28 Feb. 2017.

"Panel to Evaluate Direction of CRAG." *Oregonian* (Portland, OR), 16 May 1972.

Papers and Discussion Outlines, Public Information Program, Urban Growth Policies Report No. 1. Urban Growth Workshop. Salem, OR: Mid-Willamette Valley Council of Governments, 1972.

Pastor, Manuel, Chris Benner, and Martha Matsuoka. *This Could Be the Start of Something Big: How Social Movements for Regional Equity Are Reshaping Metropolitan America.* Ithaca, NY: Cornell University Press, 2009.

Patterson, James T. *Congressional Conservatism and the New Deal: The Growth of the Conservative Coalition in Congress, 1933–1939.* Lexington: University of Kentucky Press, 1967.

Patton, Clifford W. *The Battle for Municipal Reform: Mobilization and Attack, 1875 to 1900.* Washington, DC: American Council on Public Affairs, 1940.

Paulsen, Kurt. "Geography, Policy or Market? New Evidence on the Measurement and Causes of Sprawl (and Infill) in US Metropolitan Regions." *Urban Studies* 51, no. 12 (2014): 2629–45.

Peirce, Neal R. *Citistates: How Urban America Can Prosper in a Competitive World.* Washington, DC: Seven Locks Press, 1993.

Pendall, Rolf, Kathryn Ann Foster, and Margaret Cowell. "Resilience and Regions: Building Understanding of the Metaphor." *Cambridge Journal of Regions, Economy and Society* 3, no. 1 (2010): 71–84.

Pendall, Rolf, Jonathan Martin, and William Fulton. *Holding the Line: Urban Containment in the United States.* Washington, DC: Brookings Institution, Center on Urban and Metropolitan Policy, 2002.

The People and the Plan: The Reactions of a Number of Organizations to the Regional Plan Report Chance and Challenge. New Westminster, BC: Lower Mainland Regional Planning Board, 1964.

Perry, H.G.T. *Reports of the Post-War Rehabilitation Council: The Interim Report (1943) and Supplementary Report (1944).* Victoria, BC: Government of British Columbia, 1944.

Peterson, Paul. *City Limits.* Chicago: University of Chicago Press, 1981.

Petter, Andrew. "Sausage Making in British Columbia's NDP Government: The Creation of the Land Commission Act, August 1972–April 1973." *BC Studies*, no. 65 (1985): 3–33.

Pierre, Jon. *The Politics of Urban Governance.* London: Palgrave Macmillan, 2011.

Pinchbeck, Raymond B. "City-County Separation in Virginia." *National Municipal Review* 29, no. 7 (1940): 467–72.

Pinel, Sandra Lee. "Regional Planning as Mediation: Inside Minnesota's Metropolitan Twin Cities Regional Plan Implementation." *Journal of Environmental Policy and Planning* 13, no. 4 (2011): 399–420.

Pisarski, Alan E. *Commuting in America III.* Washington, DC: Transportation Research Board, 2006.

Piva, Michael J. *The Borrowing Process: Public Finance in the Province of Canada, 1840–1867.* Ottawa: University of Ottawa Press, 1992.

– "Government Finance and the Development of the Canadian State." Chap. 9 in *Colonial Leviathan: State Formation in Mid-Nineteenth-Century Canada,* edited by Allan Greer and Ian Radforth, 257–83. Toronto: University of Toronto Press, 1992.

Plan for the Lower Mainland of British Columbia. Burnaby, BC: Central Fraser Valley Regional District, Dewdney-Allouette Regional District, Greater Vancouver Regional District, and Regional District of Fraser Cheam, 1980.

Planning by Local Government in Oregon. Prepared for the Oregon Department of Planning and Development. Eugene, OR: Bureau of Municipal Research and Service, 1963.

"Planning Chief Metro 'Black Sheep.'" *Toronto Telegram,* 14 May 1964.

"Planning Group Begins Work Here." *Minneapolis Journal,* 30 Dec. 1928.

Planning in the CRAG Region: An Appraisal and New Direction. Portland, OR: Columbia Region Association of Governments, 1972.

Planning in the CRAG Region: The Second Step. Portland, OR: Columbia Region Association of Governments, 1973.

"Planning Is Basis." *Toronto Globe and Mail,* 17 June 1950.

"Planning Unit Head Asks Aid." *Minneapolis Journal,* 16 Aug. 1928.

"Planning's Death Sentence." *Vancouver Sun,* 18 Feb. 1969.

Plumptre, Arthur FitzWalter Wynne. *Report on the Government of the Metropolitan Area of Toronto to the Hon. David Croll, Minister of Municipal Affairs in the Province of Ontario.* Toronto: Department of Political Science and Economics, University of Toronto, 1935.

Plunkett, Thomas J. *Report of the Peel-Halton Local Government Review.* Toronto: Government of Ontario, 1966.

Polzin, Steven E., and Alan E. Pisarski. *Commuting in America, 2013: The National Report on Commuting Patterns and Trends.* Brief 4. *Population and Worker Dynamics.* Washington, DC: American Association of State Highway and Transportation Officials, 2013.

Pontusson, Jonas. *Inequality and Prosperity: Social Europe vs Liberal America.* Ithaca, NY: Cornell University Press, 2005.

Poradek, James. "Putting the Use Back in Metropolitan Land-Use
    Planning: Private Enforcement of Urban Sprawl Control Laws."
    University of Minnesota Law Review 81 (1996): 1343–75.
Portland Metropolitan Study Commission. "Anticipating the Challenges of
    Tomorrow or Continuing the Governmental Burial of Marvin Metro?"
    Brochure. Portland, OR: Author, 1968.
Powell, John A. "Addressing Regional Dilemmas for Minority
    Communities." Chap. 8 in *Reflections on Regionalism*, edited by Bruce
    Katz, 218–46. Washington, DC: Brookings Institution, 2000.
Price, Marvin James. "The Portland Boundary Commission: A Case
    Study." PhD diss., Department of Urban Studies, Portland State
    University, 1979.
Pritchett, Wendell E. "Which Urban Crisis? Regionalism, Race, and Urban
    Policy, 1960–1974." *Journal of Urban History* 34, no. 2 (2008):
    266–86.
Proposed CRAG Land Use Framework Element. Portland, OR: Columbia
    Region Association of Governments, 1976.
"Proposes Area Board to Handle Services without a Merger." *Toronto
    Evening Telegram*, 18 Jan. 1951.
Puil, George. "Regional District Must Renegotiate Skytrain Costs with the
    Provincial Government." *Vancouver Sun*, 31 July 1998, A19.
Putnam, Robert D. *Bowling Alone: The Collapse and Revival of American
    Community*. New York: Simon and Schuster, 2000.
– *Making Democracy Work: Civic Traditions in Modern Italy*. Princeton,
    NJ: Princeton University Press, 1993.
Pynn, Larry. "Richmond, GVRD Reach Compromise." *Vancouver Sun*,
    20 April 1998, B1.
Ramsay, Jack. "Restrain Planners, Minister Urges." *Vancouver Sun*,
    22 Nov. 1968.
"Rap Federation, Union Men Urge Amalgamation." *Toronto Globe and
    Mail*, 30 Feb. 1953.
"Rapid Expansion Hits Municipalities: North York Has Difficulty in
    Selling Debentures." *Toronto Globe and Mail*, 31 March 1951.
Rasch, Bjørn Erik. "Institutional Foundations of Legislative Agenda-
    Setting." Chap. 22 in *The Oxford Handbook of Legislative Studies*,
    edited by Shane Martin, Thomas Saalfeld, and Kaare W. Strøm, 455–80.
    Oxford: Oxford University Press, 2014.
Rashleigh, Ted. *A Documentary Review of the GVRD Livable Region
    Program, 1970–1975*. Burnaby, BC: Greater Vancouver Regional
    District, 1997.

- "A Progress Report on B.C.'s Regional Districts." *Community Planning Review* (Winter 1966): 9.

Rawn, A.M., Charles Gilman Hyde, and John Oliver. *Sewerage and Drainage Survey of the Greater Vancouver Area, British Columbia: A Report to the Chairman and Members, Vancouver and Districts Joint Sewerage and Drainage Board.* Vancouver, BC: Vancouver and Districts Joint Sewerage and Drainage Board, 1953.

"Ray Concedes Metro Would Lose in Vote." *Vancouver Sun*, 30 May 1961.

Ray, Hugo. *Final Report.* Vancouver, BC: Metropolitan Joint Committee, 1960.

Razin, Eran, and Mark Rosentraub. "Are Fragmentation and Sprawl Interlinked? North American Evidence." *Urban Affairs Review* 35, no. 6 (2000): 821–36.

Real Estate Research Corporation. *The Costs of Sprawl: Environmental and Economic Costs of Alternative Residential Development Patterns at the Urban Fringe.* Washington, DC: Environmental Protection Agency, 1974.

"Regional Board Starts Plan for 3,000-Mile Area." *Minneapolis Journal*, 24 June 1928.

Regional Fixed Guideway Study. St. Paul, MN: Twin Cities Area Metropolitan Transit Commission, 1972.

"Regional Leaders on Transportation Bill: Thank You State Lawmakers, 'Let's Keep Our Wheels Rolling.'" Portland Metro, 30 Aug. 2017. http://www.oregonmetro.gov/news/regional-leaders-transportation-bill-thank-you-state-lawmakers-lets-keep-our-wheels-rolling.

Regional Park System: Legislative History, Process, Capital, and Operation/Maintenance Financing. St. Paul, MN: Metropolitan Parks and Open Space Commission, 1987.

"Regional Plan a Good Beginning Despite Its Flaws." *Vancouver Sun*, 27 Oct. 1995, A22.

"Regional Plan Effect Will Be Studied." *Langley (BC) Advance*, 23 Sept. 1965.

"Regional Plan Gets Opposition." *Surrey (BC) Leader*, 19 March 1980.

Regional Urban Growth Goals and Objectives. Ord. No. 91-418b. Portland, OR: Portland Metro, 1991.

Reichert, Peggy A. *Growth Management in the Twin Cities Area.* St. Paul, MN: Twin Cities Metropolitan Council, 1976.

Relph, Edward. *The Modern Urban Landscape.* Baltimore, MD: Johns Hopkins University Press, 1987.

Report No. 1, February 20, 1969 [Broome Report]. Vancouver: Political and Administrative Structure Review Committee, Greater Vancouver Regional District, 1969.

Report of the Committee on Administrative Units. St. Paul, MN: Minnesota State Planning Board, 1934.

Report of the Committee on Taxation. St. Paul, MN: Minnesota State Planning Board, 1934.

Report of the Metropolitan Committee. St. Paul, MN: Minnesota State Planning Board, 1934.

A Report on the Minnesota Municipal Commission Submitted to Governor Harold Levander. St. Paul, MN: Minnesota Municipal Commission, 1967.

Report of the Minnesota State Planning Board. Part 1. Digest and Interpretations. St. Paul, MN: Minnesota State Planning Board, 1934.

Report of the Minnesota State Planning Board. Part 1: Digest and Interpretations. St. Paul, MN: Minnesota State Planning Board, 1936.

"Research Bureau Views Held Akin to Marxism by Forest Hill's Counsel." *Toronto Globe and Mail,* 13 Sept. 1950.

Resnick, Philip. "Neo-Conservatism on the Periphery: The Lessons from B.C." *BC Studies* 75 (1987): 3–23.

– "Social Democracy in Power: The Case of British Columbia." *BC Studies* 34 (1977): 3–20.

Rhees, Suzanne S. *Minnesota's Planning and Zoning Enabling Laws: Analysis and Options for Reform.* St. Paul, MN: American Planning Association – Minnesota, 2013.

Rich, A. McKay. Interview by Rebecca Shoemaker and Gregory Cross. Transcript. Portland Metro Oral History Project, 13 April 2007.

Rich, Amasa McKay. "The Politics of Governmental Reorganization in the Portland Metropolitan Area since 1955." PhD diss., University of Idaho, 1967.

Richardson, Arthur Herbert. *Conservation by the People: The History of the Conservation Movement in Ontario to 1970.* Toronto: University of Toronto Press, 1974.

Richardson, Nigel H. "Guest Editor's Foreword." *Plan Canada* 24, nos. 3/4 (1984): 88–91.

– "Insubstantial Pageant: The Rise and Fall of Provincial Planning in Ontario." *Canadian Public Administration* 24, no. 4 (1981): 563–85.

Richmond, Dale, and David Siegel, eds. *Agencies, Boards, and Commissions in Canadian Local Government.* Toronto: Institute of Public Administration of Canada, 1994.

"Richmond Considers Separation from GVRD." *Vancouver Sun*, 28 Oct. 1995, A14.

"Richmond Says Metro Won't Solve Problems." *Vancouver Province*, 26 Sept. 1961.

Riendeau, Roger E. "A Clash of Interests: Dependency and the Municipal Problem in the Great Depression." *Journal of Canadian Studies* 14, no. 1 (Spring 1979): 50–8.

Robarts, John C. *Design for Development: Phase Two*. Toronto: Government of Ontario, 1968.

– *Design for Development: Statement by the Prime Minister of the Province of Ontario on Regional Development Policy*. Toronto: Government of Ontario, 1966.

– *Report of the Royal Commission on Metropolitan Toronto*. Toronto: Government of Ontario, 1977.

Robbins, William G. *Landscapes of Conflict: The Oregon Story, 1940–2000*. Seattle: University of Washington Press, 2004.

– *Landscapes of Promise: The Oregon Story, 1800–1940*. Seattle: University of Washington Press, 1997.

Robin, Martin. *Pillars of Profit: The Company Province, 1934–1972*. Toronto: McClelland and Stewart, 1973.

Romney, Paul. "From the Rule of Law to Responsible Government: Ontario Political Culture and the Origins of Canadian Statism." Canadian Historical Association *Historical Papers/Communications historiques* 23, no. 1 (1988): 86–119.

Roper, Eric. "Budget Bill Could Invite More Challenges of Met Council's Regional Plans." *Minneapolis Star-Tribune*, 31 May 2017.

– "Insert in Bonding Bill Erodes Met Council Planning Power." *Minneapolis Star-Tribune*, 24 May 2018.

– "Senate OKs Bill to Overhaul the Met Council." *Minneapolis Star-Tribune*, 8 May 2017.

Rosan, Christina D. *Governing the Fragmented Metropolis: Planning for Regional Sustainability*. Philadelphia: University of Pennsylvania Press, 2016.

Rose, Albert. *Governing Metropolitan Toronto: A Social and Political Analysis, 1953–1971*. Berkeley: University of California Press, 1972.

Rothblatt, Donald N. "Summary and Conclusions." Chap. 10 in *Metropolitan Governance: American/Canadian Intergovernmental Perspectives*, edited by Donald N. Rothblatt and Andrew Sancton, 433–66. Berkeley: Institute of Governmental Studies Press, University of California, 1993.

Roy, Patricia E. "Direct Management from Abroad: The Formative Years of the British Columbia Electric Railway." *Business History Review* 47, no. 2 (1973): 239–59.

Ruble, Web. "Service District to Weigh Future." *Oregonian* (Portland, OR), 24 May 1975.

Rusk, David. *Inside Game/Outside Game*. Washington, DC: Brookings Institution Press, 1999.

Rutherford, Paul. "Introduction." In *Saving the Canadian City: The First Phase 1880–1920*, edited by Paul Rutherford, ix–xxiii. Toronto: University of Toronto Press, 1974.

– "Tomorrow's Metropolis: The Urban Reform Movement in Canada, 1880–1920." Canadian Historical Association *Historical Papers/Communications historiques* 6, no. 1 (1971): 203–24.

Samuelson, Paul A. "The Pure Theory of Public Expenditure." *Review of Economics and Statistics* 36, no. 4 (1954): 387–9.

Sancton, Andrew. *Canadian Local Government: An Urban Perspective*. Don Mills, ON: Oxford University Press, 2011.

– "Differing Approaches to Municipal Restructuring in Montreal and Toronto: From the Pichette Report to the Greater Toronto Services Board." *Canadian Journal of Regional Science* 22, nos. 1/2 (1999): 187–99.

– *Governing the Island of Montreal: Language Differences and Metropolitan Politics*. Berkeley: University of California Press, 1985.

Sandberg, L. Anders, Gerda R. Wekerle, and Liette Gilbert. *The Oak Ridges Moraine Battles: Development, Sprawl, and Nature Conservation in the Toronto Region*. Toronto: University of Toronto Press, 2013.

Satterthwaite, David, Saleemul Huq, Mark Pelling, Hannah Reid, and Patricia Romero Lankao. *Adapting to Climate Change in Urban Areas*. London: International Institute for Environment and Development, 2007.

Saunderson, P.A. *Submission to the Government of Ontario on Design for Development: The Toronto-Centred Region*. Toronto: Urban Development Institute, 1970.

Savitch, Hank V., and Sarin Adhikari. "Fragmented Regionalism: Why Metropolitan America Continues to Splinter." *Urban Affairs Review* 53, no. 2 (2017): 381–402.

Savitch, Hank V., and Paul Kantor. *Cities in the International Marketplace: The Political Economy of Urban Development in North America and Western Europe*. Princeton, NJ: Princeton University Press, 2002.

Savitch, Hank V., and Ronald K. Vogel. "Introduction: Paths to New Regionalism." *State and Local Government Review* 32, no. 3 (2000): 158–68.

Sbragia, Alberta M. *Debt Wish: Entrepreneurial Cities, US Federalism, and Economic Development*. Pittsburgh: University of Pittsburgh Press, 1996.

Schickler, Eric. *Racial Realignment: The Transformation of American Liberalism, 1932–1965*. Princeton, NJ: Princeton University Press, 2016.

Schlesinger, Arthur Meier. *The Rise of the City, 1878–1898*. New York: Macmillan, 1933.

Scott, Allen, and Michael Storper. "Regions, Globalization, Development." *Regional Studies* 37, nos. 6/7 (2003): 579–93.

Scott, Mel. *American City Planning since 1890*. Berkeley: University of California Press, 1971.

Segoe, Ladislas. *Local Planning Administration*. Chicago: International City Managers' Association, 1941.

"Sees 5,000,000 Living in Toronto in 50 Years." *Toronto Globe and Mail*, 30 Jan. 1951.

Selected Determinants of Residential Development. Background Document No. 1. St. Paul, MN: Twin Cities Metropolitan Planning Commission, 1962.

Sellers, Jefferey M. "The Nation-State and Urban Governance: Toward Multilevel Analysis." *Urban Affairs Review* 37, no. 5 (2002): 611–41.

Sellers, Jefferey M., and Sun-Young Kwak. "State and Society in Local Governance: Lessons from a Multilevel Comparison." *International Journal of Urban and Regional Research* 35, no. 3 (2011): 620–43.

Seltzer, Ethan. "Land Use Planning in Oregon: The Quilt and the Struggle for Scale." Chap. 2 in *Planning for States and Nation-States in the US and Europe*, edited by Gerrit-Jan Knaap, Zorca Nedovic-Budic and Armando Carbonell, 53–89. Cambridge, MA: Lincoln Institute of Land Policy, 2015.

– "Regional Planning and Local Governance: The Portland Story." Chap. 14 in *Sustainable City Regions: Space, Place and Govenance*, edited by Tetsuo Kidokoro, Noboru Harata, Leksono Probo Subanu, Johann Jessen, Alain Motte, and Ethan Seltzer, 277–98. Tokyo: Springer, 2008.

Seltzer, Ethan, and Armando Carbonell. "Regional Practice, Regional Prospect." Chap. 10 in *Regional Planning in America: Practice and Prospect*, edited by Ethan Seltzer and Armando Carbonell, 269–77. Cambridge, MA: Lincoln Institute of Land Policy, 2011.

"Seven New Faces on Metro Board." *Vancouver Province*, 19 Jan. 1960, 16.

Seymour, Douglas. "Board Lacks Public Trust, Solon Claims." *Oregonian* (Portland, OR), 25 Feb. 1972, 19.

Shah, Anwar, and S. Shah. "The New Vision of Local Governance and the Evolving Roles of Local Governments." In *Local Governance in Developing Countries*, edited by Anwar Shah, 1–46. Washington, DC: World Bank, 2006.

Sharifi, Amir H. "The Twin Cities Metropolitan Planning Commission: Its Background, Formation, and Early Development." BA thesis, University of Minnesota, 1960.

Shaw, Kate. "Planetary Urbanisation: What Does It Matter for Politics or Practice?" *Planning Theory and Practice* 16, no. 4 (2015): 588–93.

Shepsle, Kenneth A., and Barry R. Weingast. "The Institutional Foundations of Committee Power." *American Political Science Review* 81, no. 1 (1987): 85–104.

Sherman, Paddy. *Bennett*. Toronto: McClelland and Stewart, 1966.

Shoop, Jim. "New Government Unit Needed – Parley." *Minneapolis Star*, 11 Nov. 1966.

– "St. Paul's Byrne to Push Metro Council Plan." *Minneapolis Star*, 22 Mar. 1966.

Shor, Boris. "Polarization in American State Legislatures." Chap. 9 in *American Gridlock: The Sources, Character, and Impact of Political Polarization*, edited by James A. Thurber and Antoine Yoshinaka, 203–21. Cambridge: Cambridge University Press, 2015.

Shrubsole, Dan. "The Evolution of Public Water Management Agencies in Ontario, 1946–1988." *Canadian Water Resources Journal* 15, no. 1 (1990): 49-66.

Simeon, Richard, George Hoberg, and Keith Banting. "Globalization, Fragmentation, and the Social Contract." Chap. 10 in *Degrees of Freedom: Canada and the United States in a Changing World*, edited by Keith Banting, George Hoberg, and Richard Simeon, 389–416. Montreal and Kingston: McGill-Queen's University Press, 1997.

Simeon, Richard, and Elaine Willis. "Democracy and Performance: Governance in Canada and the United States." Chap. 4 in *Degrees of Freedom: Canada and the United States in a Changing World*, edited by Keith Banting, George Hoberg, and Richard Simeon, 150–86. Montreal and Kingston: McGill-Queen's University Press, 1997.

Siemiatycki, Matti. "Mega-Projects in the Making: A Century of Transportation Infrastructure Investment in Vancouver Canada." PhD diss., University of British Columbia, 2007.

Simpson, Scott. "Skytrain Uncertainty Angers Coquitlam." *Vancouver Sun*, 25 June 1998.

"The Single Community." *Toronto Evening Telegram*, 25 April 1950.

"Single Metro Board Oked by Probers." *Vancouver Sun*, 16 June 1960, 35.

Sinoski, Kelly. "Cost of Metro Services Could Rise 44 Per Cent over Five Years." *Vancouver Sun*, 14 July 2011.

Skogstad, Grace, and Vivien A. Schmidt. "Introduction: Policy Paradigms, Transnationalism, and Domestic Politics." Chap. 1 in *Policy Paradigms, Transnationalism, and Domestic Politics*, edited by Grace Skogstad, 1–35. Toronto: University of Toronto Press, 2011.

Skowronek, Stephen. *Building a New American State: The Expansion of National Administrative Capacities, 1877–1920*. New York: Cambridge University Press, 1982.

Smith, Alison, and Zachary Spicer. "The Local Autonomy of Canada's Largest Cities." *Urban Affairs Review* 54, no. 5 (2018): 931–61.

Smith, Barry E. "A Work in Progress: The British Columbia Farmland Preservation Program." In *Farmland Preservation: Land for Future Generations*, edited by Wayne Caldwell, Stew Hilts, and Bronwynne Wilton, n.p. Guelph, ON: Ontario Farmland Trust, 2007.

Smith, Dane. "Bill to Make Met Council Elected Is Narrowly Defeated in House." *Minneapolis Star-Tribune*, 29 April 1994.

– "House Votes to Group Metropolitan Agencies." *Minneapolis Star-Tribune*, 3 May 1994.

– "Legislators Push to Wrap up Key Bills." *Minneapolis Star-Tribune*, 6 May 1994.

Smith, Jason Scott. *Building New Deal Liberalism: The Political Economy of Public Works, 1933–1956*. Cambridge: Cambridge University Press, 2006.

Smith, Lancelot. *Report*. 3 vols. Toronto: Ontario Committee on Taxation, 1967.

Smith, Lorne. "New Development Strategy Will Give Surrey Problems." *Columbian* [n.p], 16 Feb. 1980.

Solof, Mark. *History of Metropolitan Planning Organizations*. Newark, NJ: North Jersey Transportation Planning Authority, 1998.

Sorensen, Andre, and Paul Hess. "Building Suburbs, Toronto-Style: Land Development Regimes, Institutions, Critical Junctures, and Path Dependence." *Town Planning Review* 86, no. 4 (2015): 411–36.

"Sound Financial State Reason York Opposes Merger, Reeve Testifies." *Toronto Globe and Mail*, 13 Feb. 1951.

South, Don. "The Choices We Had in the Fifties." *PIBC News* 25, no. 1 (1983): 4.

– "The Rise? And Fall? Of Regional Planning in B.C., Part Five." *PIBC News* 25, no. 3 (1983): 11.

Spanner, Donald Ross. "The Straight Furrow: The Life and Times of George S. Henry, Ontario's Unknown Premier." PhD diss., University of Western Ontario, 1994.

Spicer, Zachary. *The Boundary Bargain: Growth, Development, and the Future of City-County Separation.* Montreal and Kingston: McGill-Queen's University Press, 2016.

Spicer, Zachary. "The Rise and Fall of the Ministry of State for Urban Affairs: A Re-Evaluation." *Canadian Political Science Review* 5, no. 2 (2011): 117–26.

"Split Vote in Kent Council Defeats Final Regional Plan." *Langley (BC) Advance,* 14 July 1966.

Squire, Peverill. *The Evolution of American Legislatures: Colonies, Territories, and States, 1619–2009.* Ann Arbor: University of Michigan Press, 2014.

State Planning: A Policy Statement. Chicago: Governors Conference, Subcommittee on State Planning, Council of State Governments, 1962.

State Planning and Federal Grants: An Examination of State Comprehensive Planning in a Period of Increased State Activity and Increased Federal Funding. Chicago: Public Administration Service, 1969.

Steffens, Lincoln. *The Shame of the Cities.* New York: Hill and Wang, 1957. 1904.

Stein, David Lewis. "Nobody Is Running the Show: GTA Bound up in Confusing Patchwork of Authority." *Toronto Star,* 9 Oct. 1994.

– "What We Must Do to Prosper in the World." *Toronto Star,* 2 Oct. 994.

– "What's Wrong with the Greater Toronto Area." *Toronto Star,* 25 Sept. 1994.

Steinacker, Annette. "Game-Theoretic Models of Metropolitan Cooperation." In *Metropolitan Governance: Conflict, Competition, and Cooperation,* edited by Richard C. Feiock, 46–66. Washington, DC: Georgetown University Press, 2004.

"Step-by-Step Metro Plan Approved." *Vancouver Sun,* 12 July 1962.

Stephens, G. Ross, and Nelson Wikstrom. *Metropolitan Government and Governance: Theoretical Perspectives, Empirical Analysis, and the Future.* New York: Oxford University Press, 2000.

Stevens, Jennifer Audrey. "Feminizing the Urban West: Green Cities and Open Space in the Postwar Era, 1950–2000." PhD diss., University of California, Davis, 2008.

Stevenson, Garth. *Ex Uno Plures: Federal-Provincial Relations in Canada, 1867–1896.* Montreal and Kingston: McGill-Queen's University Press, 1993.

Stewart, Frank Mann. *A Half Century of Municipal Reform: The History of the National Municipal League.* Westport, CT: Greenwood Press, 1950.

Stiff, David, and Paul Smetanin. *Public Infrastructure Underinvestment: The Risk to Canada's Economic Growth.* Toronto: RiskAnalytica for the Residential and Civil Construction Alliance of Ontario, 2010.

Stivers, Camilla. *Bureau Men, Settlement Women: Constructing Public Administration in the Progressive Era.* Lawrence: University Press of Kansas, 2000.

Stone, Clarence N. "Reflections on Regime Politics: From Governing Coalition to Urban Political Order." *Urban Affairs Review* 51, no. 1 (2015): 101–37.

– *Regime Politics: Governing Atlanta 1946–1988.* Lawrence: University of Kansas Press, 1989.

Stone, Leroy O. *Urban Development in Canada: An Introduction to the Demographic Aspects.* 1961 Census Monographs. Ottawa: Census Division, Dominion Bureau of Statistics, 1967.

Stoney, Christopher, and Katharine Graham. "Federal-Municipal Relations in Canada: The Changing Organizational Landscape." *Canadian Public Administration* 52, no. 3 (2009): 371–94.

Stott, Greg. "Enhancing Status through Incorporation." *Journal of Urban History* 33, no. 6 (2007): 885–910.

Strachan, Alex. "Coquitlam Transit Link Defended, Richmond Argues." *Vancouver Sun*, 19 Dec. 1994, A3.

"Strength in Union." *Toronto Globe and Mail*, 25 April 1950, 6.

Strong Economy, Secure Tomorrow. Victoria, BC: Liberal Party of British Columbia, 2013.

Struthers, James. "Prelude to Depression: The Federal Government and Unemployment, 1918–29." *Canadian Historical Review* 58, no. 3 (1977): 277–93.

Studenski, Paul. *The Government of Metropolitan Areas in the United States.* New York: National Municipal League, Committee on Metropolitan Government, 1930.

"Suburban Municipalities Divided on Annexation; Hearing Plan Praised." *Toronto Globe and Mail*, 29 March 1939, 4.

Sullivan, Edward J. "The Quiet Revolution Goes West: The Oregon Planning Program 1961–2011." *John Marshall Law Review* 45 (2012): 357–95.

Sullivan, Edward J., and Ronald Eber. "The Long and Winding Road: Farmland Protection in Oregon, 1961–2009." *San Joaquin Agricultural Law Review* 18, no. 1 (2008): 1–69.

"Surrey Residents Oppose GVRD Plan." *Peace Arch News*, 9 April 1980.

Survey of Local Planning in the Twin Cities Metropolitan Area. St. Paul, MN: Twin Cities Metropolitan Council, 1978.

"Suspicion, Hostility Handicap but Law Says Way Must Be Found." *Oregonian* (Portland, OR), 15 June 1976, D20.

Swanstrom, Todd. "Beyond Economism: Urban Political Economy and the Postmodern Challenge." *Journal of Urban Affairs* 15, no. 1 (1993): 55–78.

– *Regional Resilience: A Critical Examination of the Ecological Framework*. IURD Working Paper Series, No. 2008–07. Berkeley, CA: Institute of Urban and Regional Development, University of California Berkeley, 2008.

A Tale of Three Counties: One Metropolitan Community. Portland, OR: League of Women Voters of Beaverton, Milwaukie, Oswego, and Portland, 1960.

Tassonyi, Almos T. *Municipal Debt Limits and Supervision: The 1930s and 1990s in Ontario*. Kingston, ON: School of Policy Studies, Queen's University, 1994.

"Tax Bills of Suburbanites Soar: Cost of Schools Crushing Load." *Toronto Evening Telegram*, 13 April 1951.

Taylor, Alan. *The Civil War of 1812: American Citizens, British Subjects, Irish Rebels, and Indian Allies*. New York: Vintage Books, 2011.

Taylor, John H. "Urban Autonomy in Canada: Its Evolution and Decline." Chap. 11 in *Power and Place: Canadian Urban Development in the North American Context*, edited by Gilbert A. Stelter and Alan F.J. Artibise, 269–91. Vancouver: UBC Press, 1986.

Taylor, Zack. *Good Governance at the Local Level: Meaning and Measurement*. IMFG Papers on Municipal Finance and Governance no. 26. Toronto: Institute on Municipal Finance and Governance, Munk School of Global Affairs, University of Toronto, 2016.

Taylor, Zack, and Neil Bradford. "Governing Canadian Cities." In *Canadian Cities in Transition*, 6th ed. Edited by Markus Moos, Tara Vinodrai, and Ryan Walker. Forthcoming.

Taylor, Zack, and Marcy Burchfield. *Growing Cities: Comparing Urban Growth Patterns and Regional Growth Policies in Calgary, Toronto and Vancouver*. Toronto, ON: Neptis Foundation, 2010.

Taylor, Zack, Marcy Burchfield, and Anna Kramer. "Alberta Cities at the Crossroads: Urban Development Challenges and Opportunities in Historical and Comparative Perspective." *University of Calgary School of Public Policy Research Paper* 7, no. 2 (2014).

Taylor, Zack, and Gabriel Eidelman. "Canadian Political Science and the City: A Limited Engagement." *Canadian Journal of Political Science* 43, no. 4 (2010): 961–81.

Teaford, Jon C. *City and Suburb: The Political Fragmentation of Metropolitan America, 1850–1970*. Baltimore, MD: Johns Hopkins University Press, 1979.

– *The Rise of the States: Evolution of American State Government*. Baltimore, MD: Johns Hopkins University Press, 2002.

– "Special Legislation and the Cities, 1865–1900." *American Journal of Legal History* 23, no. 3 (1979): 189–212.

– *The Twentieth-Century American City*. 2nd ed. Baltimore, MD: Johns Hopkins University Press, 1993.

– *The Unheralded Triumph: City Government in America, 1870–1900*. Baltimore: Johns Hopkins University Press, 1984.

Ten Years of Agricultural Land Preservation. Victoria, BC: Provincial Agricultural Land Commission, 1983.

Tennant, Paul. "The NDP Government of British Columbia: Unaided Politicians in an Unaided Cabinet." *Canadian Public Policy* 3, no. 4 (1977): 489–503.

Tennant, Paul, and David Zirnhelt. "The Emergence of Metropolitan Government in Greater Vancouver." *BC Studies* 15 (1972): 3–28.

Thoman, Richard S. *Design for Development in Ontario: The Initiation of a Regional Planning Program*. Toronto: Allister Typesetting and Graphics, 1971.

Thompson, Gregory L. "Taming the Neighborhood Revolution: Planners, Power Brokers, and the Birth of Neotraditionalism in Portland, Oregon." *Journal of Planning History* 6, no. 3 (2009): 214–47.

Thorpe, F.J. "Historical Perspective on the 'Resources for Tomorrow' Conference." Chap. 1 in *Resources for Tomorrow: Conference Background Papers*, edited by G.P. Boucher, 1–13. Ottawa: Queen's Printer, 1961.

"Three Assessors to Draft System for City, Suburbs." *Toronto Globe and Mail*, 31 May 1951.

The Three Basic Services. Portland, OR: Portland Metropolitan Planning Commission, 1965.

Tiebout, Charles M. "A Pure Theory of Local Expenditures." *Journal of Political Economy* 64, no. 5 (1956): 416–24.

Tollenaar, Kenneth C. *Organization for Water Distribution in the Portland Area.* Eugene, OR: Bureau of Municipal Research and Service in cooperation with the League of Oregon Cities, 1955.

Tom McCall and Oregon's Environmental Legacy. Screening of *Pollution in Paradise.* Produced by KGW-TV, 1962. Presented by William Robbins, Corvallis Science Pub, Oregon State University. http://www.youtube.com/watch?v=xJyV_eU5FzQ.

Tomalty, Ray. *The Compact Metropolis: Growth Management and Intensification in Vancouver, Toronto, and Montreal.* Toronto: Intergovernmental Committee on Urban and Regional Research, 1997.

Tomalty, Ray, and Alan Mallach. *America's Urban Future: Lessons from North of the Border.* Washington, DC: Island Press, 2016.

"Toronto, Scarboro Benefitting by Merger, Others Face Tax Boost." *Toronto Globe and Mail,* 5 April 1951.

Toronto and York Planning Board. *Report.* Toronto: Author, 1949.

"Toronto Annexation Parlay Is Proposed." *Toronto Globe and Mail,* 1 June 1939, 5.

Toward a More Resonsible Two-Party System: A Report of the Committee on Political Parties. Washington, DC: American Political Science Association, 1950.

Triadafilopoulos, Triadafilos. *Becoming Multicultural: Immigration and the Politics of Membership in Canada and Germany.* Vancouver: UBC Press, 2012.

Tsebelis, George. *Veto Players: How Political Institutions Work.* Princeton, NJ: Princeton University Press, 2002.

Tsebelis, George, and Jeannette Money. *Bicameralism.* New York: Cambridge University Press, 1997.

"12 Reassessments in Toronto Area Near Completion." *Toronto Globe and Mail,* 31 July 1952.

Twin Cities Area Metropolitan Development Guide. St. Paul, MN: Twin Cities Metropolitan Planning Commission, 1967.

"Twin City Engineers Will Organize Association to Solve Intercity Problems." *Minneapolis Journal,* 15 Sept. 1923.

"Twin City Metropolitan Area Planning Commission Proposed." *Minneapolis Journal,* 15 July 1923.

"Twin City Planning Commission Forms." *Minneapolis Journal,* 10 Dec. 1923.

"'Two-Gun Buck,' Dunbar Rated as 'Skeptic Tanks.'" *Toronto Evening Telegram*, 21 April 1950, 3.

"2 out of 3 in Twin Cities Say Met Council Should Be Elected." *Minneapolis Star*, 2 Jan. 1973.

United States. *Building the American City*. Washington, DC: National Commission on Urban Problems, 1968.

– *Financial Statistics of State and Local Governments: 1932 (Wealth, Public Debt, and Taxation)*. Washington, DC: United States Census Bureau, Department of Commerce, 1935.

– *Realty Tax Delinquency*. Vol. 1. *Current Tax Delinquency by States and Counties*. Washington, DC: United States Census Bureau, Department of Commerce, 1934.

– *Realty Tax Delinquency*. Vol. 2. *Urban Tax Delinquency*. Washington, DC: United States Census Bureau, Department of Commerce, 1934.

– *Statistical Abstract of the United States*. Washington, DC: United States Census Bureau, Department of Commerce, 1971.

– Congress. *Assessment of Community Planning for Mass Transit*. Vol. 7. *Minneapolis–St. Paul Case Study*. Washington, DC: Office of Technology Assessment, 1976.

"Urban and Rural Reserves." Portland Metro, 2 Sept. 2016. http://www.oregonmetro.gov/urban-and-rural-reserves.

Urban Area: Basic Data Maps. Portland, OR: Portland Metropolitan Planning Commission, 1960.

Urban Growth Boundary: Periodic Review Workplan. Portland, OR: Planning and Development Department, Portland Metro, 1988.

Urban Sprawl. New Westminster, BC: Lower Mainland Regional Planning Board, 1956.

Valelly, Richard M. *Radicalism in the States: The Minnesota Farmer-Labor Party and the American Political Economy*. Chicago: University of Chicago Press, 1989.

Vance, John E. *Inside the Minnesota Experiment: A Personal Recollection of Experimental Planning and Development in the Twin Cities Area*. Minneapolis: Center for Urban and Regional Affairs, University of Minnesota, 1977.

Vanderpoel, Peter. "Metro Unit Compromise Seen." *St. Paul Pioneer Press*, 24 March 1967.

– "The Twin Cities Metro Council: A Major Accomplishment Is Getting Regional Decisionmaking out in the Open." *Nation's Cities*, Nov. 1972. 21–7.

Vipond, Robert Charles. *Liberty and Community: Canadian Federalism and the Failure of the Constitution.* Albany: State University of New York Press, 1991.

Visser, James A. "Understanding Local Government Cooperation in Urban Regions: Toward a Cultural Model of Interlocal Relations." *American Review of Public Administration* 32, no. 1 (2002): 40–65.

Voorsanger, Eric J. "Problems of Annexation: A Case Study of Annexation in Portland." BA thesis, Reed College, 1955.

Walker, Peter A., and Patrick T. Hurley. *Planning Paradise: Politics and Visioning of Land Use in Oregon.* Tuscon: University of Arizona Press, 2011.

Walks, R. Alan. "New Divisions: Social Polarization and Neighbourhood Inequality in the Canadian City." Chap. 10 in *Canadian Cities in Transition: New Directions in the Twenty-First Century*, edited by Trudi Bunting, Pierre Filion, and Ryan Walker, 171–90. Toronto: Oxford University Press, 2010.

Wallis, Allan D. "Governance and the Civic Infrastructure of Metropolitan Regions." *National Civic Review* 82, no. 2 (1993): 125–39.

Wallis, John Joseph. "Constitutions, Corporations, and Corruption: American States and Constitutional Change, 1842 to 1852." *Journal of Economic History* 65, no. 1 (2005): 211–56.

Walth, Brent. *Fire at Eden's Gate: Tom McCall and the Oregon Story.* Portland, OR: Oregon Historical Society, 1994.

"Want Legislature to Give City Seven Suburbs." *Toronto Daily Star*, 5 Dec. 1949, 4.

Ward, Stephen V. "The International Diffusion of Planning: A Review and a Canadian Case Study." *International Planning Studies* 4, no. 1 (1999): 53–77.

Ware, Alan. *Political Conflict in America.* New York: Palgrave Macmillan, 2011.

Washington County. *Comprehensive Framework Plan.* Hillsboro, OR: Washington County, 1973.

The Way Ahead: A Report on the State of the Lower Mainland. Burnaby, BC: Lower Mainland Plan Review Panel, 1979.

Weaver, John C. "Order and Efficiency: Samuel Morley Wickett and the Urban Progressive Movement in Toronto, 1900–1915." *Ontario History* 69, no. 4 (1977): 218–34.

– *Shaping the Canadian City: Essays on Urban Politics and Policy, 1890–1920.* Toronto: Institute of Public Administration of Canada, 1977.

- "'Tomorrow's Metropolis' Revisited: A Critical Assessment of Urban Reform in Canada, 1890–1920." Chap. 16 in *The Canadian City: Essays in Urban History*, edited by Gilbert A. Stelter and Alan F.J. Artibise, 393–418. Toronto: McClelland and Stewart, 1977.

Weaver, R. Kent, and Bert A. Rockman. "Assessing the Effects of Institutions." In *Do Institutions Matter? Government Capabilities in the United States and Abroad*, edited by R. Kent Weaver and Bert A. Rockman, 1–41. Washington, DC: Brookings Institution, 1993.

- eds. *Do Institutions Matter? Government Capabilities in the United States and Abroad*. Washington, DC: Brookings Institution, 1993.

Weaver, Timothy P.R. *Blazing the Neoliberal Trail: Urban Political Development in the United States and the United Kingdom*. Philadelphia: University of Pennsylvania Press, 2016.

Weiner, Edward. *Urban Transportation Planning in the United States: History, Policy, and Practice*. 3rd ed. New York: Springer, 2008.

Weingast, Barry R., and John Joseph Wallis. "Dysfunctional or Optimal Institutions? State Debt Limitations, the Structure of State and Local Governments, and the Finance of American Infrastructure." Chap. 11 in *Fiscal Challenges: An Interdisciplinary Approach to Budget Policy*, edited by Elizabeth Garrett, Elizabeth Graddy, and Howell Jackson, 331–65. Cambridge: Cambridge University Press, 2008.

Weir, Margaret. "Ideas and the Politics of Bounded Innovation." Chap. 7 in *Structuring Politics: Historical Institutionalism in Comparative Analysis*, edited by Sven Steinmo, Kathleen Thelen, and Frank Longstreth, 188–216. New York: Cambridge University Press, 1992.

- "Innovation and Boundaries in American Employment Policy." *Political Science Quarterly* 107, no. 2 (1992): 249–69.

- "Planning, Environmentalism, and Urban Poverty: The Political Failure of National Land-Use Planning Legislation, 1970–1975." Chap. 7 in *The American Planning Tradition: Culture and Policy*, edited by Robert Fishman, 193–215. Washington, DC: Woodrow Wilson Center Press, 2000.

- "States, Race, and the Decline of New Deal Liberalism." *Studies in American Political Development* 19 (2005): 157–72.

Weitz, Jerry. "From Quiet Revolution to Smart Growth: State Growth Management Programs, 1960–99." *Journal of Planning Literature* 14, no. 2 (1999): 266–337.

- "Growth Management in the United States, 2000-2010: A Decennial Review and Synthesis." *Journal of Planning Literature* 27, no. 4 (2012): 394–433.

"What Amalgamation Would Mean." *Toronto Daily Star*, 9 Nov. 1951.

Whebell, C.F.J. "Robert Baldwin and Decentralization 1841–9." Chap. 4 in *Aspects of Nineteenth-Century Ontario: Essays Presented to James J. Talman*, edited by F.H. Armstrong, H.A. Stevenson, and J.D. Wilson, 48–64. Toronto: University of Toronto Press, 1974.

– "The Upper Canada District Councils Act of 1841 and British Colonial Policy." *Journal of Imperial and Commonwealth History* 17, no. 2 (1989): 185–209.

White, Graham. *Change in the Ontario State, 1952–2002: Report Prepared for the Role of Government Panel.* Toronto: Government of Ontario, 2002.

White, Richard. *Planning Toronto: The Planners, the Plans, Their Legacies, 1940–80.* Vancouver: UBC Press, 2016.

– *Urban Infrastructure and Urban Growth in the Toronto Region, 1950s to the 1990s.* Toronto: Neptis Foundation, 2003.

Whitman, Richard. "Commentary." In *Planning for States and Nation-States in the US and Europe*, edited by Gerrit-Jan Knaap, Zorca Nedovic-Budic, and Armando Carbonell, 90–5. Cambridge, MA: Lincoln Institute of Land Policy, 2015.

Whyte, William H. "Urban Sprawl." Chap. 5 in *The Expoding Metropolis: A Study of the Assault on Urbanism and How Our Cities Can Resist It*, edited by the Editors of Fortune, 115–39. Garden City, NJ: Doubleday Anchor, 1958.

Wickett, S. Morley. "City Government in Canada." *Political Science Quarterly* 15, no. 2 (1900): 240–59.

Wikstrom, Nelson. *Councils of Governments: A Study of Political Incrementalism.* Chicago: Nelson-Hall, 1977.

Wilensky, Alan J. "The Twin Cities Metropolitan Council: A Case Study in the Politics of Metropolitan Cooperation." BA thesis, Princeton University, 1969.

Wilson, James Wood. "A Land Use Plan for Chapel Hill." Master's thesis, University of North Carolina at Chapel Hill, 1951.

Wilson, James Wood, and J.T. Pierce. "The Agricultural Land Commission of British Columbia." Chap. 14 in *The Pressures of Change in Rural Canada*, edited by Michael F. Bunce and Michael J. Troughton, 272–91. Toronto: York University, 1984.

Wilson, Norman D. *A Transportation Plan for Metropolitan Toronto and the Suburban Area Adjacent.* Toronto: Toronto and York Planning Board, 1948.

Wilson, Woodrow. *Congressional Government*. Boston: Houghton-Mifflin, 1900.

Winfield, Mark. *Blue-Green Province: The Environment and the Political Economy of Ontario*. Vancouver: UBC Press, 2012.

Wiseman, Nelson. *In Search of Canadian Political Culture*. Vancouver: UBC Press, 2007.

Wolfe, David A. *21st Century Cities in Canada: The Geography of Innovation*. Toronto, ON: Conference Board of Canada, 2009.

Wolman, Harold. "Looking at Regional Governance Institutions in Other Countries as a Possible Model for US Metropolitan Areas: An Examination of Multipurpose Regional Service Delivery Districts in British Columbia." *Urban Affairs Review* Online (2017).

Wood, Andrew. "Comparative Urban Politics and the Question of Scale." *Space and Polity* 9, no. 3 (2005): 201–15.

World Bank. *Cities and Climate Change: An Urgent Agenda*. Washington, DC: World Bank, 2010.

Wrong, Dennis H. "Ontario Provincial Elections, 1934–55: A Preliminary Survey of Voting." *Canadian Journal of Economics and Political Science* 23, no. 3 (1957): 395–403.

Young, Alex. "Three Accused of Hatchet Job." *Vancouver Province*, 31 Jan. 1969.

Young, Walter D. *The Anatomy of a Party: The National CCF, 1932–61*. Toronto: University of Toronto Press, 1969.

Zachary, Kathleen Joan. "Politics of Land Use: The Lengthy Saga of Senate Bill 100." Master's thesis, Portland State University, 1978.

Zagorsky, Jay L. "Was Depression Era Unemployment Really Less in Canada Than in the US?" *Economics Letters* 61 (1998): 125–31.

Zusman, Mark. "John Gray, the Quiet Lion, Dies at 93." *Willamette Week (Portland, OR)*, 23 Oct. 2012.

Index